Understanding the Multi-Dimensional Nature of Poverty

EMERALD STUDIES IN SUSTAINABLE APPROACHES TO POVERTY ALLEVIATION

Series Editors:
Dr Richa Goel
Symbiosis Centre of Management Studies, Noida;
Symbiosis International Deemed University, Pune, India

Dr Tilottama Singh
Uttaranchal University, India

Md. Mashiur Rahman
Bank Asia Ltd., Bangladesh

Quazi Tafsirul Islam
North South University, Bangladesh

Dr Sukanta Kumar Baral
Indira Gandhi National Tribal University (A Central University of India), India

Emerald Studies in Sustainable Approaches to Poverty Alleviation serves as a hub for researchers, professionals and practitioners to share innovative research and effective solutions aimed at reducing global poverty.

Poverty is a major global issue that affects millions of people around the world. It poses a serious threat to human development, well-being and social fairness. Global poverty is a complicated and complex issue driven by different economic, social, political and environmental elements that vary by location. As per UNDP, today, one in every five people on the planet (1.2 billion) lives on less than a dollar a day. Fifty-six percent of the developing world lacks basic sanitation, and over 50 nations now have poorer real per capita incomes than they did a decade ago.

Drawing on a global authorship, *Emerald Studies in Sustainable Approaches to Poverty Alleviation* tells the stories of effective interventions and programmes that have made a difference, providing hope and inspiration for those working in the area and inspiring others to become involved. Also using various indicators like HDI, MDPI, Income Consumption index, Poverty headcount ratio, Ginni coefficient data & Welfare index this book series will try to cover even those masses who do not fall in the above criteria and will touch poverty from its grassroots level. It is critical to employ a combination of these methodologies and indicators when assessing poverty in order to present a full picture of the worldwide poverty situation.

This series will include economics, sociology, development studies, public policy and other disciplines to present a comprehensive and multidimensional assessment of worldwide attempts to eradicate poverty. Each work provides policy-makers, practitioners, scholars and concerned citizens with insights, research findings, case studies and practical help in the battle against poverty. *Emerald Studies in Sustainable Approaches to Poverty Alleviation* will allow for in-depth investigation of numerous elements of poverty and its core causes, including income disparity, access to education, healthcare and economic opportunities, social justice, child marriages, micro rural finance, food security, resource mobilisation, women entrepreneurship, war-impacted countries and more.

Forthcoming Titles

Creating Pathways for Prosperity
Richa Goel, Tilottama Singh, Md. Mashiur Rahman, Quazi Tafsirul Islam, Sukanta Kumar Baral

Understanding the Multi-Dimensional Nature of Poverty

EDITED BY

RICHA GOEL

Symbiosis Centre of Management Studies, Noida; Symbiosis International Deemed University, Pune, India

TILOTTAMA SINGH

Uttaranchal University, India

Md. MASHIUR RAHMAN

Bank Asia Ltd., Bangladesh

QUAZI TAFSIRUL ISLAM

North South University, Bangladesh

AND

SUKANTA KUMAR BARAL

Indira Gandhi National Tribal University (A Central University of India), India

emerald PUBLISHING

United Kingdom – North America – Japan – India – Malaysia – China

Emerald Publishing Limited
Emerald Publishing, Floor 5, Northspring, 21-23 Wellington Street, Leeds LS1 4DL

First edition 2025

British Library Cataloguing in Publication Data
A catalogue record for this book is available from the British Library

ISBN: 978-1-83753-293-3 (Print)
ISBN: 978-1-83753-292-6 (Online)
ISBN: 978-1-83753-294-0 (Epub)

Printed and bound by CPI Group (UK) Ltd, Croydon, CR0 4YY

INVESTOR IN PEOPLE

Dedicated to all who played an important role in the development of this edition of the book: our families, friends, readers, authors, reviewers and of course the Emerald Team with whom this seems to be a true success and we are deeply grateful to all of them.

– Prof (Dr) Sukanta Kumar Baral & Dr Richa Goel

To my father, Quazi Takdirul Islam, and my mother, Samina Islam, whose sacrifices, aspirations and support have shaped me, and to Sonali Islam, Suhana Zaman and Taslima Haque, who have loved me like a son – each of you inspires me to become a better version of myself every day.

– Quazi Tafsirul Islam

To the Almighty who gives me a life on earth, my parents, wife, kids and siblings, those are inspiring and supporting me as and when required – I am grateful to you all.

– Md. Mashiur Rahman

For my kids, Aayra and Aveer, who inspire me to tell stories that matter.

– Dr Tilottama Singh

Contents

List of Contributors

Asma Ahmed	InterResearch, Bashundhara, Bangladesh
Jashim Uddin Ahmed	North South University, Bangladesh
Dr Sukanta Kumar Baral	Indira Gandhi National Tribal University, India
Shelli Brunswick	Space Foundation, USA
Sanjeev Chaturvedi	DY Patil University, India
Anindita Das	ASTHA School of Management, India
Dr Shilpa Deo	DES Pune University, India
Michela Floris	University of Cagliari, Italy
Mohammad Osman Gani	The University of British Columbia, Okanagan Campus, Canada
Dr Richa Goel	Symbiosis Centre of Management Studies, Noida; Symbiosis International Deemed University, Pune, India
Syed Far Abid Hossain	BRAC Business School, BRAC University, Bangladesh
Sarika Iqbal	InterResearch, Bashundhara, Bangladesh
Sunaina K	Kannur University, Kerala, India
Chitra Krishnan	Symbiosis Centre of Management Studies, Noida; Symbiosis International Deemed University, Pune, India
Blanca Luz	Xi'an Jiaotong University, China
Dhamodharan M	SRM University AP, India
Jasmine Mariappan	University of Technology and Applied Sciences, IBRA, Oman
Kazi Mohiuddin	Shanghai Maritime University, China
Dr Sudhansu Sekhar Nanda	Sri Sri University, India
Ankita Nayak	KIIT University, India

Dr B. C. M. Patnaik	KIIT University, India
Dr Rabinarayan Patnaik	Siksha 'O' Anusandhan (SOA) Deemed to be University, India
Dr Durga Prasad Samontaray	King Saud University, Saudi Arabia
Dr Anjali Sane	Dr. Vishwanath Karad MIT World Peace University, India
Dr Ipseeta Satpathy	KIIT University, India
Mohd Asif Shah	Kebri Dehar University, Ethiopia
Dr Sushil Sharma	Texas A & M University, USA
Neeru Sidana	Amity University, India
Bibi Sarah Majidi	Kardan University, Afghanistan; Technical Standards and Safety Authority, Canada
Tushar Soubhari	NSS College, India
Dr Saeed Tabar	Ball State University, USA
Dr Kyla L. Tennin	Lady Mirage Global, Inc, USA
D. D. Tewari	University of Zululand, South Africa
Hasanuzzaman Tushar	International University of Business Agriculture and Technology, Bangladesh
Nassir Ul Haq Wani	Kardan University, Afghanistan; Kashmir Research Information System (KRIS), India; Presidency University, India

Foreword

The book *Understanding the Multi-Dimensional Nature of Poverty* is a comprehensive reference source that will provide personalised, accessible and well-designed experiences. 'No Poverty' is the most crucial of the 17 Sustainable Development Goals (SDGs). Research perspectives, approaches and topic integration of studies on poverty reduction have significantly extended with the growth of practice in the 21st century.

This book's first volume in *Emerald Studies in Sustainable Approaches to Poverty Alleviation* will bring the related topics of poverty eradication and comprehension to the forefront, as well as demonstrate how emerging economies are dealing with poverty challenges at their core. It focuses on the key concerns that nations throughout the world are experiencing, such as pandemic-related poverty, environmental-related poverty, energy crisis, implementation issues, and so on, and how new creative models and methods that use current technology may help make economies and enterprises more sustainable. Poverty is the greatest barrier to long-term development, which is why eradicating it has become one of the most pressing global concerns of the 21st century. It also provides an overview of current research and suggest that, in the future, cross-disciplinary collaboration and attention to the contribution of marginal fields to poverty reduction research should be prioritised. There has been a lot of debate on how developing economies' economic development and structural transformation influence poverty. This book revisits these themes, using a newly constructed dataset of global poverty measures.

I assume that this book is anticipated to be highly valuable for a wide range of readers with a variety of interests, and it is not limited to academics, postgraduate students and research associates, but also to corporate executives, entrepreneurs and other professionals and masses in all fields who can improve and expand their knowledge with the learning of the basic trends and activities in this book. This book will have an edge over the other few existing books as it presents customised economic models, essential policy tools, suggestions and strategies designed to eradicate poverty with respect to innovative technology, sustainable development, Industry 5.0 especially within the context of the 2030 Agenda.

I am pleased to write this foreword as the editors of this book has given full hearted effort for a great solution and innovation. All chapters in this book have been selected based on peer review where reviewers were very much expert in the sector.

Prof (Dr) Mohammad Saeed
Professor Emeritus, Department of Business Administration
Minot State University, Minot, ND 58707, USA

Preface

This first book in *Emerald Studies in Sustainable Approaches to Poverty Alleviation* talks about poverty as lack of sufficient material assets or money to meet a person's fundamental human requirements, which might include food, clothes and shelter. The poverty rate is the proportion of persons in a specific age group who earn less than the poverty threshold which may be a vicious cycle. It uses a variety of statistical techniques to examine past research on poverty alleviation conducted since 2000. It focuses on several economic research on growth and inequality as well as environmental studies on environmental management and protection systems. It also emphasises the significance of intergovernmental collaboration in fostering international harmony.

The goal of sustainable approaches to poverty alleviation is to combat poverty in a way that encourages long-term economic and social growth while minimising adverse environmental effects. These methods acknowledge the interdependence of social well-being, the environment and poverty. A holistic strategy that takes into account economic, social and environmental variables is also necessary. While protecting the planet's resources for next generations, it seeks to end the cycle of poverty. Achieving these objectives will require cooperation from governments, non-governmental organisations (NGOs), communities and the commercial sector. Interventions may be more successful if you interact with the community and learn about its values.

This book will give an outline of the most recent studies and make the case for prioritising interdisciplinary cooperation and consideration of the peripheral fields' contributions to research on poverty reduction in the future. How structural change and economic growth in developing economies affect poverty has been a hot topic of discussion. With the use of a recently created dataset of global poverty metrics, this book revisits these concerns.

The following chapters are listed under this book.
Chapter 1 talks about Costa Rican small Business Moving towards Sustainable Future–A Case of Varcli Pinares. Among the major industries in Costa Rica, agriculture has contributed significantly to the country's economy. Felipe Vargas established 'Varcli Pinares' 11 years ago to produce good quality bananas through sustainable operations of natural systems. The company invests in circular economy by executing decarbonisation through the capture of CO2 wastes and protection of forests. The business pioneered in reducing water consumption and implementing solar energy usage in banana production through innovative tools

and technologies while engaging in no-herbicide practices. The unique, sustainable packaging created through waste makes a visual impact and guides customers to online platforms. The company adheres to sustainable practices while impacting the community positively. However, as a small business, maintaining sustainable practices throughout the entire supply chain and competing with big companies is difficult for Varcli Pinares. Nevertheless, the company believes its simplicity and adaptability will help it thrive in the competitive industry.

Chapter 2 talks about Sustainable Approaches to Poverty and Challenges from the 21st Century. The Swedish International Development Cooperation Agency (Sida) (2019) explicated there are four dimensions of poverty, and they include (1) resources, (2) opportunities and choice, (3) power and voice and (4) human security (e.g. violence issues and concerns). Contrastingly, Ellis (1984) postulated dimensions of poverty are social, economic, legal and political poverty. The Organisation for Economic Co-operation and Development (OECD) (2015) stated poverty is not always about income, indicating 'income poverty'. Deprivation factors can be broad, but reported poor health, inadequate living standards and lack of education are dimensions of poverty (OECD, 2015). Also, according to the World Bank, the world's extremely poor are people who live on less than $1.90 USD per day (Beck et al., 2020). The $1.90 amount is at 2011 purchasing power parity levels. Additionally, the $1.90USD amount has decreased significantly over the last decades (Beck et al., 2020). Nevertheless, entrepreneurship, UN SDGs and technology can be strategies for sustainable alleviation of poverty and pandemic global economic recovery, in the 21st century.

Chapter 3 talks about Disentangling Critical Factors for Enhancing Female Entrepreneurship and Women Empowerment to Alleviate Poverty: Focus on BRICS Countries. The 2030 Agenda for Sustainable Development states that eradicating poverty for people everywhere is a pivotal goal (Goal#1), as well as empowering women and girls (Goal#5), for creating sustainable and inclusive communities (Goal#11). Contemporarily, the World Bank suggests that female entrepreneurship can contribute to economic growth and poverty reduction and, at the same time, can represent a suitable means to promote gender equity and inclusion. This chapter aims to deepen the knowledge on this fascinating and challenging topic by uncovering the main barriers that inhibit female entrepreneurship and impede women from actively collaborating to alleviate poverty and create sustainable and inclusive communities worldwide. Public–private efforts that aid women in setting up start-ups, embracing new technologies, innovating, honing their digital skills and gaining improved access to financing and financial support in light of Industry 4.0 need to be actively supported and promoted. Specifically, this chapter focuses on women entrepreneurship in BRICS countries because these nations are experiencing very different growth paths, and their significance in the global economy remains an open question.

Chapter 4 talks about Ubiquitous Business Model and Strategy of WeChat as A Platform in E-Commerce Development. The key purpose of the study is to determine the ubiquitous role of WeChat as a platform in social-media-based co-creation and e-commerce development. The study consists of mixed methodology approach. First, an automatic search was performed which included the

Science Citation Index Expanded (SCIEXPANDED), Social Sciences Citation Index (SSCI) and Arts and Humanities Citation Index (A&HCI) databases of the Web of Science (WoS). From this, a Systematic Literature Review (SLR) was conducted. Also, an ethnographic approach was used to measure the ubiquitous role of WeChat as a platform in social-media-based co-creation and e-commerce development. The study findings revealed a few interesting managerial implications. A critical result of this study discovered the social media value co-creation with WeChat as a platform for e-commerce development. In addition, social networking sites (SNSs) such as WeChat attract managers and policymakers as a tool for business development. The findings inform practitioners that social media co-creation strategies may affect e-commerce development significantly due to powerful and popular platform such as WeChat.

Chapter 5 talks about A Comparative Study of Different Poverty Alleviation Programmes undertaken in India and the Middle East: An Overview. Initiatives to reduce poverty aim to reduce the number of people living in poverty by ensuring that those with low-income households and families have appropriate access to food, assistance and essentials. According to the World Economic Forum, poverty is a significant loss of well-being that can appear in a variety of ways. Two instances of this are low wages and the difficulty to access the necessities for daily living in the form of goods and services. Poor physical and mental health, insufficient access to sanitary services, lack of a voice and a lack of resources to improve one's situation are all characteristics of poverty. The goal of this study is to provide insight into the various poverty eradication programmes undertaken in India and the Middle East, i.e. Yemen.

Chapter 6 talks about Economic Dependency Ratio as a Dimension of Poverty and Vulnerability. 'Ending poverty in all its forms everywhere' is the very first Sustainable Development Goal (SDG), to be achieved by 2030. However, the progress made in reducing poverty has been reversed due to the spread of the COVID-19 pandemic. The worsening poverty, inequality and vulnerability call for identifying the acuteness of the problem with the help of dimensions like the economic dependency ratio along with other sources like poverty line, access to social security, healthcare, basic services, food security and asset ownership and social networks at the village to name a few. The economic dependency ratio goes beyond the age dependency ratio and tries to capture the dependency better by incorporating the number of dependants and employed ones in the calculation. In this study, an attempt has been made to highlight the importance of the economic dependency ratio to measure vulnerability better in India. Unemployment data provided by the Centre for Monitoring Indian Economy (CMIE) have been utilised to understand the severity of dependency at the country level. Primary data have been collected with the help of the Proportionate Stratified Sampling method from 600 notified, non-notified slum households staying in the western part of India, and in-depth interviews have been conducted with a few homeless families. Quantitative data have been analysed using SPSS and Stata software. This study will be immensely useful as it aims to improvise the methodology to identify the poor and vulnerable. Better identification can take us a step closer to achieving SDG 1.

Chapter 7 talks about Exploring Poverty Measurement Techniques Across Diverse Economies: A Cross-Country Study. Millions of people all over the globe are impacted by poverty, which is a serious global issue. It is a complicated problem with many facets that has important consequences for society, the economy and politics. Poverty is a barrier to achieving sustainable development goals and reducing inequality across the world. Poverty can be measured in several ways, each with its strengths and limitations. Some of the commonly used measures include absolute poverty, relative poverty and multidimensional poverty. However, measuring poverty across different economies is a challenging task due to differences in social, economic and political contexts. The objective of this chapter is to examine the idea of poverty and how it is measured in various economic contexts. In this chapter, we will look at the various methods of calculating poverty, the difficulties in doing so and the efficacy of various poverty measures in capturing poverty in various economies. The chapter will also discuss how the findings may affect policy and practice and propose new lines of inquiry for future studies on how to measure poverty in various economies. The importance of this chapter lies in its potential to improve our knowledge of poverty and its measurement while also offering advice to practitioners and policymakers working to reduce poverty and promote sustainable development. Examining poverty in different economies, this chapter will help to shed light on the complex and dynamic nature of poverty and the need for tailored poverty reduction strategies in different contexts.

Chapter 8 talks about Self-Help Groups in Afghanistan: A Ploy of Economic and Social Empowerment of Women for Sustainable Development. Women's empowerment is not new; it has been recognised as a crucial component of poverty reduction and economic progress. However, it remains problematic in most developing countries, such as Afghanistan. This research evaluates women's empowerment experiences by utilising self-help groups (SHGs) as a fundamental development method to empower women economically and socially. The findings indicated that SHG involvement is closely associated with families' socio-economic well-being, meaning that SHG participants are more empowered than those who do not engage or are oblivious to SHGs. SHGs confront various obstacles in Afghanistan, including (but not limited to) erroneous cultural norms, security issues, inadequate financial assistance and poor member participation, all of which influence operations. The study suggests growing social awareness, civil society and government support, laws and regulations supporting women and strategies to enhance women's economic and social empowerment and linking groups to commercial banks as critical recommendations to foster and realise women's integration and active engagement in SHGs.

Chapter 9 talks about Factors Affecting Poverty Dynamics: A Conceptual Study. The poverty rate in India is still very high despite considerable economic reforms over the past 20 years and a rapid decline in that rate. Even if the accomplishments have received much praise, it is crucial to comprehend the dynamics of poverty by recognising those who entered and emerged from it. The literature on multidimensional poverty dynamics is not as well established as that on poverty entry and leave, despite the wealth of available empirical research on both topics. This chapter uses the multidimensional measure of issues related to health, education and infrastructure; social barriers to advancement; a lack of resources and a lack of competence to make decisions for the benefit of the household to investigate the dynamics of poverty and its underlying causes.

Chapter 10 talks about From Resist to Privilege: Rising Psychological Empowerment and Gender Equality for Poverty Alleviation. 'Poverty is well-being deprivation', declares the World Bank. There is no clear, widely accepted definition of well-being, although the World Bank provides some clues, 'to be impoverished would be to be starving, to lack shelter and clothes, to be unwell and uncared for, and to be illiterate and untutored'. Poverty is much more than this for poor people. Psychological empowerment and gender equality are among the most emphasised areas, and specific tactics will be developed to enhance psychological empowerment and gender equality. 'Psychological' empowerment, abbreviated as 'PE', denotes empowerment at the specific intensity of analysis. It is a multidimensional concept derived from the integration of various dimensions determined by three realms: (a) personality, which also includes self-attribution of the outcomes of one's actions and internal locus of control, (b) cognitive, one that contains self-efficacy perception, and (c) motivational, which describes the interest in participating in the activity and control of the factors involved. Gender equality is the equivalent involvement of males and females in utter facets of a lifetime. Gender equality manifests in business, collective relationships, politics and academics. Women's civil rights activities affiliated with the rights movements worked to establish gender equality in place of an essential human right. In many nations, indicators such as the gender-linked development indicators, the gender break index and the gender fairness index provide measurements of complete gender equivalence. Gender fairness encourages women's involvement in the above-mentioned domains, improving the quality of life for those in poverty. This chapter discusses the positive impact of psychological empowerment and gender equality on human well-being based on evidence.

Chapter 11 talks about Revamping Economic Parameters in an Innovative Digital World in 21st Century: An Interventive Study on Banking Practices. The banking sector is an essential component of any economy and plays a key role in its growth and development. The banking sector's growth and reputation can be linked to the fact that it responds to people's financial needs and correspondingly provides customised solutions. The banking sector has seen transformation in the new millennium. The pace and trend of transformation is all set to accelerate in the coming decade. The process of Liberalisation, Privatisation and Globalisation Model (LPG Model) banking practices which being unleashed a few decades back will reach to greater heights as we step into the next decade. The innovative technology has brought about a paradigm shift in all aspects of banking like routine operations, transactions, products and processes, delivery of services in terms of various e-channels, credit administration and credit management, audit and compliance and FinTech partnership. Digital transformations in the banking sector have received much needed trust because of 'The Digital India Moment'. The chapter makes an attempt to highlight the role of technology in banking and how technology-led innovations and initiatives will determine the business of banking as a whole. The significance of these technology-driven innovations and transformations is that they put both banker and customer in a win-win situation.

Chapter 12 talks about Sustainable Poverty Reduction Model – Need-Surveillance and Psycho-Social Support Practices among Migrant Workforce. Migrants have been posed with less familiarity in their new environment during COVID times, faced with various social, psychological and emotional traumas. Research indicates that they may have been originating from apprehension of being abandoned by their neighbours. Most of them were precarious with little wages, competing for their basic need fulfilment; putting them under more mental stress. Looking forward to the ancient principle, 'Athithi Devo Bhavah' (Visitors are Gods) and immediate response; measures were taken to promote community shelters and kitchens; maintaining social distancing and ensuring physical safety. The governments of different countries took proactive initiatives to study and assess their needs. The study here includes the cases being evaluated in regard to migrants' need for surveillance and psycho-social support given by the government and non-profit associations during the pandemic at the global level. Remarkably, certain countries proved the working of their sustainable poverty reduction model by evaluating factors like (i) catering to the basic necessities by providing them with free kits, (ii) providing free accommodation, (iii) providing medicines to the needy, (iv) quarantining the COVID-affected migrant patients at separate places and (v) ensuring the safe reach of migrants at their native places. The purpose behind this movement was accomplished and the model proved satisfactory, highlighting their best practices across the world.

Acknowledgements

Writing a book is harder than we thought and more rewarding than we could have ever imagined. None of this would have been possible without the efforts, hardship and of course encouragement of our entire team members, and without their experiences and support this book would not exist.

It's as challenging as it sounds to take an idea and convert it into a book. The experience is mentally taxing and satisfying. We want to express our sincere gratitude to everyone who made this possible. The success of this book was made possible by the collaboration of many outstanding researchers, who genuinely provided a new path for this book.

We still treasure the moments when our complete team, which was spread across several locations, used to communicate several times every day for months on end before producing something innovative and knowledgeable. Only by God's grace who gave us the courage to follow our aspirations and trust in our passions that we learnt how genuine this talent of writing is while putting this book together.

Our sincere and heartfelt gratitude to our family members who have been a pillar of support for us during the laborious process of finishing this book. Also, a special thanks to all the authors and reviewers who participated in the review process. This book would not have been possible without their help. We greatly appreciate the fact that many of the writers also acted as referees. Those who provided comprehensive and critical feedback on a few chapters encouraged us to clarify concepts, investigate specific aspects of insight work and explain the rationales for certain recommendations. We would also like to thank many people who have helped us learn and practice both the art and science of networking throughout the years.

Editors

Dr Richa Goel, Dr Tilottama Singh, Md. Mashiur Rahman
Quazi Tafsirul Islam, and Dr Sukanta Kumar Baral

Introduction

In order to address the enduring and complex problem of poverty while ensuring long-term societal and environmental well-being, sustainable approaches to poverty reduction are crucial. In order to be sustainable, inclusive economic growth must be encouraged. We may achieve a more equitable distribution of wealth and resources by promoting economic development that benefits all facets of society, particularly marginalised and disadvantaged communities. This strategy frequently entails spending money on healthcare, education and skill-building to enable people and communities to end the cycle of poverty. Supporting small-scale business owners and advancing sustainable agriculture can also boost regional economies, generate employment opportunities and eradicate poverty in a way that is favourable to the environment.

The preservation and prudent management of natural resources are essential components of long-term poverty reduction. Many underdeveloped communities rely largely on ecosystems for their survival, including forestry, agriculture and fishing. Sustainable resource management practices help to reduce the negative consequences of climate change, which frequently disproportionately affect the poor and ensure the long-term availability of these resources. Reforestation, clean energy sources and encouragement of sustainable agricultural methods can all help to end poverty and advance environmental sustainability.

In addition, social safety nets and focused interventions are essential parts of long-term plans to reduce poverty. These initiatives offer a safety net for the most vulnerable and can aid in ending the poverty cycle that passes down through generations. However, it's important to properly plan such programmes, taking into account their long-term effects and the ability to promote independence rather than dependence. To reduce poverty in a way that benefits both current and future generations while protecting the resources of our world, a sustainable path must ultimately combine economic growth, environmental stewardship and social support systems.

When evaluating poverty, it is important to take a global perspective and acknowledge that factors like commerce, finance and climate change frequently impact the problems that people and communities confront around the world. To accomplish this effectively, international institutions and organisations must work together to provide standardised measurements and indicators that include aspects such as access to social equity, healthcare, clean water and other non-economic resources in addition to economic metrics. A sustainable method of analysing global poverty should also stress the significance of international cooperation and development aid. Richer countries can significantly contribute to the fight against poverty by supporting efforts to enhance the capacity of underdeveloped areas, advocating fair trade and providing targeted aid. In summary, a holistic and sustainable approach to studying global poverty reduction acknowledges that poverty is a complex web of social, economic and environmental concerns that call for coordinated global action and is not just a problem of the economy.

Chapter 1

Costa Rican Small Business Moving Towards Sustainable Future: A Case of Varcli Pinares

Jashim Uddin Ahmed[a], *Asma Ahmed*[b], *Mohammad Osman Gani*[c] *and Sarika Iqbal*[b]

[a]North South University, Bangladesh
[b]InterResearch, Bashundhara, Bangladesh
[c]The University of British Columbia, Okanagan Campus, Canada

Abstract

Among the major industries in Costa Rica, agriculture has contributed significantly to the country's economy. Felipe Vargas established 'Varcli Pinares' 11 years ago to produce good quality bananas through sustainable operations of natural systems. This case study explores the complex dynamics surrounding the Varcli Pinares agricultural farming, aiming to shed light on its multifaceted nature and provide insights into its outcomes. The company invests in circular economy by executing decarbonisation through capture of CO_2 wastes and protection of forests. The business pioneered in reducing water consumption and implementing solar energy usage in banana production through innovative tools and technologies while engaging in no-herbicide practices. The unique, sustainable packaging created through waste makes a visual impact and guides customers to online platforms. The company adheres to sustainable practices while impacting the community positively. However, as a small business maintaining sustainable practices throughout the entire supply chain and competing with big companies is difficult for Varcli Pinares. Nevertheless, the company believes its simplicity and adaptability will help it thrive in the competitive industry. Through a rigorous and systematic approach, the case study aims to contribute to the existing body of knowledge in sustainable agricultural farming and provide valuable insights for practitioners and stakeholders alike.

Understanding the Multi-Dimensional Nature of Poverty, 1–11

doi:10.1108/978-1-83753-292-620241001

Keywords: Costa Rica; Varcli Pinares; sustainable practices; environmental sustainability; small business

Introduction

The United Nations (UN) is working to transform the world with progress and prosperity by establishing different goals throughout the world. The 12th Sustainable Development Goal (SDG) of the United Nations aims to foster ethical patterns of production and consumption throughout the world. This goal highlights the significance of waste reduction and the promotion of sustainable practices in both the public and private sectors. In the context of Costa Rica, a small country located in Central America, the government and private sector have implemented policies and programs to achieve this goal. Despite its relatively smaller size, it receives a bigger portion of the foreign direct investments (FDIs) in that region (Rica, 2019). Like other agro-based nations, agriculture is one of Costa Rica's main industries. It contributes significantly to the country's economy, making up about 6.5% of its total GDP and employing about 14% of its workforce. On just under 10% (505,000 hectares/1,248,000 acres) of the total land area, crops are grown. Costa Rica increased banana volume exports by 7% in 2020 generating a total of US$ 1.12 billion despite the pandemic, according to the National Banana Corporation of Costa Rica (Corbana). The 7% increase comes from 129.6 million boxes that were exported in 2020, compared to 120.7 million in 2019. This generated US$ 1.12 in 2020 compared to US$ 1.105 billion in 2019. Chiquita, Del Monte, Dole, and the local business Grupo Acon dominate the production and export of bananas in Costa Rica. Over 40,000 people are directly employed by the sector.

Costa Rica has taken significant steps to promote responsible consumption and production patterns. One of the most notable initiatives is the country's commitment to renewable energy sources. Statistics mentioned that 99.99% of Costa Rica's electricity will come from renewable sources by 2021 where hydropower, wind, and solar energy being the most significant contributors (MINAE, 2021). This focus on renewable energy has helped to reduce the country's dependence on fossil fuels and contributed to a decrease in greenhouse gas emissions. Moreover, the government has implemented a carbon neutral programme that encourages companies and organisations to reduce their carbon footprint and invest in renewable energy sources.

Rapid agricultural export production is the cause of the nation's growth and development. Two main farming techniques are used by both local Costa Rican farmers and multinational companies there: Plantation agriculture includes sustainable/permaculture methods used by multinational corporations like Dole, Chiquita, Del Monte, etc. Additionally, many indigenous communities use subsistence farming methods. With the increasing challenges of climate change, the need to adapt to sustainable business practices has become crucial. Businesses are a significant contributor to environmental pollution worldwide, yet some are recently engaging in practices to reduce their operations' impact on the environment. Implementing sustainable actions not only helps small businesses make profits but also develops a 'positive brand'. Small businesses, starting from restaurant owners to homebuilder manufacturers, are establishing sustainable operations to save money and reduce their operations' impact on the environment (Hodges, 2021). However, the reality seems to be more complicated as, according to ACCA (2021), small businesses are trying to combat the aftermath of the pandemic has had on their operations. A report on 16,300 SME clients by the SME Tracker states that businesses are tackling the financial challenges after wounding down government-backed loans post-pandemic. Only 40% of the small businesses have reported returning to their pre-pandemic productivity state. Additionally, the proprietors of SMEs have noted that they lack knowledge and understanding of how, to begin with sustainability plans. Due to the struggles of keeping their operations running smoothly, small businesses are putting sustainability as the last thing on their mind.

However, despite these efforts, Costa Rica still faces challenges in achieving SDG 12. One of the most significant challenges is the lack of awareness and education around sustainable consumption and production patterns. The government and private sector need to work together to educate the public on the importance of reducing waste, promoting sustainable practices, and supporting environmentally friendly products. These efforts require the collaborative efforts of both the government and private sector to create a sustainable and responsible future.

Sustainability in Agriculture Farming

The SDGs are a set of 17 objectives that were adopted by the UN General Assembly in 2015 with the intention of enhancing both human life and the environment of the planet. The two SDGs that support the use of sustainable agriculture are SDG 2: Zero Hunger and SDG 12: Responsible Consumption and Production.

SDG 2 expects to eradicate hunger and achieve security in food habits while promoting sustainable agriculture practices. Indicator 2.4.1 states that assessing agricultural instruments and conducting farm surveys will help the country rank the challenges and priorities aligned with sustainable agriculture's economic, environmental, and social factors. Over the past 30 years, there have been numerous discussions to clarify what is meant by sustainable agriculture. Determine whether a farm is in line with sustainable agriculture by looking at the environmental criteria of the soil quality and water management practices (Food and Agriculture Organization of the United Nations, n.d.).

Moreover, SDG 12 mentions responsible production practices where indicator 12.3 indicates reduced food losses in production and supply chain level and also to cater to post-harvest losses. The goal's aim is to ensure that consumption and production patterns are sustainable and to reduce negative environmental impacts. This includes promoting sustainable agriculture practices that minimise waste and pollution and conserve natural resources (United Nations Statistics, n.d.).

Sustainability in agriculture farming is a critical component of the SDGs in Costa Rica. The SDGs were adopted by the United Nations in 2015 as a blueprint for sustainable development, and Costa Rica has made significant progress towards achieving these goals, particularly in the area of sustainable agriculture. Costa Rica is known for its strong commitment to environmental sustainability, and sustainable agriculture is a key element of this commitment. The country has implemented a number of policies and programs aimed at promoting sustainable agriculture practices, such as the National Plan for Agroecology and Organic Agriculture, which was launched in 2017. One of the key practices of sustainable agriculture in Costa Rica is agroforestry. Agroforestry is the integration of trees into farming systems, which has been shown to improve soil health, conserve water and promote biodiversity. Costa Rica has been a leader in the promotion of agroforestry, with programs such as the Payment for Environmental Services (PES) programme, which provides incentives for farmers to plant trees on their land. Another important practice in sustainable agriculture in Costa Rica is the use of integrated pest management (IPM). IPM involves the use of a variety of techniques, such as biological control and crop rotation, to manage pests and reduce the need for pesticides. Costa Rica has been successful in promoting the adoption of IPM practices, particularly in the production of coffee, one of the country's main exports. In addition to promoting environmental sustainability, sustainable agriculture in Costa Rica also promotes social equity. For example, the Fair-Trade certification system has been successful in promoting fair labour practices and improving the quality of life for small-scale farmers in the country.

Overall, sustainable agriculture is essential for achieving the SDGs in Costa Rica. Through the promotion of practices such as agroforestry and IPM, Costa Rica is not only promoting environmental sustainability but also economic viability and social equity. As such, sustainable agriculture is an important component of the country's efforts towards achieving the SDGs and ensuring a sustainable future for all.

Case Study Methodology

This study examines the potential for sustainable business models to align with SDGs, as demonstrated by a case study of a small business in Costa Rica. The case study approach was utilised to explore the unique strategies of Varcli Pinares, which has been widely recognised as a pioneer and exceptional sustainable business within the sustainable agriculture farming (Stake, 2005). Case studies offer an advantageous approach for exploring the 'how' and 'why' questions of research inquiries (Yin, 2013). By focusing on a single instance, researchers can engage in creative problem solving and achieve a rich understanding of the organisation being studied (Denscombe, 1998; Easton, 1992). For this reason, the case study method is particularly well-suited to exploratory research of innovative and pioneering sustainable business models.

Considering the sustainable business model of Varcli Pinares is proven to be a pioneer and exceptional in the food business world with creative strategies;

therefore, this case study takes on the company as an objective of the study (Stake, 2005). The case generally involves quite different concepts on how the social world could and should be studied from those inferred approaches (Hakim, 1987; Simons, 1996), contrary to the beliefs of some researchers who view it as the study's object (Stake, 2005). Various methods like archival records, documentation, interviews, and physical artefacts are employed while conducting case studies (Ahmed et al., 2020; Fylan, 2005; Yin, 2013). Sustainable business and sustainable development regarding human beings and the planet could harmonise with each other as well as stay sustainable economically, as was found in a single case study on a small business from Costa Rica (Ahmed et al., 2023).

To gather data, the researchers employed various methods, including archival records, documentation, interviews and physical artefacts (Ahmed et al., 2020; Fylan, 2005; Yin, 2013). By using data triangulation, including email communication, documentary research and interviews, the study aimed to provide in-depth contextual information that can increase understanding levels superiorly (Seale, 2000; Yin, 1984).

In conclusion, the case study approach employed in this research provides an effective means of exploring innovative and pioneering sustainable business models. Findings indicate that sustainable business practices can align with SDGs while remaining economically sustainable. Moreover, this study highlights the potential for small businesses to serve as a model for larger businesses and corporations to adopt sustainable business practices.

The Case: Varcli Pinar*es*

Background

Family businesses are available in most of the countries of the world, but the percentage of the existing family business in Costa Rica is comparatively more. According to a study by the Chamber of Industries of Costa Rica (CICR), family businesses make up 90 out of every 100 businesses in the nation (Rico, 2013).[1] From SMEs to major corporations, there are over 30,000 family businesses in Costa Rica. According to research director Guillermo Salazar, family businesses are the driving force behind the growth of the Costa Rican economy. According to International Labour Organization (ILO), family businesses contribute 69% of Costa Rica's total gross domestic product (GDP) as well as 70% of the nation's total employment field (Arias, 2016).

Inception

The journey of Varcli Pinares started in 2009 as a family business producing bananas in Costa Rica with the motto to produce good quality bananas. By using effective management and cost-cutting measures, the company was able to expand its project

[1]The businesses in which there exist more than one member of a family having the ownership of the company.

from 30 hectares in 2009 with only 15 workers to 120 hectares in 120 days, quadrupling its size and providing employment for more than 60 families in the Matina area. The principles for the company are quality and productivity, through the three added values of innovation, sustainability and simplicity.

The founder, Felipe Olman Vargas, believes that 'waste' involves everything: waste of products, energy, time and natural resources. Therefore, the company has understood that sustainability is about doing things in the right way. Simplicity is the means to sustain key performance indicators (KPIs) such as quality and productivity in optimal conditions while reducing the consumption of resources. The goal of Varcli Pinares is to change the status quo by creating a process of sustainable innovation for the environment in addition to providing premium bananas with exquisite flavours and quality.

In addition to searching for new markets and adapting to shifting paradigms, the company is currently exporting to the Middle East, Spain, Italy, Japan and the United States. Varcli Pinares has been the only commercial off the grid farm in Costa Rica for almost 12 years now, proving that it is possible to excel in other parameters such as production (3,800 boxes a year, close to being the top performer) and with recognitions for the quality, changing the paradigms for harvesting and packing techniques; utilising only sustainable energy sources.

Sustainable Operations

Varcli Pinares ensures sustainable production of bananas through sustainable management and proper use of natural resources. This family business is ensuring sustainable operation through the use of solar energy, water consumption and reduction in the use of herbicides and chemicals. The company is fully invested in clean energies. To keep up with the growth and diversification programmes, in 2020, Varcli has renewed its solar panels and batteries doubling the packing house energy production capability. The founder has said,

> We are conscious about our carbon footprint, and in Varcli's vision, we must protect and grow. We have protected 120 hectors of forest and, as the most active way to reduce our CO2 footprint, we have set up 50 hectares of woodlands to assure that, no matter what, we can compensate for all of the CO2 that comes out from the process, capturing it with our own efforts.

Varcli Pinares ensures sustainable production of bananas through sustainable management and proper use of natural resources. This family business is ensuring sustainable operation through the use of solar energy, water consumption and reduction in the use of herbicides and chemicals.

Environmental Sustainability

Water consumption and degradation are two critical factors of human footprint in our ecosystem. The company's first step, almost 11 years ago, was to reduce consumption. For this, their team redesigned the whole system so that their packing water consumption was reduced from 145 litres to 5 litres per banana box (95% reduction). Doing this did not solve the degradation problem, so in 2020, they installed a water purification plant in their packing house which allows them to clean their water, securing the quality of water that they send back after their use. In comparison to conventional packing plants, Varcli Pinares S. A. has pioneered the reduction of water consumption from 145 litres per banana box to just 5 litres. This was made possible using a novel production technique called 'New Millennium', which entails the production of banana boxes without the use of water tanks.

By employing this methodology, the business was also able to decrease the quantity of chemicals required for the use and recycling of water in the banana tanks, as all that was required to make the water potable was the addition of chlorine.

Varcli Pinares S. A., which generates all of its energy needs using solar energy, takes pride in being a pioneer in the use of this energy to produce bananas. The management has dedicated itself to becoming a no herbicide farm, with 100% of its undergrowth being controlled only with scythes. This is because they are aware that environmental sustainability involves more than just water and energy supplies to produce bananas, including maintaining the biodiversity of the soil, preventing erosion, and reducing the acidity of the soil. This practice keeps the diversity of the soil's microorganisms intact, prevents erosion, acts as an organic fertiliser when the grass is cut, keeps the soil from drying out during droughts, lessens soil acidification and promotes soil transpiration and oxygenation.

Varcli Pinares S. A. has additionally established itself as a pioneer in the application of 'Agricultural Precision' in Costa Rica by being the first business to use a new technology introduced by the fertiliser company Abopac S. A. This technology includes all the equipment needed to know the chemical, physical, biological and electrical information of the soils of the farm, the meteorological data for roughly 100 hectares of the plantation, as well as the equipment. By utilising these technologies, the business is now able to produce knowledge on a minute-by-minute basis, assisting in deciding when and what to apply to the soil in order to become sustainable over time.

The company also owns 150 hectares of additional land that will not be used to grow bananas. Instead, 50 hectares will be set aside for cattle farming, giving the business the opportunity to produce organic matter for the upkeep of the soil of the banana plantation. Through a partnership with the Costa Rican Electricity Institute, the remaining 100 hectares will be devoted to the preservation of the fauna and flora, with a commitment to plant 5,000 trees annually.

Idea Sharing Hub

After 10 years of pushing and pulling the limits of banana production systems, the company has realised that it is not all about hi-tech solutions but about doing things the right way. The company shares the conviction that ideas come from everywhere; for which they have endorsed an 'open doors policy' to lead creativity and maximise information flow through their system.

As part of their 'Open Doors Policy', anyone coming from any background within or outside the organisation can share their ideas and knowledge. The company believes that to be better growers they need fresh ideas, so they kept their doors open with no filters or weird policies, 'If you want to learn, ask, if you want to share, we'll listen'. Any cost-effective, productive or new sustainable idea is always welcomed and encouraged within the company.

Smart Packaging

Varcli Pinares has a strong value chain, and its packaging is quite unique. Due to their work and experience in logistics, the company has spotted that most people are involved directly in the supply chain of production. Hence, Varcli has smartly designed its packaging with quick response (QR) code. Therefore, when a customer or stakeholder scans the QR code, then they can see photos and information about the company's process and know about their special neighbour, Agami Heron.[2] The company has felt that they can do something to honour this amazing bird, so they designed their packaging Agami box for Varcli's premium bananas so that all people involved in the value chain can have a close look at it by using the QR code.

Thus, by creating a box with high visual impact that integrates tools that guide them into Varcli's web page and other media platforms, the company has transformed the waste (boxes) into a media platform and has created a positive impact among the people with Varcli's message of sustainability.

Ecological Conserver

The reduction of pesticides is part of the company's core principles. For this, they have implemented agricultural practices that allow them to use insecticides in ultra-low volume, trapped in the bags to protect bunches in the fields. This helps beneficial insects to thrive in their crop areas. The company also permits its employees to start their own independent farms by giving them free access to several acres of land where they can cultivate crops like corn, cucumbers, papayas, chayote, and watermelons.

Sustainability Through Partnership

Through the sustainable partnership, Varcli Pinares is strengthening the means of implementation and creating a positive impact within the community. Varcli Pinares S. A. is helping both the community people and the wildlife by partnering with the Pacuare Reserve to maintain a sustainable ecosystem.[3] The partnership

[2]Agami heron is a rare kind of bird that honours Varcli Pinares with one of the prime nesting zones in the world at their neighbour's 'Reserva Pacuare'.

[3]Pacuare Reserve, created by John Denham, is the organisation responsible for guarding the biggest hatching post for the Leatherback turtles, from poachers that go to the beach to steal their eggs.

includes not only financial support for the educational programme for schoolchildren, but also the donation of banana boxes for the Reserve's staff and visitors to eat, as well as the provision of free tours that allow all student groups, foreign visitors and technical groups to board boats and enter the reserve via its canals.

The company gives back to the community by providing bats for the baseball teams of the canton, TVs and other prizes for the school and college raffles in Matina, as well as by welcoming groups of domestic and foreign students for tours of the farm where they grow bananas.

Discussion

Looking from an economic perspective, sustainable strategies and supply chain procedures are quite expensive. Therefore, these eco-friendly strategies are not cost-efficient for small businesses like Varcli Pinares. Although Varcli is a successful family business, it is difficult for the company to maintain sustainable procedures throughout its entire supply chain because of extra costs, added time, and other expenses. For the UK market, Costa Rica is the largest pineapple and second-largest banana supplier. Chiquita, Del Monte, Dole and the local firm Grupo Acon are the three companies that produce and export the majority of the bananas in Costa Rica. The majority of Central America's banana industry is currently under the control of American fruit companies. The three biggest banana producers – Chiquita Brands (formerly United Fruit), Dole and Del Monte – control more than 65% of global banana exports (McCracken). It is challenging for Varcli Pinares to compete with these titans and succeed in the market. Being a small family business, Varcli Pinares has to fight with the big companies to sustain itself in the industry.

Achieving SDGs is becoming one of the prime mottos of different organisations. In achieving SDGs, Varcli Pinares has taken several initiatives and made its principles focus on innovation, sustainability and simplicity. Varcli Pinares views sustainability as taking care of one's surroundings and the people around one while outperforming more conventional production methods in terms of financial gain. Varcli Pinares has successfully implemented SDG 2 and 12 and ultimately became an example in Costa Rica and worldwide. With the commitment to conserving biodiversity, sustainable production and responsible consumption, Varcli Pinares has created a space for environmental education that promotes sustainable production in agriculture. Moreover, Varcli Pinares has set a success story from the family business perspective in Central America.

The policy of biodiversity and production with environmental care, which is completely in line with the objectives of eradicating hunger, achieving food security and improved nutrition, and promoting sustainable agriculture, was successfully implemented by Varcli Pinares in order to achieve SDG 2. Varcli Pinares has also established effective resource utilisation and sustainable management to meet the UN's SDG 2. Additionally, in promoting sustainable agriculture, Varcli Pinares has taken care of smart eco-friendly packaging and established a sustainable environmental connection with its partners. Apart from the international export of bananas to the United States, Japan, Ukraine, Spain, Italy, China, and the Middle East, Varcli Pinares also fulfils the local community's demand. To minimise hunger, the company donates 102 boxes of bananas annually. On the other hand, to contribute local community, Varcli Pinares ensures the participation of women in packaging. All these initiatives helped Varcli Pinares to achieve SDG 2 in the agricultural production of bananas.

In the call of SDG 12, Varcli Pinares successfully implemented responsible consumption and production with the help of advanced manufacturing and distribution technologies. In achieving the goal, Varcli Pinares reduced the need for chemicals in the washing process. Varcli Pinares has established an innovation lab as the door of open ideas that could benefit the future production process. Innovation has become the KPI for the organisation, which comes from their co-workers and workers. Through the Idea Sharing Lab, Varcli Pinares continuously welcomes the idea for the improvement of responsible consumption.

Conclusion

Varcli Pinares strongly believes that simplicity is the new secret to innovation. Thus, the company strictly maintains the overall process starting from the banana plantation to handing over the ripe bananas to the customers, by keeping it simple, sustainable and eco-friendly. The company always encourages new ideas, and it is open and adaptable to changes. Moreover, the world is moving towards digitalisation and sustainability. Therefore, other companies can also learn from Varcli's sustainable business processes and value chain.

Funding

This work was supported by the InterResearch, Bashundhara, Dhaka, Bangladesh (2021).

References

ACCA. (2021). Small businesses say they don't have time or resources they need to be more green. https://www.accaglobal.com/an/en/news/2021/november/business-sustainability.html. Accessed on July 23, 2022.

Ahmed, J. U., Gazi, M. A., Iqbal, R., Islam, Q. T., & Talukder, N. (2020). Value co-creation through social innovation in healthcare: A case of WE CARE Solar. *World Journal of Entrepreneurship, Management and Sustainable Development*, *16*(4), 341–357.

Ahmed, J. U., Islam, Q. T., Ahmed, A., & Amin, S. B. (2023). Extending resource value-based circular economy business model in emerging economies: Lessons from India. *Business Perspectives and Research*, *11*(2), 309–321.

Arias, L. (2016). Majority of companies in Costa Rica are family affairs. https://ticotimes.net/2016/07/14/family-owned-businesses-costa-rica. Accessed on April 11, 2022.

Denscombe, M. (1998). *The good research guide for small-scale social research projects*. Open University Press.

Easton, G. (1992). *Learning from case studies*. Prentice-Hall.

Food and Agriculture Organization (FAO) of the United Nations. (n.d.). *Sustainable development goals*. https://www.fao.org/sustainable-development-goals/indicators/241/en/. Accessed on December 12, 2022.

Fylan, F. (2005). Semi-structured interviewing. In J. Miles & P. Gilbert (Eds.), *A handbook of research methods for clinical and health psychology* (pp. 65–78). Oxford University Press.

Hakim, C. (1987). *Research design: Strategies and choices in the design of social research*. Contemporary Social Research Series 13. Allen and Unwin.

Hodges, J. (2021). The role small businesses can play in building a sustainable future. *Forbes*. https://www.forbes.com/sites/forbesagencycouncil/2021/06/09/the-role-small-businesses-can-play-in-building-a-sustainable-future/?sh=2c7176452da5. Accessed on January 27, 2022.

MINAE. (2021). Renewable energy in Costa Rica. https://www.ministeriodeambiente.go.cr/energia-renovable-en-costa-rica/. Accessed on May 22, 2021.

Rica, L. T. (2019). Business culture and etiquette in Costa Rica. https://www.bizlatinhub.com/business-culture-etiquette-costa-rica/?fbclid=IwAR1HZ2ZjAXLeNPOqZhtbMe0yQh2W0_5in1MmM6gxrob5w0bcaiMmrWmx9g. Accessed on May 22, 2021.

Rico. (2013). 90% of Costa Rica business are family run. https://qcostarica.com/90-costa-rica-business-family-run/?fbclid=IwAR13wqgR6U_U_IV3RZamoexblu-9A2mXu4-F4SELkGEdZUBQkj7IaFiUGaQ. Accessed on January 10, 2022.

Seale, C. (2000). *The quality of qualitative research*. Sage Publications.

Simons, H. (1996). The paradox of case study. *Cambridge Journal of Education*, *26*(2), 225–240.

Stake, R. E. (2005). Qualitative case studies. In N. K. Denzin & Y. S. Lincoln (Eds.), *The Sage handbook of qualitative research* (pp. 443–466). Sage Publications.

United Nations Statistics. (n.d.). *SDG indicators*. United Nations. https://unstats.un.org/sdgs/metadata/?Text=&Goal=12&Target. Accessed on July 22, 2022.

Yin, R. K. (1984). *Case study research design and methods*. Sage Publications.

Yin, R. K. (2013). *Case study research: Design and methods*. Sage Publications.

Chapter 2

Sustainable Approaches to Poverty and Challenges From the 21st Century

Kyla L. Tennin[a] *and Shelli Brunswick*[b]

[a]Lady Mirage Global, Inc, USA
[b]Space Foundation, USA

Abstract

The Swedish International Development Cooperation Agency (SIDA) (2019) explicated there are four dimensions of poverty, and they include (1) resources, (2) opportunities and choice, (3) power and voice and (4) human security (e.g. violence issues and concerns). Contrastingly, Ellis (1984) postulated dimensions of poverty are social, economic, legal and political poverty. The Organisation for Economic Co-operation and Development (OECD) (2015) stated poverty is not always about income, indicating 'income poverty'. Deprivation factors can be broad, but reported poor health, inadequate living standards and lack of education are dimensions of poverty (OECD, 2015). Also, according to the World Bank, the world's extremely poor are people who live on less than $1.90 USD per day (Beck et al., 2020). The $1.90 amount is at 2011 purchasing power parity levels. Additionally, the $1.90USD amount has decreased significantly over the last decades (Beck et al., 2020). Nevertheless, entrepreneurship, UN SDGs and technology can be strategies for sustainable alleviation of poverty and pandemic global economic recovery, in the 21st century.

Keywords: Prime Minister; Prime Minister; poverty; entrepreneurship; United Nations sustainable development goals (UN SDGs); economic recovery; poverty alleviation; post-pandemic development; human security; income inequality; technology for development

Understanding the Multi-Dimensional Nature of Poverty, 13–41

Published under exclusive licence by Emerald Publishing Limited
doi:10.1108/978-1-83753-292-620241002

Introduction

Over the years, the word empower has become widely applied in the organisational sciences (House, 1988; Neilsen, 1986) in organisations. Particularly from an organisational structure, leadership and management, leaders versus subordinate, and resources access and allocation position (Roberts, 1986). Within the context of sustainable development, economies and economic growth, empowerment is defined somewhat similarly. Yet, from distinct organisational environments. Though, staying in the confines of *a business or conducting business* as the outcome. To exemplify, globally and contemporarily, economic development is generally defined as the enhancement or growth of an economy. Traditionally, economic growth concerns increasing access to jobs for people and individual's overall quality of life or well-being. Particularly, during times of crises, to lift economies going downward, out of spiraling conditions. For example, like a recession, epidemic or pandemic. Further, job creation can occur via entrepreneurship, which is someone starting a business and hiring other employees.

Moreover, economic empowerment, economic development and women's empowerment can be linked by the decision-making perspective. Making decisions about leadership, resources and even finances to improve the well-being of a group of people or person's lives. For instance, a household. Still, Rao et al. (2014) reported economic empowerment directly affects economic development and vice versa. Duflo (2012) explicated similar outcomes but claimed the *empowerment-development connection* is too weak for self-sustainment after conducting an extensive literature review. As a result, commitments related to equality policy need to be constantly reviewed and revised (Duflo, 2012). Overall, an exemplification of decision-making is presented next.

Mohyuddin et al. (2012) performed a qualitative anthropological study on village women's economic empowerment, village women who work in horticulture and agriculture. So, Mohyuddin et al. (2012) explained economic empowerment within the context of *economic empowerment of women* and contended economic empowerment is about being able to make decisions; the capacity to make decisions. To demonstrate, if women are economically empowered, they make decisions or participate in decision making (Ballon, 2018; Mohyuddin et al., 2012). Comparably, Aziz et al. (2021) argued empowered women make income, resources, leadership and even time decisions. However, in some countries, cultural norms of the nation might prevent women from making decisions. Or limit them from making decisions about household finances or income, including exerting control over finances, whether they work in agriculture inside or outside of the home (Aziz et al., 2021; Mohyuddin et al., 2012). Inside of the home to provide food for the family or outside of the household via a business (Aziz et al., 2021; Mohyuddin et al., 2012). Via a business, taking them from informal to formal employment (Mohyuddin et al., 2012).

Literature Review

The Swedish International Development Cooperation Agency (SIDA) (2019) explicated there are four dimensions of poverty, and they include (1) resources,

(2) opportunities and choice, (3) power and voice and (4) human security (e.g. violence issues and concerns). Contrastingly, Ellis (1984) postulated dimensions of poverty are social, economic, legal, and political poverty. The Organisation for Economic Co-operation and Development (OECD) (2015) stated poverty is not always about income, indicating 'income poverty'. Deprivation factors can be broad, but reported poor health, inadequate living standards and lack of education are dimensions of poverty (OECD, 2015). Also, according to the World Bank, the world's *extremely poor* are people who live on less than $1.90 USD per day (Beck et al., 2020). The $1.90 amount is at 2011 purchasing power parity levels. Additionally, the $1.90USD amount has decreased significantly over the last decades (Beck et al., 2020).

Dissimilar to Ellis (1984), Sida (2019) and OECD (2015), The Australian National University, Canberra (ANU) (2022) reported on poverty being 'material', for example, lack of food, water, clothing and sanitation. However, there are non-material dimensions of poverty too, like voice, relationships and time-use (ANU, 2022). Voice can be political voice. Likewise, education, energy, health (e.g. well-being deprivation) and employment are dimensions of poverty too (ANU, 2022). Finally, and interestingly, Kumar (2018) argued poverty can be relative, absolute, generational, situational, urban and/or rural, derived from economical, social and/or political qualities. In contrast, Beck et al. (2020) claimed poverty dimensions are deprivations of the global poor and are causally associated with the economies political contents and their economic institutions. Including international institutions related to security, trade and the country environment (Beck et al., 2020).

Each of the authors reveal that a variety of poverty dimensions exists. Beck et al. (2020) explained several multidimensional poverty indices exist too. Including the Multidimensional Poverty Index and Human Development Index (Beck et al., 2020). The focus of this chapter is to provide an overview of formative debates regarding poverty dimensions, indexes that exist, key findings (Beck et al., 2020) and solutions to the poverty dimensions of lack of education, resources and opportunities and choice. Each is connected to increasing income, which can be accomplished via entrepreneurship. Recognising these poverty dimensions as key deprivations of the global poor to resolve using United Nations 2030 sustainable development goals (SDGs) 4 (quality education), 8 (decent work and economic growth) and 17 (strategic partnerships). Decent work and economic growth via using the vehicle of entrepreneurship, to assist in alleviating poverty. Although SDG number one is no poverty.

The anthology shows in detail how such measures can be improved, from a variety of disciplinary perspectives (Beck et al., 2020). It shows that there are different methods of poverty research that require further investigation. Which could also be the reason for the many different categories of poverty dimensions of the global poor. Yet, research requires further investigation including participatory studies (value) surveys, public consensus building, the constitutional approach and financial diaries (Beck et al., 2020). Finally, we show that there is an ongoing problem of epistemic asymmetries in global poverty research and discuss responsibility for addressing poverty, including the responsibilities of academics (Beck et al., 2020).

The Current Digital Era

The 21st century digital era regards using social media, websites and the internet to perform market research and operate e-Commerce (or online) businesses, due to the recent COVID-19 pandemic (Kim, 2022). Kim (2022) proclaimed a large amount of business is completed online to avoid COVID-19 spreading. Business completed online includes gaining an education, shopping, socialisation, fitness and entertainment (Kim, 2022). Hence, decreasing physical contact between people. Kim (2022) argued performing business online *helps* individuals make decisions (Kim, 2022).

Furthermore, the present digital era has its own challenges. To explain, to suggest digital era recommendations to governments, small and medium-sized enterprises (SMEs), and entrepreneurship-based universities or business schools on how companies can elevate their brand image using a business website and/or social media Suryani et al. (2021) surveyed 400 participants. Suryani et al. (2021) found having a business website or social media does not directly affect the brand image of an SME. Still, similar to Kim (2022) and Razmetaeva et al. (2021) advised some people use the Internet less than other people due to cybercrimes. Razmetaeva et al. (2021) argued the cybercrimes and legal systems are prime issues in the current digital age because of jurisdictional challenges.

Moreover, Dr Beata Javorcik, PhD, chief economist at the European Bank for Reconstruction and Development participated in the 2021 seventh World Investment Forum United Nations Conference on Trade and Development (UNCTAD) Conference on Investing in Sustainable Development as an *academic track* panelist. Dr Javorcik advised she conducted research on technology challenges in developing economies and some of the concerns are (1) technology access, (2) skills for using technology and (3) payment security concerns and knowing how to make purchases online. Regarding skills for using technology, particularly older individuals need technology skills because it has been found that they do not know how to use the internet (B. Javorcik, personal communication, 18 October 2021).

Dr Javorcik contended some excellent points. However, what should also be discussed, possibly even first, is do older people own a computer, know how to use a computer or have finances to purchase a computer or some other device with internet access if they current do not own a computer? Including, if internet access is available in the area where they live or conduct business, do they have monetary resources to purchase Internet access? Each question is important to discuss, especially when considering how to alleviate poverty and empower people. For example, empowering people during COVID-19 since digitisation of products and services have become increasing important. Digitisation being highly necessary for current entrepreneurs, potential entrepreneurs and corporate workplaces. As a monetary resources example, Medina-Vicent (2018) argued, in rural areas, like Africa, women are poor and excluded from political and economic resources.

Additionally, at the same conference, on a different panel, a high-level panel discussing *MNEs and women empowerment*, Dr Marie-France Paquet, PhD and Ms Asa Regner, deputy executive director of United Nations (UN) Women had differing perspectives. Dr Marie-France Paquet, PhD, is a chief economist at Global Affairs Canada and recommended women corporate executive's empowerment strategies should centre on promoting women onto boards of directors and the motion should be a legal mandate for public companies (M.-F. Paquet, personal communication, 19 October 2021). Ms Regner advised women's empowerment can occur by putting women in senior leadership positions in MNEs (A. Regner, personal communication, 19 October 2021). Former female president of Mauritius, Madame President Dr Gurib-Fakim stated there is a difference between women and leadership and women in power, like board directors. Women in power contain the ability to promote women in leadership.

Dissimilar to Ms Regner and Dr Paquet, Dr Anne Harrison, PhD, is the Bank of America dean at University of California, Berkeley Haas School of Business and contended women, for example, even women entrepreneurs, can be empowered by teaching them how to use technology. Digitisation skills are needed for the current times nations are in (A. Harrison, personal communication, 19 October 2021). However, typically, if internet access is available to the women in or near where she lives or conducts business in, she doesn't have the financial resources to pay for it (A. Harrison, personal communication, 19 October 2021). Based on extension and severe past personal experiences and why entrepreneurship as a solution to poverty alleviation is the focus of the chapter herein, Dr Harrison's stance is precise. Also, women entrepreneurs who are non-traditional entrepreneurs like farmers, rural village sewers, jewelry makers, and sales-women United Nations Women (UN Women) works with via their WE Accelerate programme highlighted such entrepreneurs do not have access to mobile phones, so likely not a [laptop] computer.

Conclusively, the G20 Women's Forum for the Economy & Society (WFES) (2021) advised *automation* is a part of the digital era. Plus, alternative remedies for women to generate income and be included in the decision making for economies needs to be strategised. Women have encountered financial inclusion and gender equality challenges for decades, and still during the COVID-19 pandemic. The WFES (2021) explicated with the G20 Barometer 2021 report reskilling programs to educate women should occur. In addition to reskilling, upskilling and cross-skilling too (WFES, 2021). Particularly for corporate professions in science, technology, engineering and mathematics (STEM) fields (WFES, 2021). Specifically for women who are at risk of losing employment their country of work because of non-automated jobs shifting to automated (WFES, 2021) or robotic jobs. However, *entrepreneurship* can occur within such fields too, for poverty alleviation which is discussed next in the *How Space Creates Opportunity* section. A discussion of space technology, patents, patent transfers, commercialisation research and technology for entrepreneurial opportunities.

Dell Technologies (2017) postulated 85% of 2030 STEM jobs have yet to exist, but can be developed by STEM professionals now since they are innovative. However, inequalities in businesses do exist. For example, 35% of companies around the world are woman-owned (WEConnect International, 2021), a small percentage. Further, only a small number of woman-owned firms receive contract awards (WFES, 2021). To compare, WFES (2021) reported through its World

Development Indicators, World Bank Group posited globally, only 1% of private and public funding goes to women-owned firms to fund their projects. To compete in the global marketplace and economy, funding is critical. Most notably, WFES (2021) argued prime contractors who list planned subcontracting to women-owned firms during procurement processes, in their submitted bids, should be given extra points (WFES, 2021). Nevertheless, entrepreneurship is the key to economies recovering in times of crises, economic growth, and launching innovative ideas (WFES, 2021).

Last, for the G20 Barometer 2021 report, 88% of survey respondents agreed G20 countries need to invest in educating girls and women in STEM professions (WFES, 2021). Yet, of primary importance is 11% of women's STEM professions, which is approximately 180 million jobs in the STEM workforce, are at risk of automation (Brussevich et al., 2018). Automation puts jobs at risk of being lost, women losing employment (Brussevich et al., 2018), possibly leading to poverty. Most companies included in the report advised they plan to substantially decrease their labour force because of automation (WFES, 2021). All of the commentary herein *can suggest* women-owned enterprises via entrepreneurship should be considered to save jobs and assist with alleviating poverty.

Objectives

The aim of the chapter herein is to emphasise (1) resources, (2) opportunities and choice, (3) power and voice and (4) human security is needed to address sustainable poverty alleviation. Additionally, sustainable poverty alleviation and pandemic global economic recovery in the 21st century, which can increase economic development. Specifically, this can be accomplished by exercising the vehicle of entrepreneurship, UN SDGs, and digital business transformation. The chapter is placed mainly within the context of women's entrepreneurship and empower to exemplify poverty and solutions to alleviation.

How Space Creates Opportunity to Move Beyond Poverty

One of the things many people don't realise is just how big the global space ecosystem is. The global space economy is estimated to be $469 billion and is forecasted to grow to $1.4 trillion by 2030 (Space Foundation Editorial Team, 2023). More than 90 countries are operating in space today, with additional countries on their way to establishing space programs.

Some people think, 'What does space have to do with poverty?' Quite a lot actually. The modern space ecosystem provides boundless opportunity to improve quality of life, alter one's career trajectory, and transform economic circumstances. Space changes everything!

Research shows that commercial expansion in the space ecosystem accounts for 80% of new opportunities, making it fertile ground for women and other underrepresented groups to become active participants in and beneficiaries of the space economy. Importantly, the space industry and space technologies have also grown resilient to the economic shock and uncertainty that have become hallmarks of the last few years. Space provides stability.

Chief among reasons why space is well-positioned to lift people out of poverty is the fact that an increasing number of industries rely on space technologies. Uses are broad and intersect in exciting ways that we'll discuss later in this chapter. And space becomes even more exciting because traditional barriers to entry are disappearing. We need everyone from rocket scientists to project managers to welders – from virtually every community around the world. This creates an enormous talent pool that can be put to work to solve Earth's– and humanity's – greatest challenges.

Yet, to make this vision of using space to lift people out of poverty a reality, we first must be honest about where we are so that we can address the issues that hinder progress. We have to acknowledge that the challenges for women and other underserved groups are deeply rooted in the systemic limitations of the traditional educational system, insufficient lifelong learning programs, and the absence of mentoring programs and role models.

So, how do we overcome these challenges? Space Foundation's Centre for Innovation and Education created a workforce development road map that outlines five core disciplines that address the issues to truly make space for all. (1) awareness of space technology impact and opportunities, (2) access that opens doors to space industry jobs, careers, and contracts, (3) training for lifelong learning at every stage, (4) connections to people through a vast network and (5) mentorship of young leaders to develop role models for the next generation. Taken at the macro level, these disciplines can be viewed as an on-ramp to space and a better life for all.

Awareness of Space Technology's Impact and Opportunities

For a brighter future, we must broaden awareness of space technology, its impact on virtually every facet of daily life on Earth and of the plethora of jobs, careers and business ventures available. Most people simply do not have any idea of the role space technologies play. And why should they?

Space has generally been portrayed solely within the box of space exploration – rockets, astronauts and missions. Yes, space exploration is wonderful and exciting; yes, it contributes to science, but that's not all space is good for. Space exploration is only a fraction of what comprises the global space ecosystem. What it brings us or enables, however, is extraordinary. Satellites that help defend our respective countries and power our mobile phones, medical imagery for diagnostic testing, precision agriculture and new ways to grow food, and so much more.

By raising awareness of what the space sector has to offer, we can inspire lifelong learners to pursue studies, careers and new business ventures across a broad range of space technology-based industries which further fuels innovation and creates the necessary lift to bring people out of poverty.

Access That Opens Doors to Space Industry Jobs, Careers and Contracts

One of the ways Space Foundation (and others) aspires to break down the barriers to entry and allow access for all people to jump into the space ecosystem is through *models of partnership and sponsorship*. By aligning on goals and uniting resources and connections, organisations can open the door to demographics previously shut out from good paying jobs, jobs that will enable advancement and that provide a path to growth.

Sponsor or partner-initiated contacts may not guarantee a job for an individual, but they can make the process of proving one's skills and worth possible; they make connections possible and facilitate conversations. To develop the workforce necessary to grow the space ecosystem to its full potential, support from partners and sponsors will be required. And it is not a one-way street. Collaboration benefits individuals and suppliers as well as the organisations that hire and contract with them by building a robust pipeline of qualified space technology contributors that will continue to grow over time.

Training for Lifelong Learning at Every Stage

While education often begins in school, it certainly doesn't end there. For space innovation to take place, the current and future workforce needs training. Space Foundation and other international organisations endeavour to assist lifelong learners from the student to professional levels.

Because space needs all skill levels, ages, demographics, and because space work happens all over the world, training programs will never be one-size-fits-all. And thanks to modern technology, they don't have to be. Transitioning to a career in space doesn't have to mean a specialised degree or going to graduate school. It could be based around a wide range of multimodal training options, like hands-on camps, field excursions, self-guided online webinars and collaborative regional workshops for training. It may mean a more formal online certificate course or taking advantage of a company's professional development programs. Reskilling to keep knowledge fresh and up-to-date or upskilling to learn new skills is vital to not only growing and retaining a vibrant space workforce, but also to empowering people to improve their circumstances. It is never too late to partake in learning opportunities.

Connections to People Through a Vast Network

Space Foundation has the largest global network of any nonprofit in the space ecosystem. As such, the co-author of this chapter has a front-row seat to the connections made through this network and the types of collaborations that are created. She sees it as the ultimate resource to connect aspiring space enthusiasts to workforce and career opportunities. Other organisations share similar goals and can also serve as connective tissue.

These networks are where large enterprises meet small businesses and entrepreneurs to fill the vital supply chain. They make it possible for important space initiatives to become a reality for both the future of space exploration as well as advancing the quality of life on Earth. They also ensure that people are seen and valued, and that they have contributions that can be applied, and this in turn has a positive effect on alleviating poverty.

Mentorship of Young Leaders to Develop Role Models for the Next Generation

As we reconsider what 'space' is, what jobs are available and to whom, representation matters. Workers often fail to see themselves in space; space has not been a career option considered by many people, which goes back to the awareness problem. Workers, especially those who've been marginalised or fall into underrepresented groups, need mentors to show them what they can accomplish and to help them understand what it takes to get there.

Space Foundation offers programmes designed to ensure a healthy, balanced progression of mentorship at all levels – from aspiring workforce candidates to space professionals – effectively providing role models for the next generation of space industry contributors. Other organisations have quality, well-developed mentoring programs as well. Mentorship is a step on the road map that really should not be missed. We all have a lot to learn from one another, and through mentorship, knowledge is passed in meaningful ways.

How Space Creates the Opportunity to Move Beyond Poverty

Now that we've explored the workforce development road map, at least on the surface, let's look at a few examples of the specific opportunities it has created, of what it looks like in action. With some time spent talking with Nicole Wagner, President and CEO of LamdaVision, a company that makes protein-based artificial retinas, their process for doing so utilises a light-activated protein, bacteriorhodopsin, to restore functional sight to those who would otherwise be blind due to retinal degenerative diseases (Space Foundation, 2022a).

However, it was discovered that microgravity affects the ability to make artificial retinas. After participating and winning at MassChallenge in 2016 (Mass Challenge, 2022), this small group of scientists was paired up with Space Tango, an R&D and manufacturing company specialising in microgravity. The two teams collaborated to create something that will change the lives of millions of people – potentially keeping them out of poverty by allowing them to continue to work and live as normal. Yet, it almost didn't happen. Before MassChallenge, the LambdaVision team had no real idea how to access the space ecosystem.

Another great example that involves microgravity is Zibrio. Neuroscientist Dr Katherine Forth utilised NASA technology that originally measured astronauts' balance during and after space flight to help medical staff assess their fitness (Space Foundation, 2022b). The Zibrio team used this technology to develop a really sensitive algorithm that can predict when a person will fall over the next 12 months– just from someone standing for 60 seconds. These data can then be used for preventative balance therapy, saving a lot of people from pain and emergency room visits. If you had asked this World Champion Elite Ultimate Frisbee player if she had ever thought about becoming a space entrepreneur, the answer would be a resounding no.

Aside from providing jobs in exciting fields that probably wouldn't be associated with space, pulling entrepreneurs into the space ecosystem and partnering with space companies to improve the lives of others, many space advances are taking aim at poverty itself. For instance, freeze-dried food is commonplace today, but it wasn't always. In the early days of the space programme, a solution was needed to allow astronauts to take food with them that was long lasting and shelf-stable, hence freeze-drying.

Upon being invited to speak at AstroCon21 in Doha, Qatar last October, the co-author of this chapter met three university students from Qatar University who were using freeze-drying to attack a new problem. In Qatar, 83% of its population does not meet nutritional requirements for fruits and vegetables (Al Thani et al., 2018). Yet, many farms face the problem of surplus produce. Which is left unsold and eventually is wasted (ReFED, 2023).

Revive, a startup impact enterprise founded by Kateba al-Ghazali, Sumaya Yusuf and Nosheen Zehra rethought conceptions of nutritional food and built the foundations of a venture that will create jobs, stimulate economies, reimagine supply chains and improve the overall outcome for an estimated 10 million people by 2030. By using freeze-drying technology from NASA, they can provide a healthy, delicious snack and help our planet by reducing food waste and food insecurity. They use the fruits and vegetables that would normally be discarded and instead wash, sanitise, and slice it before freeze drying it for commercial use. This allows citizens to eat healthy, helps our planet and produce is redistributed to the needy.

Taking Action

The examples above should have sparked your enthusiasm, demonstrating the vast potential of the global space ecosystem. There are so many others, proving that entrance to the global space ecosystem is only limited by one's imagination.

So how do everyday people become space entrepreneurs? Through access programmes, like incubators such as MassChallenge that encourage and fund entrepreneurship, great ideas and fantastic people. Through mentorship programmes, like the United Nation's Space4Women Mentorship Programme (United Nations, 2023) in which women gain connections and learn which skills they need to be successful. Through training and collaboration programmes and partnerships designed to help people to acquire those skills. And through tech transfer programmes that eliminate a lot of the hard work associated with technology development.

Let's double-click on this last point for a second because it could be one of the most important to an entrepreneur's journey out of poverty or to alleviate the effects of poverty others may be experiencing. You may have noticed some of the examples above mention NASA's technology. NASA has poured so much time and money into technology development for specific space-related needs, yet the agency does not want to lock all its discoveries and testing away. Folks at NASA realise that space technology can be commercialised for the good of the world.

The agency itself would never have the resources to productise all its inventions, so it created the Technology Transfer Programme (National Aeronautics and Space Administration, 2022) through which entrepreneurs and organisations can licence NASA's patents and develop new applications. NASA is not alone. The European Space Agency (ESA) has created something similar; its Technology Transfer Programme Office (TTPO) (The European Space Agency, 2022) has transferred more than 200 space technologies for use in other sectors. The Japan Aerospace Exploration Agency (JAXA) is another great programme. In fact, there are smaller agencies all over the world engaging in technology transfers. By leveraging them, not only does it cut down on costs and time to market, but it underscores that innovation doesn't happen in a vacuum. We are in this together.

Space technology has the capacity to end poverty as we know it – as well as solve many other Mother Earth problems. The structures are being put in place to bring more people– especially women and underserved groups – into the fold and provide the training, mentorship, and connections they need. Now, we just must galvanise those willing to take a leap. Paraphrasing and co-opting the words of Neil Armstrong. By taking one small step as man or woman, we will take one giant leap forward for humankind.

Analysis: The Dimensions of Poverty

Kara et al. (2021) conducted a systematic review on how finance is handled across the globe, to evaluate if access to credit directly impacts accomplishing UN SDGs, like decreasing inequality and increasing education. Particularly, do individuals, socio-economic (education and current income level) and demographic (gender and race) characteristics prevent them from receiving financing (Kara et al., 2021)? Kara et al. (2021) found individuals *and* entrepreneurs' socio-economic and demographic features directly affect their ability to gain credit.

As mentioned above, The Swedish International Development Cooperation Agency (Sida) (2019) explicated there are four dimensions of poverty, and they include (1) resources, (2) opportunities and choice, (3) power and voice and (4) human security (e.g. violence issues and concerns). The OECD (2015) claimed deprivation factors can be broad, but reported poor health, inadequate living standards and lack of education are dimensions of poverty. Nevertheless, entrepreneurship, UN SDGs and technology can be strategies for sustainable alleviation of poverty and pandemic global economic recovery, in the 21st century.

Dimension of Poverty: Resources

DeJoseph et al. (2021) explicated examples of resources include psychosocial, material and socio-cognitive. Dissimilarly, Kim (2016) reported on economic resources, along with it is the most significant factor discussed within a poverty alleviation context. Especially compared to social capital and health (Kim, 2016). In comparison, Nolan and Whelan (2010) mentioned such resources too, but stated such resources are *financial resources*, placing the resources within the context of monetary and non-monetary resources. Meanwhile Brady and Bostic (2015) implied financial resources are acquired from employment. Employment can be a poverty reduction method (Brady & Bostic, 2015). Entrepreneurship is a form of work.

Wagle (2014) also discussed economic resources within the context of multidimensional poverty. For instance, Wagle (2014) evaluated the Alkire and Foster (AF) approach to measure the multidimensional aspects of poverty and proposed poverty includes economic and relational resources, and inner capabilities. Inner capabilities could be capacity or ability, which sometimes can come from education, mentorship or training. Before someone can do something, they have to know how to do it, which means they need to be taught how to do it, building capacity or ability to be able to do it. Further, Wagle (2014) evaluated the AF approach alongside measuring poverty in the United States using data from the General Social Survey, comparing the outcomes of both. Wagle (2014) reported such an evaluation is a two-step approach which allowed greater insight to be revealed about the structure and form of poverty, assisting with a more comprehensive analysis of issues, to inform better policy decision-making. This is what led to the conclusion of confirming is poverty being multidimensional and includes an economic resources element.

In comparison, Kim (2016) highlighted, poverty is multidimensional like past literature has claimed, which is accurate today. However, Kim (2016) stressed what needs more development is which dimensions of poverty are most important, noted within an agreeable list? Likewise, there are socio-cultural measures of poverty (DeJoseph et al., 2021). Yet, overall, poverty is also driven by education, income and cumulative risks (DeJoseph et al., 2021). Like Kim (2016), Dewilde (2004) stated the concept of poverty is multidimensional, but most studies base the ideation primitively on income. For example, poverty indicators used by the European Union in the National Action Plans on Social Inclusion (NAPIncl). However, Dewilde (2004) proposed poverty consists of both non-monetary and monetary constructs. Poverty manifests itself in different ways and among different subgroups within populations.

Last, resources could be thought of as ownership. Which is an activity or asset that includes a financial component. Not much research is found on listing financial resources that include land, except some. Financial resources are sometimes grouped with economic resources in literature. Inclusive, resources of identification cards, specific women's inclusion in financial decision making and receiving finances, like for entrepreneurship, and even owning bank accounts should be discussed in poverty alleviation research. For example, according to the World Economic Forum Global Gender Gap Report 2022, several gender equality gaps need closing and are currently being worked on globally. However, overall, gender parity is not recovering (World Economic Forum (WEF), 2022b).

The WEF (2022c) advised gender equality gaps can be closed via empowering and educating women with technology, obtaining an online education.

Nevertheless, public–private partnerships are critical to assist with closing gender gaps (WEF, 2022c). Also, women are shifting into entrepreneurship for various reasons. WEF (2022d) stated the amount of female representation in leadership roles within the workforce is very low. As an exemplification, in manufacturing, 19% of women are in leadership roles and 16% in infrastructure (WEF, 2022d). WEF (2022a) found systematic shocks and systematic difficulties in economies and workforces in the course of economic issues are what cause when to pursue entrepreneurship. Also, the number of women founders grew by 45% in 2020, but by 32% for men (WEF, 2022a).

The 2022 Global Gender Gap Report compared the economic profiles of numerous nations, composed of global gender gap index indicators. Complementary targets and contextual indicators. The target and indicators included categories, ranks and examples of each one. For example, (1) education and skills – whether STEM graduates, health and welfare, natural sciences, education, vocational training, business or graduates from tertiary education, (2) civil and political freedom – access to justice and more, (3) family and care – unmet family planning, (4) access to finance rights – access to land assets, non-land assets, financial services, (5) access to educational attainment – enrolment in primary, secondary or tertiary education and even (6) economic participation and opportunity – estimated earned income and more (WEF, 2022b).

The four pillars of the Global Gender Gap Index 2022 edition include: (1) economic participation and opportunity, (2) educational attainment, (3) access to health and survival and (4) political empowerment seats (to address policy issues) (WEF, 2022b). Each to consider when discussing *how to* alleviate poverty; approaches to alleviating poverty, by gaining access to particular resources.

Mackey and Petrucka (2021) proclaimed an appealing standpoint on women's empowerment in the digital era by advising technology can be utilised as an *intervention* to women with a lack of technology and education to empowerment. For example, technology can be solicited for improving women's health literacy, in promotion health education, contacting authorities through intimate partner violence apps, for accomplishing daily tasks in women's lives (Mackey & Petrucka, 2021), but most importantly, regarding this chapter of text, for financial literacy promotion. Hence, technology can improve both, women's resources and capabilities (Mackey & Petrucka, 2021).

As previously mentioned above in this chapter, job automations are underway in workforces. Likewise, recall Dr Anne Harrison, PhD, Bank of America dean at University of California, Berkeley, Haas School of Business statement above of women needing to exercise technology to be empowered and Mackey and Petrucka (2021) advising technology and education as an empowerment intervention tools. Equally, Dhanamalar et al. (2020) claimed to empower women in rural areas, technology trainings can be applied via Internet centres. Especially since radical changes in information technology and workforces are happening (Dhanamalar et al., 2020).

However, there is a problem with women's empowerment in the digital era, in rural areas with rural women, particularly one out of 10 rural women Dhanamalar et al. (2020) found even use the internet. Also, Sajeev (2021) argued higher education and learning technical skills can help add a source of income to women's lives, boosting the prosperity, socio-economic conditions and living standards of an economy and reducing illiteracy rates. Similarly, Dhanamalar et al. (2020) proclaimed digitisation is the most critical element of digital literacy and to empower women, which is connected to understanding mobile technology to be empowered economically and to keep abreast with daily national and global news. As a result, women in any community where rural or not can benefit from learning how to use technology and the Internet. Perhaps part of the training should be educating women on the benefits of technology and Internet access, including in parts of the world where people are leery of the Internet because of fraud (cybercrimes) as Razmetaeva et al. (2021) highlighted. Dhanamalar et al. (2020) claimed similar commentary by stating rural women can benefit from learning to use the Internet by smartphones to stay up to date on global trends and conduct financial transactions online, to become self-reliant. Financial transactions and even tracking financial activities, for example, using a spreadsheet, note taking tool or banks online banking platform can be completed using Apple and Android 'apps'.

Remember, Civera et al. (2019) argued entrepreneurship, internet and capacity-building trainings and seminars are *empowerment actions*, and the internet access is critical for the current times we are in (A. Harrison, personal communication, 19 October 2021) especially in the pandemic. However, if internet centres and internet access is available to the woman in or near the area she lives or does business in, she normally cannot get to it or afford to pay for it (A. Harrison, personal communication, 19 October 2021).

Dimension of Poverty: Power and Voice

Chakravarti (2012) argued voice in alleviating poverty is necessary for interventions. For example, having a voice in academia, industry and even governmental policy conversations (Chakravarti, 2012). Having a voice in such arenas will provide opportunity to improve human condition(s) (Chakravarti, 2012). Comparably, Arnot and Swartz (2018) explicated a nexus of poverty-gender-education exists. Particularly, *moral education* plays a vital role in women having a voice and working towards alleviating poverty (Arnot & Swartz, 2018).

Moral education is education that encourages *gender respect* and respectful relations among sexes (Arnot & Swartz, 2018). Gender respect, a highly contextualised form of struggle (Arnot & Swartz, 2018). Arnot and Swartz (2018) seem to imply the gender imbalance discussed throughout wider society pertains to poverty situations too. Like Arnot and Swartz (2018), Miller et al. (2010) reported children have voices too. Many children are being raised within intergenerational poverty. Miller et al. (2010) expounded around the globe, programmes called *cash transfer programs* within *social protection frameworks* were constructed to assist with alleviating poverty, both in the short-term and for the long-term. For the long-term to interrupt intergenerational poverty cycles (Miller et al., 2010), and discussed more in the *previous approaches to alleviate poverty section* below.

Exercising qualitative data from 16 focus groups and 163 participants, which were children, Miller et al. (2010) reported on the opinions of children who encountered intergenerational poverty. As a result, a framework was developed because it was found that social, cultural, environmental, financial, political and even material capital are significant for elder generations to transfer capital to the forthcoming generations to alleviate lifelong poverty (Miller et al., 2010). Miller et al. (2010) found focus group participants stated they experienced dramatic changes in their lives as a result of receiving a *cash transfer*, in practically every area of the framework's dimensions (Miller et al., 2010).

Participants stated cash transfers gave them the capacity to gain access to a variety of materials and goods, like healthcare (purchasing medicine), clothing, school supplies, food (high-quality foods too), housing, blankets and even livestock (Miller et al., 2010). Such an increase in capacity is symbolic of being able to begin to acquire resources and wealth. Like the wealth accumulation World Economic Forum (2022e) discussed, a cash transfer possibly enabling them to gain access to having a bank account. The cash transfer programme can be seen as empowering. Empowering participants with power. For example, Miller et al. (2010) reported participants stated the cash transfers enhanced their mental health, providing them with new dreams and hopes for the future, which assists with disrupting the intergenerational cycle of poverty.

Interestingly, the sixth and First Female President of the Republic of Mauritius, Madame President Dr Ameenah Gurib-Fakim stated at a 2022 Forbes Business School Centre for Women in Leadership USA conference *a woman leader is different from a woman in power*. Women in power can create leadership positions for women leaders and work with them, using their power, skills, connections, influence, abilities and talent to construct or provide access to programs, finances, policies, mentorship, basic life necessities, scholarships, new platforms and even into global connections and business networks. For opportunities, to advance (A. Gurib-Fakim, personal communication, 8 March 2022). Such a process will help shorten the time and unfavourable paths many girls and women would have to pursue to advance in life, economies would have to take to achieve sustainable development, and/or become successful for each.

Further, Arnot and Swartz (2018) conveyed a concept of *gender power* exists too. Gender power is where a particular gender works to put restraints on an opposite gender, like women, and create conditions where gaining respect is a struggle, and violence can even occur (Arnot & Swartz, 2018). So, how can poverty be resolved, among women, men, communities, groups of people, families, cities or nations if gender inequality, power and having a voice are issues? Arnot and Swartz (2018) did claim within the context of gender power, especially among poor persons, it is difficult for women to accomplish gaining respect and power. Inclusive, gender power and gender respect, women possessing respect and power, is no longer a part of poverty alleviation programs (Arnot & Swartz,

2018), which is a problem. Yet, the Mary Robinson Foundation (MRF) (2017) advised gender equality, skills, non-discrimination, capacity, and education due to location, religion, ethnicity, age, *unequal power relations*, and/or disability empower people too.

Moreover, Fenwick (2013) conducted qualitative research in Brazil and Argentina and argued to alleviate poverty, some strategies that can be used are current *policies or policymaking*. Dissimilarly, Chirisa and Matamanda (2016) performed research in Africa and utilised data analysis strategies of content analysis and textual analysis and found, to begin working towards alleviating poverty, urban local governments should design techniques and strategies for *sustainable housing*. Also, to do this and achieve sustainable housing, in Africa, an affordable and effective housing stock should be constructed (Chirisa & Matamanda, 2016). To work towards alleviating poverty for example.

Tiba and Frikha (2020) performed a quantitative study on 26 African countries and reported sustainable development is where environmental, social and economic development, and governance relate, begin to work together and cohesively. Inclusive, Tiba and Frikha (2020) stated, sustainable development is a part of building legacy for future generations. To accomplish sustainability, an institutional pillar connected with governance, social, environmental and economic development working cohesively is necessary (Tiba & Frikha, 2020). In comparison to Tiba and Frikha (2020), Mora (2019) highlighted a pillar of ecology to build legacy is important. Each author makes some important points to consider. Still, biodiversity needs to be preserved because it's needed to create food and medicine.

Conclusively, Menon et al. (2020) claimed global problems like *discriminatory laws* governing owning property and/or land, marriage and women being *underrepresented* in making decisions contribute greatly to women's empowerment (Menon et al., 2020) and gender gap problems. Each of these is of critical concern and needs to be addressed to accomplish poverty alleviation. Still, one of the main global problems causing the gender gap is *male dominance* (Gupta, 2021) in organisations and industries. Likewise, as demonstrated throughout this writing, *women in political power, lack of education, financial inclusion for women*, and now, during the worldwide COVID-19 crisis, *internet access*. Remember, as mentioned in the background section of this piece, political roles were revealed as powerful positions, and platforms that can be harnessed to empower other women. Also, Deininger et al. (2020) argued political roles are positions that come with decision-making and economic power. For political empowerment, in parliament only 26.1% of political seats worldwide are taken by women (World Economic Forum, 2021).

Last, Tennin (2022) conducted a global mixed methods survey on women entrepreneurs, with textual analysis for data analysis for the qualitative strand and found obtaining financial power is problem for women. Including in Turkey (Tennin, 2022). Women pursue businesses for a variety of reasons, including being laid off from work and needing income. However, banks ask women for past financial experience, look for legal deficiencies, market research conducted by the woman founder, the woman not being taken seriously, and more, just to fund their enterprise so they can startup and begin to generate profit (Tennin, 2022). Nevertheless, opening a business out of necessity was the main factor identified because women wanted to take control over their career more, possess greater flexibility, generate income and/or because of the lack of work opportunities (WEF, 2022a).

Dimension of Poverty: Human Security

Human security can consist of a variety of factors that lead to poverty or because of poverty. To exemplify, school shootings and community movements started by one person or a group of people. Sometimes, the movements lead to riots depending on the outcome of a certain court ruling and how the group feels the outcome should have been. As a result of riots due to disagreement with legal rulings, in the past, for example, in the United States of America for the George Floyd case, businesses were destroyed. Including destroyed due to looting as Lighty et al. (2021) of the Chicago Tribune highlighted. Comparably, Kingson (2020) displayed a table of the total damage insurance companies reported and stated cities across the United States were totaling $1B in damage to businesses because of violent George Floyd protests.

Similar violence occurred with the Trayvon Martin case, protests turned violent via physical fighting, throwing hammers into restaurant windows, and protestors blocking highways in California (BBC, 2013). Mcllwaine and Moser (2003) explicated some violence's arises because of feeling like one isn't protected, deaths, mistreatment, lack of money, lack of work, and even social rejection. To exemplify, when someone cannot provide for their family, the result is typically theft from businesses (Mcllwaine & Moser, 2003). Mcllwaine and Moser reported (2003) stealing via desperation. Mcllwaine and Moser (2003) reported one focus group participant stated they are pushed into robbery when they cannot work, allowed to work in some parts of their country.

Mcllwaine and Moser (2003) conducted primary research in Colombia and Guatemala employing inductive participatory urban appraisal (PUA) methodologies and reported when poverty is concerned livelihood security needs to be considered. Particularly regarding personal and physical security that can manifest in the form of conflict and violence in some people and areas of residence because of poverty. For example, lack of resources. So, physical safety and violence are critical issues for poor people (Mcllwaine & Moser, 2003). In many cases, more of a major concern than income poverty (Mcllwaine & Moser, 2003). In the eyes of the poor, security, poverty and violence are interrelated.

Comparable to Mcllwaine and Moser (2003), Moussa (2008) explicated violence is a threat to human security and in turn negatively impacts the achievement of gender equality, poverty alleviation and recognising women as the most vulnerable populations in society. Thus, the capacity of women needs to be elevated (Moussa, 2008). Which can assist with poverty alleviation if entrepreneurial skills are taught and implemented (Moussa, 2008).

Table 2.1. Mind Map of the Causal Impact of Poverty.

Result of Poverty	Result of Poverty Explained
Unemployment	There's no money to eat
Lack of housing	No money, overcrowding
Aggression/desperation	From having no food
Robberies	To get money
Low quality of life	No money
Gangs	Desire for money
Lots of children	Machismo, ignorance, lack of planning
Malnourishment	There's no money for food
Economic model	Policies favour the rich; subsidies are removed from the poor
Closure of business	Unemployed workers
Inequality in salaries and family food basket	Money doesn't stretch to cover basic necessities

Note: This table demonstrates a reconstructed word cloud of the impact of poverty on various people, places and things, and the nature of the poverty impact is explained.

Furthermore, Mcllwaine and Moser (2003) argued the poor defined poverty multidimensionally, stating poverty involves autonomy, self-respect, access to land and more, not only a lack of income or income alone. Additionally, Mcllwaine and Moser (2003) displayed an excellent mind map (e.g. word cloud) of the causal impact of poverty. Instead of reiterating the mind map, a table of the reconstructed elements of the mind map is inserted in Table 2.1.

Previous Approaches to Alleviate Poverty

As a continuation from the *dimension of poverty: power and voice section* above, an example cash transfer programme is the Social Cash Transfer Scheme (SCTS), designed to interrupt the cycle of intergenerational poverty in labour-constrained and ultra-poor households (Miller et al., 2010). Although, it is still unknown if this tactic is long-term beneficial to assist with poverty alleviation (Miller et al., 2010).

Moreover, with the previous discussion within the *dimension of poverty: power and voice* section about women needing financial power, a comparison can be made with Hundekar and Munshi's (2020) claims. Hundekar and Munshi (2020) claimed an excellent point regarding *microfinance loans* empowering women by helping them build their financial status and gain confidence and become self-sufficient. Durr-e-Shahwar et al. (2021) performed quantitative empirical research on 300 agricultural women entrepreneurs throughout the rural Pakistan of Punjab applying the agricultural index (WEAI), gender parity sub-index (GPI) and five empowerment domains (5DE) value sub-index. Throughout the north, central and south Punjab (Durr-e-Shahwar et al., 2021).

Somewhat like A. Harrison (personal communication, 19 October 2021), Durr-e-Shahwar et al. (2021) explicated the issues that contribute the most to women becoming or feeling disempowered are when women do not have access to resources and do not have control over finances or income. Durr-e-Shahwar et al. (2021) could mean lacking control over generating income. For instance, as previously mentioned, various nations have their own laws, policies and national and sub-cultures. Further, the absence of [proper] community leadership is a hindrance to women's empowerment (Durr-e-Shahwar et al., 2021).

Compared to Hundekar and Munshi (2020), Ab-Rahim and Shah (2019) argued microfinance programs are approaches to alleviating poverty. To demonstrate Ab-Rahim and Shah (2019), 37.9% of the population of Pakistan lives in poverty. There is a major lack of governmental resources and non-governmental organisations (NGOs) like microfinance institutions are being used to work on alleviating poverty in *rural* Pakistan (Ab-Rahim & Shah, 2019). Ab-Rahim and Shah (2019) conducted a quasi-experimental investigation with 465 respondents to identify if NGO microfinance organisations are breaking the cycle of poverty of poor persons in Pakistan. Ab-Rahim and Shah (2019) found the microfinance programs positively impacted borrowers' income, but had a negative impact on assets and savings. Yet, microfinance programs being harnessed to alleviate poverty are effective and have improved the well-being of borrowers who utilised the programme(s) (Ab-Rahim & Shah, 2019). Other approaches to alleviating poverty are innovation for farmers (Gunnarsson, 2021), Rural Land Consolidation (RLC) programs in China (Wang et al., 2022), and even an 18-month-long economic development programme called the Ultra-Poor Graduation approach in rural Bangladesh (Volpenhein et al., 2022).

Challenges to Sustainable Poverty Alleviation in the 21st Century

As mentioned in the introduction, technology can be used as a resource to empower individuals (Eitzel et al., 2018). Eitzel et al. (2018) asserted technology and technology transfer can be exploited for sustainability initiatives, especially in poverty-ridden areas, to reduce poverty where some of the most vulnerable populations live. Such an initiative can improve not only the confidence of, but the well-being of vulnerable populations (Eitzel et al., 2018). To do so, Eitzel et al. (2018) recommended collaborations between technology development engineers or alike corporations with local communities need to be created, so problems can be solved. For example, SDG problems, like SDG numbers 1 (no poverty), 4 (quality education) and 17 (partnerships for the goals).

However, Mia et al. (2018) conducted research on the microfinance approach to alleviating poverty like Eitzel et al. (2018) and reported microfinance programmes' success depends on their productivity. The programmes can only last and remain in effect if they are produced (Mia et al., 2018). One problem with such programmes performing is the lack of technology some communities have

(Mia et al., 2018). Particularly, keeping up with technological change. The efficiency of technology (Mia et al., 2018). As a result, Mia et al. (2018) recommended microfinance institutions participate in innovation activities to adopt technological change and be efficient.

Findings and Implications

Women's Empowerment and Education

Overall, it seems as if entrepreneurship, via (1) education, (2) financial inclusion and (3) strategic partnerships, can help address empowerment, and in turn, SDGs of the 2030 agenda. Including poverty alleviation. Hence, if people gain access to resources, education, entrepreneurship and strategic partnerships, financial status could possibly increase. Or put another way, finances can provide people with access to gaining resources, an education, strategic partnerships (e.g. contracts or procurement opportunities) or even to start a business. Education could be entrepreneurship education, like at Space Foundation. Education can also be financial. Also, if people, for example women, can obtain access to property, bank accounts, credit, investments and other resources, poverty can start to be solved.

Moreover, since the pandemic, in the United States of America on national television news, various news stations reported millions of Americans do not want to go back to the labour force. Workers would rather stay away from a stressful work environment. Also, when COVID-19 relief checks or stimulus packages are given, sometimes people can make more from such income monthly than from employment. Stressful work environments can lead to burnout. Nevertheless, people still need to generate income to provide for their homes or to have a back-up plan on how to gain income because unemployment and government benefits are temporary. Inclusive, the national deficit and talks of social security running out in the United States by 2037 should be taken into consideration.

Challenges and Opportunities to Education

Training and education empower people. Gupta (2021) claimed NGOs should play a significant role in training and empowering women. Still, women have not been trained, and in some countries educated, like they should have been due to deficiency of education, male domination and lack of sufficient government support (Gupta, 2021). Gupta's (2021) research was a case study where five cases were exercised along with in-depth interviews, to study women who obtained training from NGOs and launched an enterprise. Effective leadership and motivation played a primary role in women gaining confidence to network with others, network with potential customers to build relationships, comprehend government policies as women started businesses, and accomplish goals (Gupta, 2021). Gupta (2021) seems to imply entrepreneurship can be utilised as a strategy to alleviate poverty, but training and education for empowerment needs to occur first.

Government Programmes to Alleviate Poverty and Women's Empowerment

Sahu et al. (2015) reported although some government programmes are developed to empower people, for example, women economically, the government programmes do not guarantee a considerable empowerment. Based on each author's claims discussed throughout the content herein, it seems like the writers are in consensus about empowering deriving from increase in resources, materials or some sort of financial advantage. Further, Sahu et al. (2015) advised government programmes created to empower rural women economically actually *educate* women, but only partially *empower*.

The scholars seem to imply education alone is not enough to fully empower someone. Additional aspects need to be implemented. In most cases, including resources, materials or a financial component. This is interesting since various authors throughout poverty literature stated finances or income aren't the only poverty factors. Recall, the OECD (2015) argued poverty isn't always about income. Which seems accurate based on all literature reviewed and discussed herein. Other factors poverty regards are lack of resources, materials, healthcare, education, and more. Plus, comparable to the OECD (2015), Mcllwaine and Moser (2003) advised not only lack of income, but violence, access to land, self-respect issues and autonomy challenges can lead to poverty.

Last, if people are being partially empowered, it's likely that the programmes being used to alleviate poverty need to be revitalised. From research literature, it seems as if programmes need to contain multiple components, including education and finances.

Solutions and Recommendations

A variety of solutions can be realised to apply to poverty alleviation. Particularly, by using SDGs in conjunction with entrepreneurship promotion and the digital era. For first consideration, general education, financial literacy, entrepreneurship education and mentorship, investor education and executive education should be implemented widespread to improve economic and women's empowerment. This will cause economic and women's empowerment to align with SDGs. Including using SDGs to assist with the alignment. Derera et al. (2020) achieved such alignment by completing research on women's economic empowerment and entrepreneurship in Zimbabwe. Along with connecting the results to addressing how to alleviate poverty, associating with SDGs.

Further, what also must be considered is the country of implementation. Some nations do not allow women to have identification cards, drive, work, own land or participate in obtaining an education (BBC News, 2018; Safi, 2022; Specia, 2019; The World Bank, 2019; World Economic Forum, 2017; World Economic Forum, 2018). Hadid (2022) reported there is already a humanitarian crisis in Afghanistan, and it is worsening. Numerous Afghans are skipping eating meals because financial resources are declining, *and they do not have enough money to purchase food* (Hadid, 2022). In comparison to Hadid (2022), Clarke (2000) argued Afghans do have a decline in food, particularly a decrease in farm labour availability, which is also causing economic and social dislocation. Currently, food security is a major issue in Afghanistan (Clarke, 2000).

Next, to assist with working towards poverty alleviation, WEF (2022e) advised on women being promoted to leadership positions in countries. For example, by increasing the number of women in such leadership positions like policymaking and board of director seats, which can assist with helping women accumulate wealth (WEF, 2022e). Additionally, the World Economic Forum (2022e) stated access to investments, banking and property ownership is wealth accumulation. The number of women who occupy ministerial positions is increasing (WEF, 2022e). Between the years of 2006 and 2022, the number of ministerial positions for women doubled; the number of women occupying ministerial positions doubled. For instance, between 2006 and 2022, the number of women in ministerial positions increased from 9.9% to 16.1% (WEF, 2022e).

Moreover, WEF (2022e) explicated nations with the greatest percentages of women filling ministerial positions (not heads of state) in 2022 are Belgium (57.1%), Sweden (57.1%) and Nicaragua (58.8%). Inclusive, the WEF (2022e) stated the global average for women occupying parliament seats increased, from 14.9% to 22.9%. Further, the highest number of women in parliament are in Mexico (50%), Nicaragua (50.6%) and Rwanda (61.3%) (WEF, 2022e). Also, quotas were developed in various nations to require organisations to fund women led and owned businesses. Lucy Chow, a World Business Angels Investment Forum general partner, advised this too in a recent article for the Arabian Gulf Business Insight (McGinley, 2022). United Arab Emirates FlatoLabs (a Cairo-headquartered VC firm) general manager Riaan Sharif despised the quota requirement by arguing quotas are controversial and would initiate backlash from investors since quotas can be looked at as gender-oriented scheme (McGinley, 2022). However, required quotas seem appropriate to begin to help women acquire work including if via entrepreneurship, to alleviate poverty.

Including since the co-founder and general partner of the Artemis Fund (venture capital fund for women) stated at the 2021 World Business Angel Investors Week (WBAW) US summit 1%–2% of women-owned businesses in the United States received financial backing in 2013, which was the same amount a decade later in 2021 (L. Goldman, personal communication, 22 October 2021). Only receiving 1% of funding is a serious problem. How can economies recover from economic issues or poverty when half of the persons (women) who are a part of the economy, work and live in the economies are excluded from financial inclusion, making decisions, procurement opportunities for their enterprises and more? (L. Goldman, personal communication, 22 October 2021) This can include resources, owning land and having bank accounts and/or credit too.

Conclusion

Entrepreneurship, technology and UN SDGs can be strategies for sustainable alleviation of poverty and pandemic global economic recovery in the 21st century. Education, training and partnerships for women entrepreneurship are proven to be necessary for launching or growing an enterprise. Particularly for women's empowerment, to increase economic empowerment. Still, women face a number of barriers when trying to obtain an education, access start-up capital, secure partnerships, generate income and start and scale organisations and come out of poverty. Including women, a gender, being the most laid off during the current COVID-19 pandemic.

While maintaining households, completing errands, homeschooling and looking for avenues to replace income, dealing with equal opportunity problems in nearly every area of life, mostly finances, ownership and decision-making should not be the case. Empowering women can be easier if discrimination (e.g. main bias and domination) can be eradicated. Women possess the capacity to add value to economies through entrepreneurship as another small, small-medium-enterprises or even large corporate, so economies can circulate revenue.

Governments, policymakers, corporations, academia, lawmakers, nonprofits, industry leaders and regulators, not just NGOs, must take part in developing and exercising measures to empower women using financial inclusion, education and strategic partnerships. Various organisations around the globe are working on this and much progress has been made, but since numerous barriers still exist, only 1%–2% of women receiving funding for ventures and the percentage remains the same for decades, clearly, hidden issues still reside. So, there is still a long way to go; technical education is critical in this era, especially to survive unforeseen catastrophic epidemics or pandemic events, can be used as a tool to avoid burnout and can help economies grow and recover like entrepreneurship.

Acknowledgements

This research received no specific grant from any funding agency in the public, commercial or not-for-profit sectors.

References

Ab-Rahim, R., & Shah, S. (2019). Does NGO microfinance alleviate poverty in Pakistan? A quasi-experimental approach. *International Journal of Business & Society*, *20*(3), 888–907.

Al Thani, M., Al Thani, A. A., Al-Chetachi, W., Al Malki, B., Khalifa, S., Bakri, A. H., Hwalla, N., Naja, F., & Nasreddine, L. (2018). Adherence to the Qatar dietary guidelines: A cross-sectional study of the gaps, determinants and association with cardiometabolic risk amongst adults. *BMC Public Health*, *18*, 503. https://doi.org/10.1186/s12889-018-5400-2

Arnot, M., & Swartz, S. (2018). Gender respect: Empirical insights for (moral) educators about women's struggles for respect in the global south. *Journal of Moral Education*, *47*(4), 481–497.

Aziz, N., Ren, Y., Rong, K., & Zhou, J. (2021). Women's empowerment in agriculture and household food insecurity: Evidence from Azad Jammu & Kashmir (AJK), Pakistan. *Land Use Policy*, 1–18. https://doi.org/10.1016/j.landusepol.2020.105249

Ballon, P. (2018). A structural equation model for female empowerment. *Journal of Development Studies*, *54*(8), 1303–1320.
BBC. (2013). Trayvon Martin case: Los Angeles protest turns violent. https://www.bbc.com/news/world-us-canada-23332602
BBC News. (2018). Saudi Arabia's ban on women driving officially ends. https://www.bbc.com/news/world-middle-east-44576795
Beck, V., Hahn, H., & Lepenies, R. (2020). Interdisciplinary perspectives on poverty measurement, epistemic injustices and social activism. In V. Beck, H. Hahn, & R. Lepenies (Eds.), *Dimensions of poverty. Philosophy and poverty* (Vol. 2). Springer. https://doi.org/10.1007/978-3-030-31711-9_1
Brady, D., & Bostic, A. (2015). Paradoxes of social policy: Welfare transfers, relative poverty, and redistribution preferences. *American Sociological Review*, *80*(2), 268–298.
Brussevich, M., Dabla-Norris, E., Kamunge, C., Karnane, P., Khalid, S., Kochhar, K., & Gasper, V. (2018). Gender, technology, and the future of work. *International Monetary Fund*, *2018*(7), 1–36. https://doi.org/10.5089/9781484379769.006
Chakravarti, A. (2012). *Institutions, economic performance and the visible hand: Theory and evidence*. Edward Elgar Publishing.
Chirisa, I., & Matamanda, A. R. (2016). Addressing urban poverty in Africa in the post-2015 period. Perspectives for adequate and sustainable housing. *Journal of Settlements & Spatial Planning*, *7*(1), 79–87.
Civera, C., de Colle, S., & Casalegno, C. (2019). Stakeholder engagement through empowerment: The case of coffee farmers. *Journal of Business Ethics: A European Review*, *28*, 156–174. https://doi.org/10.1111/beer.12208
Clarke, P. (2000). Food security and war in Afghanistan. *Development*, *43*(3), 113–119.
Cross, R., Woodall, J., & Warwick-Booth, L. (2019). Empowerment: Challenges in measurement. *Global Health Promotion*, *26*(2), 93–96. https://doi.org/10.1177/1757975917703304
Deininger, K., Nagarajan, H. K., & Singh, S. K. (2020). Women's political leadership and economic empowerment: Evidence from public works in India. *Journal of Comparative Economics*, *48*(2), 277–291.
DeJoseph, M. L., Sifre, R. D., Raver, C. C., Blair, C. B., & Berry, D. (2021). Capturing environmental dimensions of adversity and resources in the context of poverty across infancy through early adolescence: A moderated nonlinear factor model. *Child Development*, *92*(4), e457–e475.
Dell Technologies. (2017). *The next era of human-machine partnerships: Emerging technologies impact on society & work in 2030*. Institute for the Future. https://www.delltechnologies.com/content/dam/delltechnologies/assets/perspectives/2030/pdf/SR1940_IFTFforDellTechnologies_Human-Machine_070517_readerhigh-res.pdf
Derera, E., Croce, F., Phiri, M., & O'Neill, C. (2020). Entrepreneurship and women's economic empowerment in Zimbabwe: Research themes and future research perspectives. *The Journal for Transdisciplinary Research in Southern Africa*, *16*(1), 11–12.
Dewilde, C. (2004). The multidimensional measurement of poverty in Belgium and Britain: A categorical approach. *Social Indicators Research*, *68*(3), 331–369.

Dhanamalar, M., Preethi, S., & Yuvashree, S. (2020). Impact of digitization on women's empowerment: A study of rural and urban regions in India. *Journal of International Women's Studies*, *21*(5), 1–7.

Duflo, E. (2012). Women empowerment and economic development. *Journal of Economic Literature*, *50*(4), 1051–1079.

Durr-e-Shahwar, K., Jhan, A. I., Farah, N., & Shahbaz, B. (2021). Obstacles and challenges for women empowerment in agriculture: The case of rural Punjab, Pakistan. *Pakistan Journal of Agricultural Sciences*, *58*(3), 1075–1080.

Eitzel, M. V., Mhike, H., Emmanuel, S. J., Madzoro, S., Changarara, A., Ndlovu, D., Chirindira, A., Ndlovu, A., Gwatipedza, S., Mhizha, M., & Ndlovu, M. (2018). Sustainable development as successful technology transfer: Empowerment through teaching, learning, and using digital participatory mapping techniques in Mazvihwa, Zimbabwe. *Development Engineering*, *3*, 196–208. https://doi.org/10.1016/j.deveng.2018.07.001

Ellis, G. F. R. (1984). The dimensions of poverty. *Social Indications Research*, *15*, 229–253. https://doi.org/10.1007/BF00668672

Fenwick, T. B. (2013). Stuck between the past and the future: Conditional cash transfer programme development and policy feedbacks in Brazil and Argentina. *Global Social Policy*, *13*(2), 144–167.

Gunnarsson, J. (2021). Pathways to innovation for Gambian farmers through supplier contracts. *Scientific African*, *14*, 1–14. https://doi.org/10.1016/j.sciaf.2021.e00990

Gupta, M. (2021). Role of NGOs in women empowerment: Case studies from Uttarakhand, India. *Journal of Enterprising Communities: People and Places in the Global Economy*, *15*(1), 25–41.

Hadid, D. (2022). *The Taliban took our last hope: College education is banned for women in Afghanistan*. https://www.npr.org/sections/goatsandsoda/2022/12/20/1144502320/the-taliban-took-our-last-hope-college-education-is-banned-for-women-in-afghanis

House, R. J. (1988). Power and personality in complex organizations. In L. L. Cummings & B. M. Staw (Eds.), *Research in organizational behavior* (Vol. 10, pp. 305–357). JAI Press.

Hundekar, V. R., & Munshi, M. M. (2020). The economic impact of SHG-BLP on the empowerment of rural women in India. *Journal of Bank Management*, *19*(3), 52–72.

Kara, A., Zhou, H., & Zhou, Y. (2021). Achieving the United Nations' sustainable development goals through financial inclusion: A systematic literature review of access to finance across the globe. *International Review of Financial Analysis*, *77*, 12–23. https://doi.org/10.1016/j.irfa.2021.101833

Kim, S.-G. (2016). What have we called poverty? A multidimension and longitudinal perspective. *Social Indicators Research*, *129*(1), 229–276.

Kim, M. (2022). How can I be as attractive as a fitness YouTuber in the era of COVID-19? The impact of digital attributes on flow experience, satisfaction, and behavioral intention. *Journal of Retailing and Consumer Services*, 63–64. https://doi.org/10.1016/j.jretconser.2021.102778

Kingson, J. A. (2020). Exclusive: $1 billion-plus riot damage is most expensive in insurance history. https://www.axios.com/2020/09/16/riots-cost-property-damage

Kumar, G. (2018). What is poverty and its types? https://www.jagranjosh.com/general-knowledge/what-is-poverty-and-its-types-1523453034-1

Lighty, T., Marx, G., Gutowski, C., & Lee, W. (2021). Chicago's 2020 unrest: A Tribune investigation documents the scope of the damage and its lingering impact on neighborhoods, businesses. https://www.chicagotribune.com/investigations/ct-chicago-2020-looting-unrest-damage-george-floyd-police-killing-20210602-olbvgmfylna3jarumzonp5zkqe-htmlstory.html

Mackey, A., & Petrucka, P. (2021). Technology as the key to women's empowerment: A scoping review. *BMC Women's Health*, *21*(1), 1–12.

Mass Challenge. (2022). Mass challenge: The global network for innovators working to solve massive challenges. https://masschallenge.org/

McGinley, S. (2022). *Quotas for funding women-led startups could address male bias.* https://www.agbi.com/analysis/quotas-for-funding-female-startups-could-address-male-bias/

Mcllwaine, C., & Moser, C. (2003). Poverty, violence and livelihood security in urban Colombia and Guatemala. *Progress in Development Studies*, *3*(2), 93–178. https://doi.org/10.1191/1464993403ps056ra

Medina-Vicent, M. (2018). Repudiating feminism: Young women in a neoliberal world. *Filanderas*, (3), 129–132.

Menon, S., Ranjitha, M., & Sharma, S. (2020). A study on the status of women's empowerment in urban Bangalore, India. *Journal of International Women's Studies*, *21*(5), 1–12.

Mia, M. A., Zhang, M., Rasiah, R., & Alam, A. F. (2018). Evaluating productivity of Chinese microfinance institutions: A malmquist approach. *Chinese Economy*, *51*(5), 432–445.

Miller, C. M., Tsoka, M., Reichert, K., & Hussaini, A. (2010). Interrupting the intergenerational cycle of poverty with the Malawi social cash transfer. *Vulnerable Children and Youth Studies*, *5*(2), 108–121.

Mohyuddin, A., Chaudhry, H., & Ambreen, M. (2012). Economic empowerment of women in the rural areas of Balochistan. *Pakistan Journal of Women's Studies*, *19*(2), 239–257.

Mora, F. (2019). The use of ecological integrity indicators within the natural capital index framework: The ecological and economic value of the remnant natural capital of Mexico. *Journal for Nature Conservation*, *47*, 77–92.

Moussa, G. (2008). Gender aspects of human security. *International Social Science Journal*, *59*(193), 81–100.

National Aeronautics and Space Administration. (2022). Technology transfer program. https://technology.nasa.gov/

Neilsen, E. (1986). Empowerment strategies: Balancing authority and responsibility. In S. Srivastva (Ed.), *Executive power* (pp. 78–110). Jossey-Bass.

Nolan, B., & Whelan, C. T. (2010). Using non-monetary deprivation indicator to analyze poverty and social exclusion: Lessons from Europe? *Journal of Policy Analysis and Management*, *29*(2), 305–325.

Organisation for Economic Co-operation and Development (OECD). (2015). *Keeping the multiple dimensions of poverty at the heart of development.* https://www.oecd.org/dac/POST-2015%20multidimensional%20poverty.pdf

Rao, S., Vlassoff, C., & Sarode, J. (2014). Economic development, women's social and economic empowerment and reproductive health in rural India. *Asian Population Studies*, *10*(1), 4–22.

Razmetaeva, Y., Ponomarova, H., & Bylya-Sabadash, I. (2021). Jurisdictional issues in the digital age. *Ius Humani*, *10*(1), 167–183.

ReFED. (2023). *Food waste is a solvable problem – and here's how to do it.* https://refed.org/food-waste/the-problem/

Roberts, N. C. (1986). Organizational power styles: Collective and competitive power under varying organizational conditions. *The Journal of Applied Behavioral Science*, *22*(4), 443–458. https://doi.org/10.1177/002188638602200407

Safi, T. N. (2022). Afghanistan: The only country that bans girls' education. https://genevasolutions.news/explorations/dispatches-from-women-in-afghanistan/afghanistan-the-only-country-that-bans-girls-education

Sahu, K., Jha, S. N., & Gajpal, L. S. (2015). Economic development and empowerment of rural women through development program with special reference to Chhattisgarh state. *International Journal of Research in Commerce & Management*, *6*(10), 66–69.

Sajeev, M. J. (2021). Women empowerment through technical education in India. *Ilköğretim Online*, *20*(4), 2045–2051.

Space Foundation. (2022a). Space commerce entrepreneurship: Nicole Wagner president & ceo of LamdaVision. https://www.youtube.com/watch?v=_NlWvGpdV9U&t=10s

Space Foundation. (2022b). Space commerce entrepreneurship interview: Dr. Katharine Forth, CEO of Zibrio. https://www.youtube.com/watch?v=3XfnjszikZQ&t=15s

Space Foundation Editorial Team. (2023). Space foundation releases the space report 2022 Q2 showing growth of global space economy. https://www.spacefoundation.org/2022/07/27/the-space-report-2022-q2/

Specia, M. (2019). Saudi Arabia granted women the right to drive. A year on, it's still complicated. https://www.nytimes.com/2019/06/24/world/middleeast/saudi-driving-ban-anniversary.html

Suryani, T., Amar Fauzi, A., & Nurhadi, M. (2021). Enhancing brand image in the digital era: Evidence from small and medium-sized enterprises (SMEs) in Indonesia. *Gadjah Mada International Journal of Business*, *23*(3), 314–340.

Team Stage. (2021). *27 enlightening women in the workforce statistics for 2021.* Team Stage IO. https://teamstage.io/women-in-the-workforce-statistics/

Tennin, K. (2022). *The access to smart finance – Female entrepreneurship survey: A white paper to shape the future of female.* Unpublished manuscript. World Business Angels Investment Forum: Global Women Leaders Committee.

The Australian National University, Canberra (ANU) (2022). *Dimensions of poverty.* https://immp.crawford.anu.edu.au/content/dimensions-poverty

The European Space Agency (ESA). (2022). Technology transfer and business incubation. https://www.esa.int/Applications/Technology_Transfer/Technology_Transfer_and_Business_Incubation

The Japan Aerospace Exploration Agency. (2022). Global JAXA. https://global.jaxa.jp/

The Swedish International Development Cooperation Agency (Sida). (2019). Poverty toolbox. https://www.sida.se/en/for-partners/methods-materials/poverty-toolbox

Tiba, S., & Frikha, M. (2020). Sustainability challenge in the agenda of African countries: Evidence from simultaneous equation models. *Journal of Knowledge Economy*, *11*, 1270–1294. https://doi.org/10.1007/s13132-019-00605-4

United Nations. (2023). About the Space4Women mentorship program. https://space4women.unoosa.org/mentorship-program

Volpenhein, P., Kim, H. S., Kim, Y., Hussein, M. I., Biswas, J., Byun, S., & Kang, Y. (2022). Impact of a livelihood promotion program on income generation and food consumption among ultra-poor households in rural Bangladesh. *Global Health Action*, *15*(1), 1–12.

Wagle, U. R. (2014). The counting-based measurement of multidimensional poverty: The focus on economic resources, inner capabilities, and relational resources in the United States. *Social Indicators Research*, *115*(1), 223–240.

Wang, Z., Wang, W., Yu, L., & Zhang, D. (2022). Multidimensional poverty alleviation effect of different rural land consolidation models: A case study of Hubei and Guizhou, China. *Land Use Policy*, *123*, 1–12. https://doi.org/10.1016/j.landusepol.2022.106399

WEConnect International. (2021). *Lead, and others will follow*. Rise to the Challenge Campaign. https://weconnectinternational.org/lead-and-others-will-follow/

Women's Forum for the Economy and Society (WFES). (2021). *A she-covery for all: Towards the zero gender-gap*. A Call to Action to the G20 Leaders. https://www.womens-forum.com/wp-content/uploads/2021/10/WFG_CALLTOACTION_2021_proposal-01_rev-06.10_final.pdf

World Economic Forum (WEF). (2017, January 11). Land. It's time to give them equal property rights. https://www.weforum.org/agenda/2017/01/women-own-less-than-20-of-the-worlds-land-its-time-to-give-them-equal-property-rights/

World Economic Forum (WEF). (2018, August 13). 104 countries have laws that prevent women from working in some jobs. Workforce and Employment. https://www.weforum.org/agenda/2018/08/104-countries-have-laws-that-prevent-women-from-working-in-some-jobs/

World Economic Forum (WEF). (2021, March 31). Global gender gap report 2021. Gender Gap Index. https://www.weforum.org/reports/ab6795a1-960c-42b2-b3d5-587eccda6023

World Economic Forum (WEF). (2022a). What the rise of female founders tell us about the state of the gender gap. https://www.weforum.org/agenda/2022/07/rise-of-female-founders-gendergap-22/20

World Economic Forum (WEF). (2022b). Global gender gap report 2022. https://www.weforum.org/reports/global-gender-gap-report2022?utm_source=sfmc&utm_mediumm=email&utm_campaign=2780358_Agenda_weekly15July2022&utm_term=&emailType=Agenda%20Weekly21

World Economic Forum (WEF). (2022c). Business perspectives, the digital economy: To educate and empower women we must close the digital divide. https://www.weforum.org/?utm_source=sfmc&utm_medium=email&utm_campaign=2780358_Agenda_weekly-15July2022&utm_term=&emailType=Agenda%20Weekly22

World Economic Forum (WEF). (2022d). Closing the gender gap for women could help economies out of crisis: Here's how. https://www.weforum.org/agenda/2022/07/closing-the-gendergap-could-help-economies-out-of-crisis/23

World Economic Forum (WEF). (2022e). Global gender gap report 2022. https://www3.weforum.org/docs/WEF_GGGR_2022.pdf

Additional Reading

Abril, D. Y. O., Lopez, A. M. C., & Bravo, I. M. R. (2021). Empowerment of women in entrepreneurship and innovation. *Poblacion y Desarrollo*, *27*(52), 69–91.

Adendorff, C. M., Keown, H., & Amansure, R. (2020). The development of a socio-economic model to promote women's empowerment initiatives in the renewable energy sector of South Africa. *Journal of Energy in Southern Africa*, *31*(2), 34–47.

Aldossari, M., & Calvard, T. (2021). The politics and ethics of resistance, feminism and gender equality in Saudi Arabian organizations. *Journal of Business Ethics*, 1–18. https://doi.org/10.1007/s10551-021-04949-3

Alkhaled, S., & Berglund, K. (2018). "And now I'm free": Women's empowerment and emancipation through entrepreneurship in Saudi Arabia and Sweden. *Entrepreneurship & Regional Development*, *30*(7–8), 877–900.

Alrubaishi, D., McAdam, M., & Harrison, R. (2021). Culture, Islamic capital and the entrepreneurial behavior of family firms in Saudi Arabia. *International Journal of Entrepreneurial Behavior & Research*, *27*(6), 1476–1501.

Bass, B. M. (1985). *Leadership and performance beyond expectations*. Free Press.

Bass, B. M., & Avolio, B. J. (1990). The implications of transactional and transformational leadership for individual, team, and organizational development. In R. W. Woodman & W. A. Pasmore (Eds.), *Research in organizational change and development* (Vol. 4, pp. 231–272). JAI Press.

Bass, B. M., & Riggio, R. E. (2006). *Transformational leadership* (2nd ed.). Erlbaum.

Shikha, K. (2019). Entrepreneurship for economic and social empowerment of women: A case study of a self-help credit program in Nithari Village, Noida, India. *Australasian Accounting, Business, and Finance Journal*, *13*(2), 123–142.

Steffens, N. K., Yang, J., Jetten, J., Haslam, S. A., & Lipponen, J. (2018). The unfolding impact of leader identity entrepreneurship on burnout, work engagement, and turnover intentions. *Journal of Occupational Health Psychology*, *23*(3), 373–387.

Tahir, M. W., Kauser, R., Bury, M., & Bhatti, J. S. (2018). "Individually-led" or "female-male partnership" models for entrepreneurship with the BISP support: The story of women's financial and social empowerment from Pakistan. *Women's Studies International Forum*, *68*, 1–10. https://doi.org/10.1016/j.wsif.2018.01.011

The World Bank Group (WBG). (2019, March 25). *Women in half the world still denied land, property rights despite laws*. The World Bank. https://www.worldbank.org/en/news/press-release/2019/03/25/women-in-half-the-world-still-denied-land-property-rights-despite-laws

The World Bank Group (WBG). (2021, June 15). *Labor force participation rate, female (% of female population ages 15+) (modeled International Labour Organization estimate)*. The World Bank. https://data.worldbank.org/indicator/SL.TLF.CACT.FE.ZS?end=2019&start=1990&view=chart

Chapter 3

Disentangling Critical Factors for Enhancing Female Entrepreneurship and Women Empowerment to Alleviate Poverty: Focus on BRICS Countries

Michela Floris[a] *and Richa Goel*[b]

[a]University of Cagliari, Italy
[b]Symbiosis Centre of Management Studies, Noida; Symbiosis International Deemed University, Pune, India

Abstract

The 2030 Agenda for Sustainable Development underscores eradicating global poverty (Goal#1) and empowering women and girls (Goal#5) to foster sustainable, inclusive communities (Goal#11). The World Bank recognises female entrepreneurship as a catalyst for global economic growth, poverty reduction and gender equity. This chapter delves into the challenges hindering female entrepreneurship, obstructing poverty alleviation and community sustainability efforts worldwide. Public–private collaborations are crucial to support women in launching start-ups, adopting new technologies, enhancing digital skills and accessing financing in the era of Industry 4.0.

Our focus is on women entrepreneurship in BRICS nations due to their diverse growth trajectories and global economic significance. Employing a qualitative approach, we analyse public and private initiatives promoting female entrepreneurship in BRICS countries. Our findings highlight both commonalities and distinctions in their strategies and policies, implicitly contributing to poverty reduction and social and economic growth. This chapter not only identifies barriers faced by women entrepreneurs but also underscores factors fuelling their ventures. It offers a practical toolkit for scholars, policymakers and practitioners (entrepreneurs and consultants) to devise tailored strategies and actions for local growth and intervention. The study comprises four parts: the introduction, setting the chapter's goal and

Understanding the Multi-Dimensional Nature of Poverty, 43–65

doi:10.1108/978-1-83753-292-620241003

previewing outcomes; the second part, exploring female entrepreneurship as a key to poverty alleviation and community sustainability; the core, the third part, unveiling in-depth BRICS country analysis; and the conclusion, summarising implications and highlighting avenues for further research.

Keywords: UN agenda 2030; female entrepreneurship; socio-economic growth; poverty reduction; sustainable and inclusive communities

Introduction to the Study

The Sustainable Development Goals for 2030 consider eradicating poverty for people everywhere as a key goal (Goal#1), as well as empowering women and girls (Goal#5), for creating sustainable and inclusive communities (Goal#11). In such a scenario, the World Bank suggests that a powerful engine for contributing to economic growth, poverty reduction and women empowerment and inclusion is the expansion of female entrepreneurship. With this perspective in mind, the International Finance Corporation underlines that female entrepreneurship and *women's access to finance* can impress global economic enhancement.

Although there is a wide agreement that female entrepreneurship can represent an engine of growth and global social and economic change, there are still few women who challenge the prejudices and clichés related to 'think manager-think male'. Several studies have shown that women meet more difficulties in creating new start-ups, or rivalled to their male colleagues, women are more likely to continue a business family (Allen & Langowitz, 2003; Díaz-García & Jiménez-Moreno, 2010; Langowitz & Minniti, 2007).

With the aim of uncovering the reasons for this situation and thus the causes of *gender differences* in entrepreneurship, scholars have mainly focused on the micro-level, that is, *self-esteem, attitudes*, and other characteristics that lead individuals to become entrepreneurs (Schlaegel & Koenig, 2014). Additionally, focusing on the macro-level, other scholars have found that women struggle to obtain finance and experience credit market discrimination (Muravyev et al., 2009). Contemporarily, other studies have underlined that gender differences are particularly evident in defined industries (Anna et al., 2000), generating the existence of industries male-dominated and industries female-dominated. To find suitable solutions to these mentioned issues, worldwide policy interventions have been launched, with controversial results, sometimes positive (Marlow et al., 2008), others not satisfactory (Aljarodi et al., 2022), but anyway necessary to spread women entrepreneurship, especially in poor countries (Obianuju & Okeke-Uzodike, 2019). Leveraging the abovementioned concepts, this chapter aims to deepen the knowledge on this fascinating and challenging topic by problematising the topic (Alvesson & Sandberg, 2011) to uncover which barriers tend to inhibit women entrepreneurships and thus to identify critical factors apt to sustain female entrepreneurship to alleviate poverty and create sustainable and inclusive communities worldwide.

In line with these assumptions, our research questions are:

(*RQ1*) What are the main barriers restraining female entrepreneurship thereby leading to poverty? (*RQ2*) Which are the research gaps and further research areas to better understand the phenomenon?

We concentrate on the BRICS nations – Brazil, Russia, India, China and South Africa – to discover appropriate solutions to our study concerns which are experiencing very different growth paths, and their presence in the global socio-economic scenario is particularly relevant. Their worldwide significance still remains an open question.

Keeping in view the research questions, the study aims to focus primarily on:

- Uncovering barriers that, on the one side, inhibit women entrepreneurship and identifying critical factors that, on the other side, foster and sustain women entrepreneurship.
- Identifying the relation between identified critical factors and sustained women growth and empowerment, identifying scholarly and practical implications, as well as suggesting policy strategies that can aid policymakers in building sustainable and inclusive communities.

In detail, highlighting the main factors that stimulate female entrepreneurship in developing countries, this study offers a toolbox for scholars, policymakers and practitioners, *identifying a developing model* embedded in specific contexts able to improve growth and reduce poverty through the enhancement of women entrepreneurship. In-depth research reveals that socio-economic background, or the macro-level or the individual level, can be used to recover aspects that influence women's entrepreneurship. These factors appear to contribute directly to gender equality and, implicitly, concur to alleviate poverty and create sustainable and inclusive communities.

Women Entrepreneurship as a Powerful Engine to Alleviate Poverty

Women entrepreneurs have been acknowledged as having added much to the development of an economy, as has been quantitatively demonstrated and accepted (Hassan et al., 2020). By contributing more to the workforce, women have bettered millions of families overcome poverty and generate jobs. Women dominate more recent industries like electronic manufacturing, where they account for more than 50% of the workforce, thanks to their greater productivity and acknowledged leadership skills. Women in leadership positions are viewed as bringing originality to their organisations (Balhara & Singh, 2015). The value of women's entrepreneurship is highlighted by their professional, enthusiastic ethical display of tasks and impressive work skills.

In their researches, Abd Rani et al. (2019) asserted that there are still questions regarding the traits that add to the victory of female entrepreneurship. As a result, research on traits like self-esteem, ambition, risk-taking, self-assurance and creativity is necessary because, according to earlier studies, these traits were most frequently cited in comparison to others (Hassan et al., 2014; Hoe et al., 2012; Lai et al., 2010; Mendryk & Dylon, 2014; Ummah & Gunapalan, 2012). Tambunan (2009) emphasised the need for female innovators to be aware of the traits necessary for their initiatives to be successful.

Female Driven Entrepreneurship

Although entrepreneurship with innovation can aid in knowledge development that may be used for cross-border entrepreneurship and value co-creation, innovation is vital since it represents the achievement of women entrepreneurs (Lai et al., 2010). In addition, the calibre of the entrepreneurial activity adds value (Nair, 2016; Saiz-Alvarez & Martínez, 2019). Women may contribute creative ideas to the table because of their unique viewpoint on society, the community and their polished management skills. This benefits the economy by reducing unemployment and promoting economic growth (Kovid et al., 2021; Kumari & Mor, 2021).

Barriers to Female Entrepreneurship

Obstacles such as a lack of entrepreneurial skills, financial constraints and other challenges regularly stymie women's innovative business practises. While Neumeyer et al. (2019) reported on differences in the entrepreneurship ecosystems of male and female entrepreneurs, Chatterjee and Ramu (2018) cited factors such as a lack of access to better research opportunities, funding, laboratory equipment and facilities, opportunities for knowledge exchange and so on that prevent women entrepreneurs from innovating. Nählinder et al. (2015) discovered no significant differences between male and female entrepreneurs in terms of innovativeness.

Financial Barriers

Women are recognised to be at a higher risk of not being able to afford potential expenses and to have less access to credit (Kumari & Mor, 2021; Suseno & Abbott, 2021). Land, property and inherited wealth are examples of assets that produce financial capital yet are only passed down through inheritance in many emerging and undeveloped nations. The main impediment to women's financial independence and agency in these countries is the difficulty in asserting a claim to their fair share of inherited property. This is because there is a pervasive social custom that restricts a woman's fair portion to her dowry. It also places the woman under the obligation of marriage, and frequently even having children, in addition to restricting the amount of financial assets that are in her name. Such financial obstacles limit the woman's independence and freedom of choice.

Social and Institutional Barriers

In their study, Fenwick and Hutton (2000) provided evidence that many women have subjectively defined success as right to choose your daily activities, being able to maintain work–life balance and family obligations, giving back to the community, building one's reputation, having children and achieving a high quality of life. Women are disincentivised from investing in exploring new career and advancement opportunities if their capacity to work and innovate compromises delicate this work–life balance. The lack of access to education and knowledge during the earliest stages of life is another typical social barrier to women-led innovation. While 82% of men are literate in India, only 64% of Indian women are.

Women's ability to lead visionary decisions is further hampered by social restraints including predetermined expectations about the roles that women should play in society. According to Bijedić et al. (2016), women self-select into female-typed occupations and working arrangements, like part-time work, as a result of institutional constraints and conventional role models. This becomes the main cause of women's reluctance to pioneer new directions in learning and exploration, which stifles creative and critical thought.

To combat the absence of entrepreneurial and mentality training that has persisted due to decades of traditional role management in societies, women also require ongoing incubatory support and training. The possibilities of women innovating are therefore rather small in situations where there is a dearth of institutional and vocal support for fostering women-driven initiatives through government-aided programmes (Al-Razgan et al., 2021; Badstue et al., 2018; Kumari & Mor, 2021). According to the study's findings, social constraints such as a lack of institutional support, a lack of education and training and outdated social standards might limit women from attaining their full potential and supporting innovative growth.

Critical Factors Enhancing Female Entrepreneurship and Empowerment

It was discovered that a variety of elements, both widespread and specific to each person, contribute to the emergence of female-driven entrepreneurs (Badstue et al., 2018; Kumari & Mor, 2021; Marvel et al., 2015; Nair, 2020; Suseno & Abbott, 2021). According to a 2007 study by Nurwahida, an innovator's attitude towards taking chances when making an unclear decision is known as risk taking. According to Schumpeter (2013), entrepreneurs' ingenuity and knowledge are what make them creative (LeBlanc, 2013; Śledzik, 2013). Entrepreneurs must be inventive, according to Peprah et al. (2022), because a lack of these qualities may result in a low survival rate for women business owners.

Women leaders are inspired to grow when they receive social recognition in the forms of regard, fame and admiration. Gaining social capital and status for oneself and one's family is a key motivator for women entrepreneurs to take risks with new businesses, claim Kumari and Mor (2021). According to certain research,

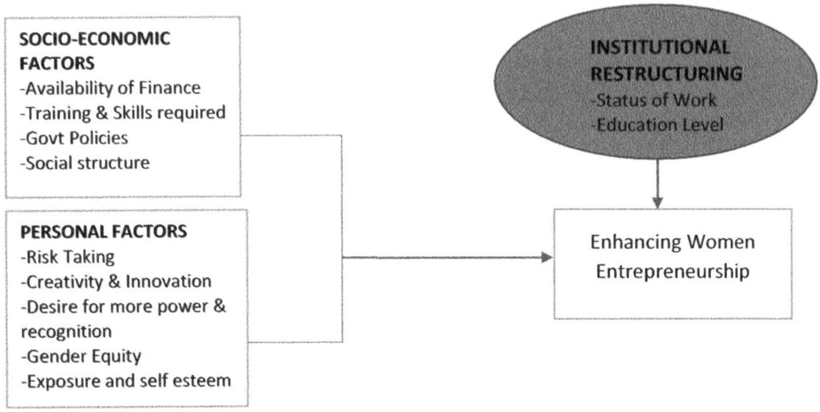

Fig. 3.1. The Conceptual Framework. *Source:* Authors' elaboration.

women are better able to understand complicated emotions, which helps them lead their teams to greater success. Teams with more women on them are more likely to make a breakthrough because diversity fosters better creativity and unique styles of looking at problems (Friedman et al., 2016; Hewlett et al., 2013; Khursheed et al., 2021; Kwakwa & Adu, 2015).

Several solutions have been proposed in various research as ways to address the hurdles to women innovating. For example, the authors of Badstue et al. (2018) and Al-Razgan et al. (2021) argue that as most rural enterprises are labour-intensive and require skills and innovation, the government should aggressively promote skill training. In order to provide a favourable environment for local businesses and to promote effective market support services in terms of product marketing, market accessibility and networking, governments must also create the appropriate investment infrastructure (Al-Razgan et al., 2021; Badstue et al., 2018; Kabasheva et al., 2015; Kariv, 2013). Fig. 3.1 depicts the conceptual framework.

Table 3.1 provides a literature review summary of some active factors and sub-factors that impact female entrepreneurship in light of UN Agenda 2030 for poverty alleviation.

Research Method

Research Design and Data Collection

This study is based on a multiple case approach (Eisenhardt & Graebner, 2007). The instances studied are representative of a modern phenomenon based on actual situations; there is no clear distinction between the phenomenon and its contexts; each case is singular and revelatory (Yin, 2008).

It also aligns with Patton's (1990) guidelines, which emphasise that 'the logic and power of purposeful sampling lies in selecting information-rich cases

Table 3.1. Literature Review Summary.

Critical Factors	Sub-Factors	References
Socio economic factors	Availability of finance	Suseno and Abbott (2021) and Kumari and Mor (2021)
	Training and skills required for entrepreneurship	Nair (2020), Lai et al. (2010), Jovanović and Lazić (2018) and Sarker and Palit (2014)
	Government policies	Nawaz (2009), Kelley et al. (2016), Al-Razgan et al. (2021) and Badstue et al. (2018)
	Social structure	Suseno and Abbott (2021) and Bijedić et al. (2016)
Personal factors	Risk-taking capacity	Marvel et al. (2015), Idris (2008), Hassan et al. (2014), and Sarker and Palit (2014)
	Creativity and innovation	Nair (2020) and Neumeyer and Santos (2018)
	Desire for more power and recognition	Nair (2020), Hassan et al. (2014) and Kumari and Mor (2021)
	Gender equity	
	Exposure and self-esteem	
Control factors	Status of work	
	Education level	Rani and Chaturvedula (2018), Mendryk and Dylon (2014) and Peprah et al. (2022)

Source: Authors' elaboration.

for in-depth study'. Cases with a lot of information provide for a lot of learning on subjects that are important to the study's purpose.

The study was conducted from October to December 2022. Primary data consisted of several documents for understanding the context of BRICS countries (demographic, technological and socio-economic features), several official documents of the diverse countries (available online) and several official websites and social media. Secondary sources comprised archival data from business publications and other documents related to BRICS entrepreneurial practices and policies. Because of the exploratory nature of this study, additional documents were retrieved and analysed until theoretical saturation was reached (Glaser & Strauss, 1979; Sebele-Mpofu, 2020; Suddaby, 2006; Walsh & Bartunek, 2011).

Research Context

According to Vieira and Veríssimo (2009), the term 'BRICS' refers to a group of developing nations that may, during the next 50 years, dominate the world economy. These countries include South Africa, Brazil, Russia, India and China. As stated on page 65 of the International Monetary Fund's (IMF's) 2017 report, 'emerging markets and developing economies account for 75% of global growth in output and consumption'. The BRICS nations are considered as investment opportunity regions as a result of their strategic locations in the Americas, Europe, Asia and Africa, which are so important to this economic growth and change. According to current research, the IMF's 2017 study that identified Brazil, Russia, India and China as the top four developing economies is what sparked interest in the BRICS nations. Despite BRICS's economic significance, there are a number of pertinent issues that need to be addressed, including a significant gender gap, a lack of affordable and sustainable energy, low capital, environmental degradation, a high rate of unemployment, a lack of infrastructure in the education sector and poverty (Anand et al., 2020; Anghinoni et al., 2021; Lustig et al., 2020; Troyano & Martín, 2017). For this reason, focusing on the BRICS countries is encouraging and can help to identify effective development tools that, starting from the improvement of women's entrepreneurship, can positively sustain the achievement of other fundamental goals, mostly focused on reducing poverty and building inclusive communities.

In a general overview, it is possible to affirm that the performance of individual countries within the bloc in addressing issues of empowerment, equality and women's rights has varied. South Africa is outperforming its BRICS rivals in terms of worldwide progress towards gender equality, coming in at number 19 in the World Economic Forum's Annual Gender Gap Report 2022. The other BRICS countries are far behind, with Russia at number 71, Brazil at number 90, China at number 100 and India at number 108. Even though South Africa has rules requiring equal gender participation in the legislature, especially for the poorer women, these regulations don't always translate into equality for the country's women.

Findings

This section briefly describes the results, firstly focusing on the single countries and secondly identifying common aspects to conceive our interpretive developmental model.

Brazil

Brazil is, by extension and population, the most important country in South America and borders most of the continent's other nations. Brazil is a federation comprised of 26 states and one federal district, and the urbanisation rate is 85%, which is relatively high. Many cities exceed a million inhabitants, starting from one of the densely populated cities in the world as well as the first in South

America, São Paulo (12,214,000 inhabitants., 22,495,000 urban agglomerates), which exceeds 10 million people considering the urban area also Rio de Janeiro (6,748,000 inhab., 12,486,000 urban aggl.). In this ranking also the capital Brasilia (2,951,000 inhabitants, 3,429,000 urban aggl.), Salvador (2,886,000 inhab., 3,430,000 urban aggl.), Fortaleza (2,687,000 inhab., 3,621,000 aggl. urban), Belo Horizonte (2,522,000 inhab., 5,271,000 urban aggl.) and Manaus (2,208,000 inhab., 2,308,000 urban aggl.).

Since gaining its independence in 1822, Brazil has come a long way (da Silva Dias, 1995). Among other goals, independence aimed to advance women in a variety of societal spheres. Brazilian women now make up 43% of the working labour force, up from 13% in the 1940s, according to the World Bank.

However, Brazil still experiences a relevant gender gap, and women in apical roles are less than men. Removing gender inequality is tough what the consulting company Oliver Wyman defined in a recent report, that is the 'sub-optimal equilibrium trap' suffered by society where women do not have the right chances to develop their talents and, thus, to know their potential to enhance social, economic and political facets of Brazil (Corrêa, 2022). This situation has concurred in building barriers and gender bias that have shaped social and cultural norms, labour conditions and workplaces. For this reason, Brazil is a fertile place to study women entrepreneurship (Allen et al., 2007). Studying Brazilian women's entrepreneurial behaviour is also justified by the status of women in that country.

An interesting study (Smith-Hunter & Leone, 2010) shows the main characteristics of Brazilian women entrepreneurs like concentration of women entrepreneurs in the services industry.

Main motivations related to the desire of self-employment, manage a firm and family responsibilities.

Main obstacles: governmental regulation and competition.

Human capital characteristics: high levels of education, professionalisation, training, previous job experience.

Financial capital: difficulties to obtain bank loan, thus, capital stemming from personal savings, money from partners and family support.

A more recent study that looked specifically at the COVID-19 era discovered that women used a variety of strategies, such as believing in societal associations in family, to manage the expectations related to running a home-based business. They also demonstrated entrepreneurial resilience and adaptability during the crisis, which is a hallmark of how women entrepreneurs overcome obstacles along the way (Ayatakshi-Endow & Steele, 2021).

Concerning the government interventions, Brazil can encounter many initiatives. There are specific federal programmes for small and medium enterprises (SMEs) and entrepreneurship, with a specific focus on women entrepreneurs. Along with SEBRAE and Rede Mulher Empreendedora (RME), the National Secretariat for Women's Policies, which has its headquarters in the Ministry of Woman, Family, and Human Rights, is working to support female entrepreneurs. This government body places a strong emphasis on equality and fairness in the workplace and the labour market as a subcomponent of its primary areas of interest, which include women's safety and rights in society. The bulk of Brazilian institutions don't seem to be doing anything to support female entrepreneurs, though. The majority of government agencies hold the opinion that specific programmes for women are superfluous, if not discriminatory against everyone else, because all products and programming are created for everyone, including women and other minority groups (OECD, 2020).

The pillar to improve women entrepreneurship is the creation of an Entrepreneurship Supportive Ecosystem, based on inclusiveness, involvement, public supports and role models (OECD, 2020).

Russia

All 86 of Russia's republics, provinces, regions and districts are under the control of the government in Moscow. The head of state is a president selected by the populace. The basis of the economy is a plentiful supply of natural resources, including oil, coal, iron ore, gold and aluminium. Its territory is roughly twice as big as that of Canada, the second-largest nation in the world. It includes all of northern Asia, 11 time zones and the eastern half of Europe. There are many different habitats and landforms present, such as deserts, semiarid steppes, thick forests and Arctic tundra. Russia has increasing numbers like 120 other ethnic groups living there, talking numerous languages and being a part of numerous civilisations. Russian entrepreneurship is strongly influenced by its historic heritage and culture (Wells et al., 2003), and entrepreneurship, as generally considered, is a relatively new concept. This concept is gendered. The entrepreneurs are often young men, and entrepreneurship is a perceived as a masculine phenomenon (Yurchak, 2003). While today's workforce is highly divided, during the old Soviet era, the Russian gender order saw women as a resource who were educated and prepared to work in traditionally masculine sectors like engineering and technology (Aaltio & Peltonen, 2009). Men typically hold the apical positions in both works for men and women (Ashwin, 2006).

Many studies underline that women's share in growth industries is increasing in numbers. According to Gale and Polnareva (2004) and Verkhovskaya et al. (2010), women entrepreneurs still frequently work in traditionally feminine industries such as beauty salons, consulting, training and small-scale production and trade. Additionally, their businesses are frequently viewed as hobby-like pursuits rather than primary competitors to those of males (Yurchak, 2003).

An interesting study (Logren & Löfgren, 2008) highlights some features that the Russian women entrepreneurs possess: awareness of individual differences, dissatisfaction with the federal-level bureaucracy, willingness to risk-taking, relevance of family–work balance, obstacles in access to credit and necessity to training and networks.

Russia exhibits a number of attempts to help female entrepreneurs on the side of official action. In particular, the federal 'Promotion of entrepreneurship' project, which is a part of the SME national project, encourages entrepreneurial education to evaluate women's entrepreneurial competencies.

In detail, the main projects are the following:

- Women's Industrial Development for Sustainability (to enhance the proportion of women working in sustainable industrial development, to entice more women into science, technology, engineering and mathematics [STEM] fields, to boost the number of socially significant projects headed by women and to entice more women to carry out industrial projects at the regional level).
- STEM Project for Women in the Digital Economy (to bring attention to women-led projects in social, cultural, financial and economic, scientific and other areas, to educate the public about the role of women in a country's socio-economic development).
- Women's Cooperation in International Trade (to increase the number of women-led businesses, including SMEs, engaged in export activities, to increase export in women-led businesses engaged in international trade, to develop effective tools to encourage export activities by offering incentives to the most successful women-led businesses engaged in non-resource exports).
- Women's Financial Literacy (to advance women's financial knowledge and skills in the age of the digital economy).
- Development of Women's Entrepreneurship (to support women's business ownership in the digital economy, give women business owners access to information, education, finance and the market).
- Most volunteers are female. Partnership for Development (to advance the volunteerism of women in association with the Federation Council and other national and local authorities).
- The Eurasian Women's Community Web Portal (to foster global ties between the Eurasian women's community and the Federation Council); Women Developing Corporate Philanthropy (to incorporate new technologies in philanthropy by raising awareness of the role of women in the development of private and institutional philanthropy, corporate social responsibility).

India

South Asian nation India, also known as the Republic of India. Its land area is the seventh-largest in the world. Its western border is drawn by Pakistan, its northern border by China, Nepal and Bhutan and its eastern border is drawn by Bangladesh and Myanmar. Its borders are the Arabian Sea to the southwest, the Indian Ocean to the south and the Bay of Bengal to the south-east. There are 36 entities in the federal union of India, which is made up of 28 states and 8 union territories. India's urbanisation rate was 1.34% in 2021, up 1.5% from the previous year. It increased 19.6% from 2010 to 2021. In India, there are 405 cities with fewer than 100,000 residents and 48 with more than one million.

In ancient India, an Indian lady had a position of honour, which was signified by the Vedic term maata. Women, like Manu Smriti, were seen as valuable entities, and girls were well-cared for throughout the early Vedic period. The practice of bigamy weakened women's positions, and the dowry and sati systems evolved during the Middle Ages. Indian society is male-dominated, and a woman still requires an anchor-person and a family. Women's domineering temperament has caused them to stroll with their heads down. It was all done from the start and is still done today. However, the reservation for women in parliament is one of the noteworthy steps done by the Government of India to address these discrepancies.

Since gaining independence in 1947, India has made significant progress in every sector, including the economy, infrastructure, science and education. Women's educational rights were promoted, and they were made aware of the importance of education, which altered women's place in Indian culture. After acknowledging women's plight in society, the government launched massive attempts to better their social, economic and political standing.

This steep fall in female labour market participation is due to a number of crucial causes, including gender inequities, wage discrimination, societal view, economic considerations, lack of knowledge, personal factors, lack of education and a lack of efforts.

According to ILO data, while the gender wage gap is gradually closing, it will take more than 70 years to close completely at the current rate of advancement. Accelerated and decisive action is required to prevent the gender wage gap from increasing and to close the present imbalance.

The two main factors contributing to gender inequality in developing countries like India, educational attainment and labour force participation, have been discussed by Jayachandran (2015), who also highlighted the predicament of women from lower socio-economic classes. As a result, empowering women and elevating their status can considerably contribute to the success of many development programmes and positive societal change (Gupta, 2006). Even though studies in developing countries have shown that empowering women is important in and of itself, it can also improve children's health and education, lower child mortality, improve organisational effectiveness in businesses, increase agricultural productivity, boost economic growth and lessen poverty.

Additionally, engaging in entrepreneurial activities can assist women in obtaining higher success, fighting prejudice in the workplace and overcoming issues connected to employability in major businesses. It also supports women's emancipation in some way.

Only about 14% of Indian women are entrepreneurs or business owners, according to the Sixth Economic Census, which was conducted in 2014. Over 90% of women's firms are microenterprises, and 79% of them are self-funded. India came in 52nd place out of 57 countries in the 2018 Mastercard Index of Women Entrepreneurs, behind Tunisia and ahead of Iran. The index considers factors including financial accessibility and ease of doing business.

According to Aparna Saraogi, cofounder of the Women Entrepreneurship and Empowerment (WEE) Foundation, there are frequently pressures and resistance from inside the family as a result of cultural preconceptions that push women to limit their responsibilities to taking care of the home. Additionally, the absence of child care support structures hinders women. According to a 2018 IMF study, raising GDP and encouraging female entrepreneurship would result in equitable access to credit and a decrease in unemployment.

Women owned only 10.11% of micro and small businesses and managed only 9.46% of them, according to the third all-India Small Scale Industries census. Despite the fact that there are more women than ever starting their own businesses, there are still many obstacles standing in their way, including a lack of funding, stringent social restrictions and a lack of time and expertise. Rather than simply establishing opportunities for women, overcoming barriers to women's entrepreneurship requires a substantial shift in people's traditional ideas and mindsets. As a result, it is critical to develop programmes that target attitude adjustments, training and supportive services. Making women aware of their existence, distinct identities and contributions to national economic progress is a critical first step.

China

China is the most populous country in the world, with a total of 1.44 billion people. Within a short period of time, it rose to the third-largest country in terms of both land area and economic output.

China's size is matched by its geographic and cultural diversity. China has a wide range of geographic locations, historical trends, economic activities and resources. China's important regions include the Loess Plateau, the Southeast Coast and Shanghai, the Yangzi Valley, the Sichuan Basin, the Southwest Uplands, Xinjiang, Northeast (Manchuria), Qinghai and the Tibetan Plateau. Shanghai, Beijing, Tianjin, Chongqing and Hong Kong are just a few of the cities that play important political and economic roles in China. The country has long accepted the distinctiveness of geographical regions.

In China, political organisation plays a crucial role in developing a common culture and uniting the nation and its regions. Exports and labour-intensive manufacturing are the pillars of the Chinese economy. In addition to moving from investment to consumption, China's economy is transitioning from low-end manufacturing to higher-end manufacturing and services. The government is fostering new growth drivers in a number of industries, including manufacturing IoT, biotech, smart cities, artificial intelligence and high-tech materials.

China has recently undertaken significant efforts to support and foster entrepreneurship, acknowledging it as one of the key forces guiding economic development (He et al., 2019). China's quick development over the past 40 years has been largely attributed to the private sector's phenomenal expansion (Atherton & Newman, 2017).

Although, as is the case in the majority of countries, males are more likely than women to engage in entrepreneurial activity, Huang et al. (2020, p. 356) assert that female entrepreneurs are 'a force to be reckoned with'. The proportion of Chinese women between the ages of 18 and 64 who are either beginning entrepreneurs or owner-managers of new firms is consistently higher when compared to the same percentage for their male counterparts. Compared to their counterparts worldwide, Chinese women are more business-minded. In China, opportunities are just as likely to motivate women as they are men in terms of percentage. The percentage of women starting businesses is, however, on the decline, which is concerning.

In 2011, it peaked at 22.4%; by 2018, it was down to 9.2%. In other words, even though Chinese female entrepreneurs appear to be in a good situation and that people consider their talents to be on par with those of their male counterparts, the intents of female entrepreneurs are intrinsically negative. A growing number of female graduates are starting their own start-up companies, particularly in Beijing, Shanghai and other eastern regions (Cooke & Xiao, 2021). Women-owned firms are most prevalent in the light manufacturing and service sector, which includes telecommunications, professional technology services, the internet and other information services. Work–life balance, career progression and self-actualisation, according to studies on entrepreneurial motivations (Li et al., 2020; Zhu et al., 2019), are what motivate women to start their own businesses.

According to Wang (2015), China has launched a national childcare programme to encourage female entrepreneurship, and more women are becoming opportunity-driven business owners as they have access to higher quality education (Deng et al., 2011).

The government agencies have been implementing several initiatives for encouraging women to become entrepreneurs. These public organisations have promoted a long series of actions in the diverse Chinese areas. The most relevant can be synthesised as follows:

- Launch of a network for female entrepreneurs managed by committee and volunteers to sustain female entrepreneurship. This network helps the collaboration and cooperation among women entrepreneurs and the exchange of useful information.
- Establishment of platforms to exchange information for start-ups. Similar to the previous initiatives, this platform helps collaboration, focusing especially on start-up needs.
- Organising of consulting service. This service allows women to be supported by professionals and consultants.
- Enhancement of women entrepreneurship skills through ad hoc educational programmes and trainings. These initiatives have the merits to create solid entrepreneurial skills and concur to develop a shared entrepreneurial mindset.
- Promotion of financial support. This initiative is particularly relevant to allow women facing prejudices and obstacles that generally they meet when need loans and external financial resources.
- Actions to promote the work–life balance. Several initiatives have been done to favour women in balancing their efforts within work and family, to give them more time to invest in their entrepreneurial activities.

South Africa

Africa's most southerly nation, South Africa, has a coastline that stretches over 2,850 km from the desert border with Namibia on the Atlantic coast, around the continent's southernmost point, and then northeast to the border with

Mozambique on the Indian Ocean. By 8 June 2023, Worldometer's study of the most recent United Nations data predicts that there will be 61,495,987 people living in South Africa. It has a 27.6-year-old median age in South Africa. It is a developing nation and has the seventh-highest score on the continent, placing it in position 109 on the Human Development Index (HDI).

The second largest in all of Africa, the most industrialised and the most technologically advanced on the continent, according to the World Bank, its economy is the 39th largest in the world. It is also viewed as a nation that is only beginning to industrialise. It is one of the top exporters of gold, platinum and other natural resources worldwide, and its financial, legal, communications, energy and transport industries are all thriving.

In South Africa, the agriculture sector is highly regarded. Despite frequently limited land and water resources, it generates a sizeable amount of exports and contributes to the domestic economy, mostly as an employer. In South Africa, 30.5 million females and 28.89 million males are projected to dwell there in 2021.

In 2022, men will make up 63.6% of the labour force and women 50.6%. Workers in precarious employment are more likely to become impoverished because they are less likely to have formal employment agreements, social security and safety nets to cushion against economic shocks. As of 2019, 10.6% of women and 10.7% of males in South Africa work in vulnerable professions.

Women spend 2.4 times more time performing unpaid household and care activities than men do. Owning property grants access to economic empowerment for women in particular and provides protection in the event of divorce or desertion.

Increasing amounts of research show that women who own property do better in terms of their children's nutrition, health and educational outcomes as well as their personal empowerment. Inequality between the sexes is a significant problem in South Africa. South African women's ability to enjoy the same privileges and rights as South African men continues to be a problem.

According to the Department of Trade and Industry (2006), the majority of women in South Africa who own businesses do not have access to loans, land ownership, educational opportunities or skill development. Women entrepreneurs work in South Africa's subsistence industries, such as handicrafts, candlemaking, gardening and sewing cooperatives.

The term 'micro-enterprise initiatives' refers to all of these firms founded by female entrepreneurs.

They were jointly formed by women's community organisations that promote women's skills in domestic work and other sources of income. Studies indicate that there is a dearth of support from the public and private sectors for these activities, putting women at risk of poor results (Kassim & Hendriks, 2002). By assisting them and encouraging a shift in their ideas towards the nature of employment, the government has recognised the worth of their contribution to their communities (The World Bank, 2008). As a growing nation, South Africa faces challenges like high unemployment rates, insufficient formal and higher education standards and the migration of people from rural to urban areas. The nation desperately needs owners of small, micro and medium-sized businesses (SMMEs) to combat unemployment and crime and advance the economy (Maas & Herrington, 2006).

In addition to providing capital equipment under the cooperative Incentive Scheme, the Department of Trade and Industry helps women cooperatives by facilitating their registration. A nationwide effort called Technology for Women in Business (TWIB) makes it easier for businesswomen to access science and technology. It was created to hasten business growth through collaborations, teaching, training and mentoring.

The government created the Isivande Women's Fund (IWF) in an effort to increase women's access to institutional funding in light of the lack of personal savings and gender bias in current lending institutions. By lending to and investing in women-owned businesses, the Fund increases and enhances the access of female entrepreneurs to financing, raising money that could boost their standard of living. The main goal of the Bavumile Skills Development Initiative (BSDI) is to assist women who run home businesses in developing their essential skills so they may produce high-quality, marketable crafts and other items with a cultural foundation. Thus, it was learned that the government had a lot of programmes designed to support the success of women-owned enterprises.

Discussion and Conclusion

Findings show that women entrepreneurship in BRICS countries encounters several barriers due to financial constraints and social and institutional obstacles, and benefited from specific initiatives oriented to enhance female-led enterprises.

Table 3.2 synthesises what happens in each country, focusing on the main barriers and the main critical factors able to promote and sustain women entrepreneurship.

Table 3.2 answers the *RQ1* (What are the main barriers restraining female entrepreneurship thereby leading to poverty?), by underlying that obtaining loans and accessing to credit remain a challenge for women, as well as gender stereotypes and prejudices that concur to create a gender effect on industries, by generating industries that are male-dominated and female-dominated. This situation probably also worsens the possibility of accessing credit since the industries in which women are mainly engaged are those with lower added value and, consequently, those which invoice less and present fewer guarantees to potential creditors and investors.

At the same time, Table 3.2 underlines that BRICS countries are particularly attentive towards gender policies, with a specific focus to women entrepreneurship improvement, perceived as an important tool to create better socio-economic conditions and, thus, to contribute in alleviating poverty and inequality. Despite profound differences in government, policies and socio-economic conditions, the analysed countries highlighted growing attention towards female entrepreneurship. This results from the numerous initiatives promoted at the level of public policies and private interventions. Specifically, governments are launching several initiatives to sustain female entrepreneurship through ad hoc programmes such as

Table 3.2. Women Entrepreneurship in BRICS Countries: Difficulties and Opportunities.

Country	Financial Barriers	Social and Institutional Barriers	Critical Factors Enhancing Women Entrepreneurship
Brazil	Difficulties in obtaining loans and credit	Gender stereotypes Industries female-dominated	Governmental programmes
Russia	Difficulties in obtaining loans and credit	Industries female-dominated Governmental bureaucracy	Governmental programmes Training and entrepreneurship education programmes
India	Low financial literacy Difficulties in obtaining loans and credit	Gender stereotypes	Governmental programmes Training and entrepreneurship education programmes Change in mindsets and traditional views
China	Difficulties in obtaining loans and credit	Industries female-dominated	Governmental programmes
South Africa	Difficulties in obtaining loans and credit	Gender stereotypes	Governmental programmes

Source: Authors' elaboration.

financial support, the creation of networks, simplification of processes, specific training and entrepreneurship education actions. This means that BRICS countries are aware of women-entrepreneurship barriers and, in front of these, are trying to remove these with public interventions. Moreover, China appears inspiring concerning policies of childcare to sustain women's work–life balance. This attention produces positive effects because allows women to work and, consequently, contribute to alleviating poverty. Additionally, with reference to removing financial barriers, government programmes that finance women-led businesses appear helpful in fostering a culture more receptive to the ideas and contributions of women by increasing the number of women in leadership positions. In other words, sustaining women entrepreneurship helps shifting from a

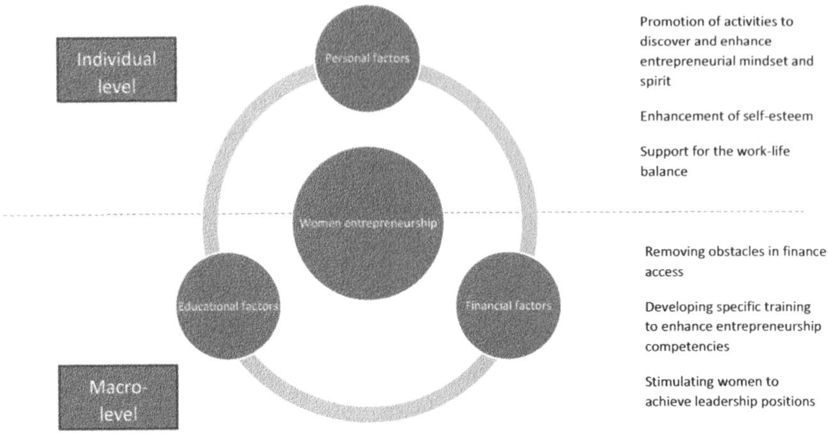

Fig. 3.2. The Interpretive Framework. *Source:* Authors' elaboration.

masculine to an inclusive culture, that represents the first step to embrace women in the fight against poverty.

In light of these considerations, we propose an interpretive model (Fig. 3.2) that can suggest public and private policies, with a specific attention on those areas that need more attention.

In this perspective, our findings suggest further studies, answering the *RQ2* (Which are the research gaps and further research areas to better understand the phenomenon?). From the literature review and the multicase analysis, the proposed framework highlights a relevant attention towards the individual perspective, focusing on women entrepreneurial intentions and attitudes, while less has been done on the role of institutional contexts and governmental policies, especially with reference to finance, education and work conditions. Further studies can fill this gap by focusing on the link among public interventions, women entrepreneurship, and effects on poverty reduction. Specifically, further research can identify effective tools to intervene, suggesting governments which actions to undertake.

References

Aaltio, I., & Peltonen, H. (2009). Portraits of Russian women entrepreneurs: Identification and ways of leadership. *Journal of Enterprising Culture*, *17*(04), 443–471.

Abd Rani, S. H., Hashim, N., & Abd Rani, S. H. (2019). The impact of networking among women entrepreneurial success. *Voice of Academia*, *15*(3), 65–71.

Aljarodi, A., Thatchenkery, T., & Urbano, D. (2022). Female entrepreneurial activity and institutions: Empirical evidence from Saudi Arabia. *Research in Globalization*, 100102.

Allen, E. E., & Langowitz, N. S. (2003). *Women in family-owned businesses*. Massachusetts Mutual Life Insurance Company and affiliated Companies.

Allen, I. E., Langowitz, N., & Minniti, M. (2007). Global entrepreneurship monitor. *2006 Report on Women and Entrepreneurship*, *3*(1), 54–88.

Al-Razgan, M., Alrowily, A., Al-Matham, R. N., Alghamdi, K. M., Shaabi, M., & Alssum, L. (2021). Using diffusion of innovation theory and sentiment analysis to analyze attitudes toward driving adoption by Saudi women. *Technology in Society*, *65*, 101558.

Alvesson, M., & Sandberg, J. (2011). Generating research questions through problematization. *Academy of Management Review*, *36*(2), 247–271.

Anand, P. B., Fennell, S., & Comim, F. (2020). *Handbook of brics and emerging economies*. Oxford University Press.

Anghinoni, G., Anghinoni, F. B. G., Tormena, C. A., Braccini, A. L., de Carvalho Mendes, I., Zancanaro, L., & Lal, R. (2021). Conservation agriculture strengthen sustainability of Brazilian grain production and food security. *Land Use Policy*, *108*, 105591.

Anna, A. L., Chandler, G. N., Jansen, E., & Mero, N. P. (2000). Women business owners in traditional and non-traditional industries. *Journal of Business Venturing*, *15*(3), 279–303.

Ashwin, S. (2006). The post-Soviet gender order: Imperatives and implications. In S. Ashwin (Ed.), *Adapting to Russia's new labour market: Gender and employment behaviour* (pp. 32–56). Routledge.

Atherton, A., & Newman, A. (2017). *Entrepreneurship in China: The emergence of the private sector*. Routledge.

Ayatakshi-Endow, S., & Steele, J. (2021). Striving for balance: Women entrepreneurs in Brazil, their multiple gendered roles and Covid-19. *International Journal of Gender and Entrepreneurship*, *13*(2), 121–141.

Badstue, L., Lopez, D. E., Umansteva, A., Williams, G., Elias, M., Farnworth, C. R., Rietveld, A., Njuguna-Mungai, E., Luis, J., Najjar, D., & Kandiwa, V. (2018). What drives capacity to innovate? Insights from women and men small-scale farmers in Africa, Asia, and Latin America. *Journal of Gender, Agriculture and Food Security*, *3*(1), 54–81.

Balhara, S., & Singh, A. (2015). Women entrepreneurship: A big motivation. *Business and Economic Research*, *5*(2), 207–216.

Bijedić, T., Maaβ, F., Schröder, C., & Werner, A. (2016). *Individual and structural influences on the entrepreneurial activities of academics* (No. 08/16). Working Paper.

Chatterjee, C., & Ramu, S. (2018). Gender and its rising role in modern Indian innovation and entrepreneurship. *IIMB Management Review*, *30*(1), 62–72.

Cooke, F. L., & Xiao, M. (2021). Women entrepreneurship in China: Where are we now and where are we heading. *Human Resource Development International*, *24*(1), 104–121.

Corrêa, M. F. (2022). *Fintechs as promoters of women's financial inclusion: A comparative case study between Brazil, China and Kenya*. https://hdl.handle.net/10438/31622

da Silva Dias, M. O. L. (1995). *Power and everyday life: The lives of working women in nineteenth-century Brazil*. Rutgers University Press.

Deng, S., Wang, X., & Alon, I. (2011). Framework for female entrepreneurship in China. *International Journal of Business and Emerging Markets*, *3*(1), 3–20.

Department of Trade and Industry. (2006). *Strategic framework of gender and women's economic empowerment*. https://static.pmg.org.za/docs/2006/060517dti.pdf

Díaz-García, M. C., & Jiménez-Moreno, J. (2010). Entrepreneurial intention: The role of gender. *The International Entrepreneurship and Management Journal*, *6*(3), 261–283.

Eisenhardt, K. M., & Graebner, M. E. (2007). Theory building from cases: Opportunities and challenges. *Academy of Management Journal*, *50*(1), 25–32.

Fenwick, T., & Hutton, S. (2000). Women l/earning themselves: Exploring relations between desire and knowledge production of women entrepreneurs. *Proceedings of "Engendering Education"*. The Canadian Association for the Study of Women and Education International Institute, 78-84.

Friedman, H. H., Friedman, L. W., & Leverton, C. (2016). Increase diversity to boost creativity and enhance problem solving. *Psychosociological Issues in Human Resource Management*, *4*(2), 7.

Gale, A., & Polnareva, L. (2004). Women in management in Russia. In *Women in management worldwide. Facts, figures and analysis*. Ashgate.

Glaser, B. G., & Strauss, A. L. (1979). *The discovery of grounded theory* (10th ed.). Aldine Publishing.

Gupta, S. (2006). Her money, her time: Women's earnings and their housework hours. *Social Science Research*, *35*(4), 975–999.

Hassan, F., Ramli, A., & Desa, N. M. (2014). Rural women entrepreneurs in Malaysia: What drives their success? *International Journal of Business and Management*, *9*(4), 10.

Hassan, S. H., Zeqiri, J., Ramadani, V., Zhen, T. S., Azman, N. H. N., & Mahmud, I. (2020). Individual factors, facilitating conditions and career success: Insights from Malaysian female entrepreneurs. *Journal of Enterprising Culture*, *28*(04), 375–400.

He, C., Lu, J., & Qian, H. (2019). Entrepreneurship in China. *Small Business Economics*, *52*(3), 563–572.

Hewlett, S. A., Marshall, M., & Sherbin, L. (2013). How diversity can drive innovation. *Harvard Business Review*, *91*(12), 30.

Hoe, C. H., Isa, F. M., Hin, C. W., Hashim, N., Yunus, J. M., & Abdullah, H. H. (2012). Development of women entrepreneurs: The case of Malaysia. *World*, *2*(6), 124–145.

Huang, Q., Liu, X., & Li, J. (2020). Contextualization of Chinese entrepreneurship research: An overview and some future research directions. *Entrepreneurship & Regional Development*, *32*(5–6), 353–369.

Idris, A. (2008). A profile of innovative women entrepreneurs. *International Business Research*, *1*(2), 3–10.

IMF, S. (2017). *World economic outlook: Gaining momentum*. International Monetary Fund.

Jayachandran, S. (2015). The roots of gender inequality in developing countries. *Annual Review of Economics*, *7*(1), 63–88.

Jovanović, O., & Lazić, M. (2018). Women entrepreneurship in Serbia: Potentials and constraints. *Journal of Women's Entrepreneurship and Education: Twice a Year Scientific Journal*, (3/4), 60–72.

Kabasheva, I. A., Rudaleva, I. A., Bulnina, I. S., & Askhatova, L. I. (2015). Organizational factors affecting employee innovative behavior. *Mediterranean Journal of Social Sciences*, *6*(1), S3.

Kariv, D. (2013). *Female entrepreneurship and the new venture creation: An international overview*. Routledge.

Kassim, M., & Hendriks, S. (2002). False hope from micro-enterprise. *Agenda*, *17*(52), 33–39.

Kelley, D., Singer, S., & Herrington, M. (2016). *2015-2016 global report*. GEM Global Entrepreneurship Monitor, Babson College, Universidad del Desarrollo, Universiti Tun Abdul Razak, Tecnológico de Monterrey, International Council for Small Business (ICSB).

Khursheed, A., Khan, A. A., & Mustafa, F. (2021). Women's social empowerment and microfinance: A brief review of literature. *Journal of International Women's Studies*, *22*(5), 249–265.

Kovid, R. K., Bhati, B., & Sharma, G. M. (2021). Entrepreneurial competencies, institutional voids and performance of small and medium enterprises: Evidence from an emerging economy. *Vision*. https://doi.org/10.1177/09722629211058809

Kumari, P., & Mor, S. (2021). Entrepreneurship and source of finance: The case of Indian women microentrepreneurs. *Strategic Change*, *30*(4), 331–340.

Kwakwa, P. A., & Adu, G. (2015). Effects of income, energy consumption, and trade openness on carbon emissions in sub-Saharan Africa. *Journal of Energy and Development*, *41*, 85.

Lai, K. P., Nathan, R. J., Tan, K. S., & Chan, B. B. (2010). Effect of innovation to the success of female entrepreneurs. *Journal of Innovation Management in Small and Medium Enterprise*, *2010*(1), 1–14.

Langowitz, N., & Minniti, M. (2007). The entrepreneurial propensity of women. *Entrepreneurship Theory and Practice*, *31*(3), 341–364.

LeBlanc, A. A. (2013). *The effect of education and knowledge, experience, mentoring, and risk on the successful entrepreneur: A qualitative study*. Doctoral dissertation, Capella University.

Li, J., Sun, J. Y., Wang, L., & Ke, J. (2020). Second-generation women entrepreneurs in Chinese family-owned businesses: Motivations, challenges, and opportunities. *Advances in Developing Human Resources*, *22*(2), 124–136.

Logren, J., & Löfgren, J. (2008). Women entrepreneurs in Russian Karelia: Hooked on entrepreneurship. In *Managers in Russia: Still so different*. Aleksanteri Institute.

Lustig, N., Pabon, V. M., Sanz, F., & Younger, S. D. (2020). *The impact of COVID-19 lockdowns and expanded social assistance on inequality, poverty and mobility in Argentina, Brazil, Colombia and Mexico* (Vol. 558). Center for Global Development.

Maas, G., & Herrington, M. (2006). *Global entrepreneurship monitor: South African report*. University of Cape Town Graduate School of Business.

Marlow, S., Carter, S., & Shaw, E. (2008). Constructing female entrepreneurship policy in the UK: Is the US a relevant benchmark? *Environment and Planning C: Government and Policy*, *26*(2), 335–351.

Marvel, M. R., Lee, I. H., & Wolfe, M. T. (2015). Entrepreneur gender and firm innovation activity: A multilevel perspective. *IEEE Transactions on Engineering Management*, *62*(4), 558–567.

Mendryk, I., & Dylon, D. (2014). Factors of professional success for self-employed women. *Human Capital without Borders: Knowledge and Learning for Quality of Life*, 933–938.

Muravyev, A., Talavera, O., & Schäfer, D. (2009). Entrepreneurs' gender and financial constraints: Evidence from international data. *Journal of Comparative Economics*, *37*(2), 270–286.

Nählinder, J., Tillmar, M., & Wigren, C. (2015). Towards a gender-aware understanding of innovation: A three-dimensional route. *International Journal of Gender and Entrepreneurship*, *7*(1), 66–86.

Nair, S. R. (2016). Women entrepreneurship across nations: Opportunities and challenges. In N. Baporikar (Ed.), *Handbook of research on entrepreneurship in the contemporary knowledge-based global economy* (pp.189–216). IGI Global.

Nair, S. R. (2020). The link between women entrepreneurship, innovation and stakeholder engagement: A review. *Journal of Business Research*, *119*, 283–290.

Nawaz, F. (2009, December). Strategy for improving human capital in Bangladesh and Nepal: Does it help for women empowerment? In *Network of Asia-Pacific Schools and Institutes of Public Administration and Governance (NAPSIPAG) annual conference Malaysia*.

Neumeyer, X., & Santos, S. C. (2018). Sustainable business models, venture typologies, and entrepreneurial ecosystems: A social network perspective. *Journal of Cleaner Production*, *172*, 4565–4579.

Neumeyer, X., Santos, S. C., Caetano, A., & Kalbfleisch, P. (2019). Entrepreneurship ecosystems and women entrepreneurs: A social capital and network approach. *Small Business Economics*, *53*, 475–489.

Obianuju, U., & Okeke-Uzodike, E. (2019). Sustainable women's entrepreneurship: A view from two BRICS nations. *Journal of International Women's Studies*, *20*(2), 340–358.

OECD. (2020). *SME and entrepreneurship policy in Brazil 2020*. https://www.oecd-ilibrary.org/sites/cc5feb81-en/1/2/4/index.html?itemId=/content/publication/cc5feb81-en&_csp_=a785eb8de77c906eb32397f9c2e77129&itemIGO=oecd&itemContentType=book

Patton, M. Q. (1990). *Qualitative evaluation and research methods*. Sage.

Peprah, A. A., Giachetti, C., Larsen, M. M., & Rajwani, T. S. (2022). How business models evolve in weak institutional environments: The case of Jumia, the Amazon.com of Africa. *Organization Science*, *33*(1), 431–463.

Rani, E. K., & Chaturvedula, S. (2018). Psychological capital: Gender differences and its relationship with job involvement. *Defence Life Science Journal*, *3*(4), 383–387.

Saiz-Alvarez, J. M., & Martínez, A. C. (2019). Entrepreneurial quality and economic crisis in the Eurozone countries driven by innovation. In S. R. Nair & J. M. Saiz-Alvarez (Eds.), *Handbook of research on ethics, entrepreneurship, and governance in higher education* (pp. 414–432). IGI Global.

Sarker, S., & Palit, M. (2014). Determinants of success factors of women entrepreneurs in Bangladesh – A study based on Khulna region. *Business and Economic Research*, *4*(2), 237.

Schlaegel, C., & Koenig, M. (2014). Determinants of entrepreneurial intent: A meta-analytic test and integration of competing models. *Entrepreneurship Theory and Practice*, *38*(2), 291–332.

Schumpeter, J. A. (2013). *Capitalism, socialism and democracy*. Routledge.

Sebele-Mpofu, F. Y. (2020). Saturation controversy in qualitative research: Complexities and underlying assumptions. A literature review. *Cogent Social Sciences*, *6*(1), 1838706.

Śledzik, K. (2013). Schumpeter's view on innovation and entrepreneurship. In S. Hittmar (Ed.), Faculty of Management Science and Informatics, University of

Zilina & Institute of Management by University of Zilina, *Management trends in theory and practice*.

Smith-Hunter, A. E., & Leone, J. (2010). Evidence on the characteristics of women entrepreneurs in Brazil: An empirical analysis. *International Journal of Management and Marketing Research*, *3*(1), 85–102.

Suddaby, R. O. Y. (2006). From the editors: What grounded theory is not. *Academy of Management Journal*, *49*(4), 633–642. http://aomarticles.metapress.com/content/CRA0TWNT83U3T4GJ

Suseno, Y., & Abbott, L. (2021). Women entrepreneurs' digital social innovation: Linking gender, entrepreneurship, social innovation and information systems. *Information Systems Journal*, *31*(5), 717–744.

Tambunan, T. (2009). Women entrepreneurship in Asian developing countries: Their development and main constraints. *Journal of Development and Agricultural Economics*, *1*(2), 27–40.

The World Bank. (2008). *Women in Africa doing business*. https://documents1.worldbank.org/curated/en/570471467990304087/pdf/4bc1q8xk38n6g4l9g5y20mm5ez9tkguat9pv7szu9edIC1.pdf

Troyano, M. C., & Martín, R. D. (2017). Poverty reduction in Brazil and Mexico. Growth, inequality and public policies. *Revista de economía mundial*, (45), 23–42.

Verkhovskaya, O. R., Dorokhina, M. V., Shirokova, G. V., Tsyganova, T., & Aray, I. (2010). Global entrepreneurship monitor. Russia 2009. https://dspace.spbu.ru/bitstream/11701/751/1/GEM_2009_eng.pdf

Vieira, F. V., & Veríssimo, M. P. (2009). Crescimento econômico em economias emergentes selecionadas: Brasil, Rússia, Índia, China (BRIC) e África do Sul. *Economia e sociedade*, *18*, 513–546.

Walsh, I. J., & Bartunek, J. M. (2011). Cheating the fates: Organizational foundings in the wake of demise. *Academy of Management Journal*, *54*(5), 1017–1044.

Wang, Q. (2015, October 4). *Child care, work-family policy and female entrepreneurship*. https://doi.org/10.2139/ssrn.2669282

Wells, B. L., Pfantz, T. J., & Bryne, J. L. (2003). Russian women business owners: Evidence of entrepreneurship in a transition economy. *Journal of Developmental Entrepreneurship*, *8*(1), 59.

Yin, R. K. (2008). *Case study research* (4th ed.). Sage.

Yurchak, A. (2003). Russian neoliberal: The entrepreneurial ethic and the spirit of "true careerism". *The Russian Review*, *62*(1), 72–90.

Zhu, L., Kara, O., & Zhu, X. (2019). A comparative study of women entrepreneurship in transitional economies: The case of China and Vietnam. *Journal of Entrepreneurship in Emerging Economies*, *11*(1), 66–80.

Ummah, S., & Gunapalan, S. (2012). Factors influencing on entrepreneurial success: An empirical study on women headed families in Ampara and Batticaloa districts in Sri Lanka. *International Journal of Business, Economics and Law*, *1*(1), 141–148.

Chapter 4

Ubiquitous Business Model and Strategy of WeChat as a Platform in E-Commerce Development

Syed Far Abid Hossain[a], *Kazi Mohiuddin*[b], *Hasanuzzaman Tushar*[c] *and Blanca Luz*[d]

[a]BRAC Business School, BRAC University, Bangladesh
[b]Shanghai Maritime University, China
[c]International University of Business Agriculture and Technology, Bangladesh
[d]Xi'an Jiaotong University, China

Abstract

This study investigates the ubiquitous business model and e-commerce strategy of WeChat as a platform. The potential of WeChat as a tool for sustainable entrepreneurial development has received limited attention from researchers. The purpose of this study is to uncover the hidden issues associated with WeChat's role in e-commerce development. It also examines the opportunities and limitations of using WeChat for e-commerce. The study employs a qualitative research approach, including an extensive literature review and ethnographic study. The results demonstrate that leveraging mobile apps like WeChat can greatly enhance entrepreneurial tendencies and foster sustainable entrepreneurship, thus contributing to poverty eradication in emerging nations.

Keywords: WeChat; business platform; e-commerce; strategy; emerging nations

Introduction

Among a few popular social networking sites (SNSs), WeChat has gained massive popularity, boasting an impressive 1.0825 billion monthly active subscribers

Understanding the Multi-Dimensional Nature of Poverty, 67–85

Published under exclusive licence by Emerald Publishing Limited
doi:10.1108/978-1-83753-292-620241004

(Tencent, 2019) in China. Due to attitudinal and behavioural loyalty (Khajeheian & Ebrahimi, 2020), social media platforms become an increasingly popular method for e-commerce development. In terms of value co-creation, (Hamidi et al., 2019), this kind of platform is still a challenge as there is no strategic procedure to conduct the business; however, a recent scholarly article investigated the regulatory issues in controlling social media (Khajeheian, 2020a) to ensure sustainable e-commerce development. Previous research has primarily centred around investigating the influence of social media on entrepreneurship development, as well as examining the role of enterprises in media management (Hossain et al., 2020; Khajeheian, 2020b), but how WeChat innovated its business model and entered the new markets with the strategic advantage for media entrepreneurs (Hossain, 2019) has been extensively ignored. This chapter focuses on the unique way that WeChat innovated to build a ubiquitous business model and entered the competitive market. This chapter used a bibliometric analysis followed by an ethnographic study to reach in-depth of the phenomena and find the hidden gap.

Literature Review

WeChat is an open-source application launched in February 2011 that offers free voice messaging, sharing videos, images and texts. This application also offers other functionalities like 'Moments' that allow sharing the story within the friends and intimates. Through the 'Official Accounts', the WeChat users can enjoy numerous services like reading newspapers, booking air tickets and hotels, etc. Moreover, WeChat has a significant contribution to online business and e-commerce development. Users are buying and selling numerous products through WeChat. It has become the most popular social media platform over the mobile phone which adopted various contexts like restaurant services (Jing, 2015), public libraries (Gan, 2016) and open relationships (Tsai & Men, 2018). WeChat has contributed to organisational settings by promoting community education and activities (Chen, 2017a). For example, the youth league campus (YLC) is a union that works for college students' counselling, management and organisational works (Chen et al., 2020). The mass people are sharing information and ideas, commenting and taking part in the discussion over the organisations utilising the fast growing and widespread use of digital communication technology (Wirtz et al., 2010) – the consequences in consumer activism and co-creation. Due to the extreme competition business, consumer engagement became a prevalent research topic in various departments like marketing, advertisement and public relationships. For instance, the marketing scholars have focused on the interaction with consumers with multiple touch points of consumer movement utilising the value-adding services to satisfy the consumer's demand. They suggested that consumer engagement consequences in interactive results (consumer satisfaction, commitment and loyalty), advocacy and purchase (Brodie et al., 2013). They have examined the engagement effects on the supportive manners for the organisation and organisation–public relationships (OPRs). According to the public relations, scholars studied that the consumers' engagement means of involvement (1) activities of organization (Slater et al., 1992), (2) decision-making or collaboration (Kang, 2014).

The perception of social media engagement and absence of constant conceptualisation, although, engagement usually defined as interaction; 'deep involvement', or 'both alignment' which impacts interactions as well as the method that leads the process of connection among groups' (Taylor & Kent, 2014). The researchers have recognised three proportions of consumer engagement like behavioural engagement, affective engagement and cognitive engagement (Brodie et al., 2013; Hollebeek et al., 2014). Affective engagement states to the emotional bond of a customer or connection to a corporation (Gustafsson et al., 2005). Behavioural engagement discusses the behavioural interactions of a consumer with a corporation. Cognitive engagement talks about the thinking of consumers towards an organisation or anxiety or absorption of organisational attachment (Paek et al., 2013; Slater et al., 1992; Slater & Rouner, 2006).

WeChat Wallet is a mobile phone-based application that provides a secure and modern way of payment. Users are able to link bank cards to their account, enabling them to receive and send money to friends, as well as make payments for goods and services. The application doesn't require any subscriptions for downloading and installation and using, and it is supported by all smartphones like iPhone, Android and windows.

At the age of information technology, the researchers paid more attention to synchronise the traditional retail channels and direct internet marketing together. At the same time, plenty of research accomplished in supply chain marketing. For instance, Niraj et al. (2001) established a model and assessment method that provides a relationship between customer characteristics and profitability in a supply chain. Narasimhan and Zhang (2000) examined the strategies of the market with independent businesses (Niraj et al., 2001). Chan et al. (2012) investigated sustainable supply chains, green industrial marketing and interaction of these components in green industrial branding.

Jüttner et al. (2010) assessed the integration of supply chain and marketing literature. Sebastiao and Golicic (2008) examined the growing firms that have an impact on modern technology and supply chain strategy, and Jüttner and Christopher (2013) studied the role of marketing in generating a supply chain direction. According to the research, customers use different tendencies and channels. As a result, the synchronisation of several channels is necessary.

The encouragement of using social media on the expansion of e-commerce is increasing day by day. Sharing information on social media by someone leads to browse by others. Thus, information spreads out through the connections, and many people receive the product or service information. For example, according to Open Threat Exchange's (OTX's) report in 2018, 70% of consumers browse the different social media platforms like blogs, message boards, social networking sites to get products, brand and company information. Moreover, at approx. 50% of consumers take a purchase decision according to social media information. Despite the fact, recently, there are more studies on the influence of social media and e-commerce. The achievement of modern wireless technology made immense progress in social networking that enabled the growth of social media users.

Nowadays, a vast number of people are relying on mobile technology to make everyday tasks more straightforward. As a result, technology has brought a revolutionary change in lifestyle, communication and decision-making.

Research shows a model on WeChat transaction how it is based on the technology acceptance model (TAM) (Davis, 1989) and social theory. The social exchange theory clarifies different factors that influence the behaviour of a person when the person makes and maintains relationships (Hsu & Lu, 2004). A perceived social impact can distinguish social influences and make reciprocating interactions as well. It's the type of social inspiration that consequences in the word of mouth marketing (Ng, 2013). Furthermore, according to the previous research, networking is marked as a factor of maintenance of the individual relationships (de Janasz & Forret, 2007). However, loss or theft of devices may discourage the use of the mobile application (Tu et al., 2015).

Bibliometric Analysis

In 2011, the Chinese tech giant Tencent developed Weixin ('micro-message'), a mobile-oriented instant messaging application. It was later rebranded in 2012 for international markets and became known as WeChat in English. The number of active users of WeChat is increasing steadily since 2011, and it has exceeded 1.2 billion in the first quarter of 2020 and globally ranks fifth based on active users (Thomala, 2020). Majority of WeChat users are from China; however, it has also users beyond the border of China (e.g. in Hong Kong, Taiwan, Malaysia and some part of Africa). As of 2019, the product WeChat Pays is being accepted by 25 countries merchants; notably, these transactions are made by Chinese expats or travellers (Iqbal, 2020).

From the beginning year 2011, WeChat is offering different features and services in the application to its users to provide better experiences (see Table 4.1). These unique features and bundled services (e.g. messaging, newsfeed, e-wallet, search engine, WeChat stores, WeChat work, workplace communication tools and many more led the people in mainland China to stay connected with this platform. Living in China has become increasingly challenging without a WeChat account (Plantin & de Seta, 2019). Besides, the heavy-handed ban on global digital platforms (e.g. Facebook, YouTube, Instagram, Twitter, WhatsApp and few others) and high infrastructural ambitions of Tencent aligned with government needs made WeChat famous and successful in China.

The above-selected articles (Table 4.2) investigated business on WeChat, which is an emerging business model in China. WeChat mingled traditional e-commerce with social media networking, competing with the most significant Chinese e-business website Taobao and other platforms (Yang et al., 2016). In this point, a question may arise why WeChat is becoming so popular than other rivalry e-commerce site. The existing literature informed that the mechanism of WeChat business model enhances consumer's trust, shopping experiences and satisfaction towards the business through providing quality information, visual attractiveness, secured privacy, shared preferences and customised recommendation services

Table 4.1. Year-wise Active Users and Major Features in WeChat Interface.

Year	Active Users (Million)	Introduced Features
2011	50	The messaging platform, initially known as Weixin, was introduced, offering features such as messaging, photo sharing and the ability to share voice and video clips. Additionally, users could search for others based on their location.
2012	160	For the global market, the platform underwent a rebranding and became known as WeChat. Along with this rebranding, new features were introduced, including Moments and Official Accounts functions. Users could now utilise QR codes, engage in voice and video calls and access WeChat via the web version.
2013	355	WeChat evolved with social games, stickers, personalised emoticons, group chats and the introduction of WeChat Wallet.
2014	500	WeChat forged partnerships with pickup, a South African courier service and the taxi-hailing app Didi Dache. It also introduced in-app stores, enabled money transfers and collaborated with Ayla Networks and Caesar's LINQ Hotel & Casino to enable control of smart rooms through WeChat.
2015	697	WeChat expanded with City Services, partnered with global brands, introduced virtual 'Red Envelopes' for Chinese New Year and launched a Windows version.
2016	889	WeChat introduced 'WeChat Out' for global calling and implemented a service charge for transfers between WeChat Wallet and debit cards for transactions exceeding 1,000 RMB.
2017	963	Users were able to generate their own reward code. The search function was added to the news feed. The friend radar function was implemented. WeRun fitness official account was added.
2018	1,000	Official Accounts app announced, Selfie Stickers, 580,000 published Mini Programs.
2019	1,100	Redesigned Look & Feel, Time Capsule added in the WeChat camera, Urgent chat alerts, 'Wow' Feature in Top Stories.

(Continued)

Table 4.1. *(Continued)*

Year	Active Users (Million)	Introduced Features
2020	1,200	Added go-to-tool for workplace communication, WeChat live streaming in official accounts; new look with lighter colours for better readability, improved search engine.

Note: Summarised from Wang (2020).

(Chen (2017b); Chen et al., 2019; Cheng et al., 2017; Peng, 2017; Plantin & de Seta, 2019; Qiujin et al., 2016; Yu et al., 2019). Digital entrepreneurs utilized these infrastructural evolutions of social media platform predominantly WeChat is utilised in China for business purposes, enabling the development and maintenance of networks for accessing resources, seeking advice, acquiring information, maintaining existing connections, and expanding into new markets (Hansen, 2020). The result from a qualitative inquiry (Liu et al., 2019) identified that m-commerce (WeChat), rather than e-commerce, is the predominant communication channel for Chinese luxury consumers which help them to enable interaction with brands at a more personal level and also enable word-of-mouth effect in China.

However, other rival e-commerce sites failed to develop trust and relationship with consumers towards the business. Notably, Yang et al. (2016) also recommended that this Chinese business model might be applied in other country contexts with similar trust issues on the online business platform. On the other hand, if this business model were to be put in the matured market (e.g. the United States or United Kingdom) to build trust in online product sales, the result might be weakened.

This extensive literature search process informed that there are large number of studies conducted on WeChat on different aspects; however, research on WeChat associated with the business has yet to be getting considerable attention to the scholars, educators and practitioners. Most of the research on WeChat associated with business focused on the context of China because of majority users are from its home market of China; however, there is only one study conducted outside of China (e.g. South Africa- Matemba & Li, 2018). The study predicted that consumers in South Africa might adopt WeChat Wallet with assurance of TAM construct (i.e. trust, security, relative advantages and ease of use).

Ethnographic Study

The rapid growth and development of technology have changed how people carry out their normal activities. Social networks, for example, allow information to be

Table 4.2. Literature on WeChat Associated With Business.

Author(s)	Tittle	Context	Methodology	Key Findings
Chen (2017b)	Perceived values of branded mobile media, consumer engagement, business-consumer relationship quality and purchase intention: A study of WeChat in China	China	Quantitative (online survey)	The study revealed that engaging consumers on branded WeChat accounts positively influenced business–consumer relationship quality and purchase intention. Branded WeChat accounts were also found to boost public trust, commitment, control mutuality and satisfaction, aiding organisations in cultivating public relations.
Chen et al. (2019)	How Do Product Recommendations Affect Impulse Buying? An Empirical Study on WeChat Social Commerce	China	Quantitative	The study found that non product-related posts with high information quality enhance users' affective trust in WeChat official accounts. Additionally, product recommendation posts strongly influence consumers' impulse buying behaviour and product affection.
Cheng et al. (2017)	Understanding trust influencing factors in social media communication: A qualitative study	China	Qualitative	The study created a trust cognitive onion model based on qualitative feedback from Chinese WeChat users, identifying key trust factors such as information quality, shared preferences, familiarity, privacy, chatting topic, convenience and time-saving.

(Continued)

Table 4.2. *(Continued)*

Author(s)	Tittle	Context	Methodology	Key Findings
Hansen (2020)	'From guanxi to WeChat?': new social networking technologies and digital entrepreneurship in Beijing	China	Qualitative (Case Study)	This study's findings verified that entrepreneurs in urban Beijing primarily utilise the popular social networking technology WeChat to expand their business network. They use WeChat to access resources, seek advice, acquire information, maintain existing connections and enter new markets.
Liu et al. (2019)	The implications of digital marketing on WeChat for luxury fashion brands in China	China	Qualitative (Case Study)	The result from the qualitative inquiry of this study identified that m-commerce (WeChat), rather than e-commerce, is the predominant communication channel for Chinese luxury consumers which help them to enable interaction with brands at a more personal level and also enable word of mouth effect in China.
Matemba and Li (2018)	Consumers' willingness to adopt and use WeChat Wallet: An empirical study in South Africa	South Africa	Quantitative	The study revealed that South African consumers are likely to embrace WeChat Wallet by considering factors such as trust, security, privacy, relative advantages and ease of use, as per the TAM.

Peng (2017)	Affective networks: How WeChat enhances Tencent's digital business governance	China	Qualitative	This study demonstrated that WeChat's affective design, including stranger social plug-ins and Moments updates, enhances a company's ability to govern young people. The circulation of user-generated content through personal digital devices within the network is particularly captivating for Chinese college students, leading to their sustained attention.
Plantin and de Seta (2019)	WeChat as infrastructure: The techno-nationalist shaping of Chinese digital platforms	China	Qualitative	The study found that the level of trust, wording attraction and WeChat activities have a significant effect on consumer attitudes.
Qiujin et al. (2016)	A study on the influence of WeChat marketing on attitudes of supermarket consumers	China	Quantitative	The study concludes that level of trust, wording attraction and active degree of WeChat have a direct impact on supermarket consumer attitudes. The findings also suggested that WeChat marketing (i.e. information quality, vivid, practical and timely content) plays an important role to enhance degree of activeness and wording attraction that leads to build trust of a consumer towards the supermarket.

(Continued)

Table 4.2. *(Continued)*

Author(s)	Tittle	Context	Methodology	Key Findings
Ren and Li (2015)	Enterprise's WeChat use and its impact on firm performance-from the perspective of value co-creation	China	Quantitative	This study identified that continuous improvement of the mechanism of WeChat use in a company might develop value co-creation, which is significant for enhancing firm performance.
Song et al. (2019)	Impact of the usage of social media in the workplace on team and employee performance	China	Qualitative	The study found that the combination of work-oriented social media (DingTalk) and socialisation-oriented social media (WeChat) yields better results in creating business value and enhancing employee and team performance.
Yang et al. (2016)	The role of business and friendships on WeChat business: An emerging business model in China	China	Field Experiment	The findings of this study suggested that developing friendship with new customers can boost product sales in WeChat business. However, it is also found that building such relationships with experienced customers may lead counterproductive for the independent strategy.

Yu et al. (2019)	Can data-driven precision marketing promote user ad clicks? Evidence from advertising in WeChat moments	China	Quantitative	The results revealed that using a higher product involvement, brand familiarity, visual attractiveness and information quality increase consumer ad click-through intention, mediated by trust. Additionally, higher product involvement accelerates consumer privacy concerns.
Zhang (2018)	Analysis on Customer Behaviour and interest in mining on WeChat Business	China	Quantitative	The study concluded based on quantitative data of shopping behaviour that customised recommendation service for consumers in WeChat business may improve their shopping experience and satisfaction.

shared with large masses, instant messaging, exchange and express ideas and comment on them (Chen, 2017b), activities that are transforming everyone's life. The evolution in the way people communicate and carry out their activities in the digital age allowed businesses to expand the scope of their products and services.

WeChat in China, initially launched as an instant messaging app in 2011, has transformed into a social networking platform facilitating business activities. WeChat serves as a platform where established businesses and entrepreneurs can utilise its various tools to effectively promote their brands, products and services. Yang et al. (2016) addressed how WeChat offers a groundbreaking approach for companies to cultivate customer relationships in an attempt to cultivate friendships. Engaging customers and their products and services by sharing product-related information on their 'moments' – as it is called in the WeChat app and shares the same attributes as Instagram where users can post text and pictures.

WeChat moments have continuously been related to its importance for entrepreneurs and overall businesses using WeChat (Chen et al., 2018). Despite the research around WeChat moments, other tools can enhance the usability of this platform to carry out businesses which are not highlighted around literature regarding WeChat business.

With this in mind, ethnographic research was performed in China, to understand how WeChat support firms and entrepreneurs in their businesses and the interaction with its potential customers. Also, on identifying which media drive e-commerce using WeChat, as more of them have been incorporated since its creation in 2010 such as video calls, payment transactions, document sharing, etc.

In this research, both observation and interviews were performed to have a better understanding of the phenomenon. The observation was gained through 3 years (2017–2020) of using WeChat as a customer to those businesses who offer their products and services in this platform. The interviews asked entrepreneurs and established businesses who use WeChat as a way to display, promote and sell their different products.

In order to immerse oneself into the WeChat world of business, it is necessary for the user to create an account, as easy as generating it in any other app around the world. As far as a person has a cellphone number and access to the internet, it will be easy and fast. When you become a user, you will be provided with an ID for the platform that is automatically created, or you can modify it as you prefer. Also, WeChat will generate a unique QR code for your user.

There are several ways of adding contacts into your WeChat account such as adding them by their phone number, WeChat ID, scanning their personal QR code (mentioned above), finding people nearby or by shaking your phone to see those other users who are also trying to find new friends within this app. There is another option, widely used when engaged in business or any transaction, where contacts can be added from a group, clicking on the users' name or photo and then selecting the option 'add'.

In order to be actively involved in business or any monetary transaction using WeChat, your WeChat pay or wallet should be enabled. Unfortunately, here is where the usage and popularity of this platform are limited as it only connects its services to Chinese bank cards. In China, it is this tool that helps businesses carry out transactions as it is easy to use and understand once connected to it. Just as one of our female entrepreneurs who started to sell her homemade cheese in China said:

> . . .the wallet is really useful and easy to understand.

Identifying it as the most useful tool for her business. It is not only for businesses that the use of WeChat Wallet makes it easier to handle transactions, also to customers who do not have the need of carrying an actual wallet or money to buy products or pay for services. Bank accounts are directly connected to their phones through WeChat, and by three simple steps, transactions can be done both in physical businesses as those made only through WeChat.

As an example, in order to buy homemade cheese, after adding the female entrepreneur, asking for the cheese of preference and giving the delivery address, the user can click on the 'transfer' or 'red packet' option, input the amount that it is needed to be transferred and hit the 'transfer' button. The female entrepreneur will receive the message of the transfer, which she can accept or return by just clicking on the option, and the transaction process will be complete.

Although the process to complete a transaction seems to be simple and fast, as previously mentioned, it is the linkage restrictions of bank cards other than the Chinese ones that affect the usability for the business of this platform internationally.

Just as several entrepreneurs remarked, they would not use WeChat for businesses internationally as they stated:

> . . .few people use it; WeChat doesn't work well outside of China.

Also, it is not only the perceived number of people using WeChat but also the availability of certain tools such as those important for businesses:

> . . .if the tool for payments existed, of course I would use it, this platform streamlines the entire process.

Despite the importance of WeChat Wallet for payments and transactions among the social network, business with WeChat can be achieved by the use of several of its tools which complement each other as its users describe it.

Just as everyone understands the importance of WeChat moments to display and promote products and services, there is also another way users have for these purposes called groups.

WeChat groups just as it happens with any other instant messaging platform are part of the daily communication among users. These chats are created based on different criteria such as a certain circle of friends, for specific events, ethnic background, for promotions to potential customers, faculties, courses, related interests or to share and discuss information about the business. There is a vast amount of reasons why a WeChat group can be created, and all of them could be sources of potential customers. As any member can add a person to the group and once inside, it represents an excellent market for those who start and do business through this platform, especially because each group can have up to 500 users in it.

When asked to one of the entrepreneurs in WeChat about how this platform helped in his business, he mentioned:

> ...both WeChat moments and groups help me to promote my products through pictures or short videos, by sending them to groups or sharing them in my moments.

As many of businesses see it and they comment on it:

> ...it is a great marketing tool.

> ...it helps me get more clients.

Both WeChat groups and moments help on developing a different marketing strategy since they can get 'closer' to its customers building a relationship marketing where there is not only a fixed transaction between buyer–seller but more of a long-term relationship. By having constant update and promotion of products right in customers' hands, they are persuaded to purchase more.

Through the interviews and observations carried out in the study, we explored how WeChat supports entrepreneurs and established firms to carry out their businesses through WeChat. Understanding that it is a combination of several tools offered by this platform that enhances the promotion and selling of a product or service. Having each tool, a specific role in the business such as groups and moments for marketing, instant private messaging for ordering and WeChat Wallet as a payment method, allowing businesses to grow and adapt to the digital area. This research also provided an insight into why WeChat business is carried out inside China and still lacks international popularity.

Discussion

From the above analysis which is based on literature review, bibliometric analysis and ethnographic study, an innovative business opportunity emerged which is embedded with unique functions which can contribute to a diverse business model as presented in Fig. 4.1 above. Our analysis found that using WeChat, marketers tried to engage the prospective buyers; however, information sharing can be a unique tool which is still under shadow. Some people continuously seek information within their known SNSs channel. This is an advantage for some online sellers to grab those potential buyers if there is a math of product or service. If not, there might be a recommender system which can be more effective due to trust. People usually believe the word of mouth within a common channel rather than traditional media such as a TV commercial. During the information-seeking stage, the final decision can be taken instantly due to the facility of WeChat

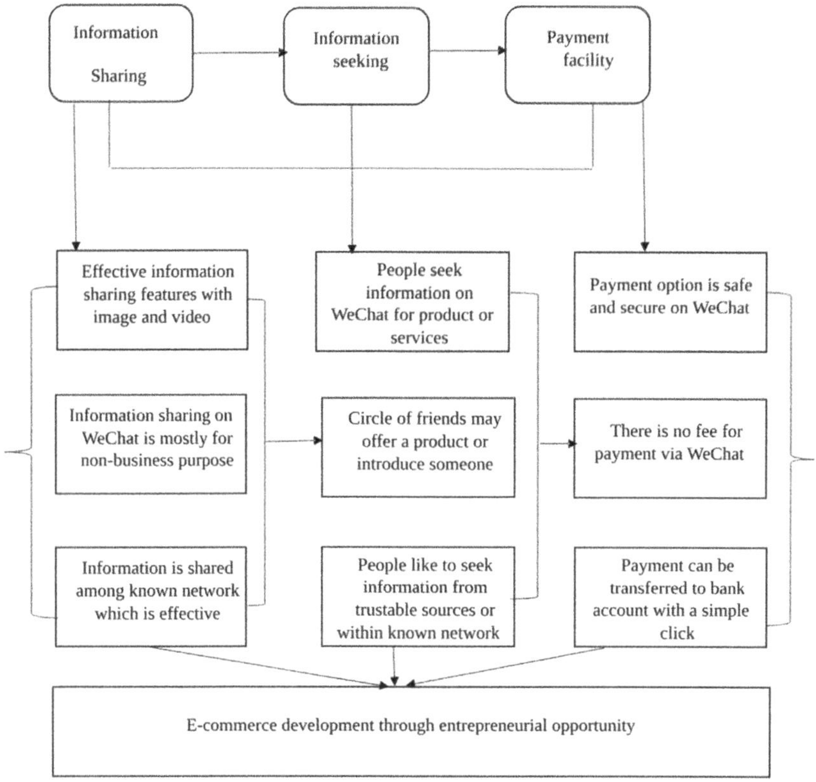

Fig. 4.1. Structure of WeChat Business Model.

payment. WeChat has its own secure payment system without any fee. As a result, potential buyers can make an instant decision to purchase products online.

In terms of sharing information, WeChat is unique than relevant SNSs. For example, gratification system such as likes and comments are not open except among mutual friends. Most of the time, users share non-business kind of information, likes dislikes, funny moments or video clips just for fun and here is the trick. With only information sharing, some people from the same SNSs group show their interest in a particular product or service. The shared information is usually very useful due to trust. Information sharing is the outcome of information seeking. People nowadays rely more on the actual buyers who have experience in purchasing a similar product. However, information sharing and information seeking is not the end of this matter. The final part is the payment. WeChat has a secure payment option where people may pay with direct money transfer or with red packet system. Red packet is the same way to transfer money with a little surprise. The surprise is sending cash in a hidden way so that the receiver doesn't know the exact amount until they open it. Red packet is also used for distribution of some random money as a reward in the WeChat group. Although WeChat group is limited to 500 members only at the moment, it's quite easy for online sellers to involve themselves in multiple groups, and this is how the business activity takes place. All the payments via WeChat are linked with a bank account, and the money can be transferred within a few seconds. This is consistent with the ethnographic analysis conducted in this study.

Conclusion

In this book chapter, the authors attempted to investigate how WeChat innovated a unique business model which can be very effective with the powerful media and SNSs. The result of this study ensures a new venture creation opportunity for prospective entrepreneurs which is consistent with existing literature (Khajeheian, 2012). In this way, WeChat emerged in the market as not just a social networking site but also as a distinctive business model, offering numerous opportunities for marketers in a competitive business environment. The emergence of WeChat can be considered as a key trend in the contemporary business era because WeChat offers unique features which are enjoyable for the buyers. In terms of legal or ethical consideration, there might be many issues which can be contradictory based on different geographical locations; however, the marketers and policymakers may think about the fruitful implementation of WeChat usage in terms of customer and sellers' side. Lack of consideration or lack of knowledge about this virtual trend may be harmful to some intermediaries or stakeholders. As a result, the involved parties in any business may become aware of the reality of this kind of business using WeChat as a tool. The framework proposed in this article is a simple guideline or example of the new business model. This is limited with few factors. Future research may discover more about the other relevant factors such as international or global marketing using WeChat. This book chapter can be a cornerstone for the development of virtual business using SNSs such as WeChat and a base for uniquely conducting e-commerce in this competitive market to exploit more opportunities.

References

Brodie, R. J., Ilic, A., Juric, B., & Hollebeek, L. (2013). Consumer engagement in a virtual brand community: An exploratory analysis. *Journal of Business Research*, *66*(1), 105–114. https://doi.org/10.1016/j.jbusres.2011.07.029

Chan, K. M., Guerry, A. D., Balvanera, P., Klain, S., Satterfield, T., Basurto, X., Bostrom, A., Chuenpagdee, R., Gould, R., Halpern, B. S., Hannahs, N., Levine, J., Norton, B., Ruckelshaus, M., Russell, R., Tam, J., & Woodside, U. (2012). Where are cultural and social in ecosystem services? A framework for constructive engagement. *BioScience*, *62*(8), 744–756.

Chen, J. (2017a). Can online social networks foster young adults' civic engagement? *Telematics and Informatics*, *34*(5), 487–497. https://doi.org/10.1016/j.tele.2016.09.013

Chen, Y. R. R. (2017b). Perceived values of branded mobile media, consumer engagement, business-consumer relationship quality and purchase intention: A study of WeChat in China. *Public Relations Review*, *43*(5), 945–954. https://doi.org/10.1016/j.pubrev.2017.07.005

Chen, T., Guo, H., & Luo, Y. C. (2018). When E-commerce meets social media: Identifying business on WeChat moment using bilateral-attention LSTM. In *International World Wide Web Conference Committee*, Lyon (pp. 343–350).

Chen, Y., Lu, Y., Wang, B., & Pan, Z. (2019). How do product recommendations affect impulse buying? An empirical study on WeChat social commerce. *Information & Management*, *56*(2), 236–248. https://doi.org/10.1016/j.im.2018.09.002

Chen, X., Ma, J., Wei, J., & Yang, S. (2020). The role of perceived integration in WeChat usages for seeking information and sharing comments: A social capital perspective. *Information & Management*, 103280. https://doi.org/10.1016/j.im.2020.103280

Cheng, X., Fu, S., & de Vreede, G. J. (2017). Understanding trust influencing factors in social media communication: A qualitative study. *International Journal of Information Management*, *37*(2), 25–35. https://doi.org/10.1016/j.ijinfomgt.2016.11.009

Davis, F. D. (1989). Perceived usefulness, perceived ease of use, and user acceptance of information technology. *MIS Quarterly*, *13*(3), 319–340. https://doi.org/10.2307/249008

de Janasz, S. C., & Forret, M. L. (2007). Learning the art of networking: A critical skill for enhancing social capital and career success. *Journal of Management Education*, *32*(5), 629–650. https://doi.org/10.1177/1052562907307637

Gan, C. (2016). A survey of WeChat application in Chinese public libraries. *Library Hi Tech*, *34*(4), 625–638. https://doi.org/10.1108/LHT-06-2016-0068

Gustafsson, A., Johnson, M. D., & Roos, I. (2005). The effects of customer satisfaction, relationship commitment dimensions, and triggers on customer retention. *Journal of Marketing*, *69*(4), 210–218. https://doi.org/10.1509/jmkg.2005.69.4.210

Hamidi, F., Shams Gharneh, N., & Khajeheian, D. (2019). A conceptual framework for value co-creation in service enterprises (Case of tourism agencies). *Sustainability*, *12*(1), 213. https://doi.org/10.3390/su12010213

Hansen, B. (2020). 'From guanxi to WeChat?': New social networking technologies and digital entrepreneurship in Beijing. *International Journal of Entrepreneurship and Small Business*, *39*(3), 430–454. https://doi.org/10.1504/IJESB.2020.104978

Hollebeek, L. D., Glynn, M. S., & Brodie, R. J. (2014). Consumer brand engagement in social media: Conceptualization, scale development and validation. *Journal of Interactive Marketing*, *28*(2), 149–165. https://doi.org/10.1016/j.intmar.2013.12.002

Hossain, S. F. (2019). Social networking and its role in media entrepreneurship. *Journal of Media Management and Entrepreneurship*, *1*(1), 73–86. https://doi.org/10.4018/jmme.2019010105

Hossain, S. F., Nurunnabi, M., Hussain, K., & Shan, X. (2020). Smartphone-based M-shopping behavior and innovative entrepreneurial tendency among women in emerging Asia. *International Journal of Gender and Entrepreneurship*, *12*(2), 173–189. https://doi.org/10.1108/ijge-03-2019-0054

Hsu, C.-L., & Lu, H.-P. (2004). Why do people play on-line games? An extended TAM with social influences and flow experience. *Information & Management*, *41*(7), 853–868. https://doi.org/10.1016/j.im.2003.08.014

Iqbal, M. (2020). *WeChat revenue and usage statistics (2020)*. Business of Apps. https://www.businessofapps.com/data/wechat-statistics/. Accessed on July 5, 2020.

Jing, M. (2015). Restaurant social media usage in China. *Worldwide Hospitality and Tourism Themes*, *7*(3), 251–265. https://doi.org/10.1108/WHATT-03-2015-0014

Jüttner, U., Christopher, M., & Godsell, J. (2010). A strategic framework for integrating marketing and supply chain strategies. *International Journal of Logistics Management*, *21*(1), 104–126. https://doi.org/10.1108/09574091011042205

Jüttner, U., & Christopher, M. (2013). The role of marketing in creating a supply chain orientation within the firm. *International Journal of Logistics Research and Applications*, *16*(2), 99–113. https://doi.org/10.1080/13675567.2013.799636

Kang, M. (2014). Understanding public engagement: Conceptualizing and measuring its influence on supportive behavioral intentions. *Journal of Public Relations Research*, *26*(5), 399–416. https://doi.org/10.1080/1062726X.2014.956107

Khajeheian, D. (2012). New venture creation in social media platform; Towards a framework for media entrepreneurship. *Handbook of Social Media Management*, 125–142. https://doi.org/10.1007/978-3-642-28897-5_8

Khajeheian, D. (2020a). Enterprise as the central focus in media management research. *Nordic Journal of Media Management*, *1*(1), 1–5.

Khajeheian, D. (2020b). The struggle to regulate social media platforms. *Nordic Journal of Media Management*, *1*(2), 123–127.

Khajeheian, D., & Ebrahimi, P. (2020). Media branding and value co-creation: Effect of user participation in social media of newsmedia on attitudinal and behavioural loyalty. *European Journal of International Management*, *1*(1), 1. https://doi.org/10.1504/ejim.2020.10020735

Liu, S., Perry, P., & Gadzinski, G. (2019). The implications of digital marketing on WeChat for luxury fashion brands in China. *Journal of Brand Management*, *26*(4), 395–409. https://doi.org/10.1057/s41262-018-0140-2

Matemba, E. D., & Li, G. (2018). Consumers' willingness to adopt and use WeChat wallet: An empirical study in South Africa. *Technology in Society*, *53*, 55–68. https://doi.org/10.1016/j.techsoc.2017.12.001

Ng, C. S.-P. (2013). Intention to purchase on social commerce websites across cultures: A cross-regional study. *Information & Management*, *50*(8), 609–620. https://doi.org/10.1016/j.im.2013.08.002

Narasimhan, C., & Zhang, Z. J. (2000). Market entry strategy under firm heterogeneity and asymmetric payoffs. Marketing Science, *19*(4), 313–327.

Niraj, R., Gupta, M., & Narasimhan, C. (2001). Customer profitability in a supply chain. *Journal of Marketing*, *65*(3), 1–16. https://doi.org/10.1509/jmkg.65.3.1.18332

Paek, H.-J., Hove, T., Jung, Y., & Cole, R. T. (2013). Engagement across three social media platforms: An exploratory study of a cause-related PR campaign. *Public Relations Review*, *39*(5), 526–533. https://doi.org/10.1016/j.pubrev.2013.09.013

Peng, Y. (2017). Affective networks: How WeChat enhances Tencent's digital business governance. *Chinese Journal of Communication*, *10*(3), 264–278. https://doi.org/10.1080/17544750.2017.1306573

Plantin, J. C., & de Seta, G. (2019). WeChat as infrastructure: The techno-nationalist shaping of Chinese digital platforms. *Chinese Journal of Communication*, *12*(3), 257–273. https://doi.org/10.1080/17544750.2019.1572633

Qiujin, Z., Zhixia, D., Haitang, Z., & Anxin, X. (2016). A study on the influence of WeChat marketing on attitudes of super-market consumers. *Journal of*

Interdisciplinary Mathematics, *19*(5–6), 1077–1093. https://doi.org/10.1080/09720502.2016.1262458

Ren, S. J. F., & Li, R. N. (2015, December). Enterprise's WeChat use and its impact on firm performance-from the perspective of value co-creation. In *2015 IEEE international conference on industrial engineering and engineering management (IEEM)* (pp. 1747–1751). IEEE. https://doi.org/10.1109/IEEM.2015.7385947

Sebastiao, H. J., & Golicic, S. (2008). Supply chain strategy for nascent firms in emerging technology markets. *Journal of Business Logistics*, *29*(1), 75–91.

Slater, M. D., Chipman, H., Auld, G., Keefe, T., & Kendall, P. (1992). Information processing and situational theory: A cognitive response analysis. *Journal of Public Relations Research*, *4*(4), 189–203. https://doi.org/10.1207/s1532754xjprr0404_1

Slater, M. D., & Rouner, D. (2006). Entertainment-education and elaboration likelihood: Understanding the processing of narrative persuasion. *Communication Theory*, *12*(2), 173–191. https://doi.org/10.1111/j.1468-2885.2002.tb00265.x

Song, Q., Wang, Y., Chen, Y., Benitez, J., & Hu, J. (2019). Impact of the usage of social media in the workplace on team and employee performance. *Information & Management*, *56*(8), 103160. https://doi.org/10.1016/j.im.2019.04.003

Taylor, M., & Kent, M. L. (2014). Dialogic engagement: Clarifying foundational concepts. *Journal of Public Relations Research*, *26*(5), 384–398. https://doi.org/10.1080/1062726X.2014.956106

Tencent. (2019). 2018 annual report. http://www.tencent.com/en-us/articles/17000441554112592.pdf

Thomala, L. (2020). *Number of monthly active WeChat users 2011–2020*. Statista. https://www.statista.com/statistics/255778/number-of-active-wechat-messenger-accounts/. Accessed on July 5, 2020.

Tsai, W.-H. S., & Men, R. L. (2018). Social messengers as the new frontier of organization-public engagement: A WeChat study. *Public Relations Review*, *44*(3), 419–429. https://doi.org/10.1016/j.pubrev.2018.04.004

Tu, Z., Turel, O., Yuan, Y., & Archer, N. (2015). Learning to cope with information security risks regarding mobile device loss or theft: An empirical examination. *Information & Management*, *52*(4), 506–517. https://doi.org/10.1016/j.im.2015.03.002

Wang, S. (2020). Product/features | WeChat Blog: Chatterbox. https://blog.wechat.com/category/features/. Accessed on July 4, 2020.

Wirtz, B. W., Schilke, O., & Ullrich, S. (2010). Strategic development of business models: Implications of the Web 2.0 for creating value on the internet. *Long Range Planning*, *43*(2), 272–290. https://doi.org/10.1016/j.lrp.2010.01.005

Yang, S., Chen, S., & Li, B. (2016). The role of business and friendships on WeChat business: An emerging business model in China. *Journal of Global Marketing*, *29*(4), 174–187. https://doi.org/10.1080/08911762.2016.1184363

Yu, C., Zhang, Z., Lin, C., & Wu, Y. J. (2019). Can data-driven precision marketing promote user ad clicks? Evidence from advertising in WeChat moments. *Industrial Marketing Management*. https://doi.org/10.1016/j.indmarman.2019.05.001

Zhang, X. (2018). Analysis on customer behavior and interest in mining on WeChat business. *Proceedings of Business and Economic Studies*, *1*(4). https://doi.org/10.26689/pbes.v1i4.678

Chapter 5

A Comparative Study of Different Poverty Alleviation Programmes Undertaken in India and the Middle East: An Overview

Ankita Nayak[a], *Ipseeta Satpathy*[a], *B. C. M. Patnaik*[a], *Sukanta Kumar Baral*[b] *and Durga Prasad Samontaray*[c]

[a]KIIT University, India
[b]Indira Gandhi National Tribal University, India
[c]King Saud University, Saudi Arabia

Abstract

Efforts and initiatives aimed at poverty reduction are motivated by the ultimate objective of reducing the prevalence of people living in poverty. The primary goal of such efforts is to ensure that individuals and families living in low-income households have fair access to basic essentials such as food, vital resources and critical services. According to the World Economic Forum, poverty is a significant loss of well-being that can appear in a variety of ways. Two instances of this are low wages and the difficulty of accessing the necessities for daily living in the form of goods and services. Poor physical and mental health, insufficient access to sanitary services, lack of a voice and a lack of resources to improve one's situation are all characteristics of poverty. The goal of this study is to provide insight into the various poverty eradication programmes undertaken in India and the Middle East, i.e. Yemen. This exploratory study aims to give an overview comprising an analysis of more than 52 published research articles on this topic. The evaluation covers papers from prominent publications as well as general management journals with significant links to the topic. This chapter makes a significant contribution to theory by understanding different challenges leading to poverty, giving insights into the various programmes taken to eradicate poverty and suggesting measures to mitigate poverty through various literature reviews; this study is a general review in the context of the paper type. This study will give discernment for academicians and executives of different organisations.

Understanding the Multi-Dimensional Nature of Poverty, 87–108

Published under exclusive licence by Emerald Publishing Limited
doi:10.1108/978-1-83753-292-620241005

Keywords: Poverty alleviation; poverty; poverty eradication; poverty alleviation programmes; relative poverty

Introduction

By giving low-income households and families enough access to food, financial support and essentials, poverty alleviation programmes work to reduce the rate of poverty in the nation. Poverty is defined by the World Bank as a significant loss of well-being shown in a number of ways. Other causes include a lack of money and the difficulty to access the necessary goods and services for a decent living. Extreme poverty presents itself in many ways, including a lack of physical protection, access to sanitary facilities and water, a voice, the capacity and opportunity to better one's lot in life and a lack of access to healthcare and education (Xu et al., 2019). The Millennium Development Goals (MDGs) were adopted by world leaders at the United Nations in September 2000 as the centrepiece of the worldwide agenda in order to address poverty, hunger, disease, illiteracy and environmental degradation against women (MDGs). Reducing child mortality, ending severe poverty and famine, achieving universal primary education, expanding women's rights and gender equality suffrage were among the Millennials Convention's eight main objectives (Alexander et al., 2022). Make sure the environment is sustainable for the long run and foster international cooperation for advancement. To track the convention's objectives progress on a global scale, national and subnational levels, and 18 distinct objectives derived from the wide eight. Goals were established. Several indicators for tracking progress towards these specified quantum objectives for the period years 1990 through 2015 were also recognised. The definition of poverty is the absence of resources to meet necessities like food, clothing and shelter. On the other hand, poverty is a far broader concept than merely a lack of resources. The World Bank Organization claims that poverty and hunger are related. Poverty is defined as not having a place to live. Being sick and unable to visit a doctor is a sign of poverty. Lack of educational opportunities and the incapacity to read are two characteristics of poverty. Lack of a job, surviving in fear of the future and living each day as it comes are all considered signs of poverty (Davidai, 2022; Ochilov & Najibullah, 2021). The inability to pay for medical expenses and participate in leisure activities, such as taking kids on a field trip with their classmates or to a birthday party, are other aspects of poverty. These are the expenses of poverty. People who are already struggling to pay for their housing and food cannot think about these additional costs. People who are isolated from society, lack a good education and get sick more frequently have a negative impact on society. Poverty impacts everyone, with increased expenses to the court system, healthcare system, and other non-profits that aid individuals in need (Atkinson, 2019; Heard-Garris et al., 2021). Despite significant advancements in measuring and assessing poverty, the World Bank Organization is working harder to offer indicators for the various aspects of poverty. As part of this endeavour, social indicators are being identified to assess social exclusion, service accessibility, service availability and education (Woo et al., 2020). Poverty has no one cause, and the results differ from case to situation. Poverty varies widely based on one's situation. Living in poverty in Canada is not the same as being impoverished in Russia or Zimbabwe. Within a country, there may be substantial differences between the wealthy and the impoverished. Whatever classifications are used, it is clear that destitution is a difficult socio-economic problem. Whatever its definition, poverty is universally acknowledged to exist (Allen & Farber, 2019). One of the features of poverty, a global issue, is a lack of personal wealth. When people cannot achieve their basic requirements for sustenance and existence, it occurs. Poverty may have a social and psychological influence on people. Poverty is more severe in emerging countries, where there is a growing population, scarcity of goods, infrastructures and services such as education and healthcare (Heshmati et al., 2015). Poverty is a complex concept that pertains to many fields, not only economics. The impoverished do not have access to credit, as well as services like public transportation, public utilities, healthcare and education. All spheres of social, economic and political decision-making exclude the poor. When the affluent and powerful violate and exploit the poor's rights, this exclusion makes them feel helpless. According to the World Bank's 2016 report, 836 million people worldwide are still living in severe poverty. In the world, one in every four children under the age of five suffers from malnutrition. More than 50% of people living in underdeveloped nations in 1990 were making less than $1.25 per day. Nearly a billion people have now been lifted out of extreme poverty, and this percentage has decreased to 14%. There is a gender gap in the distribution of possibilities for paid employment, education and property, claims the World Economic Forum 2015. The number of undernourished people has fortunately fallen at the same rate as poverty and statistics, dropping from 23.3% in 1990–1992 to 12.9% in 2014–2016, which is good news given how severe hunger is in emerging economies (Hassan et al., 2019). Poverty has a variety of consequences in real life, including (i) socio-economic burden on the congregation, (ii) poor quality and production efficiency of the community, (iii) low community involvement, (iv) decreasing public order and public peace, (v) reducing public trust in the bureaucratic system in providing community services and (vi) the potential of decreasing the quality of future generations. All of these indicators are interconnected situations that impact each other (Achmad, 2022; Choiriyah, 2018). Since India actively supported Yemen's freedom from the British, the two countries have a common historical link. In 1962 and 1967, India was one of the first nations to recognise both the People's Democratic Republic of Yemen (PDRY) and the Yemen Arab Republic (YAR). The YAR and the PDRY merged to form the Republic of Yemen in 1990. Instead of economic opportunities in urban areas, the country's urbanisation is mostly the result of acute poverty in rural areas. Furthermore, poverty is not dispersed equally across the nation. States with high rates of poverty include Orissa, Bihar and Madhya Pradesh, and this rate hasn't changed much during the economic reform era. Thus, it is evident that while economic changes have increased the nation's prosperity, the rewards have not been divided fairly, and some people have even suffered from them. The fact that some of them are unable to engage in economic reform or the process of economic growth should also be acknowledged (Mohamed & Fauziyyah, 2020). In 2021, the Bonyan Organisation conducted a poll and discovered that Yemen has one of the highest percentages of poverty in the world. The United Nations Development Programme (UNDP) estimates that 18.4% of Yemenis live in extreme poverty, making up 55.0% of the country's total population. More people live in poverty in rural areas than in cities, and women are more likely to be poor than men. Yemen's population is one-third illiterate, and there is a significant prevalence of unemployment, with 20% of people either jobless or underemployed (Bishaw & Posey, 2021). The term 'poverty alleviation' describes the economic and humanitarian efforts made to alleviate poverty in a nation. According to the World Bank, extreme poverty, which presently impacts 767 million people globally, is defined as having a daily income of $1.90 or less. Fig. 5.1 gives a visual insight into people struggling to meet their basic needs; many poverty-relief programmes were established in developing nations during the 1980s and 1990s. Evaluations of such programmes have usually focused on their success in improving members' income levels, rather than on the broader aims of human well-being.

The first necessity for addressing the problem of poverty and unemployment is to impose strict controls on the pace of population increase as well as the illegal migration of population from neighbouring nations (Idemudia & Boehnke, 2020).

How Poverty Is Gauged?

The UN created both the absolute and relative definitions of poverty as shown in Fig. 5.2. Absolute poverty is the term used to describe the level of poverty in emerging nations like India. Relative poverty is a common way to quantify poverty in industrialised nations like the United States. Based on the absolute bare minimum of income, a degree of absolute poverty has been established. A household is referred to as destitute or living below the poverty line if its income is less than this amount. The monthly maximum is 1,286 Indian rupees in urban areas and 1059.42 Indian rupees in rural areas if a family's daily income is higher than this cap.

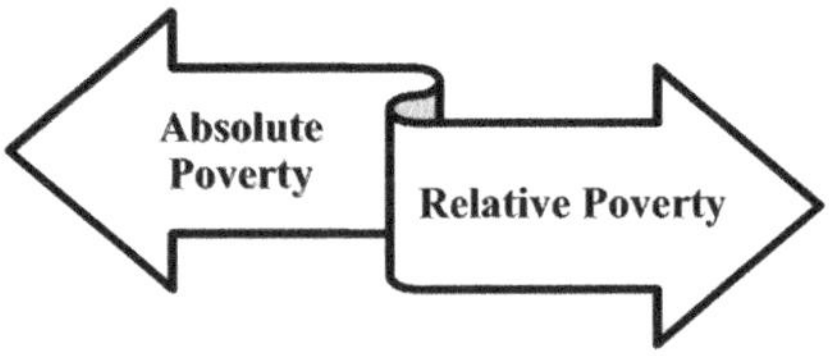

Fig. 5.1. Metrics to Measure Poverty. *Source:* Authors' framework.

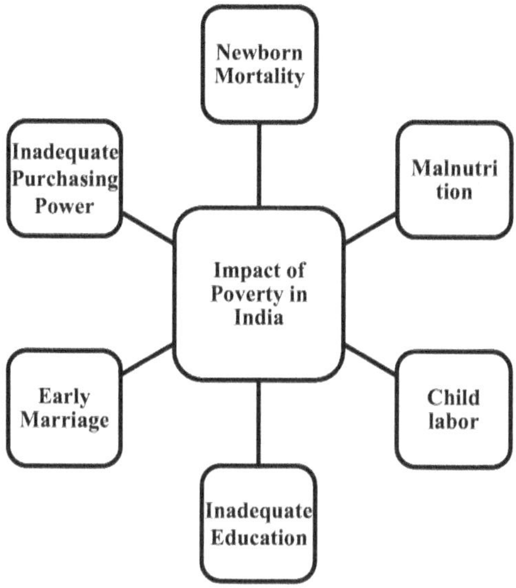

Fig. 5.2. Repercussions of Poverty in India. *Source:* Authors' framework.

Causes of Poverty

Poverty 'is not natural; it is produced', according to Nobel Peace Prize recipient Nelson Mandela. Since poverty is virtually always caused by human action, the aforementioned statement is true. There are many causes of poverty, but population growth is the primary one. Resources and finances are strained as a result of population growth. Governments are finding it difficult to feed, house and employ a population that is only growing. Other contributing causes include a lack of education, violence, calamities naturally occurring, a lack of employment, a lack of infrastructure, political instability and so forth. For instance, when a person is jobless and unable to make enough money to provide for his family's fundamental necessities, poverty results. A person is forced by ignorance to for instance, when a person lacks job possibilities, he is unable to earn enough money to meet his family's basic needs and is forced to live in poverty. A person becomes impoverished as a result of being forced to work in lower paying jobs due to ignorance. A lack of infrastructure is a sign that a nation lacks businesses, financial institutions and other organisations, which leaves few job opportunities. Natural disasters in certain countries, especially African ones like Somalia, and a lengthy civil war have led to widespread poverty. This is because all resources and funds are going into fighting the war rather than providing for the general welfare. Cyclones and other natural disasters are frequent in nations like Bangladesh, Pakistan and India. Each year, terrible disasters occur (Brady, 2018).

Poverty alleviation programmes undertaken by different countries are proof of the effort and measures countries take up to eradicate poverty from their respective countries. Reduced poverty has many positive societal effects. These include easier access to jobs, better educational opportunities (due to increased income levels and the capacity to pay for tuition and materials) and better eating options (which results in better nutrition and health) (Tontisirin, 2019). The goal of poverty alleviation is to make individuals who are already living in poverty more comfortable. The phrase 'poverty alleviation' is also widely used. The 1990 World Development Report advocated a poverty-reduction approach that combined increased economic expansion with the provision of basic social services to the impoverished. Four categories of measures are used to reduce poverty: Microfinance in the community, ability, social security, business and good governance. The long-term viability of these programmes, however, is a big worry. These social safety nets and protection mechanisms help to lessen the severity, vulnerability and social inequities of poverty in emerging nations. It is possible to lessen the global poverty of poor and vulnerable communities, according to several programmes for eradicating poverty, by fostering opportunities for economic growth, enabling sexual identity liberation, investing in infrastructure for high-quality healthcare and education and stepping up vulnerability reduction. Good governance in reducing poverty has moved to the top of development strategies during the last few decades (Singh & Chudasama, 2020).

Research Objectives

- To understand and do a comparative study of different poverty alleviation programmes undertaken in India and Yemen.
- To explore different challenges and issues regarding poverty in India and Yemen.

The Scenario in India When Poverty Reigned: Challenges and Issues

Two-thirds of the Indian population is impoverished: 68.8% of the Indian citizens live on less than $2 per day. India's population is becoming the main problem for the nation because poverty has spread there. With over 1.2 billion inhabitants, India is the second-most populated nation in the world and the seventh-largest by land area. There is 3,287,000 sq. km in all. The drastically diverse nation, which has one of the greatest economies in the world and a turnover of $1,644 billion US dollars, has long experienced growth rates of up to 10%. Only a small part of India's population has, to date, benefited from its remarkable economic growth, and the vast majority of its citizens still live in poverty (Durongkaveroj, 2020). People's problems include being compelled to move swiftly to urban places like Bombay, Delhi, Bangalore or Calcutta since there aren't enough jobs in rural areas that offer a decent wage. The majority of these foresee a life in the mega-slums, which are made up of several corrugated iron buildings and are frequently without adequate power, water or waste disposal, of abject poverty and despair. Diseases like cholera, typhus and dysentery, which primarily affect and kill children, are caused by unsanitary circumstances (Amah, 2021). Infant mortality is high; malnutrition, child labour, illiteracy, child marriage and AIDS/HIV are just a few of the ways that poverty has an impact on children, families and individuals in India. Over 25% of children in India do not have access to a school, according to the United Nations International Children's Emergency Fund (UNICEF). In terms of expulsion from school, girls outnumber boys. Despite the fact that men and women are treated equally under Indian law, fathers, brothers and spouses frequently consider girls and women, especially those who come from lower socio-economic classes, as inferior and subordinate. In India, the likelihood of obtaining a reasonable salary without education is almost non-existent (Prime, 2022). From the late 1800s to the 1900s, the British Raj saw a rise in poverty in India, which peaked in the early 20th century (Roy, 2020). In a series of terrible cycles in the late 19th and early 20th centuries, famines and epidemics claimed the lives of millions of people. Famine-related mortality decreased after India got independence in 1947 (Beitler, 2020). In 2009–2010, 354 million Indians (29.6% of the population) and 69 million (21.9% of the respondents) of inhabitants, respectively, lived in poverty, according to the research methods utilised in the Suresh Tendulkar Committee study. India's population increased by 1.3% between 2010 and 2015, reaching 1.28 billion, according to the Asian Development Bank. In 2014, 9.9% of the world of people aged 15 and over were employed. 6.9% of people are still living in poverty, with extreme poverty accounting for 63% of cases (December 2018). On the other side, the British Raj caused severe hardship in India, with the poverty rate seemingly tripling throughout the colonial period. World Poverty Clock illustrates current trends in India's poverty based on the most recent World Bank and other source figures. According to the most recent forecasts, the government will accomplish its sustainable development targets by 2030. The richest two-thirds of Indians now own 73% of the country's wealth, according to Oxfam, while the wages of the lowest half of the population (670 million people) have decreased (Allen, 2020). Poverty has a significant influence on people's health because of a lack of enough food, appropriate clothes, medical services and sanitary facilities. The issue for these people and their families is malnutrition. The effects of poverty on our nation's children include substandard housing, homelessness, insufficient child care, a lack of access to healthcare, hazardous neighbourhoods and underfunded schools. Fig. 5.2 depicts the different ways in which poverty impacts children, families and individuals in India (D, 2022).

- Newborn Mortality: India has one of the highest infant mortality rates in the world, with more than 1.4 million children dying before the age of five each year. The leading causes of death include influenza, schistosomiasis, watery diseases and malnutrition

- Malnourishment: India is the country with the highest rate of undernourishment, with over 200 million malnourished individuals, comprising 61 million kids.
- Child Labour: Despite estimates from the government that 12.5 million kids between the ages of 5 and 14 are employed, child labour under the age of 14 is illegal in India. Between the ages of 6 and 14, 65 million children work in fields instead of attending school.
- Inadequate Education: According to UNICEF, more than 25% of children in India do not attend school. Girls are more likely to be expelled from school than boys. Even though women must be treated equally with males under Indian law, many of them, especially those from lower socio-economic classes, nonetheless feel inferior. Due to their lack of education, their chances of earning a respectable life in India are quite small.
- Early Marriage: Even though it is against the law, a few Indian communities still practise child marriage. Young girls become mothers when they are still children. Before they become fully mature, many people pass away. Many parents force their children to get married young to improve their life because of their poverty.
- Inadequate Purchasing Power: When a nation's or household's per capita income and purchasing power fall below a particularly fundamental level, there are not enough healthcare professionals and facilities, there is low productivity and there is a high percentage of illiteracy. The end outcome was epidemiological issues and widespread disease.

Caste and religious strife have long been a source of historical poverty in India. Even during times of progress and advancement, patterns of poverty and underdevelopment show persistent intergroup inequality throughout time (Thorat et al., 2017). Not only is impoverishment a terrible condition, but it is also one of the biggest issues facing the globe today. The consequences of poverty are terrible. A spike in neonatal mortality due to poor medical treatment, economic growth and development in the nation are some additional significant effects of poverty. Fewer children attending school because parents cannot afford to pay for their children's education, low birth weight babies have both physical and mental impairments, unemployment and poverty are factors that contribute to domestic violence, families under hardship, an increase in the number of homeless people, issues with hygiene and diet and malnutrition are all on the rise (Khan & Mohanty, 2018).

Reign of Poverty in Yemen and Its Repercussions: Challenges and Issues

The major challenge in Yemen arose because of an inexorable humanitarian, military and political catastrophe that has resulted from internal strife and a Saudi-led military operation in Yemen. The Houthi rebels, who are opposed to Yemen's internationally recognised government, are backed by Iran and a military alliance led by Saudi Arabia. Two-thirds of Yemenis are currently unsure of where they will acquire their next meal. Most Yemenis continue to live in chaos as a result of the protracted and destructive conflict that started in March 2015. People's incomes have decreased, and debt has been placed on them as a result of the economy's collapse, widespread unemployment and non-payment of salaries. There are serious food shortages and hunger as a result of the absence of food in millions of families (Kaye, 2021).

The food crisis in Yemen is a deliberate and direct result of the conflict. More than 80% of Yemenis now live in poverty, and the economy has been reduced in half since 2015. Many people have been unable to buy food as a result of declining salaries and rising prices. Yemen, a nation with a high rate of hunger, has moreover long relied heavily on commercial imports. Conflict parties have deliberately damaged these, seriously disrupting the supply of food and other goods. Hunger is widespread throughout the nation, even hundreds of kilometres from the front lines. Families have little choice but to use frantic and risky coping mechanisms in order to prevent malnutrition or the possibility of it. Many people substantially cut back on their food intake or miss meals. With the limited resources they have, they put the needs of their children before their own. Additionally, some are driven to take out loans and send family members. Due to severe sickness, malnutrition and attacks on civilians, the country is believed to have one of the worst humanitarian situations in the entire globe. Inequality in the burden of hunger and food insecurity is disproportionately borne by women. They overeat in order to prioritise their kids and other family members, or they spend the money on other household necessities. They encounter greater rates of all forms of violence, are exposed to more danger, and have a tougher time accessing hospitals and other medical facilities. Gender-based poverty affects 3 million women and girls, and incidents of violence towards women have increased by more than 63% in the last 2 years (Amiri & Mirzaei, 2021). Several factors exacerbated these political schemes, leading to full-fledged and armed confrontations. Factors like gasoline price increases, Houthi takeover, military division and Saudi interference (Robinson, 2019).

Approximately 23.4 million people, including more than 13 million children, would require aid in Yemen in 2022, according to UNICEF, making it one of the biggest catastrophic events in the history of the planet. After 8 years of conflict, Yemen's national socio-economic structures are still in danger of collapsing, and families have been exposed to infectious disease outbreaks as a result of the fighting, widespread displacement and erratic weather shocks. By the end of 2022, 9.2 million children and more than 17.8 million individuals will lack access to enough water, sanitisation and hygiene services. There are still frequent outbreaks of illnesses like cholera, measles, diphtheria and others that may be avoided by immunisation all over the country. The demolition and closure of hospitals have had a profound impact on healthcare and educational access. By the end of 2022, 2.2 million children under the age of five were affected by severe wasting, affecting over 500,000 of them. According to the World Bank, Yemen, which has historically been the most undeveloped and one of the worst humanitarian crises in history is currently occurring in a Mid-East and North African (Region) country.

Since the start of 2015, fighting has destroyed crucial infrastructure, ruined the nation's economy and caused food shortages. The UN anticipated that by 2021, 24 million people will be 'in danger' of famine and illness, with 14 million in desperate need of help (Karamouzian & Madani, 2020).

Eighteen million Yemenis live in areas without adequate access to clean water and sanitation. Due to food insecurity and hunger, 16.2 million people urgently need humanitarian assistance. Epidemics of diseases including cholera, diphtheria, measles and dengue fever have often occurred in Yemen. Long-term inflationary pressure was placed on the Yemeni riyal by waves of currency devaluation in 2018 and 2019. Yemen is the Middle East and North African (MENA) country with the highest level of poverty. One of the world's countries with the greatest rates of poverty is Yemen. According to the UNDP, 55% of Yemen's population is poor, with 18.4% living in extreme poverty. Rural areas have greater poverty rates than cities, and women outnumber males. Yemen has a substantial unemployment problem, with over 20% of the working-age population unemployed or underemployed. One-third of the populace is illiterate (Dadush, 2019).

An outbreak of cholera in the country has resulted in the deaths of more than 2,000 individuals. Nearly 17 million Yemenis need humanitarian relief, and more than 7 million people are food insecure, as stated by the UN. The major repercussions of poverty are lack of employment, education, healthcare facilities, inadequate availability of food, poor purchasing power and inadequate access to essential services. Yemen is experiencing the world's greatest humanitarian disaster; according to the UN, the conflict in Yemen has resulted in over 370,000 deaths, with almost 60% of those deaths coming from indirect causes such as a shortage of food, water and medical treatment. Prices dropped significantly during the 2022 ceasefire, but many Yemenis worry that high prices will return after the truce expires. Many individuals cannot afford food because of rising costs and increasing unemployment rates. People are forced to eat leaves, animal feed and even rubbish since they cannot afford to consume anything else. According to the UN, almost 2 million children are at risk of famine. Food insecurity has put 60% of the population in danger of famine by 2017, and over one million people required emergency food assistance (Spiegel & Havas, 2019).

The reasons for poverty are many and complicated. According to some analysts, Yemen's poverty is brought on by a lack of work opportunities, high unemployment rates, rapid economic growth and rising unemployment. Since 2014, Yemen has been ravaged by war, which has caused poverty there to soar. Yemen's poverty rate was 45% in 2014. The percentage ought to have reached 75% by the end of 2019. Political turmoil in this war-torn area has not completely subsided. The UNDP claims that this has wasted 21 years of development. After 5 years of research into how the war has impacted Yemen's economic and social structure and how the international community can effectively invest in Yemen, the UNDP released a report on 26 September 2019, titled Assessing the Effects of the Yemeni Civil War on the Achievement of the Sustainable Development Goals (Sprimont, 2019). Fig. 5.3 shows the author's (Crawford & Waldman, 2020) list of seven facts about poverty in Yemen.

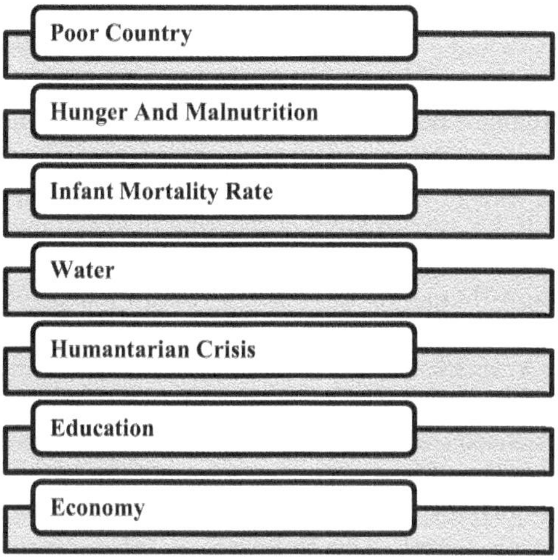

Fig. 5.3. 7 Facts About Poverty in Yemen. *Source:* Authors' framework.

- Poor Country: Prior to the current political unrest, Yemen was the poorest country in the MENA region. Yemen was the region's most impoverished country prior to its political unrest. It ranks last among Arab states in terms of the Human Development Index (HDI). Out of 189 countries, Yemen is ranked 178th on the HDI.
- Hunger and Malnutrition: Approximately 80% of Yemenis, according to the UN, are at risk of hunger. To manage malnutrition and other ailments, approximately 14.3 million individuals require medical help. Cholera, measles, dengue fever and starvation are a few of the main reasons. Over 1.5 million Yemeni children need urgent medical help due to chronic malnutrition.
- Infant Mortality Rate: Yemen's high infant mortality rate of 55.4 fatalities under the age of five per 1,000 births is exacerbated by poverty. In comparison, the infant mortality rate in the United States is 5.8 fatalities per 1,000 births. Malnutrition has a significant role in these statistics.
- Water: Simply put, there are about 18 million Yemenis who lack access to clean drinking water. Only a little more than 30% of the population has access to piped drinking water, according to UNICEF. Water contamination causes a lot of baby deaths. UNICEF makes a lot of effort to keep this issue in Yemen to a minimum. It maintains Yemen's water delivery networks. Additionally, it provides humanitarian water, sanitation and hygiene (WASH) assistance to the displaced Yemeni population as well as the analysis and disinfection of urban water sources.
- Humanitarian Crisis: Yemen's economy is being eroded by recurrent waves of currency devaluation. As a result, inflation poses a danger to the economy and

its customers. It also worsens the humanitarian issue. Yemen's legal currency, the Yemeni rial, has had a 75% decline in value during the past 4 years. Yemen, which has a GDP of almost $27 billion, is dependent on aid.

- Education: As Yemen's poverty worsens, over 2 million youngsters stay out of school. Unfortunately, this is owing to a shortage of instructors and educational resources. Yemen will remain destitute until its populace is educated. Fortunately, UNICEF was capable of securing financial incentives worth over $70 million for Yemeni teachers. Over 200,000 Yemeni children now have access to education thanks to UNICEF's restoration of 18 schools and 218 school latrines.
- The Economy: A shock to the economy of this magnitude also affected Yemenis personally. Additionally, the World Bank reports that over 40% of households experienced the loss of their primary source of income, which drove them into poverty. The nation is making a lot of effort to lift its citizens out of poverty. The World Bank has provided numerous significant emergency funds throughout Yemen's unrest. The emphasis of these awards will be on agriculture, health and nutrition.

Different Poverty Alleviation Programmes Implemented in India: Opportunities to Tackle Poverty

Poverty is a multifaceted condition that extends beyond a lack of enough money. It is defined as a state of people's social, economic and political deprivation that prevents them from participating as equals in the development phase (Quak & Luetz, 2021). While removing extreme poverty is necessary. The poverty alleviation initiative aims to alleviate poverty in the country by giving low-income households appropriate access to food, financial aid and essential utilities (Chaturvedi, 2019). Since India is a welfare state and is committed to the advancement of its residents, the government has launched a number of programmes to combat poverty and raise the living standards of the underprivileged through improvements in education, healthcare and other sensible initiatives (Zuo, 2021). According to the Geek for Geek study, attempts were undertaken following India's independence to eliminate poverty by supporting sustainable development. In 1950, a steering group was established in 1960 to create a poverty line for India and numerous other countries in the years that followed Minhas' approximation of India's poverty rates. Under the direction of Indira Gandhi, India's third prime minister, poverty was acknowledged for the first time in history following independence as a national problem. D. D. aims to abolish poverty and develop self-sufficiency ('Garibi Hatao'). Dhar devised and revealed the 55-Year Plan by encouraging rapid growth, improving income distribution and stressing rural development. In India, several poverty alleviation programmes have been implemented as shown in Fig. 5.4.

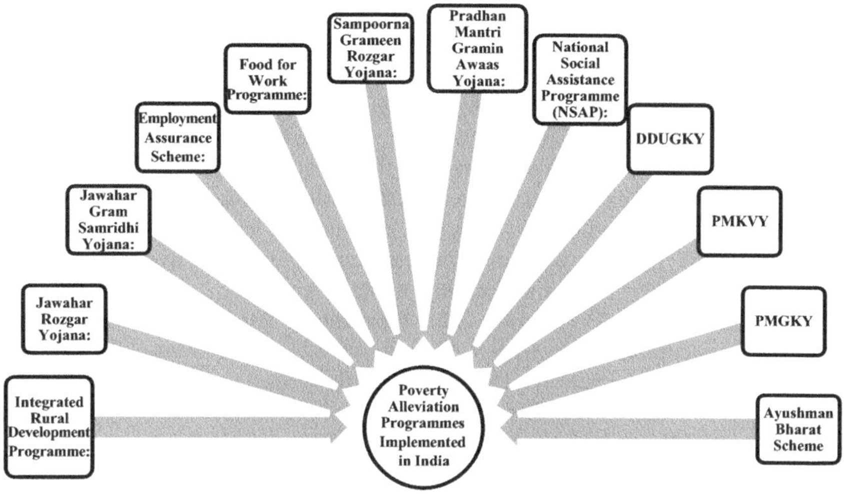

Fig. 5.4. Different Poverty Alleviation Programed Implemented in India. *Source:* Author's framework.

(1) The Integrated Rural Development Programme (IRDP): It was founded in 1980–1981 to assist poor persons in rural regions in finding self-employment. The fundamental objective of the IRDP was to permanently lower the number of impoverished households by giving them access to additional inputs and financial resources. One of the most comprehensive programmes ever created to combat rural poverty is India's IRDP, which provides the world's poorest people with assets that may generate revenue.
(2) Jawahar Rozgar Yojana: Started on 1 April 1989 by combining the National Rural Employment Programme (NREP) and the Rural Landless Employment Guarantee Programme (RLEGP), to improve the standard of living for the unemployed and underprivileged in rural areas through the generation of community and social assets. The programme's goal was to provide more attractive work for unemployed and underemployed rural residents, to generate stable employment by enhancing the rural financial system and to build assets that would benefit the area's poor residents in the long run. In this Yojana, women in rural regions are only eligible for 30% of the employment openings.
(3) Jawahar Rozgar Yojana: On 1 April 1999, the Jawahar Rozgar Yojana was once more reorganised as the Jawahar Gram Samridhi Yojana. The Sampoorna Grameen Rozgar Yojana was an even more significant modification to this plan on 25 September 2001. By developing a demand-driven community village infrastructure, it will be possible for poor rural residents to improve their long-term employment opportunities and long-term assets. Additionally, it entails offering additional employment options to the jobless in rural areas. Families living below the poverty level may be eligible for wage work (BPL).

(4) Employment Assurance Scheme: On 2 October 1993, the Employment Assurance Scheme went into effect. It covers regions that are prone to drought, desert regions, tribal regions and hill country regions. The 409 blocks in the country were covered by this system during the 1994–1995 school year, and by April 1997, the plan had been expanded to include every block. The major purpose of the initiative was to give supplement wage job possibilities to all competent adult disadvantaged individuals in rural places who needed labour on time during lean growing seasons. Its secondary purpose was to begin creating the banking system and local resources for rural India's employment and growth.

(5) Meals for Work Programme: This experiment, which began in 1977–1978, replaces compensation with food grains. This was improved in 2001 to give more jobs to the nation's 150 most underdeveloped communities while also preserving more lives. The 150 most undeveloped districts in the country are to get additional resources in addition to those provided under the Sampoorna Grameen Rozgar Yojana. This programme has the potential to provide more wage employment possibilities as well as food safety by developing need-based social, economic and communities in these underserved regions.

(6) The Sampoorna Grameen Rozgar Yojana: It was created in 2001 by combining the Ministry of Rural Development's Employment Assurance Programme with the Jawahar Gram Samridhi Yojana. The main objectives of the programme were to increase chances for wage labour, improve food safety and nutritional standards across the board, create long-term financial and social assets for the community and improve access to rural infrastructure for the underprivileged.

(7) Indira Awaas Yojana: Formerly known as Pradhan Mantri Gramin Awaas Yojana (PMGAY). The PMGAY was launched in 2015 to provide free housing for India's rural poor who fall below the poverty line. The objective is to provide affordable housing options via the use of credit-linked subsidies, rehabilitate slum dwellers through private sector involvement using land as a resource and offer acceptable homes through a combination of public and private subsidies.

(8) National Social Assistance Programme (NSAP): On 15 August 1995, the NSAP was established by Articles 41 and 42 of the Directive Principles of State Policy, which are mentioned in Part IV of the Indian Constitution, to assist widows, the elderly, the disabled and bereaved families in BPL households if the primary breadwinner passed away. It also had the following two parts:

- The National Old Age Pension Scheme (NOAPS): It became established in 1995 to offer pensions to persons who are 'destitute', meaning they have little to no access to jobs or financial support. The main objective is to give eligible recipients of social security. In this, seniors who are 60 years of age or older receive a monthly income from a quasi-person; they are not required to make any contributions to get the pension.

- The National Family Benefit Scheme (NFBS): It was founded in 1995 to provide a lump sum payout to a household below the poverty line whose head thereafter assumes parental duties after the primary wage earner goes away. It is available to anyone between the ages of 18 and 64 and offers a household of Rs. 10,000 annuities.

(9) Deen Dayal Upadhyay Gram Kaushal Yojana (DDUGKY): To fight poverty, the DDUGKY was created. Through this programme, youths in rural areas get skills and the ability to make a monthly wage. In India, there is a great programme that provides enough training for the underprivileged.

(10) Pradhan Mantri Kaushal Vikas Yojana (PMKVY) or Skill India: The PMKVY, often referred to as Skill India, was inaugurated on 16 July 2015. The eventual objective is to train around 40 million Indian kids. This government initiative encourages low-income students to explore new methods to improve their abilities.

(11) Pradhan Mantri Garib Kalyan Yojana (PMGKY): The PMGKY initiatives were announced by India's Prime Minister. This pro-poor welfare plan's purpose is to abolish poverty in the lives of the poor. The government is typically the primary factor behind parliamentarians' attempt to restore attention to the plight of the impoverished. It can be used by such members to arrange a skill-based workshop. People in need are welcome to attend for a modest cost.

(12) Ayushman Bharat scheme: The Central Government launched the Ayushman Bharat Yojana, or National Health Protection Programme, on April 14, with a concentration on the welfare of low-income persons and the offering of healthcare benefits to the needy. For secondary and tertiary care procedures, this scheme would allow 10 crore low-income households to receive cashless treatment at all government and private registered institutions nationwide and give them an annual insurance cover of Rs. 5 lakhs.

To reduce poverty, the development initiative known as microfinance provides low-cost financial services to low-income women. The Self-Help Group (SHG) model is a well-known one in South Asia. India embraced it in 2011 as part of a government effort to reduce poverty and as a supplementary strategy for including assistance for rural women to look for health literacy (Ahmad et al., 2020). Every country on the planet must address the issue of poverty. Therefore, it is not surprising that the seventeen (17) Sustainable Development Goals or SDGs framework goals place addressing poverty concerns first. Even though poverty in Indonesia is generally on the decline, it turns out that it is still challenging to identify the sign of a more severe degree of poverty index represented by both the poverty gap index and the poverty severity index (Rifa'i & Ayu, 2019). National estimates of poverty increased in urban areas from 31.8% to 13.7% between 1993–1994 and 2011–2012 but declined in rural areas, going from 50.1% to 25.7%. According to the estimates of Tendulkar committee between 1993 and 2004, poverty in India fell by 17.89% and between 2004 and 2011, it dropped by 41.3%. In 2011,

21.92% of Indians were considered to be poor, according to the SDG India Index Baseline report for 2018 (Verma & Mani, 2020).

Poverty Alleviation Programmes Implemented in Yemen: Opportunities to Combat Poverty

Yemen's Strategic Vision 2025 is a long-term strategy for improving the country. It focuses on rainfed agriculture. Agriculture, greater water harvesting, improved water-use efficiency, and cultivation all had a role in controlling khat output as well as other crops like as coffee, potatoes and vegetables. It also includes research investments to improve production, quality, and efficiency. Increasing the competitiveness of the fisheries sector by enhancing marketing infrastructure such as cooling, storage, and processing (Clapp & Moseley, 2020; Qaied & Basavaraj, 2020). According to the International Fund for Agricultural Development, the 5-year development plan and both goals of Yemen's strategic plan for reducing poverty are to lower the proportion of the population that lives in poverty. The strategy's four pillars – economic development, human resource development, improved infrastructure and social welfare protection – are the foundation for reducing poverty. Projects outlined in the most recent 5-year plan raised public awareness. With over $6 billion in investments given the serious scarcity of water supplies, the development plan understands that boosting agricultural productivity is critical to the future of agriculture, investments and efficiency improvements in both the rainfed and existing sectors irrigated. It also suggests a variety of other tasks, such as creating and enhancing access to financing and financial resources for export crops and households in remote areas. Different poverty alleviation programmes undertaken in Yemen are as follows in Fig. 5.5 (van de Walle, 2002).

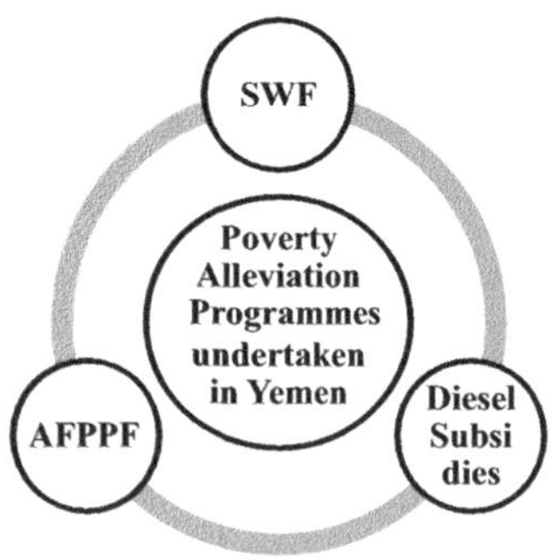

Fig. 5.5. Extended Model Different Poverty Alleviation Programmes Implemented by Govt in Yemen. *Source:* Authors' framework.

- The Social Welfare Fund (SWF) is the primary initiative of the government for delivering targeted social assistance. It was established in 1996 to compensate for the loss of subsidies for the impoverished who lacked experience. The best way to choose and contact recipients of this sort of programme has been a point of contention for the nation. In 1997, the World Bank said that the SWF was inefficient because it lacked clearly defined objective standards, adhered to unnecessary bureaucratic processes, provided insufficient follow-up on targeting and beneficiaries and underspent on programme administration. Particularly at risk are rural areas field visits revealed poor targeting, widespread misunderstanding of the plan and problems with transfer distribution, including signs that intermediaries were keeping some of the money (which was already the minimum amount). Because of their geographic reach, the following organisations are the system's targets: Orphans are the first to be counted, followed by widows with children, widows without children, divorced girls with children, divorced girls without children, unmarried girls, the poor, the elderly, the temporarily completely and temporarily partially disabled and households with a person recently released from jail. People who are now getting assistance from the Martyr's Fund or a pension, for example, will no longer be eligible in the future. There is an effort to react to shocks by considering every scenario, whether temporary or permanent. Beneficiaries in the aforementioned organisations 1 through 10 are considered permanent recipients, but those in organisations 11 through 15 are more suitable for temporary support, the maximum length of which is 3 years. Additionally, the law offers lump-sum aid to families that go through personal crises or are impacted by covariate catastrophes Help assist individuals in need financially and in kind to improve their living and social situations and prevent undesirable behaviour, such as dependency on government handouts, mendicancy, etc.
- Diesel Subsidies: The simplest consumer item that is still heavily subsidised is diesel. It appears to be used often to power fishing boats, wind turbines and irrigation pumps. Some government officials claim that the impoverished benefit from the subsidies. This is the major purpose of the government's agricultural and fishing Production Promotion Fund. Others, on the other hand, argue that the incentive has encouraged excessive pumping and inefficient water consumption, which has harmed disadvantaged farmers.
- Concerns that the lowest demographic groups in rural and coastal areas, who primarily depend on agriculture and fisheries as both consumers and producers, would suffer as a result of rising diesel prices and, eventually, the termination of the diesel subsidy, led in 1995, the Agricultural and Fisheries Production Promotion Fund (AFPPF) was established. The Fund conducts a number of operations in various sectors to try to boost the output of cultivation, varmint and fisheries. These include plans to subsidise the price of agricultural goods and machinery (such as seeds, fertiliser, tractors and so forth), water projects like dams as well as smaller initiatives to reduce the danger of drought, refill aquifers and sell output. A mechanism that deposits year 2.5 (increased from a year since 1995) for each litter of diesel sold in the nation provides funding for the AFPPF. International grants and the general budget are other sources of

support. The yearly spending plan is in the range of 25–27 million US dollars (4.5 billion JPY). The Fund's main duty is to assess, approve and fund initiatives created by others. Others include the corporate community, individuals, agricultural cooperatives and the Agriculture Cooperative Union. These co-workers will supervise the project's receipt of 4% of expenditures for overhead once it has been authorised. The AFPPF so follows a framework that is motivated by demand, even though intermediates are used to do this. It is unknown how well-known the Fund is or whether everyone who may profit from it is given the chance. The terms of financing differ significantly between projects. Some receive whole or partial grants, forgiving loans or loans with subsidised interest rates. Making non-collateralised financing more accessible is one of the objectives of the AFPPF. Farmers are struggling. The sole private source of lending in rural regions is the Cooperative Agricultural Loans Bank (CACB), which largely serves affluent farmers and agricultural organisations.

There are also other poverty alleviation initiatives, usually known as donor-supported initiatives. Several bilateral and international financial sources contribute to poverty alleviation efforts. Yemeni initiatives for the development of many donor-funded initiatives, including the government's. In the mid-1990s, efforts were launched to alleviate the negative consequences of adjustment and reform. Many donors appear to be strengthening their cooperation, such as by forming partnerships to improve outcomes and achieve their goals. Different poverty alleviation programmes like social fund development, public work projects, poverty alleviation and employment programmes, The Southern Governorates Programme and many more add up to the list of programmes in donors-assisted programmes. Cash aid, on the other hand, addresses a broader range of people's needs in a more productive and successful way of distribution that contributors may simply access. Cash assistance can be unrestricted, limited or conditional (Elayah & Fenttiman, 2022; Lyman, 2005).

Findings and Conclusion

Ending Poverty is a significant endeavour that the Indian government has undertaken, as evidenced by the fact that it has been put into practice. India's poverty rates have been steadily declining over time since the 1980s when the country switched to a high economic trajectory. The 2019 UN Human Development Report estimates that multidimensional poverty affects 27.9% of India's population. India can alleviate poverty by giving the poor the tools they need to manage their resources effectively, as long as the programmes for reducing poverty are implemented properly. These initiatives address the poor's multifarious deprivation by providing them with food security, jobs, shelter and wages. Since 1990, Yemen's government has implemented three five-year economic reform initiatives aimed at eradicating poverty and increasing growth in a variety of areas. Yemen's poverty is worse than that of other MENA nations notwithstanding a recent decline. As per the extensive literature reviews done, it has been found that India is leading Yemen in the aspect of Poverty Alleviation Programmes' rapid implementation, and the number of schemes introduced in India to reduce poverty is much alleviated than the strategies undertaken in Yemen.

Implications

The need for more focused and effective poverty reduction measures that are adapted to each country's individual circumstances needs to be noted. These initiatives should be developed with a thorough awareness of the underlying causes of poverty as well as the problems that individuals and communities confront in their specific situations. The necessity of government initiative and politics will do so in guaranteeing the effectiveness of poverty reduction efforts. As a result, governments must prioritise poverty alleviation and ensure that funds are utilised effectively. It is critical to acknowledge that poverty is a complicated issue that cannot be handled just by government initiatives. To solve the multiple issues faced by persons living in poverty, governments, NGOs and other stakeholders must work together. These might include programmes to expand education and healthcare access, encourage economic growth and assist neglected populations. The comparative research underlines the need of continuing efforts to alleviate poverty in India and Yemen, as well as the need for successful poverty reduction initiatives that are sensitive to the needs of the poor.

References

Achmad, L. I. (2022). Corporate social responsibility: Divesting from apartheid. *International Conference on Islamic Economic (ICIE)*, *1*(1), 118–135. https://doi.org/10.58223/icie.v1i1.110

Ahmad, D., Mohanty, I., Irani, L., Mavalankar, D., & Niyonsenga, T. (2020). Participation in microfinance based self help groups in India: Who becomes a member and for how long? *PLoS One*, *15*(8). https://doi.org/10.1371/journal.pone.0237519

Alexander, L., Philipp, J., & Sprimont, D. (2022). https://borgenproject.org/tag/poverty-in-yemen/

Allen, R. C. (2020). Poverty and the labor market: Today and yesterday. *Annual Review of Economics*, *12*(1), 107–134. https://doi.org/10.1146/annurev-economics-091819-014652

Allen, J., & Farber, S. (2019). Sizing up transport poverty: A national scale accounting of low-income households suffering from inaccessibility in Canada, and what to do about it. *Transport Policy*, *74*, 214–223. https://doi.org/10.1016/j.tranpol.2018.11.018

Amah, O. E. (2021). Globalization/liberalization and poverty level in Africa. In *Handbook of research on institutional, economic, and social impacts of globalization and liberalization* (pp. 138–156). https://doi.org/10.4018/978-1-7998-4459-4.ch008

Amiri, S., & Mirzaei, M. M. (2021). Iran-Yemen relations and its geopolitical crisis. International Relations and Diplomacy. *International Relations and Diplomacy*, *9*(9). https://doi.org/10.17265/2328-2134/2021.09.004

Atkinson, A. B. (2019). *Measuring poverty around the world.* https://doi.org/10.1515/9780691191898

Beitler, M. (2020). Colonial India: A legacy of neglect. https://storymaps.arcgis.com/stories/1bcfcb6b88c846f99e05ab7831669757

Bishaw, A., & Posey, K. G. (2021). https://www.census.gov/library/stories/2017/11/income-poverty-rural-america.html

Brady, D. (2018). *Theories of the causes of poverty.* https://doi.org/10.31235/osf.io/jud53

Chaturvedi, B. K. (2019). Poverty and development: Global problems from an Indian perspective. *Journal of Global Ethics*, *15*(1), 55–66. https://doi.org/10.1080/17449626.2019.1582557

Choiriyah, C. (2018). Implementasi Kebijakan publik Dalam Penanganan Kemiskinan; studi implementasi program Bantuan Langsung Tunai (BLT) di Kelurahan Kuto Batu Kecamatan ilir timur II. Islamic Banking. *Jurnal Pemikiran Dan Pengembangan Perbankan Syariah*, *3*(2), 17–30. https://doi.org/10.36908/isbank.v3i2.42

Clapp, J., & Moseley, W. G. (2020). This food crisis is different: Covid-19 and the fragility of the neoliberal food security order. *Journal of Peasant Studies*, *47*(7), 1393–1417. https://doi.org/10.1080/03066150.2020.1823838

Crawford, B. J., & Waldman, E. G. (2020). Period poverty in a pandemic: harnessing law to achieve menstrual equity. *Washington University Law Review*, *98*, 1569.

D, S. K. (2022, February 27). Impact of poverty – Indian economy notes. Prepp By College Dunia. https://prepp.in/news/e-492-impact-of-poverty-indian-economy-notes

Dadush, U. (2019). *Youth unemployment in the Middle East and North Africa, and the Moroccan case (No. 2019-4)*. Economics Discussion Papers. https://ideas.repec.org/p/ocp/rpaper/pp1812.html

Davidai, S. (2022). How do people make sense of wealth and poverty? *Current Opinion in Psychology*, *43*, 42–47. https://doi.org/10.1016/j.copsyc.2021.06.010

Durongkaveroj, W. (2020). Free trade and prosperity: How openness helps developing countries grow richer and combat poverty, by Arvindpanagariya (Oxford University Press, New York, 2019), pp. 384. *The Economic Record*, *96*(315), 540–542. https://doi.org/10.1111/1475-4932.12583

Elayah, M., & Fenttiman, M. (2021). Humanitarian aid and war economies: The case of Yemen. *The Economics of Peace and Security Journal*, *16*(1). https://doi.org/10.15355/epsj.16.1.52

Hassan, M. S., Bukhari, S., & Arshed, N. (2019). Competitiveness, governance and globalization: What matters for poverty alleviation? *Environment, Development and Sustainability*, *22*(4), 3491–3518. https://doi.org/10.1007/s10668-019-00355-y

Heard-Garris, N., Boyd, R., Kan, K., Perez-Cardona, L., Heard, N. J., & Johnson, T. J. (2021). Structuring poverty: How racism shapes child poverty and child and adolescent health. *Academic Pediatrics*, *21*(8). https://doi.org/10.1016/j.acap.2021.05.026

Heshmati, A., Maasoumi, E., & Wan, G. (2015). Introduction and summary to poverty reduction policies and practices in developing Asia. *Poverty Reduction Policies and Practices in Developing Asia*, 1–8. https://doi.org/10.1007/978-981-287-420-7_1

Idemudia, E., & Boehnke, K. (2020). Social experiences of migrants. *Social Indicators Research Series*, 119–135. https://doi.org/10.1007/978-3-030-48347-0_6

Karamouzian, M., & Madani, N. (2020). Covid-19 response in the Middle East and North Africa: Challenges and paths forward. *Lancet Global Health*, *8*(7). https://doi.org/10.1016/s2214-109x(20)30233-3

Kaye, J. L. (2021). *The business of peace and the politics of inclusion: The role of local business actors in Yemen (2011–16)* (pp. 179–202). Rethinking Peace Mediation. https://doi.org/10.1332/policypress/9781529208191.003.0010

Khan, J., & Mohanty, S. K. (2018). Spatial heterogeneity and correlates of child malnutrition in districts of India. *BMC Public Health*, *18*(1). https://doi.org/10.1186/s12889-018-5873-z

Lyman, T. R., Mahieux, T., & Reille, X. (2005). https://www.findevgateway.org/sites/default/files/publications/files/mfg-en-paper-report-of-cgap-multi-donor-mission-microfinance-in-yemen-2005_0.pdf

Mohamed, E. F., & Fauziyyah, N. E. (2020). Islamic microfinance for poverty alleviation: a systematic literature review. *International Journal of Economics, Management and Accounting*, *28*(1), 141–163.

Ochilov, A. O., & Najibullah, E. (2021). https://papers.econferenceglobe.com/index.php/ecg/article/view/398

Prime, A. (2022). Peace, poverty and betrayal, a new history of British India by Roderick Matthews. *Journal of Colonialism and Colonial History*, *23*(1). https://doi.org/10.1353/cch.2022.0008

Qaied, M. M., & Basavaraj, K. (2019). The role of microfinance for empowerment of poor women in light of the current crisis in Yemen. *International Academic Journal of Accounting and Financial Management*, *06*(01), 23–31. https://doi.org/10.9756/iajafm/v6i1/1910003

Quak, D., & Luetz, J. M. (2021). Human happiness: Conceptual and practical perspectives. In *Encyclopedia of the UN sustainable development goals* (pp. 459–475). https://doi.org/10.1007/978-3-319-95714-2_79

Rifa'i, A., & Ayu, P. (2019). Encouraging Islamic financing to achieve SDGs through poverty alleviation. *Journal of Islamic Finance*, *8*(2), 10–20.

Robinson, J. (2019). https://harris.uchicago.edu/news-events/news/fighting-poverty-and-inequality-conversation-james-robinson

Roy, T. (2020). *The economic history of India, 1857–2010*. https://doi.org/10.1093/oso/9780190128296.001.0001

Singh, P. K., & Chudasama, H. (2020). Evaluating poverty alleviation strategies in a developing country. *PLoS One*, *15*(1). https://doi.org/10.1371/journal.pone.0227176

Spiegel, K. A., & Havas, K. A. (2019). The socioeconomic factors surrounding the initial emergence of peste des petits ruminants in Kenya, Uganda, and Tanzania from 2006 through 2008. *Transboundary and Emerging Diseases*, *66*(2), 627–633.

Sprimont, D. (2019, November 21). Poverty in Yemen or potential investment? The Borgen Project. https://borgenproject.org/poverty-in-yemen-or-potential-investment/

Thorat, A., Vanneman, R., Desai, S., & Dubey, A. (2017). Escaping and falling into poverty in India Today. *World Development*, *93*, 413–426. https://doi.org/10.1016/j.worlddev.2017.01.004

Tontisirin, K. (2019). Obsolete: Community based nutrition programmes. *Reference Module in Biomedical Sciences*. https://doi.org/10.1016/b978-0-12-801238-3.03056-7

Verma, A., & Mani, D. S. (2020). An analysis of poverty alleviation programmes in India with special reference to sustainable development goals. *SSRN Electronic Journal*. https://doi.org/10.2139/ssrn.3637927

van de Walle, D. (2002). Choosing rural road investments to help reduce poverty. *World Development*, *30*(4), 575–589. https://doi.org/10.1016/s0305-750x(01)00127-9

Woo, J., Yu, R., Cheung, K., & Lai, E. T. (2020). How much money is enough? Poverty and health in older people. *The Journal of Nutrition, Health & Aging*, *24*(10), 1111–1115. https://doi.org/10.1007/s12603-020-1444-y

Xu, L., Zhang, Q., & Shi, X. (2019). Stakeholders strategies in poverty alleviation and clean energy access: A case study of China's PV poverty alleviation program. *Energy Policy*, *135*, 111011. https://doi.org/10.1016/j.enpol.2019.111011

Zuo, C. (2021). Integrating devolution with centralization: A comparison of poverty alleviation programs in India, Mexico, and China. *Journal of Chinese Political Science*, *27*(2), 247–270. https://doi.org/10.1007/s11366-021-09760-5

Chapter 6

Economic Dependency Ratio as a Dimension of Poverty and Vulnerability

Shilpa Deo[a], *Anjali Sane*[b], *Sushil Sharma*[c] *and Saeed Tabar*[d]

[a]DES Pune University, India
[b]Dr. Vishwanath Karad MIT World Peace University, India
[c]Texas A & M University, USA
[d]Ball State University, USA

Abstract

The first Sustainable Development Goal (SDG), which is to be attained by the year 2030, is to 'End poverty in all its forms everywhere'.[1] However, the progress made in reducing poverty has been reversed due to the spread of the COVID-19 pandemic. The worsening poverty, inequality and vulnerability call for identifying the acuteness of the problem with the help of dimensions like the economic dependency ratio along with other sources like poverty line, access to social security, health care, basic services, food security and asset ownership and social networks at the village to name a few. The economic dependency ratio goes beyond the age dependency ratio and tries to capture the dependency better by incorporating the number of dependants and employed ones in the calculation. In this study, an attempt has been made to highlight the importance of the economic dependency ratio to measure vulnerability better in India. Unemployment data provided by the Centre for Monitoring Indian Economy (CMIE) has been utilised to understand the severity of dependency at the country level. Primary data has been collected with the help of the Proportionate Stratified Sampling method from 600 notified, non-notified slum households staying in the western part of India and in-depth interviews have been conducted with a few homeless families. Quantitative data has been analysed using SPSS and Stata software.

[1]https://sdgs.un.org/goals/goal1

Understanding the Multi-Dimensional Nature of Poverty, 109–130

doi:10.1108/978-1-83753-292-620241006

This study will be immensely useful as it aims to improvise the methodology to identify the poor and vulnerable. Better identification can take us a step closer to achieving SDG 1.

Keywords: Poverty; vulnerability; identification; economic dependency; SDG 1

Introduction

Poverty and the risk of falling deeper into its shackles have been causing unrest in the economies for a long time. These economic problems can create havoc in societies if left unattended. Hence, the United Nations (UN) has stated 'ending poverty in all its forms everywhere' as its first SDG. Collective efforts have been taken by governments, Central Banks, non-government organisations (NGOs) and international organisations to reduce poverty and vulnerability for many years. However, changing world economic order, geopolitical tensions, the spread of the COVID-19 pandemic and the resulting stagflation, to name a few, have been posing new challenges and reversing the progress made in reducing poverty.[2]

In India, the Planning Commission had been periodically established Expert Groups (EGs) to revisit methodological questions associated with calculating poverty to make the estimates more applicable to the current state of the economy. These groups have been suggesting various poverty lines that can enable us to identify the poor (Planning Commission, 2014). However, a mere shortfall of income vis-à-vis the poverty line cannot help us to identify the poor and vulnerable sections of society. A sizeable selection of India's urban population lacks the resources to meet even the most basic necessities, and many live in slums and other informal settlements with limited access to essential services (Bapat, 2009). Identifying these urban low-income households is a prerequisite for more precisely identifying the recipients of the numerous programs the Indian Government is running to combat poverty (Planning Commission, 2012). Most people who are having poor living conditions are not actually considered impoverished by official definitions (Bapat, 2009).

With political disputes frequently claiming a scientific grounding, occasionally with reason, more frequently without, the study of Indian poverty lines historically has been the interaction between science and politics (Deaton & Kozel, 2005). There is an increasing understanding that poverty is caused by a lack of necessities including safe drinking water, proper shelter, clothing, low literacy, a short life expectancy and inadequate income (Radhakrishna et al., 2010). In India, there has been heated debate over the number of impoverished people, but not over the more crucial topic of who the poor are and how they are classified (Saxena, 2015).

[2]https://www.worldbank.org/en/news/immersive-story/2022/10/05/covid-19-dealt-a-historic-blow-to-poverty-reduction

Additionally, the potential for productive investment, innovation and the development of human resources is significantly diminished in societies where the poor encounter hurdles in the markets for land and capital, in skill acquisition and in coping with risks (Bardhan, 2013). So, while measuring and identifying the impoverished is essential, it is not adequate. Additionally, it is crucial to act in accordance with your logical, methodical thinking while considering how to improve the situation of the underprivileged (Haughton & Khandker, 2009). It is intolerable how widespread poverty is in today's world. Because so much intellectual work is invested in making it seem acceptable, the world does not rise in revolt (Basu, 2010).

The Planning Commission announced that the data collected for the Socio-Economic Caste Census (SECC) would be used as the foundation for identifying those eligible for benefits under various central government programs after receiving scathing criticism for setting such a low poverty line. The SECC had gone beyond identifying the poor only based on the poverty line and came up with three relevant sources of vulnerabilities, viz residential, social and occupational. However, the poor and vulnerable go through various other vulnerabilities like lack of access to health care, social security, access to essential services, land and social networks in villages, and food security to name a few. Hence, the present study aims to identify the poor and vulnerable based on various dimensions of vulnerability and estimate the influence of economic dependency on such vulnerabilities.

Review of Literature

According to Rowntree (1902), a family is in primary poverty if their total earnings cannot meet the 'minimum necessities of merely physical efficiency'. He went on to demonstrate that the poor were not always to blame for their circumstances. Over the years, the definition of poverty is becoming broader and encompassing furthermore deprivations. Hence, even though their earnings would be sufficient in another community, people are considered poor if they do not have access to the resources for fully engaging in the community in which they live and, in Adam Smith's words, 'are afraid to appear in public' (Deaton, 2004; Karelis, 2009).

Dandekar and Rath (1971) did a pioneering work of identifying the poor in India using the average calorie norm of 2,250 calories per person per day. They highlighted that half of the urban population could not access 2,250 calories in 1960–1961. With lifestyle changes, such definitions of poverty have also been changing. Instead of being defined as the lack of income or the inability to fulfil the 'basic needs' of certain goods, poverty should be understood as the deprivation of basic capabilities (Sen, 1992; Son, 2011). Only after contextually pertinent causes for the descent into and escape from poverty have been recognised, policies to alleviate poverty should be given shape (Krishna, 2010).

The cognitive capabilities of a person are heavily taxed by poverty alone (Mani et al., 2013; Oommen, 2015). This 'cognitive tax' results in financial choices that keep people in poverty (Oommen, 2015). However, poverty is a collection of relevant problems that may be resolved one at a time once they have been correctly identified and acknowledged (Banerjee & Duflo, 2013).

The ability to identify people who are not yet impoverished but may become so and those who will remain such makes measurement of vulnerability essential. Once they are recognised, relevant policies can be developed (Zhang & Wan, 2008). The potential to diminish people's capacities and opportunities is referred to as vulnerability. The ability of a person to reach their full potential of development can be severely compromised by a lack of timely and ongoing investments in life skills due to vulnerabilities (United Nations Development Programme [UNDP], 2014). Financial inclusion has the potential to reduce poverty and vulnerability to poverty, especially for female-headed households and for those staying in rural areas. Hence, governments are urged to create or improve regulations that support the private sector's ability to innovate and extend financial services to more remote areas. To increase financial inclusion in emerging nations, the government must invest in and regulate the mobile money sector (Koomson et al., 2020).

The condition of poor and vulnerable people can worsen further due to external shocks like natural disasters, wars, the spread of epidemics, etc. Hallegatte et al. (2020) highlight the interrelationship between disaster risk management and poverty reduction. In addition to this, the statement – 'COVID-19 does not discriminate' has been said on many occasions. This is a dangerous fallacy, however, as it ignores the rising vulnerabilities of people who are the most economically and socially disadvantaged (Patel et al., 2020). Tavares and Betti (2021) suggest that the responses to COVID-19 should prioritise vulnerable sections and emphasise the importance of integrated national action.

The age dependency ratio has been an essential demographic factor determining poverty and vulnerability. However, the growing economic dependency can shatter the lives of the vulnerable. The economic dependency ratio and its impact on poverty and vulnerability are relatively understudied (Henesy, 2021; Yip et al., 2010). Further, the economic dependency is worsening amidst increasing waves of external shocks like geopolitical tensions, repeated COVID occurrences, the lingering Russia–Ukraine war and the energy crisis to name a few. In this highly interconnected global village, these shocks are very likely to leave a devastating impact on the vulnerable sections of society. Hence, it would be very pertinent to estimate the influence of the economic dependency ratio on dimensions of vulnerability.

Methodology

Poverty and vulnerability can be traced in slums and amongst houseless households. Hence, to estimate the impact of economic dependency on vulnerability to poverty, primary data have been collected from 600 notified and non-notified slum households in the western part of India, i.e. Pune city. Pune city has been selected for data collection due to the growing urbanisation, and a lot of studies have focused on other metro cities of India like Mumbai, Delhi and Bangalore to name a few (Baker et al., 2005; Banerji, 2000; Baud et al., 2008; Benjamin, 2016; Kumar & Aggarwal, 2003; Sharma et al., 2019; Singh et al., 2002; Thara, 2017). According to the National Sample Survey Organisation (NSSO), 'a non-notified slum is a compact settlement with a collection of poorly built tenements, mostly of temporary nature, crowded together usually with inadequate sanitary and drinking water facilities in unhygienic conditions. Areas notified as slums by the respective municipalities, corporations, local bodies, or development authorities are treated as notified slums'.[3]

The total slum population is 655,494 households, according to data from the Pune Municipal Corporation (PMC) Office. The larger the sample size, the better it is to generalise the results. However, it should be kept in mind that one objective of sampling is to obtain representative data at a reasonable cost (McTavish & Loether, 2002). Hence, 0.001 of the total slum population, i.e. 655.494, was determined to be the sample size. Out of 655 households, some shared incomplete information, and a few others denied responding. Hence, the complete information was received from 600 slum households. Equal weightage was given to notified and non-notified slum dwellers (300 each) to enable comparative analysis. Snowballing technique was used to identify the slum households.

The PMC's office provided the data on the ward-wise number of notified and non-notified slums in Pune city. The sample size from each of the city's administrative wards has been calculated using these statistics. The sample size was determined using proportionate sampling method. When using proportional stratified random samples, the sample strata are drawn from the same population strata as the cases; thus, they employ the same sampling fraction and have the same number of instances. Because it assures that no stratum in the combined sample has an overwhelming influence on the overall results, this sampling technique is crucial for generalising sample results back to the population studied (McTavish & Loether, 2002).

All administrative wards were chosen for data collection because a sample must accurately represent the population. The PMC's office was contacted for information on the names of the slums and their populations to select the notified and non-notified slums. All the data acquired from the PMC's office was updated till 2009–2010. In addition, the Shelter Associates website's Spatial Slum Information was used to narrow down the list of slums.

Capturing the floating sections of the population is much more challenging. However, the decision of whether minor categories should be included in the study or not mostly depends on the research questions to be addressed (Yates, 1981). Since not all slum dwellers are impoverished and not all vulnerable people reside in slums, qualitative data from homeless households residing in different areas of Pune city have been obtained.

---

[3]https://mohua.gov.in/upload/uploadfiles/files/9Slum_Report_NBO(2).pdf

The PMC officials were unable to offer a list of the homeless people for every ward. However, they provided details on the places where the houseless households were discovered to be residing. As a result, the households that were homeless and available during the field visits and willing to provide their information served as the source of the primary data. Additionally, the definition of houseless households provided by the Indian census, which is as follows, has been used to identify the households: 'Households who do not live in buildings or census houses but live in the open on roadside, pavements, in hume pipes, under flyovers and staircases, or in the open in places of worship, mandaps, railway platforms, etc. are treated as houseless households'. The data were gathered from 39 homeless households residing in the Pune city.

A new methodology was devised to identify the poor and vulnerable based on the literature review (see Appendix A). A pilot survey was undertaken in November and December 2014. The primary sources of information were 51 slum residents. In addition, 20 homeless families were also interviewed. The final survey was conducted from March to September 2015 after specific revisions were made to the questionnaire.

The changing unemployment rate (Fig. 6.1) highlights the fluctuating economic dependency in the Indian economy.

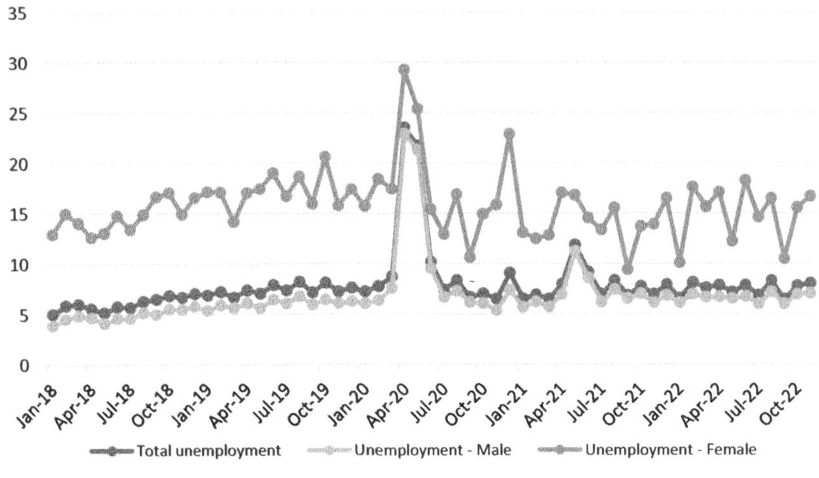

Fig. 6.1. Unemployment Rate in India (From January 2018 to November 2022). *Source:* Centre for Monitoring Indian Economy (https://economicoutlook.cmie.com/).

Economic dependency can worsen the living conditions of the underprivileged sections, and therefore, this study is undertaken to estimate how economic dependency changes according to the dimensions of vulnerability.

Results and Discussion

There is an inter-relationship between the vulnerability of a country or region to natural disasters and macroeconomic shocks on the one hand and household vulnerability to poverty on the other hand (Naude et al., 2009). Therefore, to create effective policies to address poverty, it is necessary to have a thorough understanding of the causes of vulnerability to poverty (Haughton & Khandker, 2009).

The demographic profile of the respondents has been shared in Table 6.1. It gives a clear idea about the socio-economic background of the slum dwellers. It can further be utilised to interpret better the causes of vulnerability to poverty.

Table 6.1. Demographic Profile of Slum Dwellers in Pune City.

Demographic Profile	Percentages
Household Head	
Male	91.0
Female	9.0
Religion	
Hindu	80.5
Muslim	8.2
Christian	0.7
Buddhists	7.8
Neo Buddhists	2.8
Category	
General	29.46
Other Backward Class (OBC)	15.20
Scheduled Caste (SC)	42.21
Scheduled Tribe (ST)	2.06
Vimukta Jati (VJ)	5.44
Nomadic Tribes (NT)	5.63
Household Size	
Median	4
Age Dependency Ratio	
Child dependency ratio	33.96594

(Continued)

Table 6.1. *(Continued)*

Demographic Profile	Percentages
Old age dependency ratio	6.131387
Economic dependency ratio	128.855
Level of Literacy	
Illiteracy	21.91
Primary	14.08
Secondary	46.74
Higher-secondary	9.91
Graduation	5.74
Post-graduation	1.62
Per Capita Income (PCI)	
Less than or equal to ₹ 3,000	55
Greater than ₹ 3,000	45
Headcount Ratio (HCR)	
Notified slum	9.67
Non-notified slum	11
Squared Poverty Gap Index (SPGI)	
Notified slum	0.0061
Non-notified slum	0.0067
Expenditure Inequality (Gini Coefficient)	
Notified slum	0.276
Non-notified slum	0.228

Source: Primary data.

As is evident from Table 6.1, the majority of the respondents were male-headed and belonged to OBC and SC categories. One can calculate the age dependency ratio by dividing the populations of those aged 0–14 and 65 and older by those aged 15–64. It is estimated to be 40.0973 per 100 people of working age. This age dependency ratio can be further broken down to calculate different dependency ratios because it combines the child and old age dependency ratios. We could better understand dependants' age distribution if we had separate dependency ratios. The child dependency ratio was found to be very high in comparison to the old age dependency ratio. Further, the age dependency ratio may not accurately reflect the dependency as some people who belong to the working age might not be employed and few others might be working, even if they belong to old age, to support their families. Hence, an economic dependency ratio has been calculated by dividing the number of dependants by the number of earners in the sample. The economic dependency ratio of 128.855 per 100 working-age population starkly portrays acute dependency. This economic dependency can ruin the people's lives and dig them deeper into poverty. Therefore, an attempt has been made to estimate the influence of the economic dependency ratio on the vulnerability of slum dwellers.

Majority of the slum dwellers had completed education only up to secondary school with 21.9% being illiterate. It further undermines the chances of escaping poverty (Krishna, 2010). More than half of the slum households have PCI less than or equal to ₹ 3,000. Men worked primarily as drivers, construction workers, vegetable vendors, office boys, painters, rickshaw drivers, security guards, plumbers and carriers, to name a few occupations. Most women worked as domestic helpers, tailors, nurses, beauticians, caterers, sweepers, garbage collectors, scrap collectors, vegetable and fish sellers, etc. Most of the poor work in production and service (Bardhan, 1987). The HCR is found to be only 10.335 on average. It is slightly higher for the non-notified slum dwellers vis-à-vis the notified ones.

The HCR is calculated by following the urban poverty line (₹ 1,407) stated by Rangarajan Committee Report on Poverty. As stated earlier, only measuring poverty in terms of the poverty line is not enough as it does not reveal the vulnerability that the poor go through, throughout their lives. Hence, though the HCR shows that only 10% of slum dwellers are lacking, it would be pertinent to go beyond and find out the prevailing inequality and other vulnerabilities. The HCR is inadequate because it does not measure how income is distributed among the poor (Sen, 1992). The SPGI can overcome this limitation. It is just the weighted sum of the poverty gaps (as a percentage of the poverty line), with the proportionate poverty gaps serving as the weights. The measure indirectly gives more weight to observations significantly below the poverty threshold by squaring the poverty gap index (The World Bank, 2011). The SPGI is also slightly higher for non-notified slum dwellers. An attempt has been made to identify expenditure inequality among the slum inhabitants. The Gini coefficient, which ranges from 0 (perfect equality) to 1 (perfect inequality), is a well-known indicator of inequality. It is based on the cumulative frequency curve known as the Lorenz curve, which contrasts the distribution of a given quantity (such as income or expenditure) with the uniform distribution, which symbolises equality. This most straightforward inequality measurement shows the percentage of expenditure (or income) attributable to each fifth (quintile) of the population and arranges the population from poorest to richest. Based on HCR, SPGI, and Gini coefficient values, it can be stated that in the case of the non-notified slum dwellers, poverty rather than inequality appears to be a primary problem (unlike the notified slum dwellers).

Now, let us try to answer the key research question of the study: how is the economic dependency ratio interrelated to various dimensions of vulnerability?

This question is answered with the help of the following regression model:

Economic Dependency Ratio = α_0 + α_1 Head of the household + α_2 Recent migrants + α_3 Residential vulnerability index + α_4 Asset ownership & social networks in village index + α_5 Healthcare index + α_6 Access to basic services index + α_7 Social security index + α_8 Food security index + α_9 Corruption & Harassment index + α_{10} Type of slum + α_{11} Help from politician + μ

Table 6.2. Economic Dependency Ratio and Dimensions of Vulnerability.

Economic Dependency Ratio	Coefficients	*t*	*P*>|*t*|
Head of the household	−22.60018	−0.69	0.489
Recent migrants	26.16305	1.57	0.119
Residential vulnerability index	27.94011	0.45	0.656
Asset ownership and social networks in village index	41.67262	1.25	0.213
Healthcare index	−76.37486	−1.81	0.072
Access to basic services index	180.9152	1.59	0.112
Social security index	12.65122	0.39	0.694
Food security index	163.5649	2.01	0.045
Corruption and harassment index	−95.22447	−1.81	0.072
Type of slum	−9.367706	−0.55	0.584
Help from politician	−13.42137	−0.79	0.429
Constant	−35.39721	−0.35	0.730

Source: Primary data.

Four dummy variables have been developed. So, the head of the household takes the value of 1 if it is female-headed; 0 otherwise, the variable, recent migrants takes the value of 1 if households have migrated in the last 20 years (from the year of data collection); 0 otherwise, type of slum takes the value of 1 if it is non-notified slum; 0 otherwise, and the variable help from politician takes the value of 1 if the answer is positive; 0 otherwise. Based on the methodology used by the SECC to find out the residentially, occupationally, and socially vulnerable sections, we have derived a new and improvised methodology (see Appendix A). With the help of this methodology, the indices have been computed for residential vulnerability and vulnerability concerning asset ownership and social networks in the village, corruption and harassment, and access to health care, basic services, social security, and food security. These index values range from 0 to 1, where values closer to 0 mean high vulnerability and the ones closer to 1 mean significantly less vulnerability. This is certainly not an exhaustive list of sources of vulnerability, but an attempt has been made to capture the key factors. The variable, asset ownership, and social networks in the village is incorporated to trace the availability of a fallback mechanism in case of a lack of livelihood opportunities in cities.

The adjusted *R*-squared value is found to be 0.0427 which means that 4.27% of the variation in the economic dependency ratio is explained by the dimensions of vulnerability. As can be seen in Table 6.2, the economic dependency ratio increased for recent migrants by 26 units (11% level of significance[los]), in the case of access to basic services index by a whooping 180 units (11% los), and the food security index by 163 units (4% los). Though the recent migrants try to find employment opportunities with the help of their social networks, it takes time for them to settle in the cities, so their economic dependency is higher for them. According to Gupta and Mitra (2002), people who had migrated during the last 1–5 years had the highest incidence of poverty, while those who have lived in Delhi for 12–15 years had the lowest incidence. Instead, because they can experience upward income mobility in the informal sector as well, migrants continue to live in metropolitan areas even when they are unable to find employment in the formal sector. By doing this, they can lessen the severity of poverty, if not wholly, escape it (Mitra, 2006). Also, as access to essential services and food security improves, economic dependency increases substantially. It is a novel finding as it suggests that the motivation to be an earning member decreases with improved access to essential services and food security. However, it is recommended that more rigorous research should be undertaken in this area before firmly establishing this finding. There is a negative and significant association between the economic dependency ratio, on the one hand, and the health care index and corruption and harassment index, on the other hand and the results are significant at 7% level of significance. So, as the vulnerability of households in terms of health care, corruption and harassment goes down (with increasing index values), the economic dependency ratio also declines. This is a significant finding keeping in mind the current scenario where the economic dependency has been worsening with a lack of access to health care due to the COVID-19 waves. Hence, to avoid long-term adverse health effects, the COVID-19 epidemic has made it imperative to pay holistic attention to the underprivileged and marginalised communities (Gopalan & Misra, 2020). Boo (2012) placed a significant emphasis on how corruption makes slum inhabitants extremely vulnerable to poverty. She also discussed the poor health and excessive healthcare costs that cause deaths and indebtedness.

Interestingly, in case of the sampled households that had received any kind of help from the local politician, the economic dependency ratio is decreasing by 13 units. However, the result is not significant which could be because very few people agreed to getting any kind of help from the politician. Additionally, even if the households received assistance from the politician, particularly during elections, it's probable that they kept it a secret out of fear. Instead, it has been widely noted that political patronage, particularly during election times, is frequently the source of security of tenure and the acquisition of essential community services (Singh & De Souza, 1980).

The model has also been tested for multicollinearity in Stata with the help of estat vif command, and the following are the results:

Table 6.3. Multicollinearity Test of Model.

Variables	VIF*	1/VIF
Access to basic services index	1.60	0.626093
Residential vulnerability index	1.58	0.633512
Type of slum	1.40	0.715045
Corruption & harassment index	1.28	0.781878
Social security index	1.15	0.868698
Recent migrants	1.14	0.874568

(Continued)

Table 6.3. *(Continued)*

Variables	VIF*	1/VIF
Food security index	1.13	0.884708
Asset ownership and social networks in village index	1.10	0.908687
Help from politician	1.10	0.908787
Head of the household	1.07	0.938461
Healthcare index	1.07	0.935487
Mean VIF	1.24	

Source: Primary data.

Note: *Variance Inflation Factor.

Hence, as is evident from Table 6.3, there is no multicollinearity in the model as all VIF values are less than 10.

However, both quantitative and qualitative approaches agree that, when it comes to persuading policymakers, an appealing story can frequently be worth a thousand regressions (Kanbur, 2001). Hence, a case study of a houseless household has been incorporated to highlight the role of higher economic dependency in worsening the poor and vulnerable living conditions.

Case Study: Intensifying Vulnerability to Poverty Due to Higher Dependency Ratio

HSB was staying on a pavement near Shivajinagar.[4] She belonged to the NT category. She had an alcoholic husband who did not work. So, she had to work. When she was 13 years old, she was married off, and her husband quit working after they married. He frequently beat her. They had five kids. In addition to this, because her older daughter was abandoned, she stayed with them as well as her other two daughters. One of her daughters used to attend a school in Nashik, but she had to discontinue education. Some members were illiterate, while others had only completed primary schooling. Since HSB was the sole earner in the family, there was an extremely high dependency. She worked as a construction worker and scrap collector.

With acute dependency, food security can be at stake. So, she was asked few questions regarding it. She shared that with the help of the government scheme of providing food grains at subsidised prices, they could get some wheat, rice and kerosene through the Fair Price Shop every month. However, that was barely enough to survive. They could afford to purchase only a quarter litre of milk every day and could eat fruits only if that was offered to them by some generous people. They had to undergo a lot of uncertainty due to the lack of security as the PMC officials had been visiting the place and snatching off their belongings often as a part of the eviction and demolition drive.

[4]Initial of the name is written to protect the identity.

When interrogated further about ownership of assets, HSB stated that they have a second-hand two-wheeler which was purchased by taking a loan of ₹ 5,000 from relatives. It was brought to facilitate her husband's commuting to work. However, he discontinued work. So, it has been doubly burdensome for her. She expected her children to reduce this economic dependency when they grew up. According to her, poverty is being a sole earner and living a hand-to-mouth existence. She firmly believed that coming out of the shackles of poverty was a distant dream with a single earning member supporting a family of 10 members.

Conclusion

The key economic problems of poverty, inequality and vulnerability can shatter the world economies if left unaddressed. Therefore, the local, state and national governments and international bodies have been undertaking timely measures to reduce the inequalities and vulnerabilities. One of the essential ways to eradicate it is to identify the poor and vulnerable for effective targeting. Hence, the present study has showcased a better way of identifying them. A new methodology has been devised to figure out various dimensions of vulnerability and quantify it with the help of data collected from slum dwellers. The results indicate that though very few slum households are poor, based on the poverty line, they face acute vulnerability in terms of health care, access to essential services, social security, corruption and harassment and asset ownership and social networks in the village.

Further, the interlinkages between the economic dependency ratio and the dimensions of vulnerability have been explored. It has interestingly been found that the economic dependency ratio is worsening for recent migrants. Also, the economic dependency goes down with reduced health care difficulties and corruption and harassment challenges. Hence, improved access to health care and a reduction in corruption and harassment can ensure better living conditions with less economic dependency. In addition, improved access to essential services and food security have been negatively influencing the motivation to work, resulting in a substantial increase in economic dependency. This finding needs to be corroborated further with more rigorous research. The economic dependency ratio is hardly given any importance while studying dependency. Most of the times, it is the age dependency ratio that is taken into consideration. However, the economic dependency ratio reflects the severity of dependency more clearly. Hence, it is suggested to the policymakers to rely on the economic dependency numbers and estimate its interlinkages with vulnerability to poverty at the country level for better understanding the root causes. These efforts will go a long way in eradicating poverty, minimising vulnerability and achieving the SDGs by 2030.

Limitations and Future Research Directions

A higher sample size improves the accuracy and representativeness of the sample. Hence, we intend to collect information from at least 1% of the slum population in the future. Also, the current study was restricted geographically only to Pune city. Further studies will aim to capture primary data from other metro cities. Rural dynamics, as highlighted through the rural spillover hypothesis, can also be a key determinant of economic dependency. Therefore, future studies will involve capturing other significant factors influencing economic dependency, poverty and vulnerability.

Acknowledgements

This book chapter is the outcome of the author's PhD thesis titled 'Urban Poverty & Vulnerability in Pune city'. The author is extremely grateful to Prof Dhanmanjiri Sathe, Professor & Dean of International Affairs at Gokhale Institute of Politics & Economics, and Dr Suddhasil Siddhanta, Assistant Professor at Gokhale Institute of Politics & Economics, for their timely guidance and invaluable contribution.

References

Baker, J., Basu, R., Cropper, M., Lall, S., & Takeuchi, A. (2005). *Urban poverty and transport: The case of Mumbai*. World Bank Publications. https://openknowledge.worldbank.org/server/api/core/bitstreams/63529a80-6924-5aaa-945b-ef346f86e96e/content

Banerjee, V. A., & Duflo, E. (2013). *Poor economics – Rethinking poverty and the ways to end it*. Random House India.

Banerji, R. (2000). Poverty and primary schooling: Field studies from Mumbai and Delhi. *Economic and Political Weekly*, 795–802. https://doi.org/10.2307/4408991

Bapat, M. (2009). *Poverty lines and lives of the poor – Underestimation of urban poverty – The case of India. Poverty reduction in urban areas series*. International Institute for Environment and Development. https://www.iied.org/sites/default/files/pdfs/migrate/10567IIED.pdf

Bardhan, P. (1987). Poverty and employment characteristics of urban households in West Bengal: An analysis of results of National Sample Survey, 1977–78. *Economic and Political Weekly*, 1496–1502. https://www.epw.in/journal/1987/35/special-articles/poverty-and-employment-characteristics-urban-households-west-bengal

Bardhan, P. (2013, January 20). Pranab Bardhan: How unequal a country is India? *Business Standard*. http://www.business-standard.com/article/opinion/pranab-bardhan-how-unequal-a-country-is-india-109090500021_1.html

Basu, K. (2010). *Beyond the invisible hand: Groundwork for a new economics*. Princeton University Press.

Baud, I. S. A., Sridharan, N., & Pfeffer, K. (2008). Mapping urban poverty for local governance in an Indian mega-city: The case of Delhi. *Urban Studies*, *45*(7), 1385–1412. https://doi.org/10.1177/0042098008090679

Benjamin, S. (2016). Governance, economic settings and poverty in Bangalore. *Environment and Urbanization*, *12*(1), 35–56. https://doi.org/10.1177/095624780001200104

Boo, K. (2012). *Behind the beautiful forevers – Life, death and hope in a Mumbai undercity*. Penguin Books India Private Limited.

Dandekar, M. V., & Rath, N. (1971). *Poverty in India*. Indian School of Political Economy.

Deaton, A. (2004). *Measuring poverty*. Research program in development studies. Princeton University. http://dx.doi.org/10.2139/ssrn.564001

Deaton, A., & Kozel, V. (2005). Data and dogma: The great Indian poverty debate. *The World Bank Research Observer*, *20*(2), 177–199. https://doi.org/10.1093/wbro/lki009

Gopalan, H. S., & Misra, A. (2020). COVID-19 pandemic and challenges for socio-economic issues, healthcare and National Health Programs in India. *Diabetes & Metabolic Syndrome: Clinical Research & Reviews*, *14*(5), 757–759. https://doi.org/10.1016/j.dsx.2020.05.041

Gupta, I., & Mitra, A. (2002). Rural migrants and labour segmentation: Micro – Level evidence from Delhi slums. *Economic and Political Weekly*, *XXXVII*(2), 163–168. https://www.epw.in/journal/2002/02/special-articles/rural-migrants-and-labour-segmentation.html

Hallegatte, S., Vogt-Schilb, A., Rozenberg, J., Bangalore, M., & Beaudet, C. (2020). From poverty to disaster and back: A review of the literature. *Economics of Disasters and Climate Change*, *4*(1), 223–247. https://doi.org/10.1007/s41885-020-00060-5

Haughton, J., & Khandker, R. S. (2009). *Handbook on poverty and inequality*. Rawat Publications.

Henesy, A. (2021, June 30). An alternative portrait of dependency: Esri's economic dependency ratio. https://www.esri.com/arcgis-blog/products/esri-demographics/analytics/an-alternative-portrait-of-dependency-esris-economic-dependency-ratio/

Kanbur, R. (Ed.). (2001). *Q – Squared: Combining qualitative and quantitative methods in poverty appraisal*. Permanent Black.

Karelis, C. (2009). *The persistence of poverty: Why the economics of the well – Off can't help the poor*. Oxford University Press.

Koomson, I., Villano, R. A., & Hadley, D. (2020). Effect of financial inclusion on poverty and vulnerability to poverty: Evidence using a multidimensional measure of financial inclusion. *Social Indicators Research*, *149*(2), 613–639. https://doi.org/10.1007/s11205-019-02263-0

Krishna, A. (2010). *One illness away: Why people become poor and how they escape poverty*. Oxford University Press.

Kumar, N., & Aggarwal, S. C. (2003). Patterns of consumption and poverty in Delhi slums. *Economic and Political Weekly*, 5294–5300. https://www.epw.in/journal/2003/50/special-articles/patterns-consumption-and-poverty-delhi-slums.html#

Mani, A., Mullainathan, S., Shafir, E., & Zhao, J. (2013). Poverty impedes cognitive function. *Science*, *341*, 975–980. https://doi.org/10.1126/science.1238041

McTavish, G. D., & Loether, J. H. (2002). *Social research – An evolving process*. PHI Learning Private Limited.

Mitra, A. (2006). Labour market mobility of low income households. *Economic and Political Weekly*, *XLI*(21), 2123–2130. https://www.epw.in/journal/2006/21/review-labour-review-issues-specials/labour-market-mobility-low-income-households

Naude, W., Santos-Paulino, U. A., & McGillivray, M. (2009). *Vulnerability in developing countries*. World Institute for Development Economics Research. United Nations University. https://collections.unu.edu/eserv/UNU:2548/ebrary9789280811711.pdf

Oommen, A. M. (2015). Bank and poverty reduction: A critique of World Development Report 2015. *Economic and Political Weekly*, *L*(38), 13–16. https://www.epw.in/journal/2015/38/commentary/bank-and-poverty-reduction.html

Patel, J. A., Nielsen, F. B. H., Badiani, A. A., Assi, S., Unadkat, V. A., Patel, B., Ravindrane, R., & Wardle, H. (2020). Poverty, inequality and COVID-19: The forgotten vulnerable. *Public Health*, *183*, 110. https://doi.org/10.1016/j.puhe.2020.05.006

Planning Commission. (2012). *Report of the expert group to recommend the detailed methodology for identification of families living below poverty line in the urban areas*. Government of India. http://14.139.60.153/bitstream/123456789/410/1/Report-REPORT%20OF%20THE%20EXPERT%20GROUP%20TO%20RECOMMEND%20THE%20DETAILED%20METHODOLOGY%20FOR%20IDENTIFICATION%20OF%20FAMILIES%20LIVING%20BELOW%20POVERTY%20LINEIN%20THE%20URBAN%20AREAS.pdf

Planning Commission. (2014). *Report of the expert group to review the methodology for measurement of poverty*. Government of India. https://forms.iimk.ac.in/libportal/reports/232858161-Planning-Commission-report-on-poverty-estimates.pdf

Radhakrishna, R., Ravi, C., & Reddy, S. B. (2010). *Can we really measure poverty and identify the poor when poverty encompasses multiple deprivations?* Institute for Human Development. https://doi.org/10.1177/0973703020100204

Rowntree, B. S. (1902). *Poverty: A study of town life*. Macmillan.

Saxena, C. N. (2015). Socio economic caste census – Has it ignored too many poor households. *Economic and Political Weekly*, *L*(30), 14–17. https://www.epw.in/journal/2015/30/commentary/socio-economic-caste-census.html

Sen, A. (1992). *Inequality re-examined*. Oxford University Press.

Sharma, S. V., Han, P., & Sharma, V. K. (2019). Socio-economic determinants of energy poverty amongst Indian households: A case study of Mumbai. *Energy Policy*, *132*, 1184–1190. https://doi.org/10.1016/j.enpol.2019.06.068

Singh, M. A., & De Souza, A. (1980). *The urban poor – Slum and pavement dwellers in the major cities of India*. Manohar Publications.

Singh, V., Jaiswal, A., Porter, J. D. H., Ogden, J. A., Sarin, R., Sharma, P. P., Arora, V. K., & Jain, R. C. (2002). TB control, poverty, and vulnerability in Delhi, India. *Tropical Medicine and International Health*, *7*(8), 693–700. https://doi.org/10.1046/j.1365-3156.2002.00909.x

Son, H. H. (2011). *Equity and well-being: Measurement and policy practice*. Routledge.

Tavares, F. F., & Betti, G. (2021). The pandemic of poverty, vulnerability, and COVID-19: Evidence from a fuzzy multidimensional analysis of deprivations in Brazil. *World Development*, *139*, 105307. https://doi.org/10.1016/j.worlddev.2020.105307

Thara, K. (2017). In troubled waters: Water commodification, law, gender, and poverty in Bangalore. *Gender and Development*, *25*(2), 253–268. https://doi.org/10.1080/13552074.2017.1341205

The World Bank. (2011). *Perspectives on poverty in India – Stylized facts from survey data*. Oxford University Press.

United Nations Development Programme. (2014). *Human Development Report 2014 – Sustaining human progress: Reducing vulnerabilities and building resilience*, New York. https://hdr.undp.org/system/files/documents/human-development-report-2014.human-development-report-2014

Yates, F. (1981). *Sampling methods for censuses and surveys*. Charles Griffin and Company Limited.

Yip, P. S., Cheung, K. S., Law, S. C., Chi, I., & Robine, J. M. (2010). The demographic window and economic dependency ratio in the Hong Kong SAR. *Asian Population Studies*, *6*(2), 241–260. https://doi.org/10.1080/17441730.2010.494452

Zhang, Y., & Wan, G. (2008). *Can we predict vulnerability to poverty?* World Institute for Development Economics Research. United Nations University. https://www.wider.unu.edu/sites/default/files/rp2008-82.pdf

https://economicoutlook.cmie.com/

https://www.rowntreesociety.org.uk/explore-rowntree-history/rowntree-a-z/poverty-in-york/

Appendix A

Methodology – Indices: Dimensions of Vulnerability to Poverty

Sr. No.	Dimensions of Vulnerability	Indicators	Criteria	Scores	Maximum Score
1	Residential vulnerability index	Type of house	Kutcha	0	1
			Semi kutcha	0.5	
			Pucca	1	
		Ownership of house	No	0	1
			Yes	1	
		Source of light	No electricity	0	1
			Rented	0.5	
			Own	1	
		Eviction/ Demolition	Yes	0	1
			No	1	
		Theft	Yes	0	1
			No	1	
2	Asset ownership and social networks in village index	Migration	Yes	0	1
			No	1	
		Ownership of land at village	No	0	1
			Yes	1	
		Ownership of house at village	No	0	1
			Yes	1	
		Relatives staying in village	No	0	1
			Yes	1	

(Continued)

(Continued)

Methodology – Indices: Dimensions of Vulnerability to Poverty

Sr. No.	Dimensions of Vulnerability	Indicators	Criteria	Scores	Maximum Score
3	Health care index	Chronic illness/ accident	Yes	0	1
			No	1	
		Took loan for expenditure incurred on treatment	Yes	0	1
			No	1	
4	Access to basic services index	Source of drinking water	Hand pump	0	1
			Common tap	0.5	
			Own tap	1	
		Time taken to travel for fetching water	More than 20 minutes	0	1
			Between 10 to 20 minutes	0.33	
			Between 5 to 10 minutes	0.66	
			Less than 5 minutes	1	
		Type of toilet	Open defecation	0	1
			Mobile toilet	0.33	
			Common flush toilet	0.66	
			Own toilet	1	
		Availability of bathing facility	Open air	0	1
			Canal	0.2	
			River	0.4	
			Common bathroom	0.6	
			Detached bathroom	0.8	

(Continued)

Methodology – Indices: Dimensions of Vulnerability to Poverty					
Sr. No.	**Dimensions of Vulnerability**	**Indicators**	**Criteria**	**Scores**	**Maximum Score**
			Own bathroom	1	
		Amount paid for the usage of public toilet and bathroom	Greater than median	0	1
			Less than or equal to median	0.5	
			0	1	
		Availability of drainage facility	No drainage	0	1
			Open	0.5	
			Closed	1	
		Garbage disposal	Open place	0	1
			Common dustbin	1	
		Availability of ration card	No	0	1
			Yes	1	
		Proximity of fair Price shop	No	0	1
			Yes	1	
		Sufficiency of the quantity of commodities	No	0	1
			Yes	1	
		Availability of aadhaar card	No	0	1
			Yes	1	
		Time taken to reach public hospitals	More than 20 minutes	0	1
			Between 10 to 20 minutes	0.33	
			Between 5 to 10 minutes	0.66	
			Less than 5 minutes	1	

(Continued)

(Continued)

Methodology – Indices: Dimensions of Vulnerability to Poverty					
Sr. No.	**Dimensions of Vulnerability**	**Indicators**	**Criteria**	**Scores**	**Maximum Score**
5	Social security index	Bank account	No	0	1
			Yes	1	
		Insurance policy	No	0	1
			Yes	1	
		Saving	No	0	1
			Yes	1	
		Loan	Yes	0	1
			No	1	
6	Food security index	Cooking	No	0	1
			Yes	1	
		Type of cooking fuel	Wood	0	1
			Both wood and kerosene	0.17	
			Kerosene	0.34	
			Diesel	0.51	
			Wood, kerosene and LPG	0.68	
			Both kerosene and LPG	0.85	
			LPG	1	
		Ease of availability of cooking fuel	No	0	1
			Yes	1	
		Frequency of purchasing food grains	Never	0	1
			Rarely	0.13	
			Daily	0.26	
			Weekly	0.39	
			Fortnightly	0.52	
			Monthly	0.65	
			Quarterly	0.78	

(Continued)

Methodology – Indices: Dimensions of Vulnerability to Poverty

Sr. No.	Dimensions of Vulnerability	Indicators	Criteria	Scores	Maximum Score
			Bi annually	0.91	
			Annually	1	
		Frequency of purchasing vegetables	Never	0	1
			Rarely	0.33	
			Daily	0.66	
			Weekly	1	
		Frequency of purchasing oil, spices, sugar, salt, etc	Never	0	1
			Rarely	0.13	
			Daily	0.26	
			Weekly	0.39	
			Fortnightly	0.52	
			Monthly	0.65	
			Quarterly	0.78	
			Bi annually	0.91	
			Annually	1	
		Frequency of purchasing fruits	Never	0	1
			Rarely	0.2	
			Monthly	0.4	
			Fortnightly	0.6	
			Weekly	0.8	
			Daily	1	
		Frequency of purchasing milk	Never	0	1
			Rarely	0.33	
			Weekly	0.66	
			Daily	1	
		Frequency of purchasing non – vegetarian food	Never	0	1
			Rarely	0.2	
			Monthly	0.4	
			Fortnightly	0.6	
			Weekly	0.8	
			Daily	1	

(Continued)

(Continued)

Methodology – Indices: Dimensions of Vulnerability to Poverty					
Sr. No.	**Dimensions of Vulnerability**	**Indicators**	**Criteria**	**Scores**	**Maximum Score**
7	Corruption and harassment index	Harassment for staying at the current location	Yes No	0 1	1
		Payment of bribes for staying at the current location	Yes No	0 1	1
		Payment to agent for getting ration card	Yes No	0 1	1
Total					48

Source: Authors' original work to identify the poor and vulnerable.

Chapter 7

Exploring Poverty Measurement Techniques Across Diverse Economies: A Cross-Country Study

Chitra Krishnan[a], *Sanjeev Chaturvedi*[b] *and Jasmine Mariappan*[c]

[a]Symbiosis Centre of Management Studies, Noida; Symbiosis International Deemed University, Pune, India
[b]DY Patil University, India
[c]University of Technology and Applied Sciences, IBRA, Oman

Abstract

Poverty is affecting millions of people worldwide and it is a huge global issue. It is a challenging issue with many facets that affect politics, the economy and society. Achieving sustainable development goals (SDGs) and reducing inequality around the world are both affected by poverty. There are various techniques to quantify poverty, each with advantages and disadvantages. Absolute, relative and multidimensional poverty are a few of the often-used measurements. However, measuring poverty across different economies is challenging due to social, economic and political differences. This chapter aims to examine the concept of poverty and how it is measured in various economic contexts. In this chapter, various methods of calculating poverty, the difficulties in doing so and the efficacy of various poverty measures in capturing poverty in multiple economies are also covered. This chapter will also discuss how the findings may affect policy and practice and propose new lines of inquiry for future studies on measuring poverty in various economies. The significance of this study resides in its ability to advance our understanding of poverty and its quantification while also guiding practitioners and decision-makers engaged in efforts to eradicate poverty and advance sustainable development. This chapter examines poverty in various economies in order to highlight the dynamic and complex character of poverty as well as the demand for context-specific measures to reduce it.

Understanding the Multi-Dimensional Nature of Poverty, 131–146

Published under exclusive licence by Emerald Publishing Limited
doi:10.1108/978-1-83753-292-620241007

Keywords: Absolute poverty; relative poverty; multidimensional poverty; social context; economic context; political context; challenges; policy implications; sustainable development; inequality

Introduction

In all economies, poverty is a pervasive and ongoing issue that has an impact on individuals, families and entire communities. To comprehend the extent of poverty and create practical remedies, an assessment of the problem is essential. However, determining poverty requires considering several factors, such as income, consumption, health, education and living standards. This is a difficult and complex task. The complexity of poverty itself, data scarcity, measurement issues and other factors make it difficult for developing and emerging nations to estimate poverty. Since so many emerging economies lack adequate data-gathering methods, it is difficult to compile accurate and timely data on poverty. The measurement of poverty must take a number of parameters into account since poverty in these economies typically has numerous dimensions that go beyond income or consumption levels.

Emerging economies are similarly plagued by comparable problems with data availability and quality, as well as estimating poverty. In addition, factors other than consumption and income need to be considered in order to define poverty effectively. Two multidimensional poverty indices, the Human Development Index (HDI) and the Multidimensional Poverty Index (MPI) rate the health, education and living conditions of those living in poverty (Alkire et al., 2021). These indicators provide a more complete picture of poverty and can be used to create legislation that considers the needs of low-income households.

Overview of Poverty Measurement

The process of measuring poverty is used to determine the degree and kind of poverty in a particular society. Consumption, income and multidimensional metrics that consider a variety of characteristics in addition to consumption and income, such as housing, health, education and sociological isolation, can all be used to quantify poverty. In industrialised countries, poverty is often calculated using absolute or relative poverty levels. Contrary to absolute poverty lines, which establish a predetermined minimum below which people are considered poor based on a standard of living, relative poverty lines compare an individual's wealth or income to the average wealth or income of the community.

Indicators of poverty include material deprivation and economic inequality, and multidimensional poverty assessments are more frequently used in wealthy nations, according to a 2014 study by the United Nations Development Programme (UNDP). The study also found that different countries use different measures depending on their particular situations and that there is no commonly accepted indicator for gauging poverty. For instance, the official poverty line is used to quantify poverty in the United States and is based on income thresholds that are yearly adjusted for inflation. The European Union (EU), in contrast, has a multifaceted approach to measuring poverty that considers a variety of elements, such as income, employment, health and education. Accurate measurement is necessary to grasp the nature and scale of poverty, but it can be challenging, particularly in industrialised areas. Lack of consensus on the definition of poverty, issues with data accuracy, regional variations and changes in living standards are a few of these challenges. Recognising and resolving these issues is crucial to developing effective policies and programs aimed at eradicating poverty in wealthy countries.

Purpose and Significance of the Chapter

The chapter 'Exploring Poverty Measurement Techniques Across Diverse Economies: A Cross-Country Study' examines and contrasts the various industrialised and developing nations' approaches to measuring poverty. This chapter tries to provide insights into the effectiveness of various poverty measurement approaches in order to effectively capture poverty and identify its underlying causes in a variety of economic situations.

What makes this chapter notable is its contribution to the body of knowledge on poverty measurement and its implications for policymaking. This chapter presents a thorough evaluation of the many methods for determining poverty used in various economies, emphasising the advantages and disadvantages of each technique. Additionally, it emphasises how challenging it is to quantify poverty and how it calls for a comprehensive approach to properly capture the complexities of poverty.

The chapter's conclusions are essential for policymakers in creating successful poverty reduction plans that are adapted to the unique economic, social and cultural circumstances of many nations. International development organisations can benefit from the chapter's cross-country study in their attempts to aid programs aimed at reducing poverty in emerging markets. In the end, the paper's contribution to the comprehension of poverty measurement and its implications for policymakers can result in more effective and focused poverty reduction efforts, improving the well-being of people and communities affected by poverty.

Literature Review

The literature has given considerable attention to the challenging and diverse subject of measuring poverty. One of the most widely used measures of poverty is the income- or consumption-based measure, which establishes poverty based on a household's income or consumption levels (Chen & Ravallion, 2010). Because it is simple to measure and establishes a distinct poverty line, this indicator has been widely employed in developing and emerging nations. However, because they don't take other characteristics, including health and education, into account, income- or consumption-based metrics have limitations in capturing poverty, particularly in multidimensional poverty (Alkire & Foster, 2011). Furthermore, because temporary income fluctuations might change indicators of consumption or income, it can be difficult to pinpoint long-term poverty (Chen & Ravallion, 2010).

In order to work around these restrictions, multidimensional poverty metrics – which consider poverty in a number of areas like health, education and living standards – have been established. With the use of these evaluations, public policies that consider the needs of low-income households can be developed. They provide a more complete picture of poverty. Among the most well-known measures of multidimensional poverty are the HDI, the MPI and the Basic Needs Approach (BNA).

The UNDP's HDI assesses human growth in three areas: health, education and living situations (UNDP, 2019). The MPI, which assesses poverty using 10 factors and falls into three categories (living circumstances, health and education) was created by the Oxford Poverty and Human Development Initiative (OPHI) (Alkire & Santos, 2010). Food, shelter, health and education make up the four components of the BNA, a tool created by the International Labour Organization (ILO), which measures poverty.

Although there are benefits to multidimensional poverty assessments, there can also be limitations, particularly in terms of the quantity and calibre of the data. Obtaining statistics on the various facets of poverty can be challenging, particularly in developing and rising countries where data collection methods are frequently suspect (Alkire & Foster, 2011). The calculation of multidimensional poverty indices also requires more technical expertise and resources, which limits its applicability to policymakers and practitioners (UNDP, 2019). Overall, the research highlights the importance of considering various techniques for assessing poverty in different economies and selecting the best suitable metrics based on the particular context and goals. Additionally, the research emphasises the importance of enhancing data collection methods and investing in technical capacity building to improve poverty measurement and inform policy decisions that address the needs of poor households.

Poverty in Developed Economies

People in industrialised economies are impacted by poverty, which has many different aspects. Even though developed countries are often wealthier and have greater standards of living, poverty still exists because of a number of factors, including income and wealth gaps and a lack of access to affordable housing, healthcare, education and social services. Poverty is frequently associated in industrialised nations with income disparity and social exclusion, where certain groups may face obstacles to opportunity in terms of access to opportunities for employment and education. Additionally, industrialised economies often have higher costs of living, which can be difficult for people and families with low incomes. In many industrialised nations, urban regions with high housing and living expenses and possibly few job possibilities are where poverty is most prevalent. Additionally, there are regional differences, which can result in economic and social inequality because poverty may be more frequent in some places than others.

Poverty can have detrimental effects on both individuals and society as a whole in wealthy economies. It might lead to ill health, fewer employment and educational options and social marginalisation. It is critical to address poverty in developed economies if we are to progress in social and economic equality and improve societal well-being in general. Poverty in industrialised nations can be brought on by a number of structural problems as well as human problems. Some of the major causes of poverty in prosperous economies include:

Structural and Systemic Factors

- Income inequality: When certain people and families have access to more resources than others, it might result in poverty for those who don't have as many resources.
- Unemployment: Individuals and families may find it challenging to make ends meet and earn a living salary when unemployment rates are high.
- Discrimination: When people are denied access to resources like education, employment and other resources because of their race, gender, age or other characteristics, poverty results.
- Inadequate social safety net: While social safety net programs like housing subsidies, food assistance and unemployment benefits can help to lower poverty, insufficient or underfunded programs can keep people and families in poverty.

Personal and Behavioural Factors

- Education: People with less education may have fewer work possibilities and make less money, which could put them in poverty.
- Health: Chronic health issues or poor health can make it difficult for people to work and make a living income, which adds to poverty.
- Family structure: Families with many members, especially those with little access to inexpensive daycare or flexible work schedules, may find it difficult to make ends meet.

It is important to note that these factors are often interrelated, and addressing poverty in developed economies requires a multifaceted approach that addresses both personal and systemic factors.

Overview of the Different Measures of Poverty Used in Developed Economies

Various indices, such as income poverty, relative poverty, absolute poverty and multidimensional poverty are used to measure poverty in industrialised economies. In developed economies, there are various poverty measurements that consider various characteristics of poverty. Some of the most popular techniques are listed below:

- Relative poverty: This indicator illustrates poverty in relation to the median income or standard of life for the population. A person is considered poor, for instance, if their income is below a predetermined percentage of the median income. Popular countries that use this metric include the United Kingdom, Australia and Canada. For instance, poverty is seen as falling below 60% of the median income in the United Kingdom.
- Absolute poverty: This definition of poverty is based on a predetermined standard of living, such as the price of an essential supply of goods and services. In countries like the United States, where poverty is determined by the amount of money required to purchase a minimal number of goods and services, this statistic is used. This is referred to as the poverty line in the United States.
- Multidimensional poverty: This statistic measures how much a person or household needs essential services, such as access, money, education and healthcare. In nations like Germany and France, where a variety of criteria are considered, including resource accessibility, health and education, this statistic is employed. For instance, the multidimensional poverty measure used in Germany considers the three areas of material deprivation, social isolation and employment.
- Social exclusion: This indicator measures the extent to which people or groups are prohibited from contributing fully to society and is based on elements such as money, education, employment and social networks. This measure is used in countries like Belgium where poverty is defined as a condition in which individuals or households are unable to fully participate in society because of a lack of resources and opportunities.
- Material deprivation: This indicator examines how much it costs for individuals or households to acquire needs such as quality shelter, food, clothing and medical care. In nations like Spain, where access to basic commodities and services is the primary indicator of poverty, this figure is used.
- Low-income cut-offs (LICOs) are a policy that establishes a threshold below which a household is regarded as having a low income. Utilising a proportion of the median income, the cut-off is established. This statistic is used in countries like Canada where households with income below a particular percentage of the median income are considered to have low income.
- The poverty gap is a measure of the income or resource gap from the poverty line that helps determine how much people are in poverty. This indicator, which is employed in nations like the Netherlands, ascertains the degree of poverty by comparing the income of people or households that are below the poverty line to the real poverty level.

Many countries use a variety of poverty measurements, depending on their specific economic, social and political environments as well as their political objectives. In industrialised economies, there is no standardised method for measuring poverty. The most effective method is determined by the specific environment and evaluation goals for poverty. In developed economies, the picture of poverty may be more accurately depicted by combining measurements such as income-based metrics, consumption-based metrics and multidimensional data. Identifying poverty in industrialised nations is just the start of a protracted process, it is vital to keep this in mind. Policies and programs must address the root causes of poverty in industrialised countries, such as income disparity, a lack of access to healthcare and education and a lack of social safety nets.

Comparison of the Effectiveness of Different Measures in Capturing Poverty in Developed Economies

Academics evaluate different poverty indicators for their ability to accurately depict the extent and kind of poverty in industrialised economies. Regarding the realities of individuals who experience relative poverty, some contend that income poverty assessments do not adequately capture the extent of poverty (Bradshaw et al., 1998). Bernini et al., (2023) state that relative poverty evaluations have come under fire for neglecting to consider regional variations in the cost of living and the efficacy of social safety nets. On the other hand, some contend that methods for measuring multidimensional poverty are more effective in capturing the complexity of poverty and pinpointing its underlying causes. Despite these debates, many developed countries continue to use income poverty measures as the primary measure of poverty, while also recognising the importance of multidimensional approaches in identifying and addressing poverty (Kovacevic & Calderon, 2014).

Challenges in Measuring Poverty in Developed Economies

Measuring poverty in developed economies is a complex task that has been subject to significant debate and criticism. One of the main challenges is the definition of poverty itself, which can vary widely depending on the approach taken. For instance, whereas other definitions of poverty consider broader indicators of well-being like education, health and housing, some definitions of poverty are centred on income levels (Bradshaw & Rees, 2017). Accurate income measurement is another difficulty, particularly for those whose employment is erratic or unconventional. Traditional income surveys could miss non-cash benefits like government aid or subsidised housing, which have a big impact on a family's level of living (Atkinson et al., 2017).

Furthermore, regional variations in the cost of living can make it difficult to establish a single poverty threshold that is applicable across all areas. For example, while housing costs may be higher in urban areas, other costs such as transportation and food may be lower (Mincy, 2002). Although they are more challenging to quantify than income levels, non-financial variables like access to healthcare and education can also have an impact on poverty levels. A given population's level of poverty may not be fully captured by poverty measurements that just include income (Alkire & Foster, 2011). Finally, variations in poverty levels over time can result from changes in the economy or governmental policy, making it challenging to compare poverty rates over different time periods (Gordon, 2019).

In conclusion, a multifaceted approach that considers a variety of criteria, such as income levels, non-monetary indices of well-being and geographical variations in the cost of living, is needed to effectively measure poverty in developed economies. This method is crucial for identifying those who need help the most and for creating successful strategies to combat poverty, even though it comes with a number of difficulties.

Examples of Poverty Reduction Programs and Policies in Developed Economies

There are various poverty reduction programs and policies that have been implemented in developed economies. Some examples include:

- Education and job training initiatives: These programs aim to equip participants with the skills and knowledge necessary to land better employment and increase their earning potential. Examples include adult education programs, apprenticeships and vocational training.
- Social safety net programs: These efforts aid individuals and families facing financial hardship. Examples include food assistance programs (like food stamps), housing subsidies and unemployment benefits.
- Minimum wage laws: These rules require businesses to pay their employees a certain minimum wage per hour. This makes it possible for people of all skill levels to earn a living wage and keep themselves out of poverty.
- Initiatives that aid families by lowering the cost of healthcare and child care include policies that support access to affordable healthcare and child care. Programs that offer free or discounted childcare or healthcare insurance subsidies are a few examples of how they could assist families with young children in escaping poverty.

In general, policies and programs to reduce poverty in developed countries are designed to address the root causes of poverty, including poor income, a lack of access to healthcare or inexpensive childcare, a lack of suitable education or training and destitution. These programs and policies can aid in removing people and families from poverty and fostering higher economic and social mobility by giving assistance and resources to those in need.

Poverty in Developing Economies

Poverty is a serious problem in developing countries. In 2015, the World Bank estimated that 700 million people – mostly in developing countries – were living in extreme poverty (Jolliffe & Lugo, 2018). There are many reasons why developing economies are undeveloped. One of the factors is a lack of educational and employment opportunities. Due to their low levels of education and due to a lack of information, many people in developing nations cannot compete on the international employment market. People may find it difficult to escape poverty due to a lack of employment opportunities and low wages (Freije-Rodríguez et al., 2020). Lack of access to essential services like clean water, sanitary facilities and medical attention is another element of poverty in developing countries. Over 2 billion people lack even the most basic sanitation, and the United Nations estimates that over 800 million people lack access to clean water (Carlsen & Bruggemann, 2022).

Poor health can result in lost workdays and higher medical costs, which can make poverty even worse. Infrastructure issues, corruption and political unrest can also have an impact on poverty in developing economies. These issues could make it difficult for individuals and institutions to thrive, which would obstruct the production of new jobs and economic progress (Freije-Rodríguez et al., 2020).

In conclusion, poverty is a complex problem that has a variety of effects on developing economies. By addressing these challenges, which include increasing access to necessities like education and work opportunities as well as political stability and economic success, the lives of millions of people can be improved.

Overview of the Different Measures of Poverty Used in Developing Economies

Which measurement is the most useful for capturing poverty in developing nations is a topic of continuing discussion. The selection of a measure is based on the particular context and goal, each of which has strengths and drawbacks. The effectiveness of several methods in identifying poverty in developing economies is contrasted in the following ways:

- Income poverty: The number of persons who make less than a particular income level is known as income poverty. Since it offers a clear-cut means to gauge poverty, it is an extensively used indicator in developing nations. Income poverty has drawn criticism for failing to adequately account for the multi-faceted character of poverty (Alkire & Foster, 2011). Additionally, as income does not consider non-financial components of poverty, such as access to healthcare or education, it is not necessarily a valid indication of well-being.
- Multidimensional poverty: The MPI has been utilised by a number of developing nations to pinpoint and address poverty-related problems (UNDP, 2019). The MPI considers a number of variables to give a thorough picture of poverty and can be used to concentrate on particular initiatives to combat poverty in all of its forms (Alkire et al., 2018). This index considers a number of variables, such as income, education, health and access to basic amenities, and is used in nations like Mexico and Colombia. For instance, each of the three components of the multidimensional poverty index for Mexico – standard of living, health and education – contains 10 attributes.

- The HDI measures three facets of human development: income, education and health. It not only provides a more thorough picture of poverty than income poverty alone but also allows for the monitoring of changes over time among different countries (UNDP, 2020). The HDI, however, does not adequately capture the national or subnational levels of poverty. The HDI is used in nations like South Africa and Brazil.
- The percentage of the poor's average monthly income that is below the poverty line is calculated using the poverty gap index. Both statistics on the severity of poverty and the quantity of income needed to enable the poor to escape it is given (World Bank, 2019). However, the intricacy of poverty is not considered.
- The Gini coefficient determines how much economic inequality exists within a community. It provides a gauge for the degree of societal income concentration and can be applied to assess the severity of income inequality in developing countries (World Bank, 2019). It does not, however, provide an accurate measure of poverty.

In conclusion, each approach has benefits and drawbacks, and the best one to use will vary depending on the circumstance and goal at hand. When compared to income poverty alone, multidimensional poverty measures like the MPI give a more complete picture of poverty. They can also be used to identify certain initiatives intended to fight poverty in all of its forms. The HDI offers a more complete picture of poverty than income poverty alone and can be used to track variations over time between various nations. Additional details about the degree of poverty and income inequality are provided by the Gini coefficient and the poverty gap index, respectively.

Challenges in Measuring Poverty in Developing Economies

It is difficult to measure poverty in developing economies for a number of reasons. Some of the difficulties in calculating poverty in developing economies include the ones listed below:

- Lack of reliable information: The precise level of poverty in many developing countries is difficult to estimate due to a lack of reliable data. This is because compiling statistics on poverty requires substantial resources and capacity, neither of which is common in underdeveloped countries (Ravallion, 2014).
- The multidimensionality of poverty: Poverty is a complex issue that is insufficiently captured by a single metric. Only a handful of the many facets of poverty include access to essential services, living circumstances and health. Since taking all of these factors into account makes measuring poverty challenging and time-consuming, see Alkire and Foster (2011).
- Regional differences: Poverty is not distributed uniformly across the world, with rural areas often being poorer than urban ones. Because national poverty statistics frequently hide these regional variances, the World Bank (2019)

recommends that a more granular approach to determining poverty may be required.

- Inflation and exchange rate fluctuations can affect how poverty is evaluated because poverty thresholds and income levels are usually set in local currencies. Exchange rate fluctuations have the potential to skew poverty patterns over time, making it challenging to quantify changes in poverty levels correctly (Ravallion, 2014).
- Political intervention: Governments may falsify poverty data to exaggerate levels of poverty in their nations. Political influence can occur in the assessment of poverty. Inaccurate poverty estimates could result from this, which could have negative effects on measures aimed at reducing poverty (World Bank, 2019).

In conclusion, determining the extent of poverty in developing nations is a difficult and complex process. It calls for trustworthy data that captures the multifaceted character of poverty, addresses regional inequities, considers inflation and exchange rate variations, and avoids political meddling. To effectively measure poverty and create successful poverty reduction measures, these issues must be resolved.

Poverty in Emerging Economies

Emerging economies are nations that are still regarded as developing ones but are undergoing tremendous economic growth and development. Even though these economies have reduced poverty significantly in recent years, many of them still have severe poverty concerns. More than half of the world's poor people live in developing economies as of 2021, according to the World Bank. Some of the countries in the world with the largest and fastest-growing populations are China, India, Brazil, Mexico, Indonesia and Nigeria. These countries have made progress in reducing poverty, although many of them still have significant levels of it.

One of the key causes of poverty in developing nations is income disparity. The growth and development of these countries' economies have not always led to an equitable distribution of wealth and income. As a result, a large number of people are still mired in poverty and unable to obtain basic needs like food, shelter and education. Lack of access to financial services is another facet of poverty in emerging nations.

Many people in these nations don't have access to standard financial services including savings accounts, loans and insurance. As a result, people are less able to invest, save and be ready for unforeseen circumstances like illness or job loss. In addition, one of the biggest obstacles to eradicating poverty in emerging nations is access to high-quality healthcare and education. Many citizens of these nations struggle to pay for high-quality healthcare and education, which restricts their ability to improve their lot in life and escape poverty.

In conclusion, there are still many challenges to tackle even if developing economies have made significant progress in eradicating poverty. Income inequality, a lack of access to financial services and limited access to healthcare and educational opportunities are some of the key causes of poverty in these countries. Addressing these concerns is crucial if emerging economies are to ensure that all people, not just a privileged few, benefit from economic growth and advancement.

Overview of the Different Measures of Poverty Used in Emerging Economies

A variety of metrics are used in emerging economies to gauge and monitor poverty levels. Some of the measures that are frequently applied in emerging economies are as follows:

- Income insecurity: Based on a person's income level, this indicator determines how poor they are. The national average income or consumption expenditures serve as the common bases for this measure's poverty line. Access to high-quality healthcare and education represents another significant barrier to eliminating poverty in developing countries. These countries have sizeable populations that find it difficult to pay for high-quality healthcare and education, which restricts their capacity to better their lot in life and escape poverty.
- Purchasing power parity (PPP): This metric considers variations in cost of living when comparing living levels between nations. It is used to calculate poverty rates and living standards in nations like China and Russia.
- Gini coefficient: In nations like South Africa and Mexico, this metric is used to evaluate economic disparity within a nation. For instance, the Gini coefficient for South Africa was predicted to be 0.63 in 2020, which is a significant level of economic inequality.
- Multidimensional poverty: This statistic evaluates poverty with respect to a number of factors, including housing, health and education. The UNDP's MPI serves as an example of this statistic. According to the UNDP, 1.3 billion people were classified as multidimensionally poor in 107 countries in 2021, with 80% of them residing in Asia and Sub-Saharan Africa (Oxford Poverty and Human Development Initiative, 2020). For instance, the multidimensional poverty index for Indonesia comprises 13 indicators spanning four categories: living conditions, health, education and access to services.
- Consumption poverty: This measure assesses poverty based on a person's consumption expenditure. According to the ILO, in 2018, the average daily expenditure of the poorest 20% of the population in emerging economies was \$1.90, compared to \$38.20 for the richest 20%.
- Asset poverty: This indicator of poverty looks at a person's ability to access assets including property, a place to live and useful resources. The World Bank estimates that in emerging economies, 12% of the population did not have access to power in 2018 and 30% did not have access to basic sanitation services.

- Social exclusion: This indicator of poverty evaluates it in terms of a person's social standing and accessibility to essential services. In emerging economies, 42% of the population did not have access to basic healthcare services in 2018 and 23% did not have access to basic education, according to the World Bank.

Challenges in Measuring Poverty in Emerging Economies

Measuring poverty in emerging economies can be challenging due to several factors. Here are some of the main challenges:

- Limited data: Many emerging economies have limited data on income, consumption and living conditions. This can make it difficult to accurately measure poverty levels and track progress over time.
- Inadequate measures: Poverty measures that are developed in developed economies may not be appropriate for emerging economies, where the cost of living and access to basic goods and services can vary widely. For example, using a poverty line based on the cost of goods and services in a developed country may not accurately reflect the cost of basic needs in an emerging country.
- Heterogeneity: Emerging economies can be highly diverse in terms of geography, culture and economic development. Poverty measures that do not account for this diversity may not accurately capture the experiences of different populations.
- Rapid changes: Emerging economies can experience rapid economic growth and changes in living conditions, which can make poverty measures quickly outdated.
- Informal economies: Many emerging economies have large informal economies that are not captured in official statistics. This can make it difficult to accurately measure income and consumption levels.
- Limited capacity: Many emerging economies have limited capacity to collect and analyse data, which can hinder efforts to develop accurate poverty measures.
- Corruption and political instability: Corruption and political instability can hinder efforts to collect accurate data and implement poverty reduction policies.

Investment in data gathering and analysis, as well as the creation of poverty measures that are specifically suited to the setting of rising economies, are necessary to address these issues. Additionally, efforts must be made to address the root causes of poverty, such as discrimination, insufficient social safety nets and limited economic prospects. Additionally, tackling corruption and political unrest can help increase the precision with which efforts are made to reduce poverty.

Conclusion

The difficult task of measuring poverty in industrialised economies has drawn much attention and criticism. One of the main challenges is the definition of poverty itself, which can vary substantially depending on the tactic employed. For instance, whereas some definitions of poverty focus on income levels, others consider more comprehensive well-being indicators including education, health and housing (Bradshaw & Rees, 2017). Accurately estimating income is another difficulty, particularly for persons with erratic or unconventional employment. Traditional income surveys might not account for non-cash benefits like housing subsidies or government aid, which have a big impact on a family's level of living (Atkinson et al., 2017). There is reason for optimism despite the challenges because poverty has declined. By maintaining our focus on reducing poverty and addressing its root causes, we can progress towards a more just and equal society where everyone has the opportunity to flourish. The ability of rising economies to accurately estimate poverty may be constrained by data quality and availability, which is a key finding. The lack of adequate data collection mechanisms in many emerging economies makes it challenging to get timely and accurate data on poverty.

Furthermore, a significant percentage of households that are poor are left out of official data, which could lead to an underestimation of poverty rates. Policymakers need to invest in statistical capability and data-gathering infrastructure to enhance the measurement of poverty in emerging economies. Another finding is the necessity of considering variables besides consumption and income levels when assessing poverty. Health, education and living conditions are only a few of the many aspects of poverty that are considered by multidimensional poverty metrics like the HDI and the MPI. These analyses give a fuller picture of poverty and can be used to create public policies that are considerate of the requirements of low-income households. However, since different measures of poverty can produce varying estimates of poverty rates, comparing poverty across different countries or regions can be challenging. To present a full picture of poverty and the needs of impoverished households, policymakers should consider merging objective and subjective poverty measurements.

In order to improve the assessment of poverty and guarantee that low-income households are included in official statistics, policymakers should invest in data collection methods and statistical competence. In addition to income or consumption metrics, policymakers should think about utilising multidimensional poverty indicators that consider many aspects of poverty. These metrics can be used to guide policy choices that support inclusive development and cater to the requirements of low-income households.

The development of more precise and trustworthy poverty measurements that can capture the complex nature of poverty in developing and emerging nations should be the final goal of future study. The use of various poverty measures in policy and practice, as well as how they might be used to guide decision-making, should be explored further in research. Research should also continue to solve problems with data availability and measurement, including looking into the utilisation of fresh data sources like big data and satellite images. Overall, measuring poverty is a task that calls for continual study, funding and cooperation between practitioners, scholars and policymakers.

References

Alkire, S., & Foster, J. (2011). Counting and multidimensional poverty measurement. *Journal of Public Economics*, *95*(7–8), 476–487.

Alkire, S., Kanagaratnam, U., & Suppa, N. (2018). *The global multidimensional poverty index (MPI): 2018 revision. OPHI MPI Methodological Notes, 46*. University of Oxford.

Alkire, S., Kanagaratnam, U., & Suppa, N. (2021). *The global multidimensional poverty index (MPI) 2021*. Oxford Poverty and Human Development Initiative.

Alkire, S., & Santos, M. E. (2010). *Acute multidimensional poverty: A new index for developing countries*. https://doi.org/10.2139/ssrn.1815243

Atkinson, A. B., Guio, A. C., & Marlier, E. (Eds.). (2017). *Monitoring social inclusion in Europe* (pp. 3–71). Publications Office of the European Union.

Bernini, C., Emili, S., & Ferrante, M. R. (2023). Poverty-happiness nexus: Does the use of regional poverty lines matter? *Papers in Regional Science*, *102*(2), 253–272.

Bradshaw, J., Gordon, D., Levitas, R., Middleton, S., Pantazis, C., Payne, S., & Townsend, P. (1998). *Perceptions of poverty and social exclusion*. Townsend Centre for International Poverty Research.

Bradshaw, J., & Rees, G. (2017). Exploring national variations in child subjective well-being. *Children and Youth Services Review*, *80*, 3–14.

Carlsen, L., & Bruggemann, R. (2022). The 17 United Nations' sustainable development goals: A status by 2020. *The International Journal of Sustainable Development and World Ecology*, *29*(3), 219–229.

Chen, S., & Ravallion, M. (2010). The developing world is poorer than we thought, but no less successful in the fight against poverty. *Quarterly Journal of Economics*, *125*(4), 1577–1625.

Freije-Rodríguez, S., Woolcock, M., Castañeda, R. A., Cojocaru, A., Howton, E., Lakner, C., Nguyen, M. C., Schoch, M., Yang, J., & Yonzan, N. (2020). *Poverty and shared prosperity 2020: Reversals of fortune*. World Bank.

Gordon, D. (2019). The scientific measurement of poverty: Recent theoretical advances. In *Researching poverty* (pp. 37–58). Routledge.

Jolliffe, D., & Lugo, M. A. (2018). *Piecing together the poverty puzzle*. World Bank Group.

Kovacevic, M., & Calderon, M. C. (2014). *UNDP's multidimensional poverty index: 2014 specifications*. UNDP Human Development Report Office Occasional Paper.

Mincy, R. B. (2002). Ghetto poverty: Black problem or harbinger of things to come? In *A different vision* (pp. 38–71). Routledge.

Oxford Poverty and Human Development Initiative. (2020). *Global MPI 2020 – Charting pathways out of multidimensional poverty: Achieving the SDGs*.

Ravallion, M. (2014). Poor, or just feeling poor? On using subjective data in measuring poverty. In *Happiness and economic growth* (pp. 140–178). Oxford University Press.

United Nations Development Programme (UNDP). (2019). *Human Development Report 2019. Beyond income, beyond averages, beyond today: Inequalities in human development in the 21st century*. UNDP. https://hdr.undp.org/content/human-development-report-2019. Accessed on October 13, 2022.

United Nations Development Programme (UNDP). (2020). *2020 Human Development Report: The next frontier – Human development and the Anthropocene*. UNDP.

World Bank. (2019). *Gender-sensitive poverty mapping for Timor-Leste: Policy note*. https://doi.org/10.1596/32015

Chapter 8

Self-Help Groups in Afghanistan: A Ploy of Economic and Social Empowerment of Women for Sustainable Development

Nassir Ul Haq Wani[a,d,e], *Bibi Sarah Majidi*[a,f], *Neeru Sidana*[b] *and Richa Goel*[c]

[a]Kardan University, Afghanistan
[b]Amity University, India
[c]Symbiosis Centre of Management Studies, Noida; Symbiosis International Deemed University, Pune, India
[d]Kashmir Research Information System (KRIS), India
[e]Presidency University, India
[f]Technical Standards and Safety Authority, Canada

Abstract

Women's empowerment is nothing new; it has been acknowledged as an essential element of eradicating poverty and advancing the economy. However, it remains problematic in most developing countries, such as Afghanistan. This research evaluates women's empowerment experiences by utilising Self-Help Groups (SHGs) as a fundamental development method to empower women economically and socially. This study adopts a qualitative research style, with data mainly acquired from rural areas (Kabul province). The findings indicated that SHG involvement is closely associated with families' socio-economic well-being, meaning that SHG participants are more empowered than those who do not engage or are oblivious to SHGs. SHGs confront various obstacles in Afghanistan, including (but not limited to) erroneous cultural norms, security issues, inadequate financial assistance and poor member participation, all of which influence operations. This study makes important recommendations for promoting and achieving women's integration and active participation in SHGs, including increasing social awareness, support from civil society and the government, laws and

Understanding the Multi-Dimensional Nature of Poverty, 147–170

Published under exclusive licence by Emerald Publishing Limited
doi:10.1108/978-1-83753-292-620241008

regulations that support women, strategies to increase women's economic and social empowerment and linking groups to commercial banks.

Keywords: Women; self-help groups (SHGs); economic empowerment; Afghanistan; unpaid care work

Introduction

> You can tell the condition of a nation, by looking at its women.
> (Jawahar Lal Nehru, 1949)

The statement above highlights the importance of women's involvement in national development. Women's empowerment is critical to achieving the Sustainable Development Goals (SDGs). Since the International Conference on Population and Development in Cairo in 1994, it has been the primary policy debate and discourse topic. Promoting women and increasing their engagement in economic activities is vital for long-term prosperity and development. East Asian nations like Vietnam, Thailand, China, Indonesia and others have witnessed socio-economic marvels due to their propensity to involve women in various economic sectors (World Bank, 2011). On the other hand, the inclusion of women's roles in development previously led to several community-based organisations that create initiatives to enhance women's lives in general. The Self-Help Group (SHG) programme promotes savings, communal production and social peace among the impoverished in order to empower women 'by women and for women' (Ban et al., 2020; Brody et al., 2015).

Women's SHGs are built based on the Self-Help philosophy which emphasises women's active involvement in groups and family decision-making. SHG programs are considered one of the popular development initiatives in South Asia, including Afghanistan, to encourage women based on their capability (Fernandez, 2007; Jakimow & Kilby, 2006). Mutual trust and a group approach are the fundamental tenets of SHGs, which promote women's dual (social and economic) growth, boost savings and foster entrepreneurship abilities. However, according to Greaney et al. (2013), the SHG's main target group is the poorest of the poor, notably rural women who cannot access financial aid or loan services because they lack collateral or because they do not adhere to the requirements.

In Afghanistan, four decades of civil war and chaos, rising illiteracy rates, inadequate healthcare and a variety of practises such as early marriage, reduced mobility, domestic abuse and the latest crumble of the representative democracy on 15 August 2021, have all hampered women's economic participation (Bahri, 2014; Ram & Humayun, 2022). Thus in such a situation, the ploy for enhancing women's empowerment is to engage the women in SHGs. SHGs are considered an ideal option for low-income women who are in need of loans but do not have collateral.

Credit is a common component of poverty-reduction programmes that are expressly designed for women. These programmes are heavily marketed to empower women and reduce poverty. Therefore initially, it was believed that SHGs were a strategy for empowering women economically, socially and politically by tackling poverty and issues related to women's empowerment (Wrigley-Asante, 2012). The equal participation of women is regarded as critical for enhancing real economic growth. In addition to reducing the disparate rates of female poverty, the economic participation of women is essential for raising household income and promoting national economic development (Sen & Grown, 2013). The four investment pillars that are intended to cooperate to mobilise the capability to utilise all available forces of production in order to increase women's productivity are agriculture, access to financing, the creative industries, basic skills and capacity building (NPP, 2016). According to the latest studies, SHGs are an effective programme for enhancing women's engagement, production and general livelihood (Brody et al., 2015; Rathinam & Akudugu, 2014).

Thus, economic empowerment has been a significant concern, as the quality of women's economic participation extends beyond their mere presence as workers. The status of Women in Afghanistan needs to improve as it's less favourable in relation to the men. Unfortunately, 84% of Afghani women do not have a High school diploma and are considered illiterate (Jahanmal, 2017; Rahmani, 2019). Regarding social and economic empowerment, Afghani women, particularly rural women, are more vulnerable and ostracised. For underdeveloped economies to survive and advance, the option of raising women's literacy levels, health and social standing as well as involving them in economic activity is essential (Ban et al., 2020; Hamidazada et al., 2019). Even though the government and international agencies in Afghanistan have planned and implemented many empowerment programs, such as the Women Economic Empowerment Rural Development Project (WEE-RDP), women in rural areas have been overlooked. Their socio-economic situations have been compromised (Ahmadi, 2020). However, despite these challenges, SHGs offer a ray of hope that can be counted on. SHGs do offer a solution to every issue, especially in rural areas. The quick growth of women's organisations serves as proof for this. In many instances (as the percentage of WEE-RDP districts increased exponentially from 790 to 1,010 SHGs), it has been a blind replication of success models without considering the specific results in the provinces of Parwan, Bamyan, Nangarhar, Balkh and Herat (Ministry of Rural Rehabilitation and Development Report, 2018). In order to better understand the topic of women's empowerment through SHGs and to identify obstacles to rural women's empowerment in SHGs, the current study is being carried out. The remaining five sections of this chapter are organised as follows: Section One deals with the study's background; Section Two examines pertinent literature; Section Three describes the research methodology employed; Section Four presents the findings and discussions; and Section Five wraps up the study with a discussion of policy.

Scholarship Review

Concept of Self-Help Groups

The primary concept behind a SHG is to establish a voluntary (financial) saving club comprising a small, homogeneous group of people in a local community.

However, the SHG approach's execution in practice and what it entails vary significantly across firms (Murria & Verma, 2013). Self-help organisations are the answer to every issue, particularly in rural areas. The fundamental idea is for a small group to get together on a regular basis (weekly, bimonthly or monthly) and contribute a small amount of money to a communal or common fund. This cash is kept in a savings box, tracked in a ledger and loanable to group members under pre-established conditions (PIN, 2018). It is postulated that women's participation in SHGs strengthens their economic, political, social and spiritual capacities. The ability to exert total control over one's behaviour is the most popular justification for 'women's empowerment'. Women become genuinely empowered when they have greater control over and participation in decision-making, which results in better access to resources (Muram & Wani, 2020). Women's empowerment frequently entails helping them believe in their abilities. As a result, empowerment will not be constant but somewhat variable (Cheston & Kuhn, 2002; Duflo, 2012; Trivelli & Morel, 2019). When international organisations (KNH and OPMercy) began operating in Afghanistan in 2001, SHGs were first identified there. Thomas Paul, an Indian consultant, was the one who first proposed the idea. The OPMercy first developed the SHGs approach with assistance from Indian trainers (PIN, 2018).

Most of the research now in print emphasises the value of SHGs for empowering women (Wani & Dhami, 2021), particularly in Afghanistan, India, Bangladesh and two several African nations, while also acknowledging the drawbacks of SHGs and how they affect the empowerment of women (Ferrant & Kolev, 2016; Kabeer, 2005). SHGs are frequently connected to other countries' governmental organisations or microfinance industries. For instance, SHGs are frequently connected to the conventional banking system and microfinance institutions in Bangladesh, India and Pakistan. For instance, SHGs in India are affiliated with the government and have been incorporated into the yearly strategy of the Indian government since 2000/2001 (Gugerty et al., 2019; Hall, 2013; Kumar et al., 2021). This results in assistance, simplification and guidance for the SHGs' implementation.

In Sri Lanka, for instance, providing SHGs with direct financial support is not permissible but is connected to cooperatives. This implies that they will receive a share at the end of the year in addition to their savings within their groups (Ranasinghe, 2020). The unique religious environment in Afghanistan is another way it differs from certain other nations. The SHG model allows for the charging of interest in many instances, which can improve the effectiveness of how the groups operate by causing the communal fund to expand more quickly. The majority of Afghan communities, however, are opposed to paying interest because they believe it is against Islam. There are exceptions to this rule. However, some organisations charge a 'service fee' or offer money as a 'thank you' present to the organisation for helping their small business succeed in the first place. Meanwhile, most SHGs surveyed for this study declined to express a broad, determined interest.

Women's Economic Empowerment and Rationale

Women's economic empowerment (WEE) is the process that transforms women and girls from having little power, voice and choice at home and in the economy to having the knowledge, tools and opportunities necessary to compete fairly in markets as well as the agency to manage and reap the benefits of economic gains (UN Women, 2018). A strong economic actor has three essential characteristics: control over and profit from economic gains, access to money and assets and the ability to make decisions (Galab & Rao, 2003). Realising women's rights and gender equality depends on women's economic empowerment. Economic empowerment for women encompasses equitable participation in contemporary markets, access to and control over productive assets, access to quality employment and sovereignty of their own time, lives, and bodies. Increased voice, agency and meaningful engagement in economic decision-making at all levels, from the family to international institutions, are also part of it (UN Women, 2022). Women's economic empowerment enhances productivity and economic growth. In addition to positive development outcomes, women's economic empowerment promotes productivity, diversifies the economy and increases income equality (Amin & Becker, 1998; Delechat et al., 2018). For example, raising female employment rates in Organization for Economic Cooperation and Development (OECD) countries to Sweden-like levels may boost gross domestic product (GDP) by over USD 6 trillion (PwC, 2020) while noting that improvement does not necessarily reduce gender imbalance. Gender discrepancies, on the other hand, are predicted to cost the economy 15% of GDP (Cuberes & Teignier, 2016; OECD, 2019).

Women have far less access to, control over and ownership of land and other productive assets than males. The land is perhaps the most precious economic resource, but women account for just 12.8% of agricultural proprietors globally (Fanelli, 2022). Gender equality has the highest rate of return because women devote a larger percentage of their income to supporting their families and children. According to a Brazilian study, women who manage the household's finances will see a 20% rise in children living to adulthood. This supports the hypothesis put forth by Köhlin et al. (2011) that gender and development are related. A McKinsey World Institute study found that if women participated equally in the labour market, the global GDP might increase by 26%–28 trillion dollars. The study asserts that even if every country attained gender parity at the same rate as its 'fastest-growing neighbourhood, global GDP might rise by up to $12 trillion in 2025'. Although Afghanistan is not considered in the analysis, it shows that doing so might increase GDP across South Asia, the Middle East and North Africa by up to 18% (Woetzel, 2015).

Another study found that India's GDP might rise by 8% if the ratio of women to males at work increased by 10%. In addition, Africa's overall agricultural productivity may increase by up to 20% if women had equal access to agricultural inputs to men (Agenda for International Development of the United Kingdom, 2010). Targeting women and their economic development is vital to combat poverty because they make up the majority of the world's poor (Understanding and measuring women empowerment, 2011). In addition, reducing the gender gap in agricultural inputs might prevent hunger for 100–150 million people, according to the Food and Agriculture Organization (FAO) (FAO, 2011, Women in Agriculture). Up to 38% of all small businesses registered globally are owned by women, and they are growing significantly. This expansion has a direct impact on employment generation and poverty alleviation. Men, children and society all benefit when gender equality is the norm. Higher female salaries and negotiating power lead to more great investments in children's education, health and nutrition, as women devote a larger proportion of their money to support their families. As a result it will foster economic growth over the long term (Ministry of Rural Rehabilitation and Development, 2018).

Relationship Between SHG Membership and Women's Economic and Social Empowerment

Mixed opinions have been expressed regarding the causal link between SHG involvement and women's empowerment (both economic and social) through SHGs. In the discussion of international development, empowerments, in general, and women's empowerment, in particular, have become trendy terms. A substantial plethora of literature (Goldman & Little, 2015; Gupta & Yesudian, 2006; Kabeer, 1999; Mahmud & Shah, 2012; Santillán et al., 2004; Zimmerman, 1990) is devoted to comprehending and quantifying empowerment. There is still considerable ambiguity and disagreement on the definition and assessment of empowerment (Goldman & Little, 2015). While some researchers view empowerment as a process, others see it as a result or an outcome (Batliwala, 2007; Mahmud & Shah, 2012). Others view it as both a process and a result (Goldman & Little, 2015; Kabeer, 1999). These disagreements led feminist and critical development researchers to assert that empowerment has become a development cliché that is overused and devoid of its original critical political meaning (Batliwala, 2007; Goldman & Little, 2015). However, empowerment is a slow process brought on by several variables. Zimmerman (1990) quantified the relationship between involvement in a volunteer organisation and subsequent empowerment, which is one of the pioneering works in this field (although he only considers the psychological dimension of empowerment in his works). Many academics are excited about the potential of microlending for empowering people, mainly when used in conjunction with group strategies like SHG (Al-Mamun et al., 2014). According to numerous international studies, access to group-based microcredit is said to have several advantages. The promotion of a culture of democratic participation at the grassroots level in Ethiopia (Yntiso, 2015), the creation of new jobs in Malaysia (Al-Mamun et al., 2014), the improvement of children's health in Peru (Moseson et al., 2014), the rise in female decision-making in Mexico (Angelucci et al., 2015), etc.

Nevertheless, Errais and Miles (2015) assert that corporations can enter the microlending industry. According to De Hoop et al. (2014), women's autonomy is significantly impacted by SHG membership. Even though some studies have demonstrated that SHG activities give members the tools to deal with difficulties and stressors and improve their relationships with the organisations that provide them with services and the neighbourhood where they live, according to empirical research, participating in SHG activities can reduce family stress, loneliness and guilt-feeling. On a larger scale, the advocacy work of SHG members can impact governmental policies (Moyle et al., 2006). Studies (Rappaport, 1987; Wandersman & Florin, 2003; Zimmerman, 2000) have also shown a strong correlation between participation in SHGs and political, civic and self-efficacy (1987). According to the results of the DWCRA model for poverty alleviation for women empowerment, group participation has been linked to advancement in the 'power to', 'power with' and 'power within' components of empowerment. It continues by stating that participation in SHGs has enhanced members' control over and access to productive assets, freedom to select how they wish to act towards reproduction and social well-being in their families and communities (Galab & Rao, 2003). There is evidence for specific results that are in conflict. For instance, Banerjee et al. (2015) concluded several studies that access to microcredit through SHG funds do not significantly affect the socio-economic empowerment (health, education and power to make decisions) of women members, despite increased participation-related spending on small business and profits from already-existing enterprises. The literature on SHGs and microfinance, which views SHG microfinance as a tool for economic empowerment and poverty alleviation, inspired our study (Al-Mamun et al., 2014; Errais & Miles, 2015; Kabeer, 1999; Yntiso, 2015). It is acknowledged that not all SHG members participate with the same fervour. According to Zimmerman (1990) and the trends in the literature, we suggest that different levels of SHG activity engagement lead to differing degrees of empowerment for the group's members.

Research Methodology, Operationalisation and Conceptual Framework

Research Rationale

This research aims to understand better and report the effect of the SHGs strategy in Afghanistan. An assessment of the impact and effectiveness of the SHG strategy in the Afghan rural context is required for a greater understanding of the impact on economic and social development. Furthermore, the study is dependent on documenting the shortcomings of the current SHG mechanism. The study focuses on rural centres in Kabul province (Karte Parwan, Arzanqeemat and Kartenav) where the SHG concept has been primarily implemented.

Research Methods and Instruments

The qualitative research approach and a desk-based review of existing secondary literature are employed. Academic sources, official reports, relevant governmental policy documents and strategies, published and unpublished studies and documentary sources were all included in this review. The review provided a framework for subsequent data collection and analysis. It aided in the refinement of the methodological tools and analytical framework for the interviews and focus groups, as well as the identification of information gaps in the existing literature. Key informant interviews (KIIs) and focus group discussions (FGDs) were used as data collection tools for the primary data. Four SHGs in rural Kabul city were identified for the study, and 32 members out of 50 targeted respondents were interviewed. Due to security concerns and social sensitivity towards interviewing women, we were unable to speak with each respondent in person. Observations of the same result in all groups suggest that the operation of other SHGs may be comparable, even though the research sample is too small to generalise the findings across the nation.

Key Informant Interviews

Key informant interviews were crucial in thoroughly grasping the topic and providing context. The underpinning for the interview guides was the conceptual framework created during the desk-based review. The interviews with key informants were qualitative in design and semi-structured, with interview guides highlighting the issues and subjects to be supposed to cover during the session. The interviewer framed the actual questions along the lines of such interview protocol but was allowed to follow up on any relevant concerns that arose during the discussion. This adaptability allowed for exploring previously unanticipated ideas and issues related to the study, particularly in developing suggestions and recommendations. Depending on the availability of the interviewees, an investigator could perform two or three interviews per day. The following groups and individuals were chosen as critical informants: critical members of SHGs and cluster-led association leaders.

Focus Group Discussion (FGD)

The focus groups generally have 6–12 participants, with 7–8 being adequate. As a consequence, more women often were present than had been planned. Ideally, participants could be paired as a homogeneous group based on gender, age and social position. The Focus Groups served as a space for reflection on what worked well and what could be improved. These same focus groups were led by a moderator, who was aided by a second person that took notes. The proposed format included focus groups with established SHGs. The study also included SHGs at various stages of development (newly formed, stabilised and SHGs linked to clusters and federations). The FGDs were recorded, then translated and transcribed. The note-taking was used to keep track of who spoke when and to keep a synopsis of the discussion. The questions for focus groups were designed to include primary and potential follow-up questions. The questions were designed to be fewer than those in the KII because more attendees answered them, and the focus group should last at least 2 hours. It was also hoped that the focus group questions would be simple enough for everyone to participate while arousing productive debate and introspection among participants.

Operationalisation of Variables

This study investigates the link between SHG involvement and women's economic emancipation in Afghanistan. Given the fact, that this idea cannot be simply quantified, the research's factors were chosen after a review of the literature. Group character, methods and issues are viewed as sub-variables, with participation in SHGs being the independent variable. Economic development, authority and action and accessibility and procedure are all seen as sub-variables of the dependent variable known as economic empowerment. Interview questions were adopted and employed in a FGD and five interviews with essential informants to measure the identified variables and collect data.

Conceptual Framework

Fig. 8.1 shows how involvement in SHGs enhances the economic circumstances and economic empowerment of women. According to the results of numerous research, there is a link between SHG involvement and rising economic status. The literature provides evidence that the social and economic well-being of group members improves. The nature of SHGs, the tactics they use and the obstacles women encounter when participating in economic activity are all depicted in the first section of Fig. 8.1. The economic empowerment components are consistently illustrated in the second section.

Results and Discussions

Background and Nature of Groups

The four groups being examined in this study are located in Kabul and non-governmental organisation (NGO)-sponsored initiatives. Due to societal sensitivities, the group members were given anonymous names; as a result, the study's groups were given names beginning with the letters (A, B, C and D) as discussed in Table 8.1. The member's actual name has also been substituted with a fictitious name. Group A, founded in 2009, consists of 60 people, with the age combination of participants ranging from 18 to 60 come from a variety of socio-economic situations, including six widows, 10 women of drug addicts, 20 married people with modest incomes and the remaining individuals who were single. This organisation uses elementary education, tailoring, basket weaving and food processing as strategies. The group meetings take place on Monday and Thursday each week, and each member in a week contributes 50 AFN. Group B, which was founded in 2011, has 45 members. The group's participants range in age from 18 to 55. Twenty were married people with poor incomes, 10 women were drug addicts, two were widows and the rest were single. Their primary skill set imparted was tailoring. Every Saturday and Wednesday, 20 AFN is

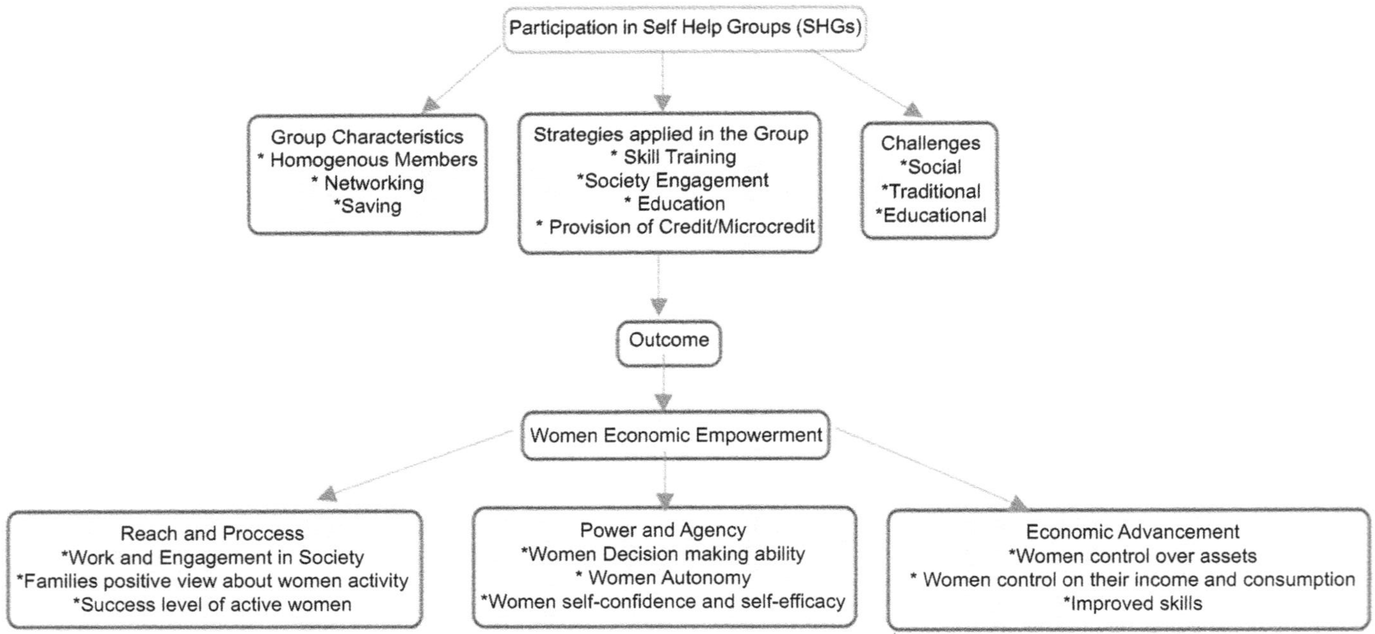

Fig. 8.1. Conceptual Framework of Women's Economic Empowerment Through SHGs. *Source:* Authors Compilation.

Table 8.1. Nature of Groups.

Group Name	Members	Age Group (Years)	Main Skills	Weekly Collection From Each Member (AFN)	Foundation
A	60	18–60	Tailoring, primary education, texturing baskets and food processing	50	2009
B	45	18–55	Tailoring	20	2011
C	49	19–40	Tailoring, carpet weaving and food processing	20	2011
D	10	15–45	Tailoring beauty parlours and carpet weaving	20	2015

Source: Authors compilation from the field survey.

contributed to the group savings. Group C, founded in 2011, comprises 29 members. Members range in age from 19 to 40, with six widows, two divorcees, 18 low-income married couples and the rest single. They donate their weekly savings of 20 AFN, and they teach others how to sew garments, weave carpets and process food. Twenty-five people made up Group D when it was first established in 2015. Their initial monthly savings amount to 20 AFN. The members' ages range from 15 to 45. The categories include 10 low-income married women, one divorcee, two women who were drug addicts and the remaining single women. They learn skills like carpet weaving and tailoring from these groups.

Women's Economic Empowerment Through SHGs

The results from the FGDs and KIIs highlighted the fact that many different techniques had been proposed to accomplish the desired aims while discussing the necessary tactics used by SHGs in supporting and promoting empowerment. These empowering techniques included granting access to education, teaching skills, encouraging social participation and advocating for their rights. It is important to note that practically all organisations have employed the access to education strategy. Teaching group members how to read and write is the main goal of primary education. Additionally, they have received a basic education in accounting so that they may apply it to their company's accounting problems. The main tactic used to economically empower women is talent transfer.

Depending on their preferences, group members receive a variety of skill training. The programme includes instruction in first aid, food preparation, beauty salons, carpet weaving and tailoring. The talents group members most desired to learn included tailoring, carpet weaving and beauty salons. In order to strengthen their presence in the community, practically all the groups have found that engaging with society and educating women about societal associations is an effective technique. Women had the opportunity to expand their networks with this tactic. In addition to getting to know other group members, by interacting with other groups and associations, members of these groups expand their networks, making it easier for them to locate a larger market to sell their goods. The members of the groups have learnt how to defend themselves against discrimination and deal with violence when it arises as a result of working to further their rights. They are also taught to defend the rights of any other women they may disagree with in their family or among their 38 acquaintances. It was discovered that access to finance proved to be a vital tool for empowering women in terms of the economic empowerment of Afghan women through SHGs. The availability of financing, which provided a foundation for women to start an income-generating activity, was the SHGs' main motivating factor. While additional funding is required to support all members, the organisations under review said that they only had access to the associations' savings from member contributions. Most of us periodically require cash but are unable to access our savings. In that case, the person whose need is more urgent receives the financial assistance. They added that even though it was less, it helped them through most of their difficult times. Golghotai, a member of the group who runs a home-based tailoring company, said:

> I had absolutely nothing when I joined this group. My husband was a soldier who had trouble making ends meet. I took over as the family's primary provider when the Taliban killed him. I took a tailoring course provided by our group, borrowed 1500 AFN from the group finances, bought a machine, and started out making clothes. I returned it when my income increased.

According to the study, group members had difficulty engaging in income-generating activities because they had restricted access to financing. The organisations' monthly funds, they claimed, are the only source of credit they have access to, but more is required to address all members' financial concerns. They have, however, noted that despite being less, it has helped numerous members begin their businesses. Other nations, such as India, Pakistan and Bangladesh, whose SHGs are affiliated with commercial banks, provide group members with microloan facilities with lower interest rates. High-interest rates and the need for collateral are the main barriers preventing these groups from obtaining any loan, even if they are neither funded by the government nor connected to banks. SHG participants' only accessible source of credit is their savings. While in other areas, the primary funding source for these groups is the supply of loans from commercial banks. Due to the need for a connection between NGOs and banks in Afghanistan, any potential support from the banking industry could be more explicit. SHGs need adequate access to credit, but they make incredible contributions in other vital areas. Women's engagement in SHGs has boosted their self-assurance and assertiveness.

Women's participation in SHGs has been correlated with increase in group members' self-assurance. They claim that joining these clubs, interacting with others and learning new skills have improved their confidence. Marya, one of the group members in Kabul, talks about how her experience of becoming a member of the SHG transformed her behaviour. She said,

> I've been a part of this organisation for a year. I was so shy that I would not even engage in conversation with strangers. But being a part of this group and talking to the other people in it gave me confidence, especially when the teacher made us speak in front of the class. Now that I'm not afraid to speak my mind, I'm overjoyed and can do so without any fear.

The resistance to classical and orthodox cultural beliefs and behaviours has been the main barrier to women's involvement in Afghanistan, among other things. The group members used to be mute bystanders since they were taught that women should not speak and should only reveal their flaws. Nearly all group members are sufficiently aware of their fundamental legal rights and are battling against their community's erroneous cultural customs to defend their daughters' rights. Marzia, one of the members, says;

> I wasted my golden years by choosing not to attend school because I was convinced that women don't need to be educated,' she said. I now understand, though, that I was misinformed. I'll see to it that my children will have a quality education.

Ferreshta, another participant from the group, remarked,

> I wedded at the age of 13. I made it through despite having no idea what marriage was since I had no choice but to follow my family members' decisions. But now that I've joined this organisation and learnt more about women's rights, I'm against my daughter's early marriage.

Other strategies that served as a foundation for further upliftment included increasing access to education, teaching skill sets and improving their decision-making ability. The most critical factor in any society's development has been declared to be primary education. The major goal of SHG formation was to give women access to primary education and literacy training. Fortunately, the study's findings indicate that the group's participants have enhanced their writing and reading abilities. After participating in the group for almost a year, about 68% of participants stated they could help their children with their schoolwork, read their books and resolve their problems. Due to the members of the SHGs learning foundational skills and gaining an elementary education, they were able to start their own income-generating ventures. Most of them could launch their businesses after completing a 6-month tailoring school. Additionally, after enrolling in these skill development classes, several group members began texturing baskets at home to sell in the market.

The study groups needed to have the decision-making element, despite this being one of the most critical aspects of empowerment. The male-dominated culture reduced women's decision-making autonomy. Women frequently consult their husbands even for minor home concerns, and over time, this habit has made them less self-sufficient in making choices. Groups practiced specific activities that pushed participants to improve their capacity for household decision-making. Members of the four groups mentioned this and were pleased with the improvement, and their skills had improved. The group members' living conditions have been enhanced by all of these tactics and procedures. SHG members who formed their own enterprises reported that their living conditions had improved somewhat. Access to healthy food, children's clothing and medical services was also improved.

Challenges in Women's Participation and SHGs Operation

The issues facing women in Afghanistan continue to be complex, as the UN Women's mandate intends, which requires adopting economic and social policies to empower all rural women and girls. Even Afghanistan's societal structure presents significant problems, as does the flexibility and participation of women in SHGs. Women's incorporation into society has long been impeded by social and traditional standards. When compared to countries where traditions are valued, those with less adherence to cultural and traditional rules have higher levels of women's empowerment (Anand, 2002; Irshad & Bhat, 2015; Lenka & Agarwal, 2017; Nichols, 2021; Sharma & Varma, 2008). Women with lower reading levels were less aware of their legal rights and more at risk of abuse and social isolation. Women's education is valued highly since it benefits society as a whole and, more importantly, because it has a positive impact on people of the same sex. For example, an educated woman is much more likely than an ignorant woman to send her daughter to school, maintain better nutrition and sanitary standards in her home and improve her family's health and well-being. All unpaid activities performed within the home, such as personal care for others, housework or community volunteer work, are referred to as 'unpaid care work'. Since one might pay to have it done, it is regarded as work.

The perception of unpaid caregiving as a female role directly affects women's capacity to engage fully in the waged economy. Worldwide, women spend three times more time providing unpaid care than men do, ranging from 1.5 times longer in North American nations to 6.7 times longer in South Asian nations (OECD, 2019). If the current rate of closing the gender gap in unpaid care work continues, it will take 210 years to close the gap among both genders according to International Labour Organization (ILO) (Charmes, 2019). Similarly,

Afghanistan has numerous difficulties, including improper cultural traditions, security issues, little member participation and little involvement from the government and other essential parties like the banking industry.

When discussing these issues in the context of SHGs in Afghanistan, the respondents pointed out that traditional and religious views play a significant role in determining membership in SHGs. Additionally, the group members expressed that other women might be interested in joining similar groups. However, their family members suggested that they should stay at home since it is not acceptable in the culture and even if they could persuade them, their relatives were still unhappy.

Poor security is another issue that has hurt the performance of SHGs in Afghanistan. Men and women have faced significant obstacles due to worries about security issues. In particular, women have long struggled to participate in social activities because of security concerns. This region is now dangerous for women, notably for those who commute to their work places, due to the activities of many terrorist organisations. The little participation of members, who are assumed to carry out the majority of home duties, limits their ability to find time for themselves and contributes to the underperformance of SHGs. Due to their commitments to running their homes and caring for their children, they have been unable to attend their meetings frequently. Shakila, one of the respondents, stated:

> I am aware that I need to attend to group more frequently since, if I did not, I would miss much of what is addressed here. But, to be able to leave my house and children alone, I do need assistance. Someone else needs to help me with this. As I have to handle everything on my own.

When government becomes disengaged from its role, the additional difficulties reach their height. Commercial banks and federations are closely linked with the SHGs method in most nations (including Bangladesh, India and Pakistan). These organisations can then offer microloans to group members so they can invest and launch any legal business. Unfortunately, this is entirely off the radar in the context of Afghanistan. Members of the group provided examples of how they occasionally come up with a tonne of great and workable ideas that could be implemented. However, their dreams are dashed by their inability to secure finance from banks and other businesses.

Discussions

Women's empowerment is a multidimensional realm that involves financial, socio-economic and political autonomy. Women's empowerment refers to the agency that women have that allows them to recognise previously denied rights. It also entails removing both formal (legislation, norms and regulations) and informal (economic and societal) obstacles that prevent women from improving their well-being, individually or collectively, and constrain their options and views. Women's participation in the advancement of societies has been regarded as a famous discourse on accomplishing their rights and responsibilities, thus symbolising their promotion as social transformation agents (Enslin, 1998; UN Women Report, 2018), which is critical to Afghanistan's advancement and progress.

SHGs, particularly for rural women, play an essential role in assisting women in seizing the opportunities which gives them the ability to use their hidden power to elevate their status in Afghanistan. Self-help organisations advocate an alternative that empowers individuals to make decisions regarding a range of social, political, economic, health and educational issues and inspires women to fight various types of oppression in the home and broader community (Irshad & Bhat, 2015; Khan & Bhat, 2022; Ndaeji, 2014). Apart from these, SHGs seek to empower women through their active participation. The most recent development agenda, the SDGs, recognise the significance of participatory processes in achieving several pragmatic, responsible and comprehensive targets, such as SDGs 5 and 7. SHGs are an exemplar of advancement as a procedure of capacity advancement at the grassroots level and thus make a significant contribution to women's economic policy priorities such as SDG 5 and Target 7 of SDG 16, which aims to ensure considerate, inclusive, cooperative and informed decision-making at all levels (United Nations, 2018). These SHGs share a common goal: to empower women through engagement and participation.

This study also made an effort to evaluate women's engagement and involvement in SHGs, which promote women's empowerment. The engagement and involvement of women in SHGs empowers them and gives them a voice.

Power, control and involvement can be seen as both a means and an end, claims Pettit (2012). Women who are aware of, associate with and participate in SHGs increase their sense of confidence, dignity and self-worth. Women become more independent as SHG membership increases.

This study has focused on the economic empowerment of women in terms of SHG involvement and empowerment. After joining SHGs, it is discovered that women are financially empowered; however this discovery is just emerging. According to the literature review, women's negotiating power within the family is reduced due to limited ownership of land and economic domains in numerous nations, including Afghanistan, which creates a sense of uneasiness and confidence. This decrease could explain why they experience less economic empowerment despite participating in SHGs. In Afghanistan, hierarchies, patriarchal structures and conservative social structures restrict women's economic participation. According to Kabeer (2001), since empowerment is a multidimensional and contextual in nature, empowerment in one area does not imply empowerment in other dimensions. The findings of the study partially support the findings of Kabeer et al. (2011), Malhotra et al. (2002), Sharma and Varma (2008), Irshad and Bhat (2015), Gugerty et al. (2019) and Ranasinghe (2020). These studies show that women have far greater authority in sociocultural domains and much less power in economic sectors. They contend that although most women have sociocultural empowerment, economic and political empowerment are still necessary for women to advance to greater levels of empowerment; however, women's political involvement in Afghanistan needs to be more active and active, given the Taliban government's organisational state and philosophy.

At the national and provincial levels in Afghanistan, there are numerous programmes and policy initiatives for marginalised populations. SHGs used empowerment strategies to facilitate and promote empowerment: access to education, skill transfer, promoting society engagement and advocacy for their rights. The relevant concerns that impact the survival and operation of SHGs in Afghanistan range from incorrect cultural practices, security concerns, low member attendance, shaky financial support from the government and the nature of their operation. SHGs are frequently linked to other countries' microfinance sectors and governmental entities.

SHGs, for example are regularly linked to the general financial system and Microfinance Banks in Bangladesh, India and Pakistan. SHGs in India, for example are linked with the government and have been included in the government of India's annual strategy since 2000–2001 (Gugerty et al., 2019; Kumar et al., 2021). This brings with it assistance and streamlining, as well as guidance in terms of SHG implementation. For example, direct financial support to SHGs is illegal in Sri Lanka. The only assistance provided to SHGs is training and access to the labour market. SHGs in Sri Lanka have historically been linked to cooperatives. This means they can expect a share at the end of the year in addition to their savings within their groups (Ranasinghe, 2020). Another distinction between Afghanistan and other countries is the religious context.

In many regions, the SHG model allows for the charge of interest, which can contribute to more effective group functioning through a faster-growing community fund. However, most Afghan groups believe paying interest to be unIslamic. Some groups charge a 'service fee' or provide money contributions as a 'thank you gesture to the group for allowing the success of their small company in the first place'. However, most SHGs polled for this study refused a broad, definite interest. Furthermore, concrete and intangible hurdles obstructing half of the population go unaddressed. SHGs might be one way to reach Afghanistan's poorest women. Women may be empowered via self-help organisations by teaching and empowering them to understand their rights better, contributing to decision-making.

Conclusion

In Afghanistan, SHGs may empower women by enabling entrepreneurial activity, boosting trust and confidence and delivering technical expertise and access to the market. These are part of the aims of sustainable development and hence assist towards long-term livelihood. To ensure women's inclusion and active engagement in SHGs, the government, civil society and women activists must collaborate. This study paves the way for a deeper comprehension of women's empowerment through participation in SHGs. Women who participate in SHGs gain self-assurance and life control.

Regarding resource control, women's emancipation may be criticised, yet involvement in SHG makes sense. Because the data is cross-sectional, the findings of this study should be carefully considered in light of the central claim that participation in SHGs empowers women. By taking part in SHGs, women can improve their capacity to make financial resource decisions, as well as their mobility, adaptability and participation in leadership and reproductive decisions. The results also show that there seems to be a variance in the responses as a result of distinct groupings, such as women representing various social classes who have limited access to and knowledge of the market.

The results suggest that SHGs support women, but to increase community knowledge and enlightenment, the government, civil society and women activists must work together about the necessity of involving women in socio-economic and political realms. According to the study's conclusions, women's economic empowerment is vital to the country's poverty reduction and economic progress. To accomplish this aim, the government and the people must collaborate. Participation of women in SHGs is one strategy for getting women into the labour field. Though achieving this aim will be challenging, the likelihood of this thought propagating is strong. The findings suggest that women's participation in SHGs increases families' social and economic well-being. The techniques utilised in groups for empowerment have been shown to be successful in achieving their objectives. Participants in a group could start small businesses and make money after participating in group discussions.

Participants also stated that having a job in the family had changed how their family members perceived them, particularly the male relatives. However, there are still challenges to be addressed. The traditional view of working women continues to cause harm on their operations. Furthermore, more financing has been needed for their economic activity. The government should also get involved in SHG initiatives that promote women's empowerment.

Recommendations

Afghanistan is a traditional country; any action that goes against the ideals and beliefs of society is exceedingly harmful. To simplify the way and overcome this difficulty, the general public's understanding of working women and how it benefits the family and the country's economy must be enhanced. One strategy may be to use the media and religious leaders to present successful examples of women who have engaged in such programs. Increasing societal awareness is thus a viable technique to pursue. The government plays a careful role in the efficient execution of every initiative. This initiative also requires government aid to be efficient and effective.

There needs to be a serious discussion about women's anti violence and harassment laws and policies. In addition, women who want to start a business should have access to microloans with the help of the government. Strategies for empowering women economically need to be developed further. Even if the techniques employed in these groups were successful, things will get better if new strategies are introduced. They can get more done and accomplish more if they receive education in entrepreneurship, financial literacy, communication skills, leadership and management.

The distribution of microloans for economic empowerment is also reciprocal and symbiotic. Therefore, connecting these organisations to commercial banks may facilitate lending and borrowing. Furthermore, by reducing interest rates at the initiative level, and simplifying the loan application process will make the process easier and accessible.

Policy Implications

Women's educational levels must be prioritised by the government organisations and NGOs operating in the field and promoting the establishment of SHGs to enhance women's living and working situations. Increased involvement in SHGs will undoubtedly result from improved education in rural regions. One of the elements impacting SHG participation is the distance from the market; the government and other organisations must engage in infrastructure development to enhance SHG participation. Non-members of SHGs must be recognised for their efforts towards membership and non-members' comprehension, and awareness must be spread. Because SHG membership contributes to women's empowerment, government institutions and NGOs must make SHGs more sustainable. They must provide financial assistance, advice and value addition to convert these activities into income-generating ventures, thereby financially and socially empowering women.

Limitations and Future Scope of Work

The study encountered significant difficulties in addressing data collection procedures. The size of the FGDs surpassed expectations as they were held within existing SHGs in familiar locations. As a result, there were often more women than expected. Women kept arriving and calling each other to participate despite smaller FGDs being recommended to include all participants in the discussion. FGDs are most popularly used in groups of strangers.

On the other hand, focus groups were implemented in this study to investigate pre-existing groups such as SHGs. As a result, rather than serving as an anonymous discussion forum, focus groups functioned as a space for reflection on what was already collaborating well or what could be improved. In most FGDs, facilitators were the organisation's point of contact with the SHGs. As evidenced by statements expressing hope for continued financial support, this influenced participants' responses in the hope of obtaining additional financial support from the organisation. According to the study, organisations running SHGs in rural and urban areas should be evaluated. Their knowledge would be used to compare data to urban SHGs, where applicable, and to comprehend the differences in constraints between these two settings. There is a need to revisit the social, political and sometimes institutional contexts in which poor women are embedded. Thus, understanding women's empowerment in Afghanistan requires understanding the sociocultural and political contexts in which they live. As a result, the findings extend the scope for a qualitative study to examine and explore the cause rationale in-depth and to contrast the position of women members before and after joining the SHGs. The findings of this study might add new aspects of promoting SHGs in purpose of women socio-economical empowerment and identifying the gaps among the empowerment components in Afghanistan.

References

Ahmadi, M. F. (2020). *Afghanistan-SOUTH ASIA-P164443-women's economic empowerment rural development project-procurement plan*. World Bank Group.

Al-Mamun, A., Mohiuddin, M., & Mariapun, S. (2014). Investigating the effects of Amanah Ikhtiar Malaysia's microcredit programs on employment in rural Malaysia. *Journal of Southeast Asian Economies*, *31*(3), 471–483.

Amin, R., & Becker, S. (1998). NGO-promoted microcredit programs and women's empowerment in rural Bangladesh: Quantitative and qualitative evidence. *The Journal of Developing Areas*, *32*(2), 221–236.

Anand, J. S. (2002). *Self-help groups in empowering women: A case study of selected SHGs and NHGs*. Centre for Development Studies.

Angelucci, M., Karlan, D., & Zinman, J. (2015). Microcredit impacts evidence from a randomized microcredit program placement experiment by Compartamos Banco. *American Economic Journal: Applied Economics*, *7*(1), 151–182.

Bahri, J. (2014). Western gender policies in Afghanistan: Failing women and provoking men. *Gender, Technology and Development*, *18*(2), 163–185.

Ban, R., Gilligan, M. J., & Rieger, M. (2020). Self-help groups, savings, and social capital: Evidence from a field experiment in Cambodia. *Journal of Economic Behavior & Organization*, *180*, 174–200.

Banerjee, A., Duflo, E., Glennerster, R., & Kinnan, C. (2015). The miracle of microfinance? Evidence from a randomized evaluation. *American Economic Journal: Applied Economics*, *7*(1), 22–53.

Batliwala, S. (2007). *Putting power back into empowerment*. Open Democracy.

Brody, C., De Hoop, T., Vojtkova, M., Warnock, R., Dunbar, M., Murthy, P., & Dworkin, S. L. (2015). Economic self-help group programs for improving women's empowerment: A systematic review. *Campbell Systematic Reviews*, *11*(1), 1–182.

Brown, A. (2012). *Empowerment and gender equality for water and sanitation in rural India: Two case studies*. Oregon State University.

Charmes, J. (2019). *The unpaid care work and the labour market. An analysis of time-use data based on the latest world compilation of time-use surveys*. International Labour Office (ILO).

Cheston, S., & Kuhn, L. (2002). Empowering women through microfinance. *Opportunity International*, *64*.

Cuberes, D., & Teignier, M. (2016, December 7). *Macroeconomic costs of gender gaps in a model with household production and entrepreneurship*. UB Economics Working Papers E16/356. SSRN: https://ssrn.com/abstract=2887252

De Hoop, T., Van Kempen, L., Linssen, R., & Van Eerdewijk, A. (2014). Women's autonomy and subjective well-being: How gender norms shape the impacts of self-help groups in Odisha, India. *Feminist Economics*, *20*(3). https://www.tandfonline.com/doi/abs/10.1080/13545701.2014.893388

Delechat, M. C. C., Newiak, M. M., Xu, R., Yang, M. F., & Aslan, G. (2018). *What is driving women's financial inclusion across countries?* International Monetary Fund.

Duflo, E. (2012). Women empowerment and economic development. *Journal of Economic Literature*, *50*(4), 1051–1079.

Enslin, E. (1998). Imagined sisters: The ambiguities of women's poetics and collective actions. In *Selves in time and place: Identities, experience, and history in Nepal*. Rowman & Littlefield.

Errais, E., & Miles, S. B. (2015). Investing in microfinance: The case of Tunisia. *Journal of Private Equity*, *18*(3), 79–96.

Fanelli, R. M. (2022). Bridging the gender gap in the agricultural sector: Evidence from European Union countries. *Social Sciences*, *11*(3), 105.

FAO. (2011). *The state of food and agriculture (2010-2011)*. https://www.fao.org/4/i2050e/i2050e00.htm

Fernandez, A. P. (2007). *History and spread of the self help affinity group movement in India: The role played by IFAD*. IFAD – International Fund for Agricultural Development.

Ferrant, G., & Kolev, A. (2016). *The economic cost of gender-based discrimination in social institutions*. Organization for Economic Co-operation and Development Center.

Galab, S., & Rao, N. C. (2003). Women's self-help groups, poverty alleviation, and empowerment. *Economic and Political Weekly*, 1274–1283.

Goldman, M. J., & Little, J. S. (2015). Innovative grassroots NGOS and the complex processes of women's empowerment: An empirical investigation from Northern Tanzania. *World Development*, *66*, 762–777.

Greaney, B., Kaboski, J. P., & Van Leemput, E. (2013, April). *Can self-help groups really be "self-help"?*. NBER Working Paper No. 18970. JEL No. O1,O12,O16.

Gugerty, M. K., Biscaye, P., & Leigh Anderson, C. (2019). Delivering development? Evidence on self-help groups as development intermediaries in South Asia and Africa. *Development Policy Review*, *37*(1), 129–151.

Gupta, K., & Yesudian, P. P. (2006). Evidence of women's empowerment in India: A study of socio-spatial disparities. *Geojournal*, *65*(4), 365–380.

Hall, C. M. (2013). *Women and empowerment: Strategies for increasing autonomy*. Routledge.

Hamidazada, M., Cruz, A. M., & Yokomatsu, M. (2019). Vulnerability factors of Afghan rural women to disasters. *International Journal of Disaster Risk Science*, *10*(4), 573–590.

Irshad, I. A., & Bhat, A. A. (2015). The vitality and role of self-help groups (SHGs) in women upliftment: Special reference to Kashmir. *International Journal of Regulation and Governance*, *3*(8), 105–110.

Jahanmal, Z. (2017, February 16). *Survey finds 84 percent of women illiterate*. Kabul, Afghanistan.

Jakimow, T., & Kilby, P. (2006). Empowering women: A critique of the blueprint for self-help groups in India. *Indian Journal of Gender Studies*, *13*(3), 375–400.

Köhlin, G., Sills, E. O., Pattanayak, S. K., & Wilfong, C. (2011). *Energy, gender, and development: What are the linkages? Where is the evidence?* https://ssrn.com/abstract=1931364

Kabeer, N. (1999). Resources, agency, achievements: Reflections on measuring women's empowerment. *Development and Change*, *30*(3), 435–464.

Kabeer, N. (2001). Conflicts over credit: Re-evaluating the empowerment potential of loans to women in rural Bangladesh. *World Development*, *29*(1), 63–84.

Kabeer, N. (2005). Gender equality and women's empowerment: A critical analysis of the third millennium development goal. *Gender and Development*, *13*(1), 13–24.

Kabeer, N., Khan, A., & Adlparvar, N. (2011). Afghan values or women's rights? Gendered narratives about continuity and change in urban Afghanistan. *IDS Working Papers*, *2011*(387), 1-39.

Khan, S. T., & Bhat, M. A. (2022). Can microfinance-backed entrepreneurship be a holistic empowerment tool for women? Empirical evidence from Kashmir Valley, India. *Journal of Business and Socio-economic Development*. https://doi.org/10.1108/JBSED-07-2021-0097

Kumar, N., Raghunathan, K., Arrieta, A., Jilani, A., & Pandey, S. (2021). The power of the collective empowers women: Evidence from self-help groups in India. *World Development*, *146*, 105579.

Lenka, U., & Agarwal, S. (2017). Role of women entrepreneurs and NGOs in promoting entrepreneurship: Case studies from Uttarakhand, India. *Journal of Asia Business Studies*. https://doi.org/10.1108/JABS-07-2015-0088

Mahmud, S., & Shah, N. (2012). Measurement of women's empowerment in rural Bangladesh. *World Development*, *40*(3), 610–619.

Malhotra, A., Schuler, S. R., & Boender, C. (2002). Measuring women's empowerment as a variable in international development. In *World Bank workshop on poverty and gender: New perspectives*. The World Bank.

Ministry of Rural Rehabilitation and Development. (2018). *Women economic empowerment rural development program (WEE-RDP)*. World Bank Group.

Moseson, H., Hamad, R., & Fernald, L. (2014). Microcredit participation and child health: Results from a cross-sectional study in Peru. *Journal of Epidemiology & Community Health*, *68*(12), 1175–1181.

Moyle, T. L., Dollard, M., & Biswas, S. N. (2006). Personal and economic empowerment in rural Indian women: A self-help group approach. *International Journal of Rural Management*, *2*(2), 245–266.

Muram, S., & Wani, N. U. H. (2020). Linkage between international political relations and foreign direct investment: A case study of Afghanistan. *Kardan Journal of Social Sciences and Humanities*, *3*(1), 1–32.

Murria, P., & Verma, S. (2013). Microfinance through self-help groups: A thematic perspective. *Productivity*, *54*(3).

Ndaeji, M. N. (2014). *Participation in self-help groups and empowerment among rural women in Niger state*. Doctoral dissertation, Universiti Putra Malaysia.

Nichols, C. (2021). Self-help groups as platforms for development: The role of social capital. *World Development*, *146*, 105575.

NPP. (2016). *Women's economic empowerment national priority programme*. World Bank Group.

OECD. (2019). *Breaking down barriers to women's economic empowerment*. Development Policy Paper, OECD.

Pettit, J. (2012, September 10–12). *Empowerment and participation: Bridging the gap between understanding and practice.* Paper presentation, The UNDESA Expert Group Meeting.

PIN. (2018). *The self-help group approach in Afghanistan.* https://resources.peopleinneed.net/documents/643-afg-self-help-group-study.pdf

PwC. (2020, March 20). *PwC Global.* https://www.pwc.com/gx/en/news-room/press-releases/2020/women-in-work-index-2020.html

Rahmani, N. (2019). *Divorced women's financial rights in Afghanistan: Does Mahr offer financial security to Afghan divorced women?* Doctoral dissertation. https://opus.lib.uts.edu.au/bitstream/10453/140526/1/01front.pdf

Ram, R., & Humayun, S. I. (2022). The Afghan Debacle and the Taliban Triumph: What India expects? *Kardan Journal of Social Sciences and Humanities*, *5*(1), 1–8. https://doi.org/10.31841/KJSSH.2022.121

Ranasinghe, P. K. G. I. L. (2020). *Social empowerment of unemployed women by providing credit facilities to start self-employments: A case study of a rural bank in Sri Lanka.* http://repository.ou.ac.lk/bitstream/handle/94ousl/1806/Article_09.pdf?sequence=3

Rappaport, J. (1987). Terms of empowerment/exemplars of prevention: Toward a theory for community psychology. *American Journal of Community Psychology*, *15*, 121–148.

Rathinam, U., & Akudugu, M. A. (2014). Self-help groups as a livelihood development for rural women: Experiences from India and Ghana. *Journal of Economics and Sustainable Development*, *5*(15).

Santillán, D., Schuler, S. R., Anh, H. T., Tran, H. M., Quach, T. T., & Duc, N. M. (2004). Developing indicators to assess women's empowerment in Vietnam. *Development in Practice*, *14*(4), 534–549.

Sen, G., & Grown, C. (2013). *Development crises and alternative visions: Third world women's perspectives.* Routledge Publishing.

Sharma, P., & Varma, S. K. (2008). Women empowerment through entrepreneurial activities of self help groups. *Indian Research Journal of Extension Education*, *8*(1), 4651.

Trivelli, C., & Morel, J. (2019). *Rural youth inclusion, empowerment, and participation.* International Fund for Agriculture Development (IFAD).

UN Women. (2018). *Promoting women's economic empowerment: Recognizing and investing in the care economy.* Issue Paper, UN Women.

UN Women. (2022). *UN women strategic plan 2022–2025.* https://www.unwomen.org/en/un-women-strategic-plan-2022-2025

United Kingdom Department for International Development. (2010). *Agenda 2010 – The turning point on poverty: A background paper on gender.* https://www.womenindisplacement.org/sites/g/files/tmzbdl1471/files/2020-11/DFID%20Agenda%202010.pdf

United Nations. (2018). *UNDP support integrating gender equality across the SDGs, including Goal 5.* https://www.undp.org/sites/g/files/zskgke326/files/migration/ye/UNDP-Gender-Equality-Strategy-2018-2021.pdf

Wandersman, A., & Florin, P. (2003). Community interventions and effective prevention. *American Psychologist*, *58*(6–7), 441.

Wani, N. U. H., & Dhami, J. K. (2021). An empirical investigation of the effects of health and education on income distribution and poverty in SAARC countries. *Kardan Journal of Economics and Management Sciences*, *4*(3), 1–15.

Woetzel, J. (2015). *The power of parity: How advancing women's equality can add $12 trillion to global growth*. (No. id: 7570). https://www.mckinsey.com/~/media/McKinsey/Industries/Public%20and%20Social%20Sector/Our%20Insights/How%20advancing%20womens%20equality%20can%20add%2012%20trillion%20to%20global%20growth/MGI%20Power%20of%20parity_Executive%20summary_September%202015.pdf

World Bank. (2011). *The World Bank annual report 2011*. http://books.google.ie/books?id=-WzEvQEACAAJ&dq=The+World+Bank+annual+report+2011+:+year+in+review&hl=&cd=1&source=gbs_api

Wrigley-Asante, C. (2012). Out of the dark but not out of the cage: Women's empowerment and gender relations in the Dangme West district of Ghana. *Gender, Place & Culture*, *19*(3), 344–363.

Yntiso, G. (2015). The self-help groups approach in Ethiopia: Promising achievements and formidable challenges. *Journal of Ethiopian Studies*, *48*(1), 33–60.

Zimmerman, M. A. (1990). Toward a theory of learned hopefulness: A structural model analysis of participation and empowerment. *Journal of Research in Personality*, *24*(1), 71–86.

Zimmerman, M. A. (2000). Empowerment theory: Psychological, organizational and community levels of analysis. In J. Rappaport & E. Seidman (Eds.), *Handbook of community psychology* (pp. 43–63). Plenum.

Chapter 9

Factors Affecting Poverty Dynamics: A Conceptual Study

Sudhansu Sekhar Nanda[a], *Anindita Das*[b] *and D. D. Tewari*[c]

[a]Sri Sri University, India
[b]ASTHA School of Management, India
[c]University of Zululand, South Africa

Abstract

The poverty rate in India is still very high despite considerable economic reforms over the past 20 years and a rapid decline in that rate. Even if the accomplishments have received much praise, it is crucial to comprehend the dynamics of poverty by recognising those who entered and emerged from it. The literature on multidimensional poverty dynamics is not as well established as that on poverty entry and leave, despite the wealth of available empirical research on both topics. This chapter uses the multidimensional measure of issues related to health, education and infrastructure; social barriers to advancement; a lack of resources and a lack of competence to make decisions for the benefit of the household to investigate the dynamics of poverty and its underlying causes. This chapter distinguishes between chronic and sporadic poverty, and emphasizes the need to focus on the unique factors that determine each type. It is stated that when one individual has lived in poverty for a longer period of time, it is morally required to help. Furthermore, the causes of chronic and temporary poverty may differ, requiring policymakers to treat them as separate categories when developing policies. The theoretical work cited in this chapter laid the groundwork for a model of poverty dynamics, which could prove useful in elucidating the root causes of and pathways out of poverty for policymakers.

The conceptual studies on poverty raise a number of concerns, most notably how poverty is quantified and defined; its origins, dynamics and causes; and where and how it is distributed geographically.

Keywords: Poverty causes; poverty dynamics; poverty distributions; factors; economic reforms

Understanding the Multi-Dimensional Nature of Poverty, 171–187

Published under exclusive licence by Emerald Publishing Limited
doi:10.1108/978-1-83753-292-620241009

Introduction

Although poverty in and of itself is discouraging, it becomes deeply concerning when it reinforces itself and makes it exceedingly tough for people to break free of poverty over and over again over successive generations. According to the International Labour Organization's Social Safety Report 2017–2019, 71% of people around the world still lack access to sufficient social protection (International Labour Organization, 2019). Officials from over the globe have asserted, 'Poverty has been diminishing', but is this an exercise in triage? Those who are barely getting by have a better chance of breaking out of poverty, whereas those who are too destitute to be helped by any policy are forgotten and do not get out. Those who have broken the cycle of poverty remain at risk because they lack the resilience to withstand negative shocks; a positive shock lifts them out of poverty, but they are vulnerable to a huge negative shock that could send them back below the poverty line. Policymakers have been striving to identify the root causes of poverty and the variables that help low-income families break the cycle of poverty and improve their quality of life.

Poverty is multifaceted, encompassing not only monetary deprivation but also limitations on health, education and other areas of life quality. The inability to make decisions that would benefit their household is a major contributor to staying in poverty and an obstacle to climbing out of poverty for households struggling with issues like poor health, illiteracy, social hurdles to development, inadequate infrastructure, etc. Multidimensional poverty indicators, which account for various forms of deprivation experienced by households, do a good job of capturing these aspects of poverty.

As the hazards of shocks and the external environment increase for the poor, researchers have moved their attention from quantifying poverty to researching its dynamics, as well as what helps and hurts their efforts to escape poverty (Norton, 2012). To comprehend the dynamic nature of poverty and to alleviate chronic poor, it is now widely agreed that static poverty assessments do not sufficiently capture the mechanisms behind poverty (Addison et al., 2008). The static analysis views the impoverished as a homogeneous population with consistent characteristics (Thomas & Gaspart, 2012). Since people fall into and out of poverty throughout time, dynamic analysis is necessary to distinguish between these two types of economic hardship.

The first part of this chapter provides a theoretical foundation for researchers interested in the dynamics of poverty. The existing theoretical literature on the causes of poverty is examined in Section 2. The third section of this chapter explores the origins of poverty's dynamics and persistence, and the final section summarises this chapter's findings.

Poverty and Its Dynamics

After 70 years of freedom and growth, India is still struggling to alleviate poverty. In 2011, 21.9% of India's population was impoverished, despite the country's high growth rates, which lifted it out of the 'low-income country' category it had occupied for decades (Bhide & Mehta, 2008). But it's encouraging that poverty has been declining so rapidly since the 1990s. The poverty rate as a share of the population fell from 45 % in 1993–1994 to 21.9 % in 2011–2012 (Government of India, 2018). Although data beyond 2011 are lacking, it is safe to assume that a sizeable portion of India's population has been lifted out of poverty.

World Bank data (Fig. 9.1) show that India's huge population meant that it had the greatest impact on global population growth in 2011. An estimated 22.5% of its population (14% urban and 26% rural) lived below $1.90 per day of purchasing power parity in 2011 India. This was up from 19.4% in Bangladesh in 2010 (World Bank Group, 2016). Fifteen per cent, 8%, and 3.4% of the populations of Nepal, Pakistan and Maldives, respectively, are living in poverty. While the South Asian region as a whole had a relatively high population growth rate, Sri Lanka and Bhutan had the region's lowest population growth rate of roughly 2%. In absolute terms, India still has the most people living below the international poverty line; however, this number has been slowly declining over the previous two decades, dropping from 30% to 26% between 2005 and 2011 (Chatterjee et al., 2016). When compared to neighbouring countries such as Pakistan, Sri Lanka, Bangladesh and Nepal, India's poverty rate made remarkable progress between 2004 and 2011.

While the number of Indians living in poverty has dropped dramatically, the bottom 40% of the country's population is still experiencing a slower increase in their discretionary income. The annual growth rate of poor people's consumption expenditure was 3.2% between 2005 and 2011, just below the 3.7% annual growth rate of the general population's consumption (Narayan & Murgai, 2016). When compared to other middle-income nations, India's shared prosperity indicator ranks on the level with Sri Lanka and Nigeria but behind China, Russia, Vietnam, Turkey and South Africa. Despite having reduced poverty faster than most emerging countries and reporting higher levels of consumption, India does not demonstrate significant progress towards equitable growth. When looking at 51 other middle-income nations, India placed 27th.

Although worldwide estimates of poverty have been made using monetary measurements, several academic works highlight the need to quantify poverty on multiple dimensions (Alkire & Robles, 2016; Tran et al., 2015; Wang & Wang, 2016). Official reporting still uses income metrics, but the Oxford Poverty and Human Development Initiative (OPHI) and United Nations Development Programme (UNDP)-created Multidimensional Poverty Index (MPI) has been adopted by a number of nations as a means of assessing poverty in a variety of ways. Between 2005–2006 and 2015–2016, India's multidimensional poverty rate dropped from 635 million to 364 million, or 42.5%, a decrease of 271 million individuals (Alkire et al., 2018).

India's rural–urban split is one of the country's most pressing social problems. Table 9.1 demonstrates that between 1993–1994 and 2011–2012, the rural poverty rate decreased from 50.10 % to 26.3%, while the urban poverty rate decreased from 32.00 % to 14.0%. India's rural areas are home to the great majority (217.1 million) of the country's poor.

The Scheduled Castes (SCs) and Scheduled Tribes (STs) have a disproportionately high poverty rate in rural India (STs). While only 18.67% and 10.83% of the rural population in 2011, respectively, belonged to SCs and STs, these groups

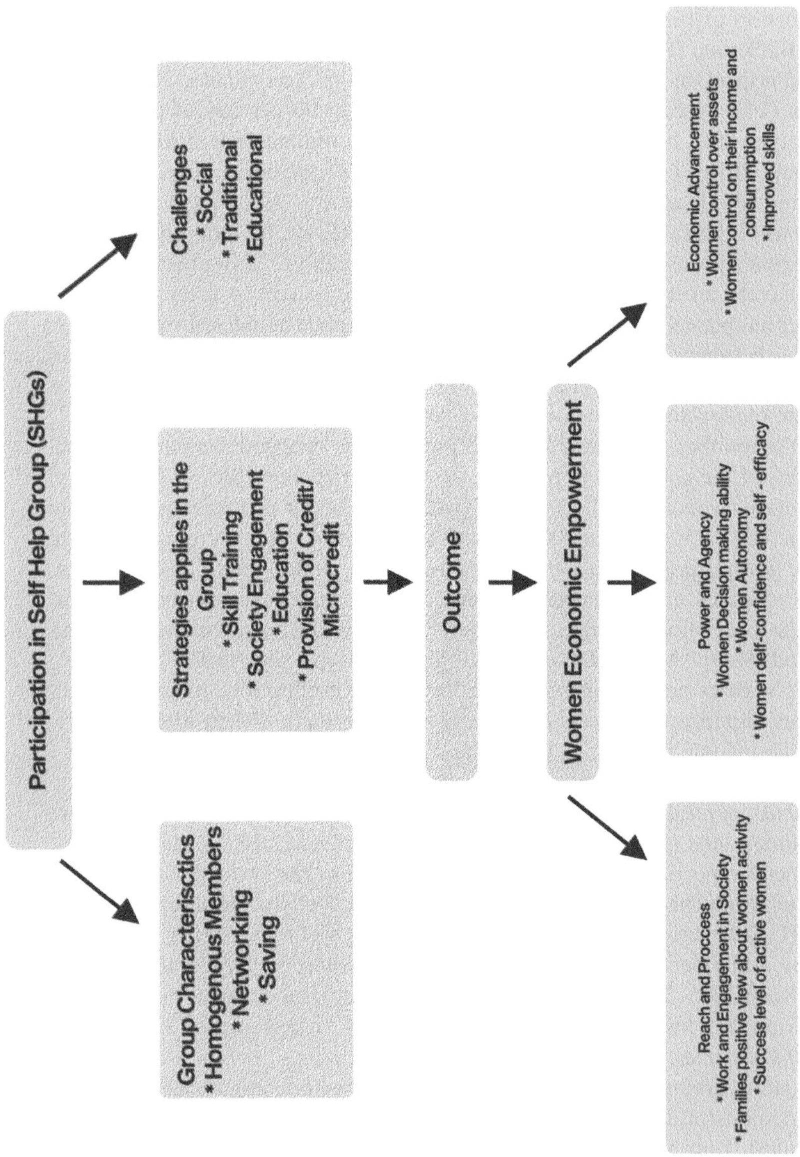

Fig. 9.1. Comparing India to Other South Asian Nations in Terms of Poverty Reduction. *Source:* World Bank's Database on Poverty.

Table 9.1. Rates of Poverty in India and the Location of Poor Households.

Year	Percentage of People Living in Poverty			Number of People Living in Poverty (Million)		
	Total	Rural	Urban	Total	Rural	Urban
1993–1994	44.23	50.10	32.00	402	327.62	73.6
2004–2005	36.21	40.18	26.01	406	325.62	81.14
2011–2012	22.02	26.3	14.0	270	217.1	53.0

Source: Government of India (2017).

made up 32.62% and 46.21% of those living in poverty in rural regions (Government of India, 2016). The SC is an amalgamation of India's lowest caste families, who were historically subjected to untouchability. Some rural residents are modest, subsistence farmers, while the vast majority are employed in the agricultural sector (Kasi, 2013). However, the STs were classified as such because of their historical and cultural distinctiveness, lack of integration into mainstream society and reliance on subsistence agriculture and other non-agricultural methods of production (Government of India, 2013).

While poverty has decreased in India as a whole, Datt and Ravallion (2002) noted that it has decreased in only a few regions/states. There was a reduction in poverty during the 1990s, but it was not proportional to the expansion of the economy, so their argument goes. Once per capita GDP averaged between 1% and 2% in the 1980s, poverty rates did not show any discernible pattern. It has been shown that the poverty rates began to decline, albeit gradually, in the 1980s, as prosperity picked up speed (Hasan et al., 2015). India's economy grew rapidly in the early 2000s, and the country's poverty rate and the absolute number of impoverished people both fell dramatically (Hasan et al., 2015). Poverty reduction has been slow in comparison to other Asian countries, despite the country's robust economy. However, rapid economic expansion is insufficient to eradicate poverty on its own. Between 1981 and 2005, India's poverty reduction elasticity was just 0.3, far lower than China's at −0.8. For example, When compared to China, India might have helped many more people escape poverty if it had the same degree of economic freedom (Ravallion, 2011).

India's low elasticity of poverty reduction to economic growth can be attributed to the country's inadequate health, education and institution systems. As per the 2019 Human Development Index (HDI), India ranked just 129th out of 189 countries in terms of human development (UNDP, 2019). This problem is exacerbated by differences in state-by-state economic growth and human development rates. States in India with a greater poverty rate experienced slower economic growth in 2011–2012. Even in terms of growth, urban and rural India are vastly different.

Almost every state had a decrease in poverty, although the north-eastern states saw either no change or a very slight decrease. However, the decline in poverty rates has occurred in vastly different ways between states. According to Table 9.2, the HDI

Table 9.2. People Below Poverty Level, by State.

States	2004–2005				2011–2012					% Change in Poverty Rural	% Change in Poverty Rural + Urban
	Rural	Urban	Rural + Urban	HDI	Rural	Urban	Rural + Urban	Economic Growth	HDI		
Andhra Pradesh	32.3	23.4	29.6	0.298	11.0	5.8	9.2	7.51	0.309	21.3	20.7
Arunachal Pradesh	33.6	23.5	31.4	0.234	38.9	20.3	34.7	4.49	0.124	−5.3	−3.6
Assam	36.4	21.8	34.4	0.234	33.9	20.5	32.0	5.33	0.138	2.5	2.4
Bihar	55.7	43.7	54.4	0.050	34.1	31.2	33.7	10.29	0.158	21.6	20.7
Chhattisgarh	55.1	28.4	49.4	0.142	44.6	24.8	39.9	6.98	0.180	10.5	9.5
Delhi	14.96	13.1	12.9	01.10	13.1	10.01	10.00	10.03	02.00	3.21	2.98
Goa	27.98	22.34	25.31	0.987	7.12	4.2	5.1	20.21	0.803	21.3	19.9
Gujarat	39.1	20.1	31.6	0.429	21.5	10.1	16.6	7.66	0.477	17.6	15.2
Haryana	24.8	22.4	24.1	0.544	11.6	10.3	11.2	8.03	0.493	13.2	12.9
Himachal Pradesh	25.0	4.6	22.9	0.605	8.5	4.3	8.1	7.31	0.647	16.5	14.8
Jharkhand	51.6	23.8	45.3	0.145	40.8	24.8	37.0	4.49	0.222	10.8	8.3
Karnataka	37.5	25.9	33.3	0.436	24.5	15.3	20.9	3.69	0.420	13	12.5
Kerala	20.2	18.4	19.6	1.000	9.1	5.0	7.1	7.96	0.911	11.1	12.6
Madhya Pradesh	53.6	35.1	48.6	0.182	35.7	21.0	31.7	9.69	0.186	17.9	16.9

Maharashtra	47.9	25.6	38.2	0.583	24.2	9.1	17.4	4.82	0.629	23.7	20.7
Manipur	39.3	34.5	37.9	0.256	38.8	32.6	36.9	9.79	0.199	0.5	1.1
Meghalaya	14.0	24.7	16.1	0.340	12.5	9.3	11.9	12.58	0.246	1.5	4.2
Mizoram	23.0	7.9	15.4	0.529	35.4	6.4	20.4	−2.55	0.408	−12.4	−5.1
Nagaland	10.0	4.3	8.8	0.403	19.9	16.5	18.9	8.32	0.257	−9.9	−9.9
Odisha	60.8	37.6	57.2	0.174	35.7	17.3	32.6	3.78	0.261	25.1	24.6
Punjab	22.1	18.7	20.9	0.640	7.7	9.2	8.3	6.52	0.538	14.4	12.6
Rajasthan	35.8	29.7	34.4	0.278	16.1	10.7	14.7	5.17	0.324	19.7	19.7
Sikkim	31.8	25.9	30.9	0.299	9.9	3.7	8.2	10.77	0.324	21.9	22.9
Tamil Nadu	37.5	19.7	29.4	0.587	15.8	6.5	11.3	7.39	0.633	21.7	17.6
Tripura	44.5	22.5	40.0	0.288	16.5	7.4	14.1	8.69	0.354	28	26.5
Uttar Pradesh	42.7	34.1	40.9	0.167	30.4	26.1	29.4	5.57	0.122	12.3	11.5
Uttarakhand	35.1	26.2	32.7	0.247	11.6	10.5	11.3	9.36	0.426	23.5	21.4
West Bengal	38.2	24.4	34.2	0.462	22.5	14.7	20.0	4.72	0.483	15.7	14.3
All India	41.8	25.7	37.2	0.507	25.7	13.7	21.9	6.69	0.554	16.1	15.3

Source: Government of India Press Release 2013.

has been consistently high in the states of Kerala, Gujarat, Himachal Pradesh and Haryana; it has been consistently low in the states of Jharkhand, Uttar Pradesh, Bihar and Madhya Pradesh. Despite experiencing economic growth at the same rate as Kerala and Himachal Pradesh, the population of Uttar Pradesh, Bihar and Chhattisgarh remains poor due to a lack of human development. There is evidence that GDP growth alone is insufficient to remove poverty, as high poverty rates are found in states with low human development. Thus, the case of multidimensional growth's significance in achieving the objective of greater poverty reduction is bolstered.

Academics and policymakers have challenged the poverty statistics provided by the Government of India because it does not accurately depict the extent of poverty in the country. India's poverty estimates have always been at odds with other indicators of social well-being, such as childhood malnutrition, maternal anaemia, educational attainment, access to public services, employment prospects, asset ownership and so on (Mitra, 2013). Moreover, when trying to understand what causes poverty, using a metric based solely on consumption costs is inadequate.

Although assessing poverty is a pressing issue in India, little has been studied in this area using publicly available data. Using data from the 1971–1972 National Survey samples for 56 regions, Subramanian and Jayaraj (2006) sought to explain the variations in prosperity between areas. They discovered that owning assets had a greater effect on poverty rates than did agricultural output. They also demonstrated that land is the single most essential factor in a family's financial well-being in India, a country with a sizeable rural population.

No research has been conducted in India that dissects multidimensional poverty into its component forms to better understand the role played by various forms of deprivation in this social phenomenon. With OPHI's approach to estimating multidimensional poverty and knowledge of the mechanisms that induce moves into and out of poverty, this chapter seeks to address this gap in the literature. The Indian government has traditionally targeted income as a means to alleviate poverty. However, many different types of deprivation contribute to poverty that must be considered for policies aimed at alleviating poverty to be effective. This dissertation takes the mixed-methods, decompositional approach to study the elements and privations that contribute to poverty's dynamic nature. This would be a huge aid in educating policymakers on where they should focus their efforts. Changes into and out of poverty, as well as periods of sustained poverty, are correlated with the following factors:

Demographic Factors: According to numerous studies, the changes in demographics have a substantial impact on the development and persistence of poverty. Having more people rely on one person for financial support makes a household more vulnerable to shocks and hardship. There is a strong correlation between the gender of the home head and the likelihood of experiencing or prolonging poverty.

According to Bhide and Mehta's (2008) research on Indian families, those with more people living in their homes in 1970–1971 were more likely to be living in poverty in 1981–1982. The likelihood of living in persistent poverty rose as household size and the dependency ratio both increased.

Economic Factors: It has been hypothesised that economic factors, such as a family's major source of income and the status of the breadwinner in the household, have a significant role in shaping poverty dynamics. Changing a family's principal source of income from agriculture to something else has been linked to a 72% rise in the likelihood of escaping poverty, according to one study (Justino & Litchfield, 2003). It has been said that leaving the agricultural sector for the non-farming, one can escape poverty (Ahmed & Tauseef, 2018; Nargis & Hossain, 2006). Most low-income households were those involved in farming or other menial labour. Those who make their living in agriculture often do so at the expense of their families since they do not have the resources to invest in modern farming methods that would lift them out of poverty.

Human Capital: Bhide and Mehta (2008) observed that while higher levels of education helped moderately poor households rise above their starting position, the same was not true for the extremely poor. When considering the causes and consequences of poverty, health and schooling are two of the most influential factors. Poor health and the associated catastrophic costs of healthcare (sometimes of low quality) are cited by Krishna (2004) as a major contributor to poverty among many Indian households.

A family's ability to maintain its standard of living after experiencing a shock between the two eras is diminished because of the interruption to its steady stream of revenue. Isolated events or widespread catastrophes can serve as shocks.

Caste is a major social norm and value that should be considered when discussing poverty, particularly in South Asian countries. Although discrimination based on caste is illegal, it is still widely practised, especially in rural areas. There is a clear distinction between the socio-economic status of different types of households, with those from higher status groups typically falling into the 'non-poor' category and those from lower status groups typically being connected with long-term, entrenched poverty.

Infrastructure and Public Resources: Human capital development is the primary mechanism by which household access to public resources, such as healthcare, education and employment opportunities and the availability of markets and public institutions affect a household's poverty status. Families that have easier access to resources like medical care, education, employment and transportation are more likely to succeed.

It was found by Jayne et al. (2011) that a 26% decrease in household wealth was associated with a 10% increase in the distance to the nearest healthcare institution. There is a higher chance of escaping poverty for households in communes with better infrastructure, as demonstrated by research by Justino and Litchfield (2003).

Majumder (2012) found that in India, raising the quality of regional infrastructure led to higher per capita consumption and a lower poverty rate. Using data from all of India's states between 1957 and 1991, Datt and Ravallion (1998) discovered that the states with the best infrastructure and human resources also had the highest rates of poverty reduction over time.

Possessions: Numerous studies have proven the importance of asset ownership in influencing poverty dynamics. Many people worry that losing their possessions will permanently alter their family's standard of living. Movements out of poverty are linked to increases in household asset ownership, land ownership, remittances and livestock ownership, while movements into poverty or continued chronic poverty are linked to decreases in these variables (Chapoto et al., 2011; Teguh & Nurkholis, 2011).

According to research by Bhide and Mehta (2008) on poverty trends in India, the likelihood of climbing out of poverty or slipping back into it is extremely sensitive to one's starting point in terms of wealth.

Poverty Dynamics: Factors

It is not just individual abilities but also institutional and social characteristics that impact whether a home is endowed with or deprived of many aspects of well-being throughout time. The dynamics of poverty are affected by households' capacity to exercise their rights within the existing framework of institutions.

Poor Governance

Wasted resources and unfulfilled promises of service are the inevitable results of ineffective administration. In a 2002 study (Grindle), Government's capacity to maintain order and provide for its people is the essence of good governance (Fukuyama, 2013). It's not so much about the outcomes that leaders intend as it is about the processes by which agents carry out those intentions (Fukuyama, 2013). The failure of governments to accomplish their goals and provide a favourable environment for their citizens is known as poor governance, and it is increasingly thought to be one of the primary causes of all societal structural issues (Sheng & Kioe, 2009).

When it comes to helping the poor, political will and good governance are crucial. The impoverished are unable to make the most of their resources because of the drag that inadequate governance creates (Ghatak, 2015). Corruption, ineffective service delivery and inadequate policy, all stem from weak governance, which has serious consequences for the poor. Consequently, high-quality political institutions and governance are the major factors in economic growth and poverty alleviation.

Limited and subpar public services (such as healthcare and schools), unclear ownership of land and other resources, unfair working conditions and outdated or non-existent infrastructure are all symptoms of inadequate leadership.

Limited Supply of Public Services: Health and Education

Whether or not low-income families are able to escape poverty depends heavily on the amount of human capital they are able to collect as a result of increased access to basic services, especially healthcare and education (World Bank, 2001).

Building up one's human resources is crucial to escaping economic suffering, as suggested by the concept of human capital and poverty. Nevertheless, poverty reinforces itself when it impedes the development of human capital (Barrett et al., 2016). The state of an individual's health and education affects their ability to work, but it also defines their outlook on the future and, by extension, their propensity to make long-term investments (Wang & Wang, 2016).

Everyone, not just the poor, deserves access to quality healthcare and education. For the poor, this is especially important since it promotes the accumulation of human capital. People who are both healthy and educated have a better chance of succeeding in the current climate. Problems like insufficient infrastructure, a dearth of qualified healthcare providers and educators and restricted access to essential services, all work against the development of human capital. Public health and education systems are often provided at no cost to low-income households in developing countries. However, research shows that these are primarily gained through spending one's own money, most frequently on prescriptions, textbooks and other supplies.

Like physical capital, human capital can be passed down from generation to generation. A child's inability to make educated decisions about their health and education at an early age can be explained by their parents' perspectives and choices (Bhalotra & Rawlings, 2009).

Land Inequality

Millions of low-income families around the world lack title to the land or buildings they rely on and hence have no legal claim to them. Rural areas are experiencing a more severe crisis due to the higher likelihood of the impoverished population relying on agriculture for their livelihood. The land is more than just a place to lay your head at night; it's also a way to make money, feed your family, build your credit, elevate your social standing and exert influence over others. Most people who farm without property belong to marginalised groups; they may be members of indigenous communities, descendants of indentured servitude, sharecroppers or tenants who aren't guaranteed a return on their investment.

It is believed that land reform programmes can help landless families escape poverty. While some research suggests that land reforms help the poor, the majority of the evidence focuses on land reforms that were only partially successful or were a complete failure. China, South Korea, Japan and Taiwan are the countries that have implemented successful land reforms that others can look to for inspiration. Successful land reforms require conducive changes in social, economic and political structures. Bolivia, Brazil, Chile and Peru, all attempted land reforms that ultimately failed due to rent-seeking behaviour and elite dominance of the policy process. Countries like India, the Philippines, Indonesia and Thailand had some success with reforms (Besley & Burgess, 2010; World Bank, 2003).

Without land as collateral, low-income families may be unable to access the credit necessary to invest in the higher yielding, productive technology necessary to lift them out of poverty. There can be no doubt that the root causes of underdevelopment and persistent poverty in developing nations are improper property rights and landlessness (Barrett et al., 2008; Hulme & Shepherd, 2003).

Labour Laws

People may be unable to climb out of poverty if there is income inequality and inefficient use of labour resources in an economy with weak or non-existent labour rules and regulations. Inadequate institutional capacity and out-of-date regulations undermine the effectiveness of labour laws in reducing poverty.

Wages in developing countries are typically not set by the market forces of supply and demand for labour; instead, workers in the same industry often have vastly varied wage levels. Reasons for this include societal discrimination and limitations on moving between different types of work and different geographical areas (Perry, 2006).

The informal economy typically accounts for a disproportionate share of employment in developing nations. When drafting labour regulations, the informal economy is often overlooked. To avoid legal scrutiny, many Indian companies prefer to operate in the unregulated informal sector, which accounts for 92% of the country's total workforce. In addition, unskilled workers make up a sizeable component of the informal sector, and they are not protected by employment regulations that provide things like a pension, health insurance and equitable working conditions. While workers in the official sector have more protections because, to labour rules, those in the informal sector have it rough too. During 2013, Oxfam found that tea pickers in India were paid less than $2 per day, which is below the World Bank's poverty line; in Malawi, workers were paid less than $1.25 per day, which is below the country's extreme poverty line (Hamilton et al., 2015). It was also discovered in the same study that in 2009, female strawberry pickers in Morocco were paid poorly and subjected to a variety of forms of sexual harassment (Hamilton et al., 2015).

Inclusion and Exclusion in Society

Poverty may be difficult to escape from because of ingrained beliefs, practices and norms as well as the stigma and discrimination that accompany them. This affects not only the family's financial stability but also the individual's ability to make educated decisions (United Nations Department of Economic and Social Affairs, 2016).

When people are already living at a disadvantage due to their socio-economic condition, the effects of social exclusion exacerbate their situation and make it more difficult for them to share in the fruits of progress (United Nations Department of Economic and Social Affairs, 2016). When people are actively discriminated against, it can have a devastating emotional impact and trap them in a cycle of poverty (United Nations Department of Economic and Social Affairs, 2016). It is well-established that caste-based social exclusion is a major contributor to economic disadvantage, vulnerability, low social status and prejudice (Deininger et al., 2009; Meerman, 2005). Because of their inability to access existing resources, the poor and marginalised continue to be at risk of poverty's debilitating effects (Meerman, 2005).

Credit Market Failure: Financial Exclusion

The poor are not impoverished because they lack education or training, but rather because they are unable to keep the fruits of their labour. They lack the authority to influence the flow of capital, which is what allows individuals to escape poverty (Yunus, 2003).

Asset endowment is important for understanding poverty patterns, and market failures are one key cause (Dercon, 2003). The credit market failures, it is argued, could have a disproportionately negative impact on the poor. This suggests that the poor are not making the best use of their resources because they do not have easy access to affordable financing (Dercon, 2003).

Providing low-income families with access to safe saving plans and insurance, as well as lending facilities during times of financial crisis, might help entice them to put their money into potentially riskier investments to boost their income. However, low-income families have difficulty accessing these services because they are either unavailable or prohibitively expensive. Many obstacles stand in the way of the impoverished being able to use banking services.

Market flaws, asymmetric knowledge and high transaction costs contribute to market failures, which can be addressed through financial inclusion and microfinance in particular (Green et al., 2008). Households are less susceptible to and more robust in the face of economic shocks and variations when they have access to financing.

Conclusion

Researchers in India have been trying to gauge the breadth and depth of poverty since at least the 1950s. The poverty threshold below which households in India are categorised as poor has been determined using data from government-conducted consumption expenditure surveys (Mehta et al., 2011). India's poverty rate is high regardless of which metric is used to assess it, even though several revisions have been made to the approach traditionally used to do so. Looking at the MPI, which considers a variety of criteria, we also see a high incidence of poverty.

The literature on poverty suggests that because of the cyclical nature of poverty, static poverty metrics fail to capture the full scope of the problem. Studies of the causes and consequences of poverty show that a sizeable fraction of American households lives below it. It is essential to track the same sample of households over time if one wants to understand the dynamics at play in people's entry into and exit from poverty. Factors including land and livestock ownership, access to inexpensive credit and insurance, health and educational achievement are key long- and short-term determinants of economic well-being, as is well acknowledged in both the empirical and theoretical literature on poverty.

Despite the abundance of literature on the topic, our understanding of the factors that contribute to and exacerbate multidimensional poverty is restricted because most of it focuses on income/consumption/expenditure as a measure of deprivation. While monetary measures of poverty are useful for revealing people's spending habits on necessities like food, shelter, healthcare and schooling, they fail to account for people's quality of life as a whole because they don't consider intangible aspects of prosperity like people's health, nutrition, level of education, the state of public infrastructure, the availability of markets and so on. Since the factors influencing upward and downward mobility in poverty go beyond income or consumption, it is important to quantify poverty dynamics by considering a wide range of non-financial factors and how they interact. It is important to stress, however, that the official monetary poverty threshold should not be completely abandoned because these indicators are just as vital to understanding the relationship between non-monetary aspects of poverty and the creation of a sustainable revenue stream. Income and other indicators go hand in hand; therefore, focusing alone on the level of living is insufficient. Non-monetary measurements of poverty should not replace monetary ones but rather serve to supplement them (Alkire & Santos, 2013).

References

Addison, T., Hulme, D., & Kanbur, R. (2008). *Poverty dynamics: Measurement and understanding from an interdisciplinary perspective*. Working Papers. Cornell University, Department of Applied Economics and Management. https://doi.org/10.2139/ssrn.1246882

Ahmed, A., & Tauseef, S. (2018). *Climbing up the ladder and watching out for the fall: Poverty dynamics in rural Bangladesh*. IFPRI Discussion Paper; No. 1791. International Food Policy Research Institute. https://www.ifpri.org/publication/climbing-ladder-and-watching-out-fall-poverty-dynamics-rural-bangladesh

Alkire, S., Oldiges, C., & Kanagaratnam, U. (2018). *Multidimensional poverty reduction in India 2005/6–2015/16: Still a long way to go but the poorest are catching up*. OPHI Research in Progress 54a. University of Oxford.

Alkire, S., & Robles, G. (2016). *Measuring multidimensional poverty: Dashboards, union identification, and the multidimensional poverty index (MPI)*. OPHI Research in Progress 46a. University of Oxford.

Alkire, S., & Santos, M. E. A. (2013). Multidimensional Approach: Poverty Measurement & Beyond. *Social indicators research*, *112*(2), 239–257. https://doi.org/10.1007/s11205-013-0257-3

Barrett, C. B., Carter, M. R., & Ikegami, M. (2008, February 1). Poverty traps and social protection. https://ssrn.com/abstract=1141881

Barrett, C., Garg, T., & Linden, M. (2016). *Well-being dynamics and poverty traps*. Centre for Climate Change and Economics and Policy.

Besley, T., & Burgess, R. (2010). Land reforms, poverty reduction, and economic growth: Evidence from India. *Quarterly Journal of Economics*, *6*(May), 225–279.

Bhalotra, S., & Rawlings, S. (2009). Gradients of the intergenerational transmission of health in developing countries. *The Review of Economics and Statistics*, *95*(2), 660–672.

Bhide, S., & Mehta, A. K. (2008, December 1). *Economic growth and poverty dynamics*. Chronic Poverty Research Centre Working Paper (No. 120 pp. 1–33). https://doi.org/10.2139/ssrn.1537189

Chapoto, A., Banda, D., Haggblade, S., & Hamukwala, P. (2011). *Factors affecting poverty dynamics in rural Zambia*. Food Security Research Project Lusaka, Zambia, Working Paper 55 (pp. 1–44).

Chatterjee, U., Murgai, R., Narayan, A., & Rama, M. (2016). *Pathways to reducing poverty and sharing prosperity in India*. World Bank Group.

Datt, G., & Ravallion, M. (1998). Why have some Indian states done better than others at reducing rural poverty? *Economica*, *65*(257), 17–38.

Datt, G., & Ravallion, M. (2002). Is India's economic growth leaving the poor behind? *The Journal of Economic Perspectives*, *16*(3), 89–108.

Dercon, S. (2003). Poverty traps and development: The equity-efficiency trade-off revisited. In *Paper prepared for the Conference on Growth, Inequality and Poverty, organised by the Agence française de développment and the European Development Research Network (EUDN)*.

Deininger, K., Jin, S., & Nagarajan, H. K. (2009). Land reforms, poverty reduction, and economic growth: Evidence from India. *The Journal of Development Studies*, *45*(4), 496–521.

Fukuyama, F. (2013, January 25). *What is Governance, Centre for Global Development*. Working Paper No. 314. https://doi.org/10.2139/ssrn.2226592

Ghatak, M. (2015). Theories of poverty traps and anti-poverty policies. *The World Bank Economic Review*, *29*, 1–29.

Government of India. (2013). *Statistical profile of scheduled tribes in India* (pp. 1–448). Ministry of Tribal Affairs, Statistics Division. Government of India.

Government of India. (2016). Rural development statistics. *Census*, *2011*, 333–358.

Government of India. (2017). Handbook on India insurance statistics. *Committee Reports: Insurance Regulatory and Development Authority of India*, *71*(5), pp. 1376–1393.

Government of India. (2018). *India in figures 2018* (p. 21). Government of India, Ministry of Statistics and Programme Implementation, Central Statistics Office.

Green, C. J., Kirkpatrik, C. H., & Murinde, V. (2008). Financial inclusion and development: A cross country analysis. In *Annual Conference of the Human Development and Capability Association*, New Delhi (Vol. 168, (10–13), pp. 1–30).

Hamilton, S., Wilshaw, R., Théroux-Séguin, J., & Gardener, D. (2015). *In work but trapped in poverty*. OXFAM Study.

Hasan, R., Lamba, S., & Gupta, A. (2015). *Growth, structural change and poverty reduction: Evidence from India*. South Asia Working Paper Series. Asia Development Bank.

Hulme, D., & Shepherd, A. (2003). Conceptualizing chronic poverty. *World Development*, *31*(3), 403–423.

International Labour Organization. (2019). *World employment and social outlook: Trends 2019*. International Labour Office. ISBN 978-92-2-132952-7 (print). ISBN 978-92-2-132953-4 (web pdf).

Jayne, T. S., Haggblade, S., Minot, N., & Rashid, S. (2011). *Agricultural commercialization, rural transformation and poverty reduction: What have we learned about how to achieve this?*

Justino, P., & Litchfield, J. (2003). *Poverty dynamics in rural Vietnam: Winners and loosers during reform*. Poverty Research Unit at Sussex Working Paper No 10 (pp. 1–46). University of Sussex.

Kasi, E. (2013). Conceptual and methodological issues of poverty and vulnerability: An ethnographic study from the South. *Advances in Anthropology*, *03*(01), 38–45.

Krishna, A. (2004). Escaping poverty and becoming poor: Who gains, who loses, and why? *World Development*, *32*(1), 121–136.

Majumder, R. (2012). *Removing poverty and inequality in India: The role of infrastructure*. Munich Personal RePEc Archive, (MPRA Paper No. 40941).

Meerman, J. (2005). Oppressed people: Economic mobility of the socially excluded. *The Journal of Socio-Economics*, *34*(4), 542–567.

Mehta, A. K., Shepherd, A., Bhide, S., Shah, A., Kumar, A. (2011). *India chronic poverty report: Towards solutions and new compacts in a dynamic context*. Chronic Poverty Research Centre.

Mitra, S. (2013). *The debate on poverty measures in India*. Featured Opinion: Centre for Budget and Governance Accountability.

Narayan, A., & Murgai, R. (2016). *Looking back on two decades of poverty and well-being in India*. Poverty and Equity Global Practice Group, The World Bank. (WPS7626).

Nargis, N., & Hossain, M. (2006). Income dynamics and pathways out of rural poverty in Bangladesh, 1988–2004. *Agricultural Economics*, *35*.

Norton, A. (2012). *The shifting dynamics of poverty – How do we research poverty and wellbeing in a changing world?* Overseas Development Institute.

Perry, G., Arias, O., Humberto López, J., Maloney, W. F., & Servén, L. (2006). *Poverty reduction and growth: Virtuous and vicious circles*. The World Bank.

Ravallion, M. (2011). A comparative perspective on poverty reduction in Brazil, China, and India. *World Bank: Development Research Group*, *26*(1), 71–104.

Sheng, & Kioe, Y. (2009). *What is good governance*. United Nations Economic and Social Commission for Asia and the Pacific.

Subramanian, S., & Jayaraj, D. (2006). *The distribution of household wealth in India*. UNU-WIDER Research Paper No. 2006/116. https://doi.org/10.1093/acprof:oso/9780199548880.003.0006

Teguh, D., & Nurkholis, N. (2011). *Finding out of the determinants of poverty dynamics in Indonesia: Evidence from panel data*. MPRA Research Paper NO 41185. University Library of Munich. https://ideas.repec.org/p/pra/mprapa/41185.html

Thomas, A. C., & Gaspart, F. (2012). Does poverty trap rural Malagasy households? *World Development*, *67*(33), 490–505.

Tran, V. Q., Alkire, S., & Klasen, S. (2015). *Static and dynamic disparities between monetary and multidimensional poverty measurement: Evidence from Vietnam* (Vol. 23, pp. 249–281). OPHI Working Paper 97.

UNDP. (2019). *Human development index ranking*. Human Development Reports.

United Nation Department of Economic and Social Affairs. (2016). *Report on the world social situation*. United Nations. ISBN: 978-92-1-130336-0. eISBN: 978-92-1-057710-6.

Wang, Y., & Wang, B. (2016). Multidimensional poverty measure and analysis: A case study from Hechi City, China. *Springer Plus*, *5*(1), 642.

World Bank. (2001). *World Development Report 2000/2001: Attacking poverty*. World Development Report. Oxford University Press. http://hdl.handle.net/10986/11856

World Bank. (2003). *The World Bank annual report 2003* (Vol. 1). ISSN: 0252-2942. ISBN: 0-8213-5594-5.

World Bank Group. (2016). *Poverty and shared prosperity 2016*. ISBN: 978-1-4648-0958-3 (paper). ISBN: 978-1-4648-0979-8 (electronic). https://doi.org/10.1596/978-1-4648-0958-3

Yunus, M. (2003). *Banker to the poor: Micro-lending and the battle against world poverty*. Public Affairs.

Chapter 10

From Resist to Privilege: Rising Psychological Empowerment and Gender Equality for Poverty Alleviation

Dhamodharan M[a] *and Sunaina K*[b]

[a]SRM University AP, India
[b]Kannur University, Kerala, India

Abstract

'Poverty is well-being deprivation', declares the World Bank. There is no clear, widely accepted definition of well-being, although the World Bank provides some clues, 'to be impoverished would be to be starving, to lack shelter, to be unwell and uncared for, and to be illiterate and untutored'. Poor people are subject to uncontrollable situations and denied voice and influence. Psychological empowerment (PE) and gender equality are among the emphasised areas which need to be catered. 'Psychological' empowerment, abbreviated as 'PE', denotes empowerment at the specific intensity of analysis. It is a multidimensional concept derived from the integration of various dimensions determined by three realms: (a) personality, which includes self-attribution and internal locus of control, (b) cognitive, that contains self-efficacy perception, (c) motivational, which describes the interest in participating in the activity and control of the factors involved. PE shows that people believe their actions are manageable and controlled, that they are transitioning from a condition of learned helplessness to a state of logical hope and optimism. Gender equality is the equivalent involvement of males and females in utter facets of a lifetime. Women's civil rights activities affiliated with the rights movements worked to establish gender equality in place of an essential human right. In many nations, indicators such as the gender-linked development indicators, the gender break index and the gender fairness index provide measurements of complete gender equivalence.

This chapter discusses the positive impact of PE and gender equality on human well-being based on evidence.

Understanding the Multi-Dimensional Nature of Poverty, 189–212

Published under exclusive licence by Emerald Publishing Limited
doi:10.1108/978-1-83753-292-620241010

Keywords: Gender equality; psychological empowerment; poverty alleviation; sustainability; women's rights

Introduction

The World Health Organization (WHO) describes deprivation as 'the failure to attain a minimum standard of living, with fundamental essentials such as provisions, accommodation, and clothing remaining unfulfilled.'

This definition emphasises the importance of elementary requirements, such as nutrition, safe water, sanitation and access to medical assistance, in determining poverty. The WHO understands that poverty is a multifaceted problem that involves social, economic and political elements that restrict people's prospects and life chances (Siddiqui et al., 2020). Therefore, poverty reduction measures should not strive to solve material deprivation but also to improve the poor and marginalised population's social inclusion, participation and empowerment. Promoting psychological empowerment (PE) and gender equality contributes significantly to poverty reduction and makes a difference in society.

PE is the method through which people acquire notable control over their life, develop a feeling of self-efficacy and become more capable of making choices that influence their well-being (Yukl & Becker, 2012). In the most profound sense, PE may assist people and communities in transcending the feelings of helplessness and discouragement that often accompany poverty (Zhou & Chen, 2021). In addition, it may lead to increased engagement in decision-making processes, better social networks and a higher feeling of control in one's life, which can promote well-being and alleviate poverty.

Gender equality is an additional crucial aspect that can influence poverty. Women are disproportionately affected by poverty, discrimination and barriers to education and career opportunities and face higher rates of gender-based violence (United Nations: Gender Equality and Women's Empowerment, n.d.). Gender equality may enable women to employ fully in community, financial and political life by addressing these inequities. It may result in improved health outcomes, increased gain access to schooling and employment opportunities and higher economic sustainability, all of which can contribute to reducing poverty (Bayeh, 2016).

In this chapter, the author discussed the importance of PE and gender equality to alleviate societal poverty.

The Notion of Empowerment

The definition of the phrase 'empowerment' is the capacity of individuals to comprehend and manage themselves then their circumstances, including communal, financial and political elements. Empowerment is extending their talents and perspectives to achieve greater degrees of success and happiness. Superior self-esteem, perceptions of identity, feelings of control of one's life, greater critical perception and heightened civic engagement are characteristics of empowered persons (Bukowski & Kreissl, 2021).

Empowerment has three types: organisational, community and individual (Zimmerman, 1995). The initial type of empowerment is organisational empowerment, which includes procedures and constructions that boost associate participation and presentation. Henceforth, it is facilitating the attainment of organisational objectives. The next stage of empowerment is communal empowerment which discusses to a collaborative effort to enhance the excellence of life in a communal and the links between communal groups. Organisational and communal empowerment remains not focused on individuals but empowers a group of people. The third empowerment is individual empowerment that encompasses the changing of individuals' lives in accomplishing goals and achieving objectives that they previously considered unattainable (Pigg, 2009). PE is another term for individual empowerment (Zimmerman, 1995).

Psychological Empowerment: Definition

The name PE is coined in industrial-organisational psychology. Individual liberty, selection, liability and participation in organisational decision-making are characterised as liberation. PE is an 'innate task motivation replicating a significance of self-control involving one's work and an energetic commitment with their work role'. (Li et al., 2021).

In simple terms, PE mentions to the individual's intellect of control over their own life, beliefs in their abilities and a significance of purpose and meaning in life. When individuals feel empowered, they are more likely to improve their lives, pursue education, training and job opportunities and engage in community activities that support their well-being.

PE may be challenging to evaluate because it presents itself in various perspectives, abilities and behaviours among individuals. Diverse situations may need the adoption of distinct ideas, skills and behaviours. Over time, PE may fluctuate. Each of these characteristics indicates that PE would be a broad concept that cannot be reduced to a uniform set of operational norms and definitions.

Role of PE in Poverty Alleviation

PE can be a powerful tool in the fight against poverty. Poverty is often associated with a sense of powerlessness and helplessness, leading to hopelessness and despair. PE can help counteract these negative effects of poverty by providing individuals with a significance of limitation over their lives and a belief in their skills to generate positive transformation (Alvarez et al., 2018).

PE consists of three main components explaining the empowerment in three directions and leading to sustainable wealth. Fig. 10.1 illustrates the role of PE in alleviating poverty.

PE has three components which include: 1. Intrapersonal components – it refers to how people think about themselves, 2. Interactional features mention to

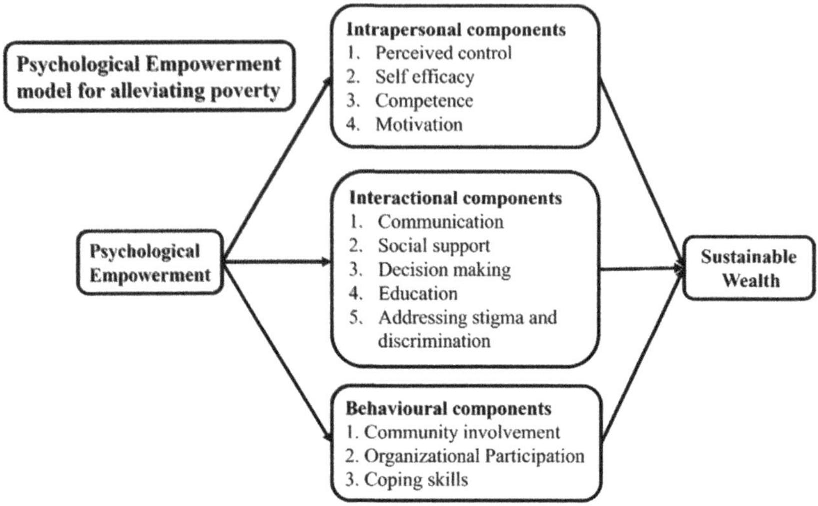

Fig. 10.1. Psychological Empowerment Model for Alleviating Poverty. *Note:* This model demonstrates the role of psychological empowerment components to achieve the sustainable wealth. *Source:* Prepared by the author.

exactly in what manner people recognise their community and sociopolitical problems and 3. Behavioural components – it relates to actions rooted to affect outcomes directly (Eisman et al., 2016; Zimmerman, 1995).

Intrapersonal Components

Intrapersonal components explain individual emotions and one's perception of being empowered. It includes perceived control, self-efficacy, competence and motivation. Intrapersonal empowerment also embraces a person's sense of autonomy and restriction over occupation and life, leading to sustainable wealth (Diener & Biswas-Diener, 2005).

Perceived Control

A fundamental component of PE in poverty alleviation is perceived control. Perceived control relates to a person's perception that they can change their environment and attain their goals (Alvarez et al., 2018). Perceived control can be essential in empowering individuals to improve their own socio-economic and social circumstances in the context of poverty reduction.

People with a strong feeling of perceived control might be more likely to take steps to improve their economic and social circumstances, such as enrolling in education or job skills training, launching their enterprises or lobbying for their rights (Becker et al., 2002). People behave with more flexibility in the face of hardship because they can overcome barriers and accomplish their goals. Those who believe they have little influence over their circumstances are more prone to suffer sentiments of pessimism and helplessness, which can add to a sense of powerlessness and prolong the cycle of poverty.

Promoting a sense of perceived control can therefore be a crucial strategy for developing PE and reducing poverty. It might include providing individuals with the knowledge and tools to change their circumstances and fostering a sense of agency and self-determination by creating supportive environments (Ayoo, 2022). In addition, policies and programmes that address more significant social and economic disparities can contribute to a fairer and more empowering environment for all people.

Self-Efficacy

Self-efficacy is an individual's belief in their ability to complete a particular task or achieve a specific ambition (Carey, 2009). In the linked poverty alleviation, self-efficacy can be vital in empowering individuals to improve their economic situation and reduce poverty. People with advanced degrees of self-efficacy are beyond expected to take proactive steps towards poverty alleviation, such as seeking education and training, starting a business or pursuing higher paying jobs (Wuepper & Lybbert, 2017).

Furthermore, self-efficacy creates the effectiveness in poverty alleviation programmes. Programmes that focus on building self-efficacy by providing education, training and resources that help individuals develop skills and increase their confidence are more effective in reducing poverty than programmes that solely provide material aid (Advani & Martellotto, 2017). For example, microfinance programmes that provide small loans to low-income individuals have successfully alleviated poverty partly because they help build self-efficacy by allowing individuals to start their own businesses and gain greater control over their economic situation. In summary, self-efficacy may empower individuals to eliminate poverty and advance economic well-being to take charge of their life and explore possibilities for economic growth.

Competence

Competence refers to an individual's self-confidence in their capabilities to effectively achieve their job tasks (Indeed Editorial Team, 2021). When individuals feel competent in their occupation, they are more probable to feel powerful. Competence is one of the highest intrapersonal factors of PE to alleviate poverty. The following strategies can be used to improve competency to achieve sustainable wealth.

- Building skills and knowledge: Competence can help individuals acquire the skills and knowledge needed to achieve their goals. It includes pursuing education and training opportunities, seeking mentors or advisors or learning from successful role models (Mccure, 2021).

- Encouraging risk-taking: Competence encourages individuals to perceive risks and pursue novel opportunities. When individuals feel self-confident in their capabilities, they may be more willing to try new things and take on challenges, leading to resolving poverty.
- Increasing self-esteem: Competence helps individuals build self-esteem and confidence, which can be necessary to overcome feelings of helplessness and hopelessness. This increased self-esteem can motivate individuals to pursue their goals and take proactive steps towards achieving them. It can be significant for impoverished individuals, who may face significant challenges and barriers to economic advancement (Mann et al., 2004). Feeling competent and capable can motivate to overcome these challenges and pursue economic opportunities.
- Enhancing decision-making: Competence can also improve an individual's ability to make effective decisions. When individuals feel confident in their abilities, they may be better operational to calculate different choices and make findings that associate with their goals and values (Bruine de Bruin et al., 2020).
- Innovation and creativity: Competence promotes innovation and creativity. Individuals may be able to identify new ways of addressing social and economic challenges through acquiring knowledge and skills (Wao et al., 2022). It can lead to the enhancement of new products, assistance or approaches that create economic opportunities and contribute to poverty alleviation.

Motivation

Motivation is the desire to act towards a particular goal or outcome (Ing, 2012). Motivation has a role in alleviating poverty from an individual level. Firstly, intrinsic motivation is the type of motivation that drives one to absorb in an action or pursue a goal since it is directly meaningful or enjoyable (Oudeyer & Kaplan, 2009). Intrinsic motivation can help individuals and communities develop a sense of purpose and meaning in their poverty alleviation efforts, which can increase their commitment and persistence. Secondly, goal setting involves identifying precise, computable, attainable, applicable and time-bound goals. Goal setting can help individuals and communities clarify their priorities and develop a path towards poverty alleviation, increasing their motivation and focus (Ing, 2012). Thirdly, self-determination implies the capacity to make selections and take actions founded on one's values and interests. Motivation can support self-determination by inspiring people and the drive needed to take control of their lives and pursue their goals and aspirations (Lopez-Garrido, 2021).

Interactional Components

The interactional aspect of PE concerns to a person's ability to empathise with the communal and primary resources necessary to attain their objectives. A person's capacity to effectively control the environment depends on their awareness of the available resources in a specific setting (Zimmerman, 1995). Interactional components refer to the social and relational factors influencing poverty alleviation efforts. These components include communication, social support, decision-making, education and addressing stigma and discrimination.

Communication

Communication involves the exchange of information and ideas between individuals and groups (ICOFB, 2018). Practical communication skills can enhance the capacity of deficient people to communicate their needs, desires and concerns. Communication can also increase the ability of deprived people to understand and respond to the needs and concerns of others, which can promote positive relationships and social support.

Social Support

Social support refers to the network of people who provide expressive, informational and influential support to people and communities (Towey, 2016). Social support can assist individuals to cope with the challenges of poverty alleviation and to stay engaged in efforts over the long term. Positive associations with relatives, friends, or communal members can provide sensitive support and a sense of belonging. Poor people with supportive relationships are more likely to be empowered and have greater control over their lives.

Decision-Making

Poor people with a voice in decisions that affect their lives are likelier to feel empowered and have better control over their lives. Participation in decision-making processes can also improve the capability of poor people to recognise and respond to the needs and concerns of others (Green & King, 2013).

Education

Access to education can provide poor people with the intelligence and expertise needed to upgrade their lives. Education can also increase self-efficacy and limitation over one's life. Poor people get empowerment through learning, improving their social network and developing their skills through education (Hadi et al., 2015). In addition, mentoring also plays a role in PE. Mentoring involves a supportive association between a skilled individual and a less skilled individual, where the experienced individual provides guidance, support and encouragement. Mentoring can enhance poor public's self-esteem, self-efficiency and perception of control (Eby et al., 2008).

Addressing Stigma and Discrimination

Stigma and discrimination can significantly impact the interactional components of PE for poor people. Stigma refers to negative attitudes and beliefs people hold towards others grounded on their distinguished differences, while difference involves the unequal treatment of people based on those differences (APA, 2020). Policies and laws addressing discrimination and promoting equality can help reduce stigma and discrimination. It can include anti-discrimination laws, policies that promote diversity and inclusion and efforts to address systemic inequalities. Community-based approaches, such as peer support groups, can provide a safe and supportive environment for poor people. It can involve creating community centres, support groups and other community-based programmes that promote social inclusion and support. Interventions addressing stigma and discrimination can help confirm that all individuals have equivalent access to prospects, resources and services, which is critical for promoting economic stability and reducing poverty.

Behavioural Components

Behavioural components refer to individuals' actions and behaviours to achieve their goals, increase their sense of control over their lives and promote their well-being. Behavioural features include community involvement, organisational participation and coping skills.

Community Involvement

Poverty and community involvement are also closely interconnected. Community involvement refers to the participation of community members in decision-making, problem-solving and collective action to improve the well-being of their community (Raditloaneng, 2015). Poverty can limit access to possessions such as schooling, healthcare and employment, reducing opportunities for community involvement. Efforts to address poverty can help to increase access to these resources and provide individuals with the assistance and comprehension needed to participate in community life. Encouraging community involvement can help individuals to feel connected to their community and to work together to create positive change.

Organisational Participation

A positive work environment can be conducive to PE. Organisations can generate a festive work atmosphere by promoting respect, support and open communication. It can help individuals feel respected and reinforced, increasing their self-efficacy and promoting sustainable wealth (Monje Amor et al., 2021). Organisations can allow individuals to participate in decision-making and collaborate with others on projects and initiatives. In addition, organisations can provide financial support to poverty alleviation programmes through donations, grants or corporate social responsibility initiatives. Furthermore, organisations can partner with other organisations working on poverty alleviation initiatives to share resources and expertise and develop more effective programmes (Golle, 2007).

Coping Skills

Poverty is a stressful and challenging experience for people. Meanwhile, coping skills are the strategies and techniques individuals use to manage the stress and challenges of daily life, such as poverty. Coping skills can be physical, emotional or cognitive and may involve seeking social support, engaging in physical activity, practicing relaxation techniques or reframing negative thoughts (Algorani & Gupta, 2022). One of the most important coping skills for impoverished people is seeking social support, including help from family, friends or community organisations (Towey, 2016). In addition, learning to manage money effectively can be an essential coping skill for impoverished people. It may involve creating a budget, tracking expenses and seeking out resources to help make ends meet. Additionally, there are often a variety of resources available to help those living in poverty, including food banks, affordable housing programmes and job training programmes. These resources can be an important coping skill. Finally, practising self-compassion can be an essential coping skill for impoverished people (Allen & Leary, 2010). It might involve being kind and supportive to oneself and recognising that poverty is not a reflection of personal worth.

Gender Equality

Gender equality pertains to individuals having identical rights, opportunities and treatment, irrespective of gender (United Nations, 1993). It comprises equivalent admittance to schooling, healthcare, employment, political representation and equal pay for equal work. Gender equality explains that people should be free to express their gender identity without the anxiety of discernment or violence and that social norms and cultural attitudes should not limit or disadvantage individuals based on gender. Ultimately, gender equality seeks to eliminate gender-based bias and foster fairness and justice for all individuals (United Nations, 2013).

Gender Equality: Definition

According to United Nations:

> Gender equality refers to the equitable rights, duties, and opportunities of men and women and girls and boys. Equality does not guarantee that women and men will become the same, but that their rights, responsibilities, and opportunities will not be contingent on their gender at birth. Gender equality requires taking consideration of the interests, requirements, and priorities of both women and men, and recognising the differing needs of various categories of women and men. UN (2021)

Inequality in Focus: a Quick Look at Gender Statistics

Women are overrepresented in global poverty. According to the UN Women, 55% of the world's highly deprived (defined as those existing on less than $1.90 per day) are women, and girls and females are 9% less likely than males to have a bank account, and this gender gap has not narrowed in recent years (UN Women, 2017). According to the World Economic Forum's 2021 Global Gender Gap Report, the global gender pay gap is currently 16%, meaning that women earn 77 cents for all dollar men earn. In addition, only 27% of managers and senior officials are women, and women hold just 22.6% of parliamentary seats worldwide (UN Women, 2021). According to the United Nations, one in three females globally has experienced physical or sexual violent behaviour. Discrimination based on gender is also widespread, affecting women's access to education, healthcare and financial opportunities (United Nations, 2020). The International Labour Organization (ILO) explains the global employment force involvement rate for females was below 47% where as 72% for males in 2022. Females are further likely to work in informal, low-paying jobs with few benefits and less job security (ILO, 2022).

According to the UN, females are more likely than males to live in scarcity in old age, partly due to lower lifetime earnings, longer life expectancies and gender-based discrimination in access to social protection programmes (Jayachandran, 2015). The COVID-19 epidemic has worsened gender differences and poverty. Females have been disproportionately affected by the pandemic, with higher rates of job loss, increased care responsibilities and increased risk of violence (Ahinkorah et al., 2021).

Gender inequality is a barrier to financial progress and expansion. The World Bank estimates that concluding the gender disruption in labour force involvement could grow global GDP by $28 trillion by 2025 (UN Women, 2018). Gender equality is also associated with improved health outcomes, lower rates of violence and greater political stability (Milner et al., 2021). These statistics highlight the urgent need for strategies and programmes that promote gender equivalence and reduce poverty. It can include initiatives such as investment in young women's education, educating women's admittance to healthcare and moneymaking opportunities and addressing the origin of gender-based viciousness and discrimination.

Role of Gender Equality in Alleviating Poverty

Gender equivalence is not a female's concern. Women's equality improves the health, income and education of society. No country has gender economic equality. Only six nations gave women equal rights in 2019 (Lamble, 2019). Systematic discrimination, harmful beliefs, lack of sexual and reproductive healthcare and poor political engagement maintain gender inequity worldwide. Gender equality is has a role to reduce the world's poverty. Therefore, the following strategies should be followed to strengthen gender equality to alleviate poverty.

Gender inequality occurs in different places and times in women's life cycles. The author suggested promoting gender equality in five dimensions to achieve sustainable wealth and zero percent of poverty in worldwide: 1. Family, 2. Workplace, 3. Education, 4. Health and 5. Politics.

Fig. 10.2 explains the gender equality model for alleviating poverty.

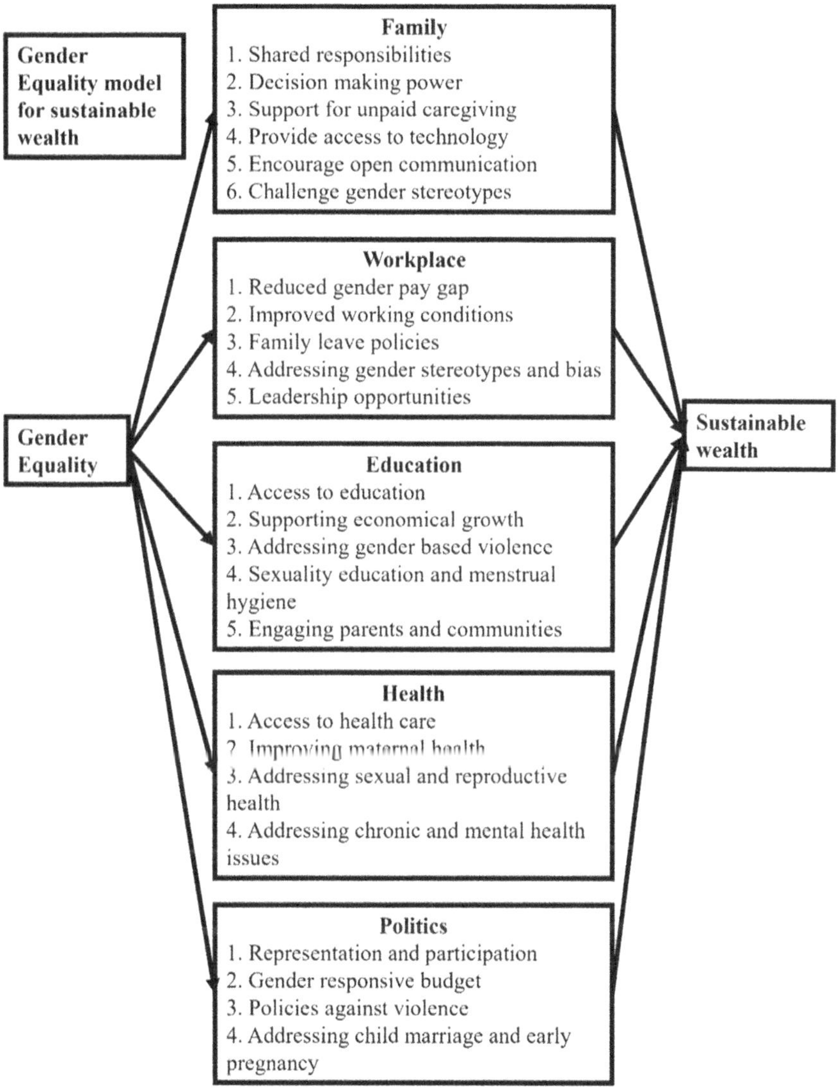

Fig. 10.2. Gender Equality Model for Alleviating Poverty. *Note:* This model demonstrates the role of gender equality in different segments to achieve the sustainable wealth. *Source:* Prepared by the author.

Gender Equality in Family

Gender equality in the family is an essential responsibility in reducing poverty, as it can improve economic outcomes for both men and women. When household work is shared equally between partners, women have more time to absorb in income-generating occupations, which can help to increase their financial freedom and lessen their helplessness to poverty. Additionally, when women can subsidise household revenue, families invest in education and healthcare for their children, which can help break the cycle of poverty (Cerrato & Cifre, 2018). Following strategies help to encourage gender equality in the family.

Shared Responsibilities

Encouraging men and women to share responsibilities for family responsibilities and caregiving can help to decrease the drain on women and allow them more time to participate in economic activities (Ferrant et al., 2014). It can be attained through education and awareness-raising campaigns and encouraging strategies that provide shared responsibilities.

Promote Women's Decision-Making Power

Empowering women to make decisions about family spending and resource allocation can help to reduce poverty and promote gender equality. It can be attained through education and awareness-raising campaigns, as well as by encouraging policies that improve women's decision-making power.

Provide Support for Unpaid Caregiving

Women often tolerate the burden of unpaid caregiving, which can restrict their capacity to contribute in economic activities. Support for unpaid caregiving, such as paid parental leave and affordable babysitting, can help promote gender equality and reduce poverty (Gammage et al., 2019).

Provide Access to Technology

In the digital world, women have various opportunities to improve their skills. But women often have limited access to technology, which can limit their economic prospects and perpetuate poverty. Supporting access to technology, such as computers and smartphones, can facilitate to promote gender equality and reduce poverty by enabling women to participate in digital economies and connect with networks of support (Pesando & Rotondi, 2020, pp. 1–13).

Encourage Open Communication

Open communication is essential for encouraging gender equality in the family. Encourage women and girls in the family to share their thoughts and feelings and create a safe and supportive environment where everyone's opinions are valued. It includes creating safe spaces where women and girls can share their opinion without fear of judgement or reprisal in family. It involves actively listening to others and being willing to consider different viewpoints (UN Women, 2019). Open communication enables family members to address encounters and misunderstandings in a healthy and productive approach. It can help to prevent these conflicts from escalating and promote more harmonious relationships within the family.

Challenge Gender Stereotypes

Challenging harmful gender stereotypes and encouraging family members to challenge them can help promote gender equality. Encourage family members to question traditional gender roles and to consider how they can work together to promote equality (UN Women, 2019).

Gender Equality in the Workplace

The workplace is the third home for women. Women face several issues in the workplace regarding pay, promotion, opportunities and violence. Meanwhile, gender inequality may stop women's growth and lead to poverty. In organisations or workplaces, the following steps help women get equal rights to alleviate poverty.

The Reduced Gender Pay Gap

Promoting gender equality in the workplace can assist in decreasing the gender pay gap, which can help to reduce poverty among women. When females are compensated the same as men for the similar work, they can better assist themselves and their children, reducing the likelihood of poverty (Gopinath, 2022). In addition, employers should conduct regular salary equity assessments to guarantee that males and females are paid similarly for identical occupation. It can help to identify and address any gender pay gaps that may exist in the organisation (UN Women, 2018).

Improved Working Conditions

Gender equality in the workplace can help to improve working conditions for all employees. Promoting equal access to job opportunities, pay and benefits, workplaces can aid in creating a fairer and additional equitable atmosphere for all employees, reducing the likelihood of poverty due to unfair working conditions (Burton & WHO, 2010, pp. 1–131). In addition, employers can offer flexible work preparations, such as freelance or remote work, that can support females with caregiving responsibilities. It can help to increase females' involvement in the workforce and reduce the likelihood of poverty.

Family Leave Policies

Working women have an issue with work–life balance. Therefore, offering paid family leave policies to men and women can help alleviate poverty and promote gender equality. The organisation makes a leave policy for women employees to take time off work to concern for a new infant or sickening family member without losing income or risking job loss (Better Care Network, 2019). In addition, family leave policies should be available to all employees, regardless of their job position or tenure with the company. Also, employers should offer a range of flexible leave options, such as part-time leave, intermittent leave and job sharing, to accommodate the diverse needs of women employees (Russell et al., 2009).

Addressing Gender Stereotypes and Bias

Gender stereotypes and biases can affect how females are perceived in the workstation and limit their opportunities for advancement. Addressing these biases can help promote gender equality by establishing a more level playing area. It can involve testing established gender roles, upgrading gender-neutral language and ensuring that all employees are calculated based on their abilities and performance (Stamarski & Son Hing, 2015). Sexual harassment and prejudice can create a hostile workplace environment, making it difficult for women to succeed. Promoting a zero-tolerance policy for sexual harassment and discrimination can help promote gender equality by ensuring all employees feel safe and respected (Ministry of Women and Child Development, 2015).

Leadership Opportunities

Women are often underrepresented in leadership positions, limiting their career advancement and earning potential. Gender equality in the workplace fosters opportunities for women to take on leadership roles. Employers can support all women employees in their professional development and career advancement (Froehlicher et al., 2021). It can involve creating leadership development programmes for women, providing mentorship opportunities and creating networks of female leaders.

Gender Equality in Education

According to the sustainable development goal report 2020, the fourth part goal is to confirm comprehensive and unbiased excellence education and encourage lifetime learning chances for everyone (UNESCO, 2019). Education is measured as a landmark for women's empowerment since it permits them to answer to encounters, provoke their outdated title role and transform their lives. Therefore, education has a significant role in gender equality and alleviating poverty. The following strategies may improve gender equality in the educational setting.

Access to Education

Girls and females have limited admittance to schooling due to social and economic barriers. Educating the girls and women helps to reduce the gender equality and increase the opportunities to the women and girls to be independent in their life (Right to Education Initiative, 2022). Education can provide individuals, particularly marginalised communities and women, aid to progress their skills, education and experience which leads to secure better-paying jobs and create a pathway out of poverty (Dahal, 2017).

Supporting Economic Growth

Education is a crucial driver of financial development and can help to create more opportunities for women and girls. Education and training are tailored to the requirements of females and girls. It helps to start a more inclusive and reasonable economy, ultimately helping to alleviate poverty (Marquez-Ramos & Mourelle, 2019). Education can foster innovation and entrepreneurship, which are important drivers of economic growth. Education provides individuals with the essential facts and skills to progress new products and services, and it can stimulate entrepreneurship and innovation, leading to economic growth and job creation (Wei et al., 2019).

Addressing Gender-Based Violence

Education can support addressing gender-based violence by teaching children about healthy relationships, consent and gender equality. Proper education improves respectful and equitable relationships (Montserrat et al., 2022). Gender-based viciousness, with internal violence, sexual violence and humanoid trafficking, is a main communal issue and destruction of human rights and gender equality (Gopinath, 2022). Furthermore, it leads to poor health outcomes and reduced economic opportunities. But education can support to decrease of the risk of gender based violence and encourage gender equality, which alleviates poverty.

Sexuality Education and Menstrual Hygiene Management

Comprehensive sexuality education can help encourage girls and boys through the acquaintance and skills they want to make well-versed outcomes about their health and relationships (UNESCO, 2011). Menstrual hygiene management is necessary for girls to stay in an educational set-up. Lack of approach to safe and hygienic menstrual products and facilities can lead to absenteeism and dropout. Education institutions can provide menstrual products, private toilets and hygiene education to promote menstrual hygiene management (Sommer et al., 2021).Sexuality education and hygienic menstrual management help girls continue their studies without disinclination which leads to alleviating poverty in future.

Engaging Parents and Communities

Parents and communities play an essential role in promoting gender equality in education. Education institutions can engage parents and communities to support girls' education. In addition, creating awareness about gender stereotypes and promoting a culture of gender equality may help the parents to understand the importance of girl children education (Li et al., 2022). Furthermore, providing financial support, such as scholarships, stipends or school feeding programmes, can help to reduce the financial burden on families and increase access to education.

Gender Equality in Health

Health is a key factor in upgrading gender equality and removing poverty, as females and girls are often excessively affected by poverty and health disparities. The following strategies help to improve the well-being of girls and females to alleviate poverty in society.

Access to Healthcare

Females and girls often face greater blockades to accessing healthcare, particularly in developing countries. These barriers include geographic isolation, lack of transportation, cultural norms and economic barriers (Habib et al., 2021). Access to healthcare services can progress the health outcomes of females and girls, leading to a more productive workforce and ultimately promoting economic growth. In such a way, healthcare support primes to prevent the poverty.

Improving Maternal Health

Maternal health is a vital issue in endorsing gender equality and reducing poverty. Women who can access quality motherly healthcare are likelier to have healthy children, better economic opportunities and a brighter future (Lassi et al., 2016). Meanwhile, motherly mortality is a foremost global health issue. Maternal mortality can be reduced with admittance to eminence maternal health attention, including expert birth attendants, reserve obstetric care and postnatal attention (Maduka & Ogu, 2020). Women can stay healthy and contribute to their families and communities with the support of proper maternal care.

Addressing the Sexual and Reproductive Health

Females and girls are often suspiciously exaggerated by sexual and propagative health issues, such as unplanned pregnancy and sexually communicated infections (Henry et al., 2012). Providing admittance to contraception, family planning services, also safe abortion services can empower womenfolk and girls to make educated decisions about their propagative health, leading to better health outcomes and increased economic opportunities (Kc et al., 2021). Therefore, addressing sexual and propagative health improves health outcomes, which promotes gender equality and reduces poverty.

Addressing Health and Mental Health Issues

Non-communicable illnesses, such as heart disease and diabetes, are a growing worldwide health concern, predominantly in low- and middle-income nations (Miranda et al., 2008). Women are increasingly affected by these diseases, and addressing them is critical for promoting gender equality and reducing poverty. Meanwhile, access to prevention and treatment services, including screening and lifestyle interventions, and healthcare can help individuals reduce their risk of non-communicable diseases and stay healthy (Budreviciute et al., 2020). Mental health problems, such as depression and anxiety, can negatively impact individuals' health, well-being and economic prospects. Women are affected by mental health issues, and addressing these issues is critical for promoting gender equality and reducing poverty. Promoting mental health services, including counselling, medication and healthcare, can help individuals address mental health issues and improve their overall health and well-being (Castillo et al., 2019).

Gender Equality in Politics

Politics has a significant role in helping gender equality and alleviating societal poverty. It can help those policies and plans be considered and executed in an approachable way to the requirements and significance of all members of society, including women and girls. Following strategies help to make gender equality in politics, directly reducing community poverty.

Representation and Participation

Women are often understated in governmental decision-making, limiting their capacity to shape policies and programmes that impact their lives (Mlambo & Kapingura, 2019). Women's representation in politics and the promotion of their participation in decision-making processes related to public policies make a significant difference and impact in poverty alleviation. In addition, the government ensures that females' perspectives and experiences are considered when making decisions about issues such as poverty reduction, social protection and economic development.

Gender-Responsive Budget

Gender-responsive budgeting is an approach that involves analysing government budgets to identify and address gender inequalities (UN Women, 2016). The government needs to include a gender perspective in budgeting processes, which explains that resources are allocated to address the precise needs and priorities of females and girls, including those related to poverty reduction.

Policies Against Violence

Gender-based violence, with sexual violence and intimate spouse violence, is a key public health alarm that marks lots of groups around the globe, particularly females and girls (Gopinath, 2022). Gender-based violence can perpetuate poverty by limiting women's education, employment and social participation opportunities. Policies and programmes addressing gender-based violence and governments can help generate a harmless and further equitable society which ensures gender equality and well-being (WHO, 2009).

Addressing Child Marriage and Early Pregnancy

Child marriage and early pregnancy are significant barriers to girls' education and economic opportunities and can perpetuate poverty and gender inequality (Parsons et al., 2015). The implementation of government policies and initiatives aimed at addressing child marriage and early pregnancy, along with the provision of comprehensive sex education at the school and college levels, has a profound impact on society. Governments can enact and enforce the existing laws that set the lowest age for wedding at 18 years and make child marriage an immediate punishable offence (Chadha & Tiwari, 2022). These laws should be supported by strong enforcement mechanisms, such as penalties for violators and awareness campaigns to educate communities about the harms of child marriage.

Conclusion

Closing the gender gap and reducing poverty are critical goals for sustainable development. There are multiple examples to understand that gender inequality and poverty are interconnected and reinforce each other. Addressing these issues needs a holistic tactic considering the societal, financial and political features that subsidise inequality and poverty. Meanwhile, the part of PE and gender equality in alleviating poverty cannot be overstated. The two concepts are closely related and work hand in hand to create a more equitable society. PE mentions to the progression of giving people the influence and properties to control their lives and make choices that affect their well-being. Gender equality indicates to equal treatment and chances for males and females in all areas of society.

PE and gender equality can alleviate poverty by creating more opportunities for women. When women are given admittance to education, healthcare and financial prospects, they are better equipped to lift themselves out of poverty. Empowering females to take control of their own lives can make them more financially independent, which can help break the cycle of poverty. When women have the opportunity to access these resources, they are more inclined to allocate resources towards their families and societies. This leads to improved health and economic results for everyone, while also advancing gender equality and confronting these preconceptions. The community can create a more inclusive environment where everyone can thrive. Once people feel that they have a regulator over their lives and can make choices that affect their well-being, it will make them more likely to take actions to improve their situation. In addition, it can increase self-esteem and confidence, improving mental health and happiness. Promoting PE can help individuals to overcome the psychological barriers that often keep them trapped in poverty. Finally, PE and gender equality are crucial to creating a more sustainable and resilient society. It can produce a more diverse and inclusive civilisation that is healthier furnished to address the complex encounters of poverty, climate change, also social inequality. Ultimately, these efforts can help break the poverty cycle and create a brighter future for all.

References

Ayoo, C. (2022). Poverty reduction strategies in developing countries. In *Rural development - education, sustainability, multifunctionality*. IntechOpen. https://doi.org/10.5772/intechopen.101472

Advani, A., & Martellotto, L. (2017). A way to reduce poverty that's so simple, it just might work. https://www.weforum.org/agenda/2017/03/a-way-to-reduce-poverty-that-s-so-simple-it-just-might-work/

Ahinkorah, B. O., Hagan, J. E., Ameyaw, E. K., Seidu, A. -A., & Schack, T. (2021). COVID-19 pandemic worsening gender inequalities for women and girls in Sub-Saharan Africa. *Frontiers in Global Women's Health*, *2*, 52. https://doi.org/10.3389/fgwh.2021.686984

Algorani, E. B., & Gupta, V. (2022). Coping mechanisms. In *Westerly* (Vol. 63, p. 102). StatPearls Publishing. https://doi.org/10.2307/j.ctvp7d4ft.131

Allen, A. B., & Leary, M. R. (2010). Self-compassion, stress, and coping. *Social and Personality Psychology Compass*, *4*(2), 107–118. https://doi.org/10.1111/j.1751-9004.2009.00246.x

Alvarez, K., van Leeuwen, E., Montenegro-Montenegro, E., & van Vugt, M. (2018). Empowering the poor: A field study of the social psychological consequences of receiving autonomy or dependency aid in Panama. *British Journal of Social Psychology*, *57*(2), 327. https://doi.org/10.1111/BJSO.12234

APA. (2020). *Psychiatry.org - stigma, prejudice and discrimination against people with mental illness*. American Psychiatric Association. https://www.psychiatry.org/patients-families/stigma-and-discrimination

Bayeh, E. (2016). The role of empowering women and achieving gender equality to the sustainable development of Ethiopia. *Pacific Science Review B. Humanities and Social Sciences*, *2*(1), 37–42. https://doi.org/10.1016/J.PSRB.2016.09.013

Becker, A. B., Israel, B. A., Schulz, A. J., Parker, E. A., & Klem, L. (2002). Predictors of perceived control among African American women in Detroit: Exploring empowerment as a multilevel construct. *Health Education & Behavior: The Official Publication of the Society for Public Health Education*, *29*(6), 699–715. https://doi.org/10.1177/109019802237939

Better Care Network. (2019, July 1). Redesigning the workplace to be family-friendly: What governments and businesses can do. https://bettercarenetwork.org/library/strengthening-family-care/parenting-support/redesigning-the-workplace-to-be-family-friendly-what-governments-and-businesses-can-do

Bruine de Bruin, W., Parker, A. M., & Fischhoff, B. (2020). Decision-making competence: More than intelligence? *Current Directions in Psychological Science*, *29*(2), 186–192.

Budreviciute, A., Damiati, S., Sabir, D. K., Onder, K., Schuller-Goetzburg, P., Plakys, G., Katileviciute, A., Khoja, S., & Kodzius, R. (2020). Management and prevention strategies for Non-Communicable Diseases (NCDs) and their risk factors, In *Frontiers in public health* (Vol. 8, p. 574111). Frontiers Media SA. https://doi.org/10.3389/fpubh.2020.574111

Bukowski, M., & Kreissl, K. (2021). Empowerment, poverty, and vulnerability 1–14. https://doi.org/10.1007/978-3-319-69625-6_131-1

Burton, J., & World Health Organization. (2010). WHO healthy workplace framework and model: Background and supporting literature and practices. In *WHO Library Cataloguing-in-Publication Data*. World Health Organization. https://iris.who.int/bitstream/handle/10665/113144/9789241500241_eng.pdf

Carey, M. P. (2009). *Self-efficacy teaching tip sheet*. American Psychological Association. https://www.apa.org/pi/aids/resources/education/self-efficacy

Castillo, E. G., Ijadi-Maghsoodi, R., Shadravan, S., Moore, E., Mensah, M. O., Docherty, M., Aguilera Nunez, M. G., Barcelo, N., Goodsmith, N., Halpin, L. E., Morton, I., Mango, J., Montero, A. E., Rahmanian Koushkaki, S., Bromley, E., Chung, B., Jones, F., Gabrielian, S., Gelberg, L., . . . Wells, K. B. (2019). Community interventions to promote mental health and social equity. In *Current psychiatry reports* (Vol. 21, Issue 5). Springer. https://doi.org/10.1007/s11920-019-1017-0

Cerrato, J., & Cifre, E. (2018). Gender inequality in household chores and work-family conflict. *Frontiers in Psychology*, *9*(AUG), 1330. https://doi.org/10.3389/fpsyg.2018.01330

Chadha, V., & Tiwari, U. (2022). Legal efforts to curb child marriage in India, USA and Australia: A comparative analysis. *Age of Human Rights Journal*, *18*, 463–489. https://doi.org/10.17561/tahrj.v18.6582

Dahal, G. (2017). The contribution of education to economic growth: Evidence from Nepal. https://doi.org/10.20472/iac.2016.023.032

Diener, E., & Biswas-Diener, R. (2005). Psychological empowerment and subjective well-being. In *Measuring empowerment: Cross-disciplinary perspectives* (pp. 125–140). https://books.google.co.in/books?hl=en&lr=&id=BzXyApyTGOYC&oi=fnd&pg=PA125&dq=Psychological+empowerment+and+subjective+well-being&ots=HQV_egSZv9&sig=1-EiNDLgpnHbO8er3JN6TjWtNHg

Eby, L. T., Allen, T. D., Evans, S. C., Ng, T., & DuBois, D. L. (2008). Does mentoring matter? A multidisciplinary meta-analysis comparing mentored and non-mentored individuals. *Journal of Vocational Behavior*, *72*(2), 254–267. https://doi.org/10.1016/j.jvb.2007.04.005

Eisman, A. B., Zimmerman, M. A., Kruger, D., Reischl, T. M., Miller, A. L., Franzen, S. P., & Morrel-Samuels, S. (2016). Psychological empowerment among urban youth: Measurement model and associations with youth outcomes. *American Journal of Community Psychology*, *58*(3–4), 410–421. https://doi.org/10.1002/AJCP.12094

Ferrant, G., Pesando, L. M., & Nowacka, K. (2014, December, 12). *Unpaid care work: The missing link in the analysis of gender gaps in labour outcomes*. OECD Development Centre.

Froehlicher, M., Griek, L. K., Nematzadeh, A., Hall, L., & Stovall, N. (2021). Gender equality in the workplace: Going beyond women on the board. In *The substainability yearbook 2021*. https://www.spglobal.com/esg/csa/yearbook/articles/gender-equality-workplace-going-beyond-women-on-the-board

Gammage, S., Sultana, N., & Mouron, M. (2019). The hidden costs of unpaid caregiving. The public and private sectors need to work together to promote gender equality. *Finance & Development*, *56*(1), 20–23. https://www.imf.org/external/pubs/ft/fandd/2019/03/pdf/gender-equality-and-costs-of-unpaid-caregiving-gammage.pdf

Golle, J.-P. (2007). *The contribution of NGOs to the fight against poverty and social exclusion in Europe* (Vol. 56). Grouping of the Conference of INGOs of the Council of Europe International Movement ATD Quart Monde.

Gopinath, G. (2022). *Gender equality boosts economic growth and stability*. International Monetary Fund. https://www.imf.org/en/News/Articles/2022/09/27/sp092722-ggopinath-kgef-gender-korea

Green, D., & King, S. (2013). What can governments due to empower poor people? https://oxfamilibrary.openrepository.com/handle/10546/305513

Habib, S. S., Jamal, W. Z., Zaidi, S. M. A., Siddiqui, J. U. R., Khan, H. M., Creswell, J., Batra, S., & Versfeld, A. (2021). Barriers to access of healthcare services for rural women— applying gender lens on tb in a rural district of sindh, Pakistan. *International Journal of Environmental Research and Public Health*, *18*(19), 10102. https://doi.org/10.3390/ijerph181910102

Hadi, R., Wahyudin, U., Ardiwinata, J. S., & Abdu, W. J. (2015). Education and microfinance: An alternative approach to the empowerment of the poor people in Indonesia. *SpringerPlus*, *4*(1), 1–9.

Henry, D. B., Deptula, D. P., & Schoeny, M. E. (2012). Sexually transmitted infections and unintended pregnancy: A longitudinal analysis of risk transmission through friends and attitudes. *Social Development*, *21*(1), 195–214. https://doi.org/10.1111/j.1467-9507.2011.00626.x

ICOFB. (2018). Communication | definition of communication - ICoFP https://www.icofp.org/blog/communication/

ILO. (2022). The gender gap in employment: What's holding women back? - InfoStories. https://www.ilo.org/infostories/en-GB/Stories/Employment/barriers-women#global-gap

Indeed Editorial Team. (2021). The 4 levels of competence: Definition and examples. In *Indeed career guide*. https://www.indeed.com/career-advice/career-development/levels-of-competence

Ing, M. (2012). Theories of motivation. In *Theory and practice of curriculum studies* (pp. 71–79). https://doi.org/10.4324/9780203814840

Jayachandran, S. (2015). The roots of gender inequality in developing countries. *Annual Review of Economics*, *7*(1), 63–88. https://doi.org/10.1146/annurev-economics-080614-115404

Kc, H., Shrestha, M., Pokharel, N., Niraula, S. R., Pyakurel, P., & Parajuli, S. B. (2021). Women's empowerment for abortion and family planning decision making among marginalized women in Nepal: A mixed method study. *Reproductive Health*, *18*(1), 28. https://doi.org/10.1186/s12978-021-01087-x

Lamble, L. (2019). *Only six countries in the world give women and men equal legal work rights | Global development | the Guardian. The Guardian*. https://www.theguardian.com/global-development/2019/mar/01/only-six-countries-in-the-world-give-women-and-men-equal-legal-rights

Lassi, Z. S., Kumar, R., & Bhutta, Z. A. (2016). Community-based care to improve maternal, newborn, and child health.

Li, T., Gupta, S., & Zhou, H. (2021). An empirical study on drivers' willingness to use automatic features of intelligent vehicles: A psychological empowerment perspective. *Frontiers in Psychology*, *12*, 794845. https://doi.org/10.3389/FPSYG.2021.794845

Li, Y., Zuo, M., Peng, Y., Zhang, J., Chen, Y., Tao, Y., Ye, B., & Zhang, J. (2022). Gender differences influence gender equality awareness, self-esteem, and subjective well-being among school-age children in China. *Frontiers in Psychology*, *12*, 6368. https://doi.org/10.3389/fpsyg.2021.671785

Lopez-Garrido, G. (2021). Self-determination theory | simply Psychology. *Simply Psychology*. https://www.simplypsychology.org/self-determination-theory.html

Maduka, O., & Ogu, R. (2020). Preventing maternal mortality during childbirth: The scourge of delivery with unskilled birth attendants. *Childbirth. IntechOpen*. https://doi.org/10.5772/intechopen.90463

Mann, M., Hosman, C. M. H., Schaalma, H. P., & De Vries, N. K. (2004). Self-esteem in a broad-spectrum approach for mental health promotion. *Health Education Research*, *19*(4), 357–372. https://doi.org/10.1093/HER/CYG041

Marquez-Ramos, L., & Mourelle, E. (2019). Education and economic growth: An empirical analysis of nonlinearities. *Applied Economic Analysis*, *27*(79), 21–45. https://doi.org/10.1108/AEA-06-2019-0005

Mccure, N. (2021). Developing specific skills, competencies, and points of view needed by professionals in the field most closely related to this course https://www.ideaedu.org/idea-notes-on-learning/developing-specific-skills-competencies-and-points-of-view-needed-by-professionals-in-the-field-most-closely-related-to-this-course/

Milner, A., Kavanagh, A., Scovelle, A. J., O'neil, A., Kalb, G., Hewitt, B., & King, T. L. (2021). Gender equality and health in high-income countries: A systematic review of within-country indicators of gender equality in relation to health outcomes. In *Women's health reports* (Vol. 2, pp. 113–123). Mary Ann Liebert, Inc. https://doi.org/10.1089/whr.2020.01141

Ministry of Women and Child Development. (2015). *Sexual harassment of women at workplace act, 2013*. (Issue 19).

Miranda, J. J., Kinra, S., Casas, J. P., Davey Smith, G., & Ebrahim, S. (2008). Non-communicable diseases in low- and middle-income countries: Context, determinants and health policy. *Tropical Medicine and International Health*, *13*(10), 1225–1234. Europe PMC Funders. https://doi.org/10.1111/j.1365-3156.2008.02116.x

Mlambo, C., & Kapingura, F. (2019). Factors influencing women political participation: The case of the SADC region. *Cogent Social Sciences*, *5*(1), 1681048. https://doi.org/10.1080/23311886.2019.1681048

Monje Amor, A., Xanthopoulou, D., Calvo, N., & Abeal Vázquez, J. P. (2021). Structural empowerment, psychological empowerment, and work engagement: A cross-country study. *European Management Journal*, *39*(6), 779–789. https://doi.org/10.1016/j.emj.2021.01.005

Montserrat, C., Garcia-Molsosa, M., Planas-Lladó, A., & Soler-Masó, P. (2022). Children's understandings of gender-based violence at home: The role school can play in child disclosure. *Children and Youth Services Review*, *136*, 106431. https://doi.org/10.1016/j.childyouth.2022.106431

Oudeyer, P. Y., & Kaplan, F. (2009). What is intrinsic motivation? A typology of computational approaches. *Frontiers in Neurorobotics*, *3*(NOV), 6. https://doi.org/10.3389/neuro.12.006.2007

Parsons, J., Edmeades, J., Kes, A., Petroni, S., Sexton, M., & Wodon, Q. (2015). Economic impacts of child marriage: A review of the literature. *Review of Faith and International Affairs*, *13*(3), 12–22. https://doi.org/10.1080/15570274.2015.1075757

Pesando, L. M., & Rotondi, V. (2020). *Mobile technology and gender equality* (pp. 1–13). Springer. https://doi.org/10.1007/978-3-319-70060-1_140-1

Pigg, K. E. (2009). Three faces of empowerment: Expanding the theory of empowerment in community development. *33*(1), 107–123. https://doi.org/10.1080/15575330209490145

Raditloaneng, W. N. (2015). Poverty and community engagement. In *Lifelong learning for poverty eradication* (pp. 19–36). Springer International Publishing. https://doi.org/10.1007/978-3-319-10548-2_2

Right to Education Initiative. (2022). Women and girls | right to education initiative. https://www.right-to-education.org/girlswomen

Russell, H., O'Connell, P. J., & McGinnity, F. (2009). The impact of flexible working arrangements on work-life conflict and work pressure in Ireland. *Gender, Work and Organization*, *16*(1), 73–97. https://doi.org/10.1111/j.1468-0432.2008.00431.x

Siddiqui, F., Salam, R. A., Lassi, Z. S., & Das, J. K. (2020). The intertwined relationship between malnutrition and poverty. *Frontiers in Public Health*, *8*, 453. https://doi.org/10.3389/FPUBH.2020.00453

Sommer, M., Caruso, B. A., Torondel, B., Warren, E. C., Yamakoshi, B., Haver, J., Long, J., Mahon, T., Nalinponguit, E., Okwaro, N., & Phillips-Howard, P. A. (2021). Menstrual hygiene management in schools: Midway progress update on the "MHM in ten" 2014–2024 global agenda. In *Health research policy and systems* (Vol. 19, Issue 1 pp. 1–14). BioMed Central Ltd. https://doi.org/10.1186/s12961-020-00669-8

Stamarski, C. S., & Son Hing, L. S. (2015). Gender inequalities in the workplace: The effects of organizational structures, processes, practices, and decision makers' sexism. In *Frontiers in Psychology* (Vol. 6, p. 1400). Frontiers Media S.A. https://doi.org/10.3389/fpsyg.2015.01400

Towey, S. (2016). Social support | taking charge of your health & wellbeing. University of Minnesota. https://www.takingcharge.csh.umn.edu/social-support

UN, W. (2021). *OSAGI gender mainstreaming - Concepts and definitions*. United Nations entity for gender equality and the empowerment of women. https://www.un.org/womenwatch/osagi/conceptsandefinitions.htm

UN Women. (2017). UN Women and the World Bank unveil new data analysis on women and poverty. UN Women – Headquarters. https://www.unwomen.org/en/news/stories/2017/11/news-un-women-and-the-world-bank-unveil-new-data-analysis-on-women-and-poverty

UN Women. (2018, January 22). Economies that work for women, work for everyone. UN Women – Headquarters. https://www.unwomen.org/en/news/stories/2018/1/feature-economies-that-work-for-women-work-for-everyone

UN Women. (2019, May 15). Gender equality starts at home: Seven tips for raising feminist kids. UN Women – Headquarters. https://www.unwomen.org/en/news/stories/2019/5/compilation-gender-equality-starts-at-home

UN Women. (2021). Equal pay for work of equal value. UN Women – Headquarters. https://www.unwomen.org/en/news/in-focus/csw61/equal-pay

UN Women. (2016). Gender responsive budgeting in the Asia-Pacific Region: A status report. UN Women – Asia-Pacific. https://asiapacific.unwomen.org/en/digital-library/publications/2016/12/gender-responsive-budgeting-in-the-asia-pacific

UNESCO. (2011). *Youth and comprehensive sexuality education*. The United nations youth.

UNESCO. (2019). *Sustainable development goal 4 and its targets*. Unesco. https://en.unesco.org/education2030-sdg4/targets

United Nations. (1993). Gender equality | United Nations https://www.un.org/en/global-issues/gender-equality

United Nations. (2015). United Nations: Gender equality and women's empowerment. In *United Nations sustainable development*. https://www.un.org/sustainabledevelopment/gender-equality/

United Nations. (2020). *Women and girls – closing the gender gap*. United Nations. https://www.un.org/en/un75/women_girls_closing_gender_gap

United Nations: Gender equality and women's empowerment. (n.d.). Retrieved February 23, 2023, from https://www.un.org/sustainabledevelopment/gender-equality/

Wao, H., Otendo, C. O., Syonguvi, J., Muriithi, P., Kadengye, D. T., & Brodin, E. M. (2022). Encouraging social innovation for combating poverty: master's students' gendered experiences with a service-learning intervention in Kenya and Uganda. *Studies in Graduate and Postdoctoral Education*, *13*(2), 171–187. https://doi.org/10.1108/SGPE-07-2021-0054

Wei, X., Liu, X., & Sha, J. (2019). How does the entrepreneurship education influence the students' innovation? Testing on the multiple mediation model. *Frontiers in Psychology*, *10*(July), 1557. https://doi.org/10.3389/fpsyg.2019.01557

World Health Organization. (2009). *Promoting gender equality to prevent violence against women* [Book]. https://www.peelregion.ca/health/youth/pdfs/PromotingGender Equality.pdf

Wuepper, D., & Lybbert, T. J. (2017). Perceived self-efficacy, poverty, and economic development. *Annual Review of Resource Economics*, *9*, 383–404. https://doi.org/10.1146/ANNUREV-RESOURCE-100516-053709

Yukl, G. A., & Becker, W. S. (2012). Effective empowerment in organizations. *3*(3), 210–231. https://doi.org/10.1057/OMJ.2006.20

Zhou, H., & Chen, J. (2021). How does psychological empowerment prevent emotional exhaustion? Psychological safety and organizational embeddedness as mediators. *Frontiers in Psychology*, *12*, 546687.

Zimmerman, M. A. (1995). Psychological empowerment: Issues and illustrations. *American Journal of Community Psychology*, *23*(5), 581–599. https://doi.org/10.1007/BF02506983

Chapter 11

Revamping Economic Parameters in an Innovative Digital World in 21st Century: An Interventive Study on Banking Practices

Rabinarayan Patnaik[a] *and Sukanta Kumar Baral*[b]

[a]Siksha 'O' Anusandhan (SOA) Deemed to be University, India
[b]Indira Gandhi National Tribal University, India

Abstract

Banking sector is an important subset of any economy and plays a very crucial and significant part in its growth and development. The expansion and credibility of banking sector is attributed to the fact that it caters to the financial needs and accordingly provides customised solutions for the people at large. The new millennium has witnessed metamorphosis in the banking sector. The pace and trend of transformation is all set to accelerate in the coming decade. The process of Liberalisation, Privatisation and Globalisation Model (LPG Model) banking practices which being unleashed a few decades back will reach to greater heights as we step into the next decade. The innovative technology has brought about a paradigm shift in all aspects of banking like routine operations, transactions, products and processes, delivery of services in terms of various e-channels, credit administration and credit management, audit and compliance and Fin-Techs partnership. Digital transformations in the banking sector have received much needed thrust because of 'The Digital India Moment'. The current study attempts to highlight the role of technology in banking and how technology led innovations and initiatives will determine the business of banking as a whole. The significance of these technology-driven innovations and transformations is that they put both banker and customer in a win-win situation as drawn from existing literature related to financial institutions. The focus is on investigating the digital innovations adopted by the different banks both public and private to understand the economic structural changes resulted out of it.

Understanding the Multi-Dimensional Nature of Poverty, 213–225

Published under exclusive licence by Emerald Publishing Limited
doi:10.1108/978-1-83753-292-620241011

Keywords: Digital innovations; indian banking system; blockchain; artificial intelligence; Fin-Tech

Introduction

At present, everyone desires a healthy, robust and sustainable banking system that is critical for the growth and development of our economy. Banking system is the mainstay of our economy, and technology has become the backbone of modern-day banking (Kaur et al., 2020). To begin with, technology was considered as business enabler and now it has become a great business driver. Practices adopted by banks have witnessed tremendous shift since 1969 after the nationalisation of commercial banks (Islam & Hasan, 2016)). During the late 1980s, Indian Banking Sector had realised the relevance of computerisation. There was a massive growth in the networking of bank branches. Under the then chairman of Reserve Bank of India, Dr C. Rangarajan, in the year 1989, one committee after a systematic study on the computerisation processes adopted by the bank recommended a report containing feasible and relevant changes to be practised in the years to come (Kumar et al., 2022). ICICI bank pioneered the internet banking services for the first time in India in the year 1997. Since then to survive in this competitive market, almost every bank has shifted from paper-based banking to paperless banking, i.e. towards digital banking. Over the years, the impact created by the services of banks can be visible and realized by masses (Kalyani, 2016). However, the customers still remain the critical factor whose perception and ultimately the satisfaction of theirs lead to the effectiveness and success rate of services provided by the banks. Majority of the banks (total 34 currently both public and private banks) are into online service facilities. Now, people can do banking from anywhere at any time with very minimal cost. The development of electronic home banking has significantly necessitated reorganisation of banking services and operations. Digital modes have replaced the brick-mortar model of branches (Andrew, 2021). However, very little has been done to understand the level of efficiency exhibited by the digital and innovative practices followed by the banks to the customers (for example, the digital banking apps). In addition to that, the safety and security concerns (e.g. in certain instances like money transfer and distribution) associated with these digital practices and modes of services need to be further addressed.

Research Objectives

With the backdrop of understanding and analysing innovative practices creating effective results to the consumers of banks, the current study aims to find out the following perspectives:

- To understand the changing digital scenario in the banks in India.
- To examine the digital banking new trends and innovations in Indian banks.
- To analyse the various digitally offered products, services as well as channels by Indian banks.
- To analyse the role of Fin-Tech in Indian banks towards digital transformation.

Review of Literature

There have been various past studies which made inroads to the current context. However, to genuinely communicate the definiteness of the current study, certain literature can be of real value and thereby extend the scope of the former (Heim, 2019). The benefits and advantages created by the innovative practices should be focused while adopting the same (Kuncoro & Suriani, 2018). Further, the results should be clearly visible and realised by the banks concerned, for example, the reduction in operating costs for the practising banks (Scott et al., 2017). Not limited to urban consumers, the banking practices in the innovative and digital stage must extend the horizon of value addition to the rural consumers and thereby boosting up the economy at large (Hempel & Hamm, 2016). This can only be possible once the banking system has an immense capacity to accelerate financial inclusion apart from offering the benefits of ease of operations and low-cost factor (Perera, 2018). It is also observed that the digital platform has helped the payments system in banks much more improvised thereby driving the banking service towards achieving the objectives of cash-less situation (Gayathri, 2017). Along with the advantages, there have been shortcomings of using online interface in banking systems as well (Vinoth et al., 2022).Thus, considering the uses of innovative technologies in banking processes, the following hypotheses has been proposed:

H0. Null hypothesis taken that digital innovation mode of banking is not providing safe and secure banking service to their esteemed customer.

H1. There is need for use of digital innovation mode of banking system for a better banking service in Fin-Tech areas of banking service.

Research Methodology

In the pursuance of expanding the scope of innovations in the banking sector, typically in the Indian context, the methods considered for the said purpose remain mostly as exploratory in nature and primarily based on secondary data. Along with the review of literature, the relevant information was collected from various sources like bank documents, RBI Working Group Reports, RBI Bulletin, RBI Annual Reports, reports published by various sites of Government of India and various other websites. For present research work, various banking journals and other financial newspapers have also been referred. Various studies on this area by several research agencies have also been considered. Following phenomena are described to make conclusive statements in the end of this study.

Innovation

Innovation is a crucial component for entities to generate value and offer competitive benefits (Porter & Kramer, 2018). Organisations adopt innovative models to re-engineer their operations and increase their competitive strengths (Spender et al., 2017). Competitive advantage can be maintained by embracing innovation. It envisages introduction of novel methods and new techniques to result in an extraordinary way expressed in services and products of superior quality mainly because of revamped processes and parameters (Ambos & Tatarinov, 2022).

Digital Banking: The Way Forward

So far as the word digital banking is concerned, in simple terms, it can be defined as digitalisation of various traditional banking operations and performance and processes that were earlier available to the customers by visit to the bank's branch or ATM only. As per Payments and Settlement Act, 2007, the definition of digital payments includes consideration of transferring funds electronically post consent, instruction and initiation from the concerned person to make banking transactions with the help of debit or credit to bank account through electronic, online, internet, mobile apps. It can also include ATM, point of sale, card payments, direct deposits, transfers and withdrawal of funds as well. Digital banking activities include online account/fixed deposit opening, funds transfer, credit card payments, request for cheque book, change/block pin number, loan application, bill payment and investments (Larsson & Viitaoja, 2017).

Digitalisation of Banking: History and Evolution

In the 1960s, banks started offering the cards and services in the form of ATMs thereby introducing the digital banking in the world. Developments of World Wide Web and internet banking have also seen the simultaneous evolution of digital banking (Shaikh et al., 2017). Online banking has emerged in 1990s. At that time, it was an idea, taking into consideration the security and safety of customer financial data. The United States was the first country in the world to start online banking in October 1994 (Raskin & Yermack, 2018). In India, the banking services have seen a revolution in a title called Infinity from the House of ICICI Bank in the year 1997. Slowly and steadily, Indian consumers have familiarised themselves with the innovative and digital tools offered by various banks synchronised with global banking systems which later advanced itself by offering the consumers the ease of omnichannel instead of earlier and traditional single channels of operations. The evolution of digital banking innovations can be understood from the four phases as cited below.

- *Phase – 1* (1998–2002): E-Banking, where there was a single touch point both for customers and bank.
- *Phase – 2* (2003–2008): Multichannel Integration, where customers got to use brand through multiple touch points with bank using advanced communication.
- *Phase – 3* (2009–2014): Omnichannel, where the concerned bank got unified view of customer, and the customer enjoyed a holistic brand experience.
- *Phase – 4* (From 2015–till date): Internet of Everything, where the focus is on the logic of market of one customer centricity.

Table 11.1. Evolution of Digital Banking in India.

1980	• Mechanisation and computerisation of processes related to payment system • Standardisation of cheques, encoders, MICR implementation and minimal use of bank draughts and cheques
1990	• Computerisation of branches, expansion of products and services, connectivity with other branches • Core banking systems, ATM's and electronic funds transfer, online banking
2010	• Internet banking, mobile banking, Real Time Gross Settlement (RTGS), National Electronic Funds Transfer (NEFT) and National Electronic Clearing Services (NECS)
2011	• Emerging financial technology (Fin-Tech), e-collaborations with Fin-Tech and adoption of new technology, biometrics and cheque truncation systems
2012	• Initiatives from NPCI in the form of Rupay (an Indian option to VISA and Master card) and with the help of National Automated Clearing House (NACH)
2013	• Aadhar Enabled Payment System (AEPS)
2017	• Initiative from NPCI in the form of bharat QR and Master card, visa – Integrated payment System – money transferred directly in user's linked account
2020	• Availability of NEFT on a 24 × 7 × 365 basis, i.e. 16.12.2019

Source: compiled by authors.

In the Indian context, the digital banking evolution can be understood even much before 1997 episode of ICICI Bank (Table 11.1).

The banking system in India has witnessed radical transformation from the conventional or traditional banking system to electronic banking system of convenience (Dandona et al., 2017). Payment systems in India keep on evolving from manual to electronic to digital banking with new emerging technologies and innovations. It started with 1980s with the need of computerisation, electronic payment systems in 2010 and move on to digital and Fin-Tech E-collaboration. The Indian Banking and Payment System is witnessing various new emerging technologies like block chain, artificial intelligence (AI), robotic process automation (RPA), biometrics, chatbots, machine learning and use of big data and predictive analysis offered by the Fin-Tech companies (Trivedi, 2019).

Emerging Technologies

Artificial Intelligence (AI): AI facilitates increased revenue, reduced costs, better compliance and higher profits. A Report by Accenture (2018) has pointed out that AI has the potential to add USD 957 billion by 2035 (1.3% of GDP) to the Indian economy. Thus, an illustrative use of AI by banks operating in India can be a real insight provider (Table 11.2).

Apart from this, there are several innovative technologies cited below used for banking services in the revamping process of economic factors.

- *Chatbots:* It facilitates quicker resolution of customer related issues. It is more effective than traditional methods like email, phone etc.
- *Big Data:* Big data technology aids in analysis, processing of various transactions and data for extracting crucial information for sustaining competitive advantage. It helps in recognising recent market movements and reorganising operational issues and process to manage risks.
- *Blockchain Technology:* It holds the potential to influence various banking transactions.
- *Cyber Security:* Sometimes, online transactions are susceptible to risk of data breach. Hence, banks need to strengthen cyber security in banking processes. Cyber security in banking transactions helps in protecting customer asset (Patnaik, 2022).
- *Robotic Process Automation (RPA):* RPA has streamlined back office processes which used to be performed by bank employees. With the shift from man to machine, banks have witnessed improvement in efficiency, cost reduction and manpower-related issues (Agarwal & Agarwal, 2017).
- *Cloud Computing:* By adopting cloud computing, services like mobile banking, card management, etc. are handled properly. Productivity, performance and profitability can be improved by cloud computing (Masdari et al., 2016). National Association of Software and Service Companies (NASSCOM) reports that the cloud market in India is also expanding and expected to grow to $7.1 billion by 2022. State Bank of India has collaborated with Oracle, and Bank of Baroda has collaborated with IBM for acceleration of Cloud Innovation in their respective Banks.
- *Distributed Ledger Technology (DLT):* A distributed ledger is a database allowing recording of the transaction of assets thus helping the efficiency of traditional databases.
- *Predictive Analytics:* Massively used in several industries and disciplines, such as insurance, banking and marketing. Predictive analytics can provide a holistic view in the customer's journey with the bank and further help strengthen the relationship (Wang et al., 2018). Banks need to embrace the capabilities of data and analytics to improve risk modelling and fraud detection.
- *Machine Learning:* This can be used by banks for risk prediction, risk prevention, fraud detection, investments, investment modelling customer services and customer modelling, etc. AI application is adopted in machine learning (Galbusera et al., 2019).

Table 11.2. Illustrative Use of Artificial Intelligence (AI) by Banks Operating in India.

Name of Banks	Number of Digital App Using	Use of AI	Percentage
State Bank of India	07	• Partnered with Hitachi for payment services that will use the AI technology of Hitachi for SBI payment services • Utilising IBM Watson to perform a variety of jobs • AI-based solution presently in use developed by Chapdex	24.28
Bank of Baroda	02	• Using AI-empowered robot 'Baroda Brainy' • Using AI solution by Quadra tyx	8.70
Allahabad Bank	01	Using AI-enabled app 'emPower' for e-commerce payments	4.35
Canara Bank	01	Using humanoid robot Mitra and Candi	4.35
ICICI Bank	03	• Using iPal, an AI-based chatbot • AI features such as facial and voice recognition, bots, etc. are being leveraged • Deployed robotics software to ease over 200 of its processes	13.58
HDFC Bank	02	• Launched IRA 2.0, an interactive humanoid • 'Eva' an AI-based chatbot, developed by Sense forth AI research	8.70
YES Bank	02	• Using YES TAG • Using AI solution by Quadra tyx	8.70
Axis Bank	03	Launched an AI-enabled app developed by Active AI	13.58
Kotak Mahindra Bank	01	Using AI solution by Quadrat yx	4.35
UCO Bank	01	Using AI solution by Quadrat yx	4.35
Total Banks – 10	**23**		**100%**

Source: Compiled by authors.

Challenges and Opportunities in Implementation of Digital Innovations

- *Sustainable Competitive Advantage:* The execution process of digital innovations in Indian banks confronts the challenges of sustainability and continuity. Customer education and financial literacy should be continued to make more people digitally inclusive (Gupta & Kinange, 2016).
- *Customer Retention:* It has become another important challenge in today's post-loyalty world. Consumers' demands are changing in this tech savvy and highly digital era as they are not tied up with traditional banks. Technology giants are offering superior digital offerings like Amazon, Face book, Google to attract the customers. Banks need to innovate or partner with them (Rikap & Lundvall, 2022).
- *Digital Native, Intelligent, Social, Connected (DISC) Approach:* needs to be adopted by the banks today to understand customer context and provide fresh, agile and relevant digital solutions to consolidate their digital leadership. Merchant acceptance and infrastructure need to be increased both in rural and urban space (Gochhwal, 2017).
- *Skilled Resources:* Automation in banking process through digitalisation brought about sociological challenges. Banks need to understand the impact on jobs and train the workforce with new IT skills (Ocen et al., 2017).
- *Cyber Security Risks:* The Centre for Software and IT Management (CSITM) in their study conducted at IIM Bangalore has pointed cyber security risks as the prime challenge in banking reforms through digital platforms. In their study, they have identified the potential risks in digital wallets, specific bank's app for account holders, direct link with user's bank and basic Unstructured Supplementary Service Data (USSD) services (Malik & Annuar, 2021). Other types of security risks are phishing, vishing, hacking, credit card frauds, cloning, etc.
- *New Innovative Product Design:* Modern customers are aware of the benefits and ready for new digital solutions. Banks need to focus more on product design, service delivery and customer support (Drasch et al., 2018). Bharat Bill Payment, Interbank Web based Platform, E-mandate part of NACH and Digital platform for high-value electronic transactions are the proposed new launches by NPCI.
- *Better Regulatory Environment:* Data Connectivity and the Spread of Smart phones have improved the digital ecosystem by providing an efficient and effective regulatory environment (Sussan & Acs, 2017).
- *Leveraging the Power of Social Media:* Social Media Technology, Digital Assistants and third party channels like Facebook, Twitter for leveraging internal capabilities are likely to become the primary channels by 2022 apart from online and internet banking (Campbell et al., 2020).

Hypothesis Testing

In the section of Hypothesis Testing, the Response model has been taken for justifying the hypothesis. For the said purpose, 10 banks of different branches with 500 customers were taken from Bhubaneswar, the capital city of Odisha, an eastern state in India (each with 50 respondents based on gender wise analysis, as well as on different professions like business, cultivator, government service, private service, company employees, etc.). After obtaining the data, it was presented in appropriate tables (Tables 11.3 and 11.4) with proper classifications used with an eye on accurate analysis and interpretation thereon.

As per the aforesaid data table, mean value for female customer is 42.0 and male customer is 58.0 and the mean difference in between is 16. 0, and the number of banks is 10d.f is ($N - 1 = 09$). It is proved that more customers preferred the use of digital innovation banking system. The significance level at 0.1 level is 0.8186 and 0.5 level is 0.8289, the obtained data is more than the table value and therefore the use of AI in digital innovation in banking sector is justified. This rejects the null hypothesis.

Findings of the Study

With a thorough analysis of earlier studies followed by the hands on study taken on the transformation process in the economic scenario because of digital intervention in banks, the following findings came to the fore:

- Digital innovations help in reducing operating costs and widening the customer base.
- Reports can be generated and analysed for various purposes at different point of time.
- It is safer way to handle financial transactions and to prevent misuse in DBT under Digital Banking.

Suggestive Remarks

With all the limitations in the current study, the results obtained in the process that lead to the recommendations common to the banking practices due to innovations adopted by the system can be cited as given below.

- Loss of data can be avoided by employing well-trained IT experts.
- Tough laws should be enacted for cyberattack.
- Technology should be developed and expanded so that the people from remote areas can also take advantages of it.

Conclusion and Future Implications

From the analysis of developments as well as advancements of innovations in banking practices with an aim to revamp the economic parameters in a digital environment, the following areas can be concluded and kept for further study in the years to come.

Table 11.3. Usage by Bank Customers.

		No Respondents			Use of digital Innovation App		Mean Value		
Serial No	**Name of Banks**	**Male**	**Female**	**Total Respondent's**	**Yes**	**No**	**M**	**F**	**Percentage**
1	State Bank of India	30	20	50	34	16	68.0	32.0	100%
2	Bank of Baroda	25	25	50	32	18	64.0	36.0	100%
3	Allahabad Bank	28	22	50	31	19	62.0	38.0	100%
4	Canara Bank	35	15	50	28	22	56.0	44.0	100%
5	ICICI Bank	32	18	50	32	18	64.0	36.0	100%
6	HDFC Bank	23	27	50	34	16	68.0	32.0	100%
7	YES Bank	36	16	50	31	19	62.0	38.0	100%
8	Axis Bank	32	18	50	27	23	54.0	46.0	100%
9	Kotak Mahindra Bank	26	24	50	34	16	68.0	32.0	100%
10	UCO Bank	25	25	50	26	24	52.0	48.0	100%
	Total Bank-10	290	210	Total-500	309	191	618	382	1,000

Source: Analysed by authors.

Table 11.4. Descriptive Statistical Representation.

Number of Banks	10	Mean Value	MD	Average MD	% Response Positive	% Response Negative
Number of respondents (F)	210	42.0	−8.0	16.0	61.8	38.2
Number of respondents (M)	290	58.0	+8.0			
Total number of respondents	500					

Source: Analysed by authors.

- The rising trends in adoption of digital innovations and new Fin-Tech emerging products. While there will always be challenges, opportunities also exist for those banks and financial institutions who are ready to innovate and offer more digital financial products to the customer.
- The Digital Payment Ecosystem with Fin-Tech collaboration and global technological giants are acting as aggregators for the retail transactions.
- Measurement of digital payments should be carried out at regular interval to study and monitor the progress.
- The new emerging financial technologies in Indian Payment System will continue to be evolving, reaching global heights with regulatory compliance and risk management.
- To understand the pace and quality with which banks are moving towards technology-intensive customer services under the aegis of various digital India programmes.
- By digital technology opportunities and challenges, the banking industry is rising along with digital innovation keeping in pace with the popularity it gained during COVID era and beyond.

References

Agarwal, H., & Agarwal, R. (2017). First industrial revolution and second industrial revolution: Technological differences and the differences in banking and financing of the firms. *Saudi Journal of Humanities and Social Sciences*, *2*(11), 1062–1066.

Ambos, T. C., & Tatarinov, K. (2022). Building responsible innovation in international organizations through intrapreneurship. *Journal of Management Studies*, *59*(1), 92–125.

Andrew, M. S. A. (2021). Digital payments, e-commerce and entrepreneurship. *The New Era of Digital Payments*, *42*.

Campbell, C., Sands, S., Ferraro, C., Tsao, H. Y. J., & Mavrommatis, A. (2020). From data to action: How marketers can leverage AI. *Business Horizons*, *63*(2), 227–243.

Dandona, L., Dandona, R., Kumar, G. A., Shukla, D. K., Paul, V. K., Balakrishnan, K., & Thakur, J. S. (2017). Nations within a nation: Variations in epidemiological transition across the states of India, 1990–2016 in the global burden of disease study. *The Lancet*, *390*(10111), 2437–2460.

Drasch, B. J., Schweizer, A., & Urbach, N. (2018). Integrating the 'Troublemakers': A taxonomy for cooperation between banks and fintechs. *Journal of Economics and Business*, *100*, 26–42.

Galbusera, F., Casaroli, G., & Bassani, T. (2019). Artificial intelligence and machine learning in spine research. *JOR spine*, *2*(1), e1044.

Gayathri, G. (2017). A study about demonetisation impact and its objectives. *Asian Journal of Development Matters*, *11*(1), 66–73.

Gochhwal, R. (2017). Unified payment interface—an advancement in payment systems. *American Journal of Industrial and Business Management*, *7*(10), 1174–1191.

Gupta, P. K., & Kinange, D. U. (2016). A study of financial literacy and its impact on customer satisfaction with special reference to banks of Bagalkot District. *International Journal of Management*, *7*(6), 43–50.

Heim, I. (2019). Definiteness and indefiniteness. In *Semantics: Noun phrases and verb phrases* (pp. 33–69). De Gruyter Mouton.

Hempel, C., & Hamm, U. (2016). Local and/or organic: A study on consumer preferences for organic food and food from different origins. *International Journal of Consumer Studies*, *40*(6), 732–741.

Islam, M. T., & Hasan, M. T. (2016). Corporate social responsibility of commercial Bank in Bangladesh: A comparative study on nationalized and private banks. *Asian Business Review*, *6*(1), 4–34.

Kalyani, P. (2016). An empirical study about the awareness of paperless E-currency transaction like E-wallet using ICT in the youth of India. *Journal of Management Engineering and Information Technology (JMEIT)*, *3*(3), 18–42.

Kaur, D., Sahdev, S. L., Sharma, D., & Siddiqui, L. (2020). Banking 4.0: 'the influence of artificial intelligence on the banking industry & how ai is changing the face of modern day banks. *International Journal of Management*, *11*(6).

Kumar, V. S., Dharmender, G., & Prasad, S. R. (2022). Magnitude of IT in Indian banking industry. *SpecialusisUgdymas*, *1*(43), 1629–1639.

Kuncoro, W., & Suriani, W. O. (2018). Achieving sustainable competitive advantage through product innovation and market driving. *Asia Pacific Management Review*, *23*(3), 186–192.

Larsson, A., & Viitaoja, Y. (2017). Building customer loyalty in digital banking: A study of bank staff's perspectives on the challenges of digital CRM and loyalty. *International Journal of Bank Marketing*, *35*(6), 858–877.

Malik, A. N. A., & Annuar, S. N. S. (2021). The effect of perceived usefulness, perceived ease of use, reward, and perceived risk toward e-wallet usage intention. In *Eurasian business and economics perspectives: Proceedings of the 30th Eurasia business and economics Society Conference* (pp. 115–130). Springer International Publishing.

Masdari, M., Nabavi, S. S., & Ahmadi, V. (2016). An overview of virtual machine placement schemes in cloud computing. *Journal of Network and Computer Applications*, *66*, 106–127.

Ocen, E., Francis, K., & Angundaru, G. (2017). The role of training in building employee commitment: The mediating effect of job satisfaction. *European Journal of Training and Development*, *41*(9), 742–757.

Patnaik, R. (2022). Data privacy policy: Cyber security implications on retail operations. In *Cross-industry applications of cyber security frameworks* (pp. 159–181). IGI Global.

Perera, A. S. A. (2018). The factors influencing on the customer adoption of internet banking system special reference to the Sampath Bank in Colombo district. *International Journal of Scientific and Research Publications*, *8*(2), 83–107.

Porter, M. E., & Kramer, M. R. (2018). Creating shared value: How to reinvent capitalism—and unleash a wave of innovation and growth. In *Managing sustainable business: An executive education case and textbook* (pp. 323–346). Springer Netherlands.

Raskin, M., & Yermack, D. (2018). Digital currencies, decentralized ledgers and the future of central banking. In *Research handbook on central banking* (pp. 474–486). Edward Elgar Publishing.

Rikap, C., & Lundvall, B. Å. (2022). Big tech, knowledge predation and the implications for development. *Innovation and Development*, *12*(3), 389–416.

Scott, S. V., Van Reenen, J., & Zachariadis, M. (2017). The long-term effect of digital innovation on bank performance: An empirical study of SWIFT adoption in financial services. *Research Policy*, *46*(5), 984–1004.

Shaikh, A. A., Glavee-Geo, R., & Karjaluoto, H. (2017). Exploring the nexus between financial sector reforms and the emergence of digital banking culture–Evidences from a developing country. *Research in International Business and Finance*, *42*, 1030–1039.

Spender, J. C., Corvello, V., Grimaldi, M., & Rippa, P. (2017). Startups and open innovation: A review of the literature. *European Journal of Innovation Management*, *20*(1), 4–30.

Sussan, F., & Acs, Z. J. (2017). The digital entrepreneurial ecosystem. *Small Business Economics*, *49*, 55–73.

Trivedi, J. (2019). Examining the customer experience of using banking chatbots and its impact on brand love: The moderating role of perceived risk. *Journal of Internet Commerce*, *18*(1), 91–111.

Vinoth, S., Vemula, H. L., Haralayya, B., Mamgain, P., Hasan, M. F., & Naved, M. (2022). Application of cloud computing in banking and e-commerce and related security threats. *Materials Today: Proceedings*, *51*, 2172–2175.

Wang, Y., Kung, L., & Byrd, T. A. (2018). Big data analytics: Understanding its capabilities and potential benefits for healthcare organizations. *Technological Forecasting and Social Change*, *126*, 3–13.

Chapter 12

Sustainable Poverty Reduction Model: Need-Surveillance and Psycho-Social Support Practices Among Migrant Workforce

Tushar Soubhari[a], *Sudhansu Sekhar Nanda*[b] *and Mohd Asif Shah*[c]

[a]NSS College, India
[b]Sri Sri University, India
[c]Kebri Dehar University, Ethiopia

Abstract

Migrants have been posed with less familiarity in their new environment during COVID times, faced with various social, psychological and emotional traumas. Research indicates that they may have been originating from apprehension of being abandoned by their neighbours. Most of them were precarious with little wages, competing for their basic need fulfilment, putting them under more mental stress. Looking forward to the ancient principle, '*Athithi Devo Bhavah*' (Visitors are Gods), and immediate response, measures were taken to promote community shelters and kitchens, maintaining social distancing and ensuring physical safety. The governments of different countries took proactive initiatives to study and assess their needs. The study here includes the cases being evaluated regarding migrants' need for surveillance and psycho social support given by the government and non-profit associations during the pandemic at the global level. Remarkably, certain countries proved the working of their sustainable poverty reduction model by evaluating various factors. The study started by introducing who migrants were, diagnosing their problems faced during the pandemic, how Sustainable Development Goals can be implemented and various measures taken at government and institutional levels to protect the migrant workforce.

Understanding the Multi-Dimensional Nature of Poverty, 227–253

Published under exclusive licence by Emerald Publishing Limited
doi:10.1108/978-1-83753-292-620241012

Keywords: Migrant workforce; stress; sustainable poverty reduction; need surveillance; psycho-social support

Introduction

Poverty eradication is a global priority after the economic and social impacts of the COVID-19 outbreak, but it is of utmost importance in rural areas. Rural areas will play an important role in bringing about the ultimate success of the Sustainable Development Goals (SDGs), given that about 80% of the world's 734 million extremely poor people reside in rural areas, and that about 70% of the SDGs targets relate to rural areas achieving the 2030 Agenda. The World Bank estimates that as many as 100 million people will be living in extreme poverty as a direct result of the COVID-19 problem by the end of 2020. There was a pronounced effect on rural people's ability to make a living, their food intake and their sense of safety in the face of the pandemic because of their lack of preparation and resilience.

It was predicted that millions of migrants, whose livelihoods were deemed to be threatened by internal displacement and lockdown measures, would see a decline in food security and nutrition as a result of income shocks. Without adequate social protections, many families may be compelled to resort to coping strategies that have long-term, detrimental effects, such as reducing the variety or quantity of food consumed, selling assets, taking children out of school and increasing child labour. Cutting back on schooling could prevent young people from learning the skills they will need to land good jobs in the future.

In keeping with the spirit of the 2030 Agenda for Sustainable Development and its central tenet of 'leaving no one behind', it is imperative that the most vulnerable individuals be given top priority in all recovery policies and initiatives, both short term and long term. Timely planning and fostering an all-inclusive socio-economic recovery process in emerging nations are two of the programme's primary goals. Considering countries' varied requirements and appropriately resolving the limitations they have faced since the spread of COVID-19, help has been provided for recovery policies, initiatives and tools.

WHO Is a Migrant?

A Migrant is defined as a person who moves across international borders or within a state away from their home location irrespective of the causes for their movement; according to the UN Migration Agency (International Organisation for Migration – IOM). Recently, migrants from various states and countries gained momentum in their residential importance in the search for better jobs, relearning new skills matching their potential, acculturation, social upliftment, housing, social adjustment and saving families from the hoarded crisis.

Problems Identified by Migrants During COVID Times

Several reasons underlie for migrant labourers' stress levels to increase during COVID times, especially vulnerable to certain queries like where to live? Where to work? Where to depend for health and education? Where to improve savings and

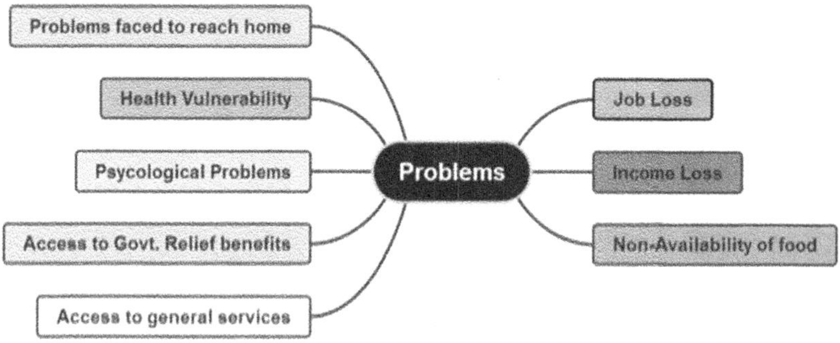

Fig. 12.1. Shows Problems Faced by Migrants During COVID Times. *Source:* Created by authors for the study purpose.

create access to insurance? Since time immemorial, migrants have been quenching hunger and thirst for poverty. Merely, money does not suffice in need fulfilment towards lowering the poverty level; rather, studies showed that it must be cured from the base level pointing to cure the psychological problems of labourers. Fig. 12.1 shown below highlights the different issues underlying the root cause for their mental tension during COVID times.

Rising issues stimulated individuals, institutions (be they public or private) and social groups to contribute following the SDGs priorities. These goals were reported in the United Nations Sustainable Development Report, which were modified and sequenced for the study as follows (as shown in Fig. 12.2):

Modus-Operandi of Making SDG a Grand Success

Attempts of the UN have never gone in vain since the 17 SDGs have been predicting a sure success to achieve sustainable development by ensuring 'No hunger, No Poverty' by 2030. The United Nations Development Programme (UNDP) hosted the support to help the COVID-19-affected people for social and economic recovery, specifically pooling funds named 'United Nations COVID-19 Response and Recovery Fund' for the lower- and middle-income countries.

Addressing the risky pandemic effects on the food and agricultural sector, the Food and Agricultural Organization (FAO) assisted the affected countries with food assistance to over 87 million vulnerable people across the world. They urged these countries to:

- Meet the adequate and immediate needs for food.
- Boosting social welfare programmes
- Proceed with global food trade.
- Proceed with the domestic supply chain.
- Support small farmers to increase food production.

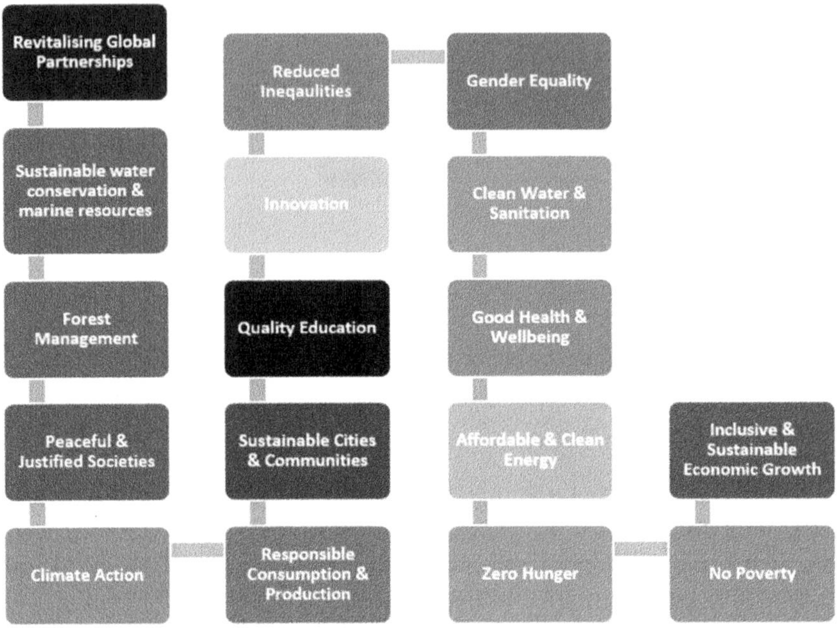

Fig. 12.2. Shows the Sequential Steps Towards Achieving SDG.
Source: Modified by authors for the study purpose based on the SDG Report of the United Nations.

Keeping in mind the strategic updates looking for guidance towards public health response and the fight against the adverse effects of the pandemic, the World Health Organization (WHO) accelerated research for inventing vaccines and maintaining the COVID-19 Solidarity Response Fund via donations. Psychological issues of migrant labourers were asked to be diagnosed at the government level through telephonic counselling, uplifting their mental health. Various public health measures and global efforts taken by the WHO to combat COVID-19 have been produced in the Strategic Preparedness and Response Plan.

Additionally, in reaction to the worldwide trend of national and localised institution closures, UNESCO organised a series of events. With the help of civil society organisations, media and IT partners, they developed and deployed a number of cutting-edge solutions to address insufficiencies in content and connectivity and to promote equal access to educational opportunities. In particular, the goal of this effort was to help countries mobilise resources and implement innovative and context-appropriate solutions, guarantee universal access to these solutions, ensure coordinated responses that don't duplicate existing efforts and make it easier for students to return to school, thereby lowering dropout rates.

Gender-based violence is on the rise which needs to be curbed. It came as a product of the COVID-19 crisis. The rapid reaction was developed by UN Women to help close the gender gap in areas such as social protection and economic stimulus packages, as well as response planning and decision-making.

In response to the pandemic outbreak, the IOM adjusted its water, sanitation and health (WASH) services to prevent the spread of further epidemics. The UN-Habitat worked with their partners repeatedly emphasising handwashing during informal settings. Also, the United Nations International Children's Emergency Fund (UNICEF) checked attempts to provide the best quality water, sanitation and health facilities for the children in slum areas. Responding to the pandemic emergency, the UN Secretary-General for Sustainable Energy prioritised the use of clean energy solutions, connecting vulnerable consumers and preparing for sustainable economic recovery via reliable and sufficient energy production. In fact, the pandemic awakened the need for becoming more mindful in using available resources more mindfully and indeed reduced the number of carbon footprints in society. The most recent reports from the United Nations Framework Convention on Climate Change (UNFCCC) have proven this to be the case. Therefore, the SDG made it possible to bring attention to the pressing issue of creating more environmentally friendly employment opportunities while also fostering inclusive and long-term growth.

Literature Review

Migrant labour is a critical component of many economies worldwide, contributing significantly to economic growth and development. However, the well-being and poverty status of the migrant workforce often remain a concern due to their vulnerability to exploitation, limited access to social services and psycho-social challenges. This literature review examines studies and research focused on sustainable poverty reduction models that incorporate need surveillance and psycho-social support practices for migrant workers. The scope for conducting this study in purview to various studies conducted in the same area accounts for various reasons being identified.

(1) Migrant Workforce and Poverty:

- Discuss the socio-economic conditions of migrant workers and their susceptibility to poverty.
- Explore how migration affects the poverty status of individuals and families.
- Examine the different factors contributing to the vulnerability of migrant workers to poverty, such as low wages, job insecurity and lack of social protection.

(2) Need-Surveillance for Migrant Workers:

- Define and describe the concept of need surveillance in the context of migrant labour.

- Explore the role of need surveillance in identifying the specific needs and challenges faced by migrant workers.
- Highlight the methodologies and tools used for effective need surveillance among migrant populations.

(3) Psycho-Social Support Practices:

- Investigate the importance of psycho-social support for migrant workers' well-being.
- Examine various psycho-social support interventions and programmes tailored for migrant workers.
- Analyse the impact of psycho-social support on reducing poverty and improving the overall quality of life for migrant workers.

(4) Sustainable Poverty Reduction Models:

- Review existing sustainable poverty reduction models that integrate need surveillance and psycho-social support for migrant workers.
- Identify successful case studies or initiatives that have effectively reduced poverty among migrant labourers.
- Evaluate the long-term sustainability of these models and their potential for replication in different contexts.

(5) Challenges and Gaps in Research:

- Discuss the challenges researchers face when studying migrant workers' poverty reduction.
- Highlight gaps in the literature, including regions or types of migration that are under-represented in current research.
- Identify areas where further research is needed to develop more effective poverty reduction models.

(6) Policy Implications:

- Explore the policy implications of the findings in the reviewed literature.
- Discuss how governments, NGOs and international organisations can implement policies and programmes that address the needs of migrant workers and contribute to sustainable poverty reduction.

Having identified the many outcomes expected through this study, the bibliometric analysis was used to design Fig. 12.3 as shown below, collected from 181 documents from the SCOPUS Database and grouped under three different clusters. The blue cluster represents most of the studies carried out in the area of sustainability and migrant workforce worldwide. Connected works were even carried out in different contexts showing different variants or applications in the fields of medicine, agriculture, business and finance, as depicted in the green cluster. The latest studies were found quoted citing studies majorly from the country contexts of China, the United Kingdom and the United States, followed by Australia, Canada, Germany, India and Vietnam. They were depicted as red clusters.

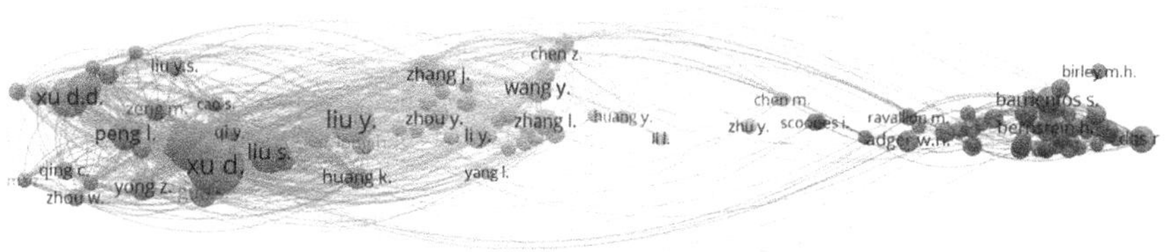

Fig. 12.3. Representing the Authors' Co-citations in the Area Being Studied. *Source:* Created by authors using Vosviewer Software based on cited literature work.

The Commendable Efforts Towards Supporting Migrants at Various Levels

(1) Regional and Countrywise Focus on COVID-19 Resilient Programmes by Fao:

- economic empowerment for rural women;
- expansion of short- and long-term social safety systems for rural residents;
- fortification of rural institutions and smallholder producer associations;
- stop the use of children as labourers in line with the Agenda 2063 of the African Union.

  Targeted countries: Botswana, Burkina Faso, Burundi, Cabo Verde, Cameroon, the Central African Republic, Chad, Comoros, Côte d'Ivoire, the Democratic Republic of the Congo, Eswatini, Ethiopia, the Gambia, Guinea-Bissau, Ghana, Kenya, Lesotho, Madagascar, Malawi, Mali, Mauritius, Niger, Rwanda, São Tomé and Príncipe, Senegal, Seychelles, Sierra Leone, Somalia, South Sudan, Sudan, Tanzania, Togo, Uganda, Zambia and Zimbabwe.

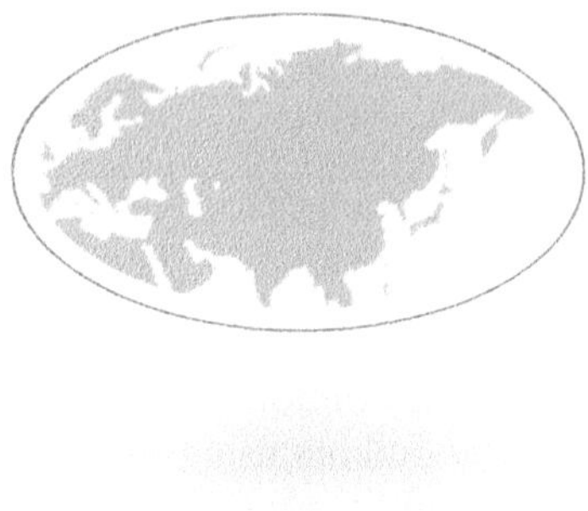

- Refugees in Afghanistan, Bangladesh and Pakistan must be safeguarded.
- Invest in expanding women's and small farmers' access to digital technology.
- Reduce reliance on child labour and empower women in rural areas.
- Regulate out-migration to cities and vice versa.
- Increase social safety nets and support for small businesses.
- And shield farmers from the effects of the weather, the economy and the environment.

- Aid the region's poorest nations (Albania, Armenia, Bosnia and Herzegovina, Kyrgyzstan, Moldova and Tajikistan) by investing in their food security, extension and advisory services, digitisation, migration, social protection and youth and female empowerment.

- Bolivia, Colombia, the Dominican Republic, Eastern Caribbean, Guatemala, Ecuador, El Salvador, Guyana, Haiti, Honduras, Jamaica, Nicaragua, Paraguay and Peru rural institutions and producers' organisations, particularly in the domains of forest and farm production.

(2) Pro-Migrants' Welfare-Based Need Fulfilment Approaches in India

- Kerala Poverty Alleviation Model:
  - *Early Preparation was the key:* The Chinese government initiated an aggressive response to the newly emergent coronavirus disease after hearing rumours of an outbreak in January 2020. The state confirmed the first case of COVID-19 in India on 30 January 2020 and two more instances on 2 and 3 February 2020, causing the government to declare a health emergency. As a first line of defence, we stepped up our screening and surveillance of all arriving Chinese travellers and anyone who had been in contact with them. The Health Department received assistance from the State Emergency Operations Centre (SEOC) and the Kerala State Disaster Management Authority's office. An outbreak of this magnitude calls for a collective and inclusive response.
  - *Health infrastructure investment as a whole:*
    As a response to the pandemic, the state government established at least two COVID-19-specific hospitals in each district, staffed by highly qualified medical professionals from a wide range of fields. To create and evaluate treatment and discharge protocols for each positive case, state and district medical boards were established.
  - *Pre-flight passenger checks:* When the number of reported cases across the country first began to rise, interstate bus and train stations began conducting random screenings of all passengers.
  - *Plan for evaluation and isolation:* The state's response to the rising number of incidents was to beef up its monitoring and control measures. The state's principal line of defence against COVID-19 is extensive contact tracing and testing. Following WHO recommendations, the state conducted extensive tracking, testing and isolation.
  - *Low-intensity interactions with high-risk people:* Owing to the state-wide closure, the authorities established hundreds of temporary shelters for migrant workers and increased the quarantine period to 28 days. In addition, COVID care centres are available in every municipality for the use of visitors and commuters. All certified isolation facilities have sufficient infrastructure to accommodate inhabitants returning from other states. As of the 29th of June 2020, there are 180,617 persons being monitored, 177,955 of whom are in quarantine at home or in an institution and 2,662 of whom are in specially designated isolation facilities. Constant follow-up via phone calls and in-person checks are being made to guarantee compliance.
  - *Giving emotional and social assistance:* The Government of India supports two state-wide telehealth networks: e-sanjeevani for general medicine and

Ottakalla Oppamundu for telepsychiatry. Frontline workers engaged in corona outbreak control activities also have access to a counselling service. As part of its all-inclusive policy, the government has made efforts to better serve people with mental illness, children with special needs, migrant workers and the elderly who live alone. To date, the state's psycho-social services have reached 11,685,500 people, providing them with a supportive setting in which to cope with the strain of the novel coronavirus epidemic.

- *Risk communication:* The 'Break the Chain' awareness campaign successfully spread the word about the value of regular hand washing, maintaining a safe distance when coughing and other measures to prevent the spread of illness. To encourage a positive behavioural shift, hand-washing facilities were placed in highly visible areas, such as public transportation hubs and airports. The Ministry of Health and Family Welfare of Kerala has released the 'Kerala Arogyam' portal, which includes extensive data on the COVID-19 pandemic. The Department of Health and Family Welfare has developed the 'Covid Jagratha' portal and the website for the Directorate of Health Services, both of which contain extensive information on COVID-19.
- *Community engagement programmes:* To teach on critical safety practices as urged by the government during the shutdown, Kudumbashree organised close to 1.9 lacks WhatsApp groups with 22 lakh neighbourhood groups (NHGs). With the help of Kudumbasree and the Local Self Government Department (LSGD), over 8,651,627 free meals have been distributed to construction workers, people in quarantine or isolation, the homeless and others in need. A thoughtful and compassionate response and relief approach are shown in the millions of prepared meals distributed and the free rations provided under the Public Distribution Scheme.

  Grassroot Innovative Strategies of Kudumbashree towards Social Upliftment:

  - Microfinancing.
  - Vanitha Bank for providing loans for new start-ups.
  - Upliftment programmes being promoted (legal literacy classes, talent development of poor children forming *Balasabhas* and *Balasangamam; Ashraya* projects for rehabilitation; *Harithashree* for lease land farming; *Akshaya* project for IT training among women; *Yuvashree* Project for employment upskilling and attitudinal changes).

    This is visually depicted in the following Fig. 12.4:

• Psycho-social Intervention Model adopted in Chandigarh (based on Maslow's Model)

A psychosocial intervention model based on Maslow's Hierarchy of Needs would typically involve the following elements:

- Assessment: Identify the specific needs of individuals or communities within the context of the hierarchy. This involves understanding which level(s) of need are not adequately met.

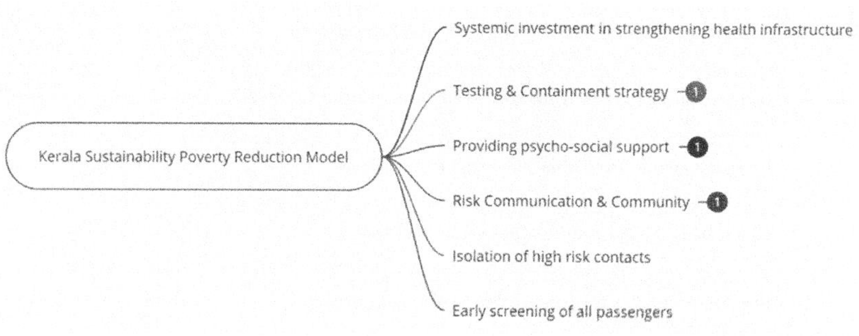

Fig. 12.4. Shows the Kerala Sustainability Poverty Reduction Model. *Source:* Created by authors based on KSDMA Report, 2022.

- Targeted Interventions: Design interventions that address the unmet needs at each level of the hierarchy. For example:
  - For physiological needs, provide access to food, clean water and safe housing.
  - For safety needs, implement safety measures, economic support and healthcare.
  - For love and belongingness, create social support systems and community-building programmes.
  - For esteem needs, offer skill-building opportunities, recognition and empowerment.
  - For self-actualisation, support personal development, education and creativity.
- Holistic Approach: Recognise that individuals and communities may have needs at multiple levels of the hierarchy simultaneously. A holistic approach ensures that interventions address all relevant needs.
- Cultural Sensitivity: Consider cultural factors that may influence how needs are perceived and met. Cultural competence is essential for effective interventions.
- Monitoring and Evaluation: Continuously assess the effectiveness of interventions and adjust them as needed to ensure that individuals and communities progress towards meeting their needs and achieving self-actualisation (as clearly depicted in Fig. 12.5 below).

• Poverty Reduction Initiatives Proposed by Central Govt, India
Initiatives taken by the Government of India represent a multifaceted approach to sustainable poverty reduction, addressing both immediate needs and long-term development goals. It is important to note that the effectiveness of these programmes may vary based on factors such as implementation, monitoring and local context. To be very specific, Fig. 12.6 depicts the effectiveness of Pradhan Mantri Garib Kalyan Yojana.

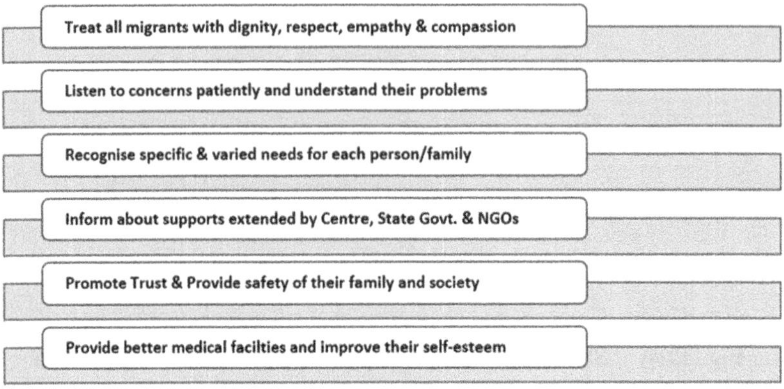

Fig. 12.5. Shows the Psycho-social Efforts of Chandigarh State, India. *Source:* Modified by authors for the study purpose based on Chandigarh Govt. Health Report, 2022.

- Social Responsive Practices in America
  Studies found that the majority of the immigrants to the US were from the parts of South East Asia, coming in venture to solve their personal financial problems. The US government has not done a good job of considering the specifics of various immigrant communities by, for example, addressing their social welfare concerns, accommodating their changing demands with a more adaptable quota system or giving more weight to their professional credentials.
- Govt. Response Towards Migrants' Need Fulfilment
  The response to the migrant crisis during COVID-19 times involved collaborative efforts between the central government and state governments. While these measures were aimed at addressing the immediate needs of migrants, they also highlighted the importance of long-term policies and mechanisms to protect the rights and welfare of this vulnerable population. The pandemic prompted discussions about improving social security nets and labour reforms to better support migrant workers in the future. A peculiar note to this noble activity was picturised in Fig. 12.7 below:
- NGOs and Pandemic Preparedness
  During the COVID-19 pandemic, several NGOs worldwide played a crucial role in pandemic preparedness and response efforts. These NGOs worked in collaboration with governments, international organisations and local communities to address various aspects of the pandemic, including healthcare, humanitarian aid, awareness campaigns and support for vulnerable populations (as shown below in Fig. 12.8).

  Various Indian NGOs which provided relief during COVID-19 are tabulated as follows:

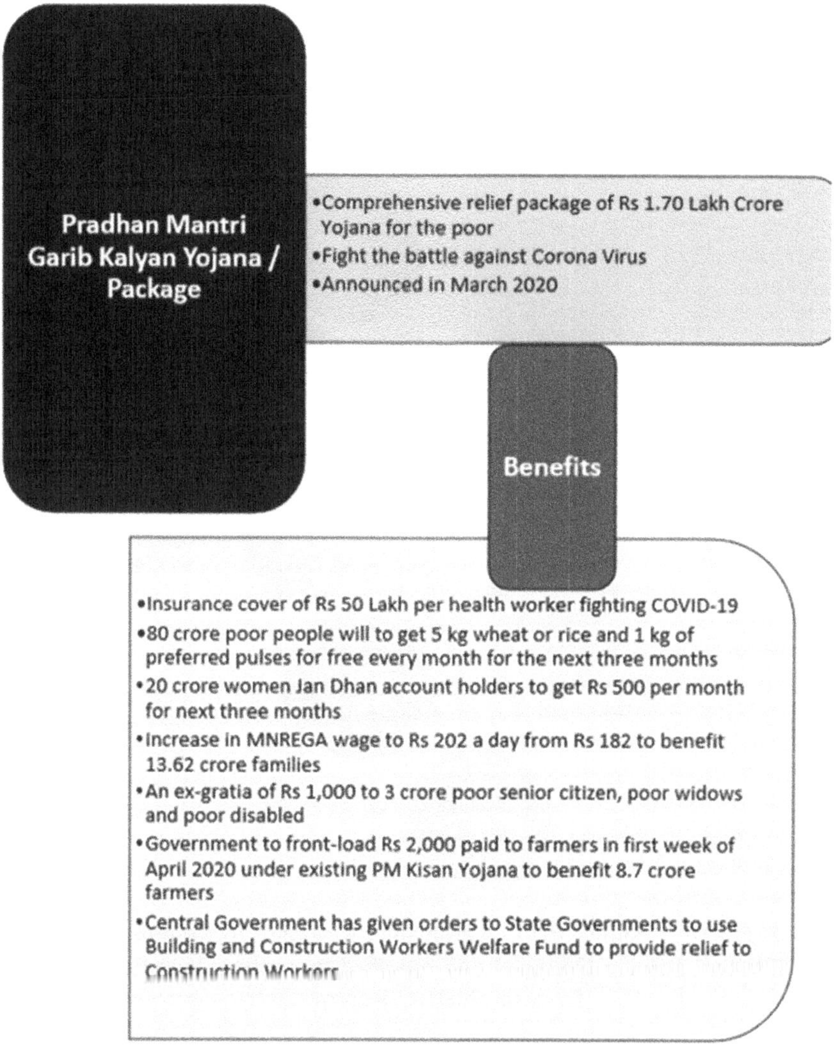

Fig. 12.6. Shows the Success Story of PM Garib Kalyan Yojana.
Source: Modified by authors for study purposes based on the PMGKY Report, MoF, 2022.

During the COVID-19 pandemic, numerous Indian NGOs played a crucial role in providing relief to vulnerable populations, including the provision of food, medical supplies, healthcare services and other forms of assistance. A few examples have been highlighted in Table 12.1 below:

Ways by which NGOs combat COVID-19 at the International level

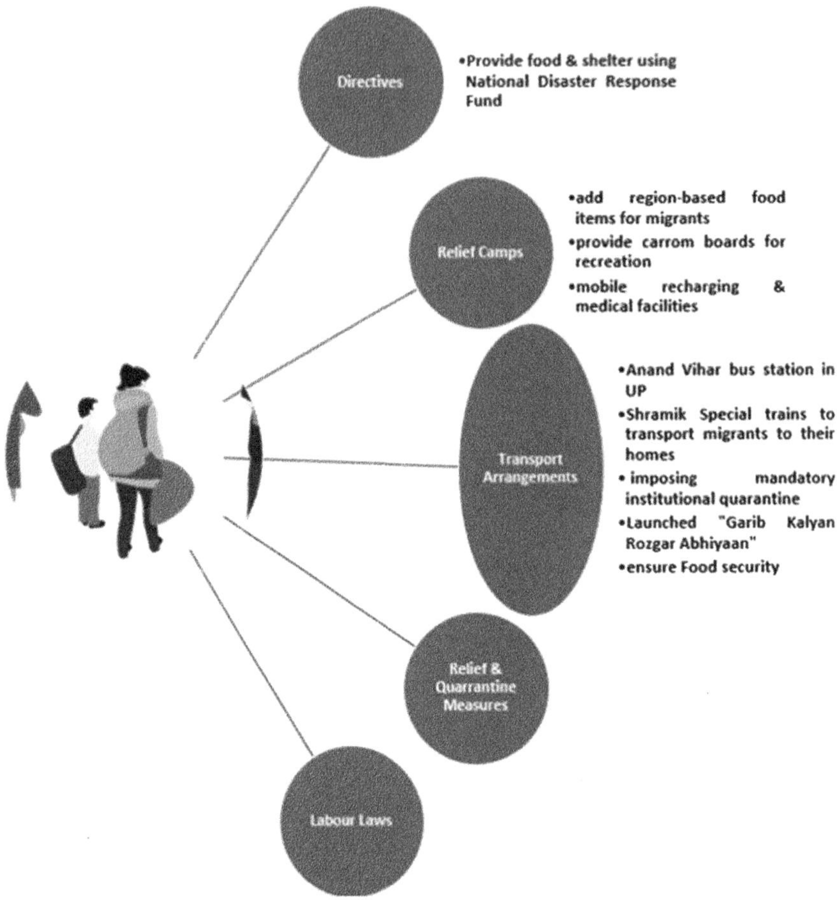

Fig. 12.7. Shows the Government's Response to Migrants' Need Fulfilment. *Source:* Designed and modified by authors based on the data from the NHRC Report, 2022.

- Provision of food, medical aid and personal hygiene kits
  - 'Action Against Hunger': Helping healthcare facilities by spreading information about disease prevention and distributing supplies like antibiotics and personal protective equipment.
- Retaining vital healthcare infrastructure
  - 'Amref Health Africa': It is crucial to maintain essential health services even if the government is closed or partially closed due to the ripple effects of COVID-19 on areas such as maternal and child

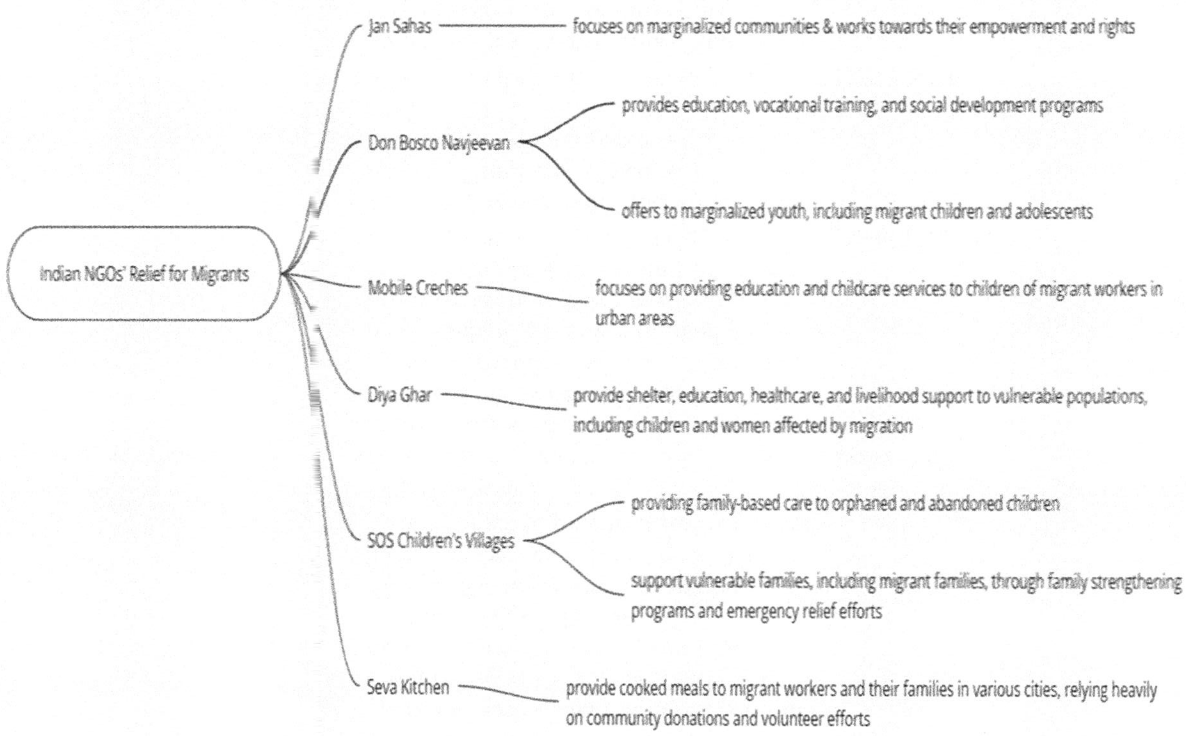

Fig. 12.8. Shows NGOs in India Providing Relief for Migrants. *Source:* Created and modified by authors based on the ICWF Report, 2022.

Table 12.1. Shows Various Indian NGOs Which Provided Relief During COVID-19.

Name of NGO	Summary	Focus Area
Mission Oxygen	*Objective:* Started as an overnight operation across Delhi and the National Capital region to help hospitals that were running low on oxygen after treating COVID-19 patients. *Efforts:* Raising money to import lifesaving concentrators, so we need to plan for their shipment, distribution and amplification.	Delhi NCR
Gautam Gambhir Foundation	*Objective:* Assistance for the disadvantaged, ensuring that frontline healthcare providers are protected. *Efforts:* Providing necessities such as food, shelter, clothing and hygiene products such as N-95 masks, nutritional supplements and bedding.	Delhi NCR
Mazdoor Kitchen	*Objective:* Supply North Delhi's daily wage employees with food and shelter. *Efforts:* Hundreds of people in North Delhi are receiving meals and food packs.	Delhi (North)
Breathe India	A group of IIT alums are collecting money to buy oxygen tanks, and they're getting help from the 'Save Life' foundation.	Delhi NCR

Chikka Foundation	COVID-19 assistance work is being carried out by a UN-accredited NGO by distributing rations, masks and soaps to the impoverished people in Muzaffarpur, as well as providing food and domestic help who have been laid off as a result of the crisis. Promote the value of personal space by spreading the word.	Delhi, Bihar
Enrich Lives Foundation	A philanthropic group, Enrich Lives Foundation (previously Annapurna Movement) *Objectives:* Hunger alleviation, education, women empowerment, poverty alleviation and public health. *Efforts:* Meal distribution, second, the distribution of grocery kits and job placements.	Mumbai
Khaana Chahiye	Started in March 2020. *Objectives:* Help the homeless, migrant workers and daily wage employees in Mumbai get the food they need during the lockdown.	Mumbai
Spoorthi Foundation – Coronavirus Relief Fund	Built a secure refuge where our kids may grow and develop in peace so they can become independent adults with the self-respect and fortitude to stop the pattern.	Telangana

(Continued)

Table 12.1. *(Continued)*

Name of NGO	Summary	Focus Area
	Do away with everything standing in the way of a child reaching his or her full potential. Food, vitamins, minerals, dry fruits and hygiene items like masks, gloves and sanitizers should be made available.	
Feeding from Far	A programme that has been providing food for the homeless and unemployed who have been struggling to sustain themselves throughout the shutdown. Since the first lockdown, we have been able to give approximately 10 lakh meals to the needy through cooked meals and ration kits.	Mumbai, Govandi
Khushiyaan Foundation	Contributed by providing food to those in need through their Roti-Ghar programme on the ground.	Delhi, Bengaluru, Hyderabad, Orissa
Help Now - Ambulance Services	Started by three IIT grads (Aditya Makkar, Shikar Agarwal and Venkatesh Amrutwar), it now operates the largest private ambulance network in the country. To purchase BLS Oxygen Ambulances and over 50,000 personal protective equipment Kits; to establish a secure,	Mumbai, Delhi, Bengaluru, Pune

	round-the-clock logistical network for the movement of COVID patients and suspects, drugs, phlebotomists, healthcare personnel (doctors, nurses) and blood/organs/medical supplies in India.	
Milaap	Crowdfunding site in India with the most users.	Delhi NCR, Hyderabad, Chennai, Bihar, Bengaluru
Sustainable environment and Ecological development Society (SEEDS)	In recognition of SEEDS' outstanding contributions to the field of disaster management and its dedication to helping those in need, the Government of India presented the organisation with the 2021 Subhash Chandra Bose Aapda Prabandhan Puraskar, India's highest civilian honour. Currently attempting to tackle the never-ending COVID-19 challenge. SEEDS is helping by easing the strain on our healthcare system in several ways: Two measures are proposed: 1) increasing the frequency of vaccination drives and 2) creating COVID care centres. Communities' Third-Party Support Line 4) using digital platforms to make oxygen distribution easier and deliver healthcare.	Delhi, Haryana, Uttarakhand, Bihar, West Bengal, Kerala, Karnataka, Maharashtra, Telangana, Punjab, Uttar Pradesh

(Continued)

Table 12.1. *(Continued)*

Name of NGO	Summary	Focus Area
Akshaya Patra Foundation	Based in Bengaluru, the Akshaya Patra Foundation works to alleviate poverty in India. *Objectives:* Put an end to students going hungry in a class by requiring that all government and government-aided schools participate in the Mid-Day Meal Scheme. Fighting child hunger and defending the right to an education for kids from low-income families. Offering healthy, freshly prepared food to students every day they attend class. They started off serving 1,500 kids in five schools in 2000, but with the cooperation of the Government of India and different State Governments, as well as consistent funding from corporations, individual contributors and well-wishers, they were able to expand their reach to include an additional 1.8 million kids.	Andhra Pradesh, Assam, Chhattisgarh, Delhi, Gujarat, Karnataka, Orissa, Rajasthan, Maharashtra, Tamil Nadu, Telangana, Tripura, Uttar Pradesh
Paytm Foundation	In light of the deteriorating COVID-19 situation in India, Paytm's charitable arm, Paytm Foundation, is attempting	PAN India

	to raise INR 10 Cr (about $200,000) to supply oxygen concentrators to hospitals and clinics around the country. Funds raised through this campaign will have their value doubled by Paytm.	
Zomato Feeding India	Non-profit division of Zomato with the support of logistics company Delhivery, Feeding India is able to procure oxygen concentrators and related supplies for hospitals and families in need across India.	PAN India
Green Dream Foundation	A platform started by IIT Graduates to reach senior citizens and physically challenged people. Connecting people using social networking groups assisted by volunteers with GPS technology for supplying emergency equipment and services.	Delhi

Source: Modified data by authors based on recent reports of Government of India.

health, sexual and reproductive health, gender-based violence and non-communicable diseases like tuberculosis and malaria.

- Health information dissemination
  - 'Health Communications Resources': Mobilises collaborators and locals then provide them with the tools they need to use media to improve community health and well-being.
- Supporting women and young people
  - 'ActionAid': Helping women and youth affected by the Syrian Refugee Crisis via humanitarian action over the course of a four-year programme.
- Disbursing funds to households so they can buy needs
  - 'Kaarvan Crafts Foundation': Send them each a sustainable PKR 4,400 every month till things settle down for everyone.
- Helping those who are disabled
- 'Motivation': Emphasising online communication with people in India and East Africa.
- The prenatal period, including prenatal check-ups and diagnostic procedures
  - 'PHASE Worldwide': Aiding local authorities in carrying out swift diagnostic tests and working along with them to keep tabs on those quarantined.
- Lockdown transportation provision
  - 'All We Can': Keeping rural Ugandans' bikes clean so they can continue to use them to travel to urban centres for things like food shopping and medical care.
- Setting up isolation and treatment centres in fragile settings
  - 'Relief International': Hygiene kits and isolation wards have been put up in numerous countries, including Syria, Iran, Bangladesh and Cox's Bazaar, Bangladesh.
- Role of Self Help Groups (SHGs) Towards combating pandemic crisis The World Bank reports quote that enormous openings for women SHGs have come during the pandemic where women from different locations learned new skills and came out with creative products and services which created great demand in the market. Creation of face masks and sanitizers, running community kitchens, fighting misinformation spreading the right information and various provisions for banking and other financial solutions.

  At the global level, the International Labour Organization (ILO) made various attempts to protect migrant workers' interests by ensuring protection against gender-based violence and workplace harassment, access to free and affordable dispute settlement mechanisms, promoting equity on the grounds of non-discrimination, prioritising health and safety protocols and conducting honest and safe recruitment practices.

- Corporate Social Responsibility (CSR) Strategy Towards Migrants' Social Support

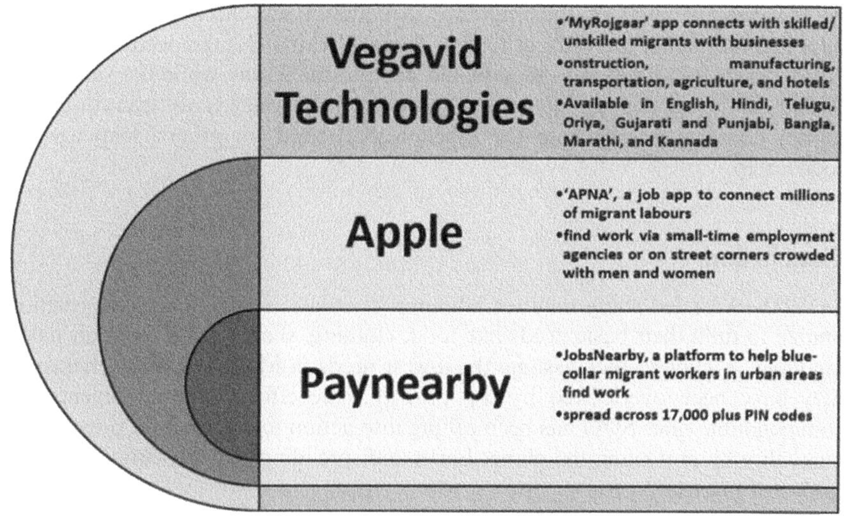

Fig. 12.9. Shows CSR Strategies of Corporates Towards Migrants' Upliftment. *Source:* Created by authors based on the Business World Report, 2020.

As per the reports of the Ministry of Corporate Affairs (MCA), every company was expected to permit avenues for CSR expenses which include eradicating hunger, poverty, malnutrition, preventive healthcare, better sanitation facilities and disaster management rehabilitation programmes, as discussed under the Schedule VII of the new Act. A few common corporate examples have been summarised in Fig. 12.9.

Findings From the Study

In times past, the term 'Poverty' was seen as horrifying impacting economic growth adversely. But now, it is seen moreover as an opportunity since after the emergence of SDG and understanding its role in providing employability with a situation of 'no hunger'. Hence, studies worldwide highlight the need for poverty reduction through economic and social sustainability and raising the productive capacity of poor migrant labourers. During the pandemic, various efforts have been taken from the sides of the government, NGOs and corporations at the global level. As we know, good jobs are easy to be lost and therefore commence the scope for migration. Though migration is one way or the other a short-term solution to alleviate poverty, it might not suffice in the long run. For which, some alternatives must be substituted for such issues. The issues are nevertheless cornered gender-wise. All are equally affected. In this competitive world, it must be the duty of each of the migrants to conduct self-check-in absorbing the opportunities available without further delay. Creativity is the need of the hour. No matter what others say, they would have to make hay while the sun shines. Situations during the pandemic merely proved that money is not everything. No money could ever substitute the psychological need for others' leap towards social help.

Conclusion

COVID-19 landed every migrant labourer in situations of physical deprivation, unable to fulfil their basic needs like food, clothing, shelter, travel to their native land, etc… Though they assume the lowest needs in Maslow's Need Hierarchy, they have been overlooked by top priority. The efforts of every agency are commendable since SDG has been calling into action to end hunger, poverty and inequality by protecting the planet Earth and spreading peace, harmony, justice, faith and prosperity.

Suggestions From the Study

Reducing poverty with resilience needs eliminating poverty through equity, eradicating poverty through education, alleviating poverty through peace and promoting climate justice by halting poverty and ending hunger in the long run. This could be the mantra to solve the migrant poverty situation despite experiencing a cashless factor. Not only individuals but institutions also must foresee stimulating inclusive economic growth balancing psycho-social support for their employees along with the promotion of microfinance initiatives.

Implications of the Study

The study discussed here included different cases from both India and globally, encrypting various reasons for how they take forward sustainable practices as a lucrative strategy in the modern era in connection to social upliftment and poverty eradication. The findings from various studies summarise the fact that migrants' problems were easily diagnosed and suggest sustainable practices were conducted not only at the individual level but despite at the institutional level. Pro-poor and gender-sensitised development strategies could surely support accelerated investments in poverty eradication programmes.

Bibliography

Anaf, J., Baum, F., Freeman, T., Labonté, R., Javanparast, S., Jolley, G. M., Lawless, A., & Bentley, M. J. (2014). Factors shaping intersectoral action in primary health care services. *Australian & New Zealand Journal of Public Health*, *38*(6), 553–559. https://doi.org/10.1111/1753-6405.12284

Archana, K., & Rutvi, M. (n.d.). Corporate social responsibility practices in the times of COVID-19: A study of India's BFSI sector. https://www.downtoearth.org.in/blog/governance/corporate-social-responsibility-practices-in-the-times-of-covid-19-a-study-of-india-s-bfsi-sector-74583. Accessed on May 31, 2022.

Ariyari, S. (2019). Partnership in surveillance: A Kerala model to emerging public health threats. *Online Journal of Public Health Informatics*, *11*(1). https://doi.org/10.5210/ojphi.v11i1.9766

Bhagat, R. B., Reshmi, R., Sahoo, H., Roy, A., & Govil, D. (2020). The COVID-19, migration and livelihood in India: Challenges and policy issues. *Migration Letters*, *17*(5), 705–718. https://doi.org/10.33182/ml.v17i5.1048

BW Online Bureau. (2020, September 16). Companies creating job opportunities for migrant workers in pandemic. https://bwdisrupt.businessworld.in/article/Companies-Creating-Job-Opportunities-For-Migrant-Workers-In-Pandemic/16-09-2020-321120/. Accessed on September 1, 2021.

Chatterjee, P., Nagi, N., Agarwal, A., Das, B., Banerjee, S. K., Sarkar, S., . . ., & Gangakhedkar, R. R. (2020). The 2019 novel coronavirus disease (COVID-19) pandemic: A review of the current evidence. *Indian Journal of Medical Research*, *151*(2), 147. https://doi.org/10.4103/ijmr.ijmr_519_20

Chen (2020, February 22). *Part of the Dotdash publishing family*. Investopedia. https://www.investopedia.com. Accessed on August 28, 2020.

Diaz, P., Murthy, S., & Lakshminarayana, R. (n.d.). *Advances in disaster mental health and psychological support*. https://hpod.law.harvard.edu/pdf/advances-in-disaster-mental-health.pdf. Accessed on March 11, 2020.

dmondson. (2020, July 7). What is Corporate Social Responsibility (CSR)? https://www.thebalance.com/corporate-social-responsibility-csr-4772443. Retrieved August 31, 2020, from.

Economic Survey of India 2017. (2017, February 28). OECD. https://www.oecd.org. Accessed on March 26, 2020.

enkins, L. S., Von Pressentin, K. B., Naidoo, K., & Schaefer, R. (2020). The evolving role of family physicians during the coronavirus disease 2019 crisis: An appreciative reflection. *African Journal of Primary Health Care & Family Medicine*, *12*(1). https://doi.org/10.4102/phcfm.v12i1.2478

Firdaus, G. (2017). Mental well-being of migrants in urban center of India: Analyzing the role of social environment. *Indian Journal of Psychiatry*, *59*(2), 164. https://doi.org/10.4103/psychiatry.indianjpsychiatry_272_15

Firdaus, G. (2017b). Mental well-being of migrants in urban center of India: Analyzing the role of social environment. *Indian Journal of Psychiatry*, *59*(2), 164. https://doi.org/10.4103/psychiatry.indianjpsychiatry_272_15

Garg, S., Bhatnagar, N., & Gangadharan, N. (2020). A case for participatory disease surveillance of the COVID-19 pandemic in India. *JMIR Public Health and Surveillance*, *6*(2), e18795. https://doi.org/10.2196/18795

Gautam, R., & Singh, A. (2010). Corporate social responsibility practices in India: A study of top 500 companies. *Global Business and Management Research: International Journal*, *2*(1), 41. http://www.gbmrjournal.com/pdf/Gautam%20&%20Singh,%202010.pdf

Government of India. Ministry of Health and Family Welfare. (2020, April 1). *Guidelines for COVID appropriate behaviour*. https://www.mohfw.gov.in/index.html.Guidelines. Accessed on June 26, 2021.

Gulia, K. K., & Kumar, V. M. (2020). Reverse quarantine in Kerala: Managing the 2019 novel coronavirus in a state with a relatively large elderly population. *Psychogeriatrics*, *20*(5), 794–795. https://doi.org/10.1111/psyg.12582

Here is how the large 50 global organisations & leaders are responding to COVID-19? (2020, May). https://csrbox.org/media/Report. Accessed on December 5, 2020.

India has 139 million internal migrants. They must not be forgotten. (2017, October 1). https://www.weforum.org/agenda/2017/10/india-has-139-million-internal Migrants-we-must-not-forget-them/ Accessed on December 25, 2021.

Joy, S. (2020, May 27). From food to hygiene kits, here is how NGOs are helping the poor fight against COVID-19. Retrieved October 3, 2021, from. https://www.deccanherald.com/national/north-and-central/from-food-to-hygiene-kits-here-is-how-ngos-are-helping-the-poor-fight-against-covid-19-818409.html

Kar, S., Rupa, K., Gupta, M., & Singh, S. K. (2003). Analyses of Orissa super cyclone using TRMM (TMI), DMSP (SSM/I) and OceanSat-I (MSMR) derived data. *Journal of Atmospheric and Ocean Science*, *9*(1–2), 1–18. https://doi.org/10.1080/1023673031000080376

Kulkarni. (2020). 6.6 lakh migrant workers in more than 21,000 camps. Retrieved June 9, 2021, from https://www.deccanherald.com/national/66-lakh-migrant-workers-in-more-than-21000-camps-centre-819809.html

Maharaj, V., Tomita, A., Thela, L., Mhlongo, M., & Burns, J. K. (2016). Food insecurity and risk of depression among refugees and immigrants in South Africa. *Journal of Immigrant and Minority Health*, *19*(3), 631–637. https://doi.org/10.1007/s10903-016-0370-x

Mandyam. (2020, April 2). *60,000 migrants in Bengaluru not getting ration kits despite Govt promise*. Retrieved June 21, 2020, from https://timesofindia.indiatimes.com/city/bengaluru/60k-migrants-in-citynot-getting-ration-kits-despite-govt-promise/article Show/74937979

Maslow, A. H. (1943). A theory of human motivation. *Psychological Review*, *50*(4), 370–396. https://doi.org/10.1037/h0054346

Mathew, G., Ramesh, N., Shanbhag, D., Goud, R., Subramanian, S., Lobo, C., Xavier, A., & Dasari, P. (2016). Quality of life and probable psychological distress among male workers at a construction site, Kolar district, Karnataka, India. *Indian Journal of Industrial Medicine*, *20*(1), 54. https://doi.org/10.4103/0019-5278.183846

Namrata, S., & Rupali, M. (2020, June 24). Companies go all out to get back migrant workers. Retrieved March 26, 2022, from https://timesofindia.indiatimes.com/business/india-business/cos-go-all-out-to-get-back-migrant-workers/articleshow/76538895.cms

Nath, D. (2020, April 4). India coronavirus lockdown | Migrant workers and their long march to uncertainty. https://www.thehindu.com/news/national/india-coronaviruslockdown-migrant-workers-and-their-long-march-to-%20uncertainty/article31251952.ece

Pw, D. (1988). Immigration and migration in America: Social impact and social response. *International Migration*, *26*(4), 441–452. https://doi.org/10.1111/j.1468-2435.1988.tb00663.x

Rajan, S. I., Sivakumar, P., & Srinivasan, A. (2020). The COVID-19 pandemic and internal labour migration in India: A 'crisis of mobility. *Indian Journal of Labour Economics*, *63*(4), 1021–1039. https://doi.org/10.1007/s41027-020-00293-8

Rangan, K., Chase, L., & Karim, S. (2015). The truth about CSR. *Harvard Business Review*, *93*(1), 12. https://dialnet.unirioja.es/servlet/articulo?codigo=5546295

Rashid, A., & Mahale, A. (2020, April 4). India coronavirus lockdown: Migrant workers and their long march to uncertainty. Retrieved September 29, 2021, from https://www.thehindu.com/news/national/india-coronaviruslockdown-migrant-workers-and-their-long-march-to-Uncertainty/article31251952.ece

Ray. (2020, May 16). Corporate social responsibility in times of COVID 19 pandemic. https://government.economictimes.indiatimes.com/news/economy/corporate-social-responsibility-in-times-of-covid-19-pandemic/75771467. Accessed on August 29, 2020.

Sharma, D. (2022, April 4). Corporate social responsibility during COVID times. https://www.actionaidindia.org/corporate-social-responsibility-during-covid-times/. Accessed on September 19, 2022.

Strategy and society: The link between competitive advantage and corporate social responsibility. (2007, April 24). *Strategic Direction*, *23*(5). https://doi.org/10.1108/sd.2007.05623ead.006

Team Sahyog. (2021, April 28). List of NGOs providing relief during Covid-19. https://www.investindia.gov.in/bip/resources/list-ngos-providing-relief-during-covid-19. Accessed on August 5, 2022.

Thorpe. (2013, May 18). Why CSR? The benefits of corporate social responsibility will move you to Act. https://www.forbes.com/sites/devinthorpe/2013/05/18/why-csr-the-benefits-of-corporate-social-responsibility-will-move-you-to-act/?sh=329b5bf865a3. Accessed on August 31, 2020.

Vijaykumar, L., Thara, R., John, S., & Chellappa, S. (2006). Psychosocial interventions after tsunami in Tamil Nadu, India. *International Review of Psychiatry*, *18*(3), 225–231. https://doi.org/10.1080/09540260600655912

Visagie, S., & Schneider, M. (2014). Implementation of the principles of primary health care in a rural area of South Africa. *African Journal of Primary Health Care & Family Medicine*, *6*(1). https://doi.org/10.4102/phcfm.v6i1.562

World Economic Forum. (2015, July 22). *3 ways governments can solve migration crises*. https://www.weforum.org/agenda/2015/07/3-things-governments-need-to-do-to-solve-migration-crises/. Accessed on May 15, 2021.

World Health Organisation. (2003a, October 1). *Emergency response manual*. https://apps.who.int/iris/bitstream/handle/10665/206816/Emergency_response_manual_eng.pdf?sequence=1&isAllowed=y. Accessed on November 21, 2022.

World Health Organisation. (2003b). Mental health in emergencies : Mental and social aspects of health of populations exposed to extreme stressors. https://apps.who.int/iris/handle/10665/67866. Accessed on February 5, 2020.

Woskie, L. R., Wellenius, L. G. A., Tsai, T. C. & Jha, A. (2020, June 16). Early impact of India's nationwide lockdown on aggregate population mobility and COVID-19 cases. https://doi.org/10.2139/ssrn.3631258

Printed and bound by CPI Group (UK) Ltd, Croydon, CR0 4YY

13/09/2026

14961026-0002